WIENER GEOGRAPHISCHE SCHRIFTEN

GEGRÜNDET VON LEOPOLD G. SCHEIDL

HERAUSGEGEBEN VON KARL A. SINNHUBER

GEOGRAPHISCHES INSTITUT DER WIRTSCHAFTSUNIVERSITÄT WIEN (HOCHSCHULE FÜR WELTHANDEL IN WIEN)

51/52

STUDIES IN THE GEOGRAPHY OF TOURISM AND RECREATION

CONTRIBUTIONS À L'ETUDE DE LA GÉOGRAPHIE DU TOURISME

BEITRÄGE ZUR FREMDEN-VERKEHRSGEOGRAPHIE

I

Editors:
KARL A. SINNHUBER and FELIX JÜLG

Wien 1978

VERLAG FERDINAND HIRT, WIEN

Publication of this series is facilitated by grants from the Austrian Federal Ministry of Science and Research and the *Österreichische Gesellschaft für Wirtschaftsraumforschung,* University of Economics, Vienna.

La publication de cette série est subventionnée par le Ministère Fédéral des Sciences et de la Recherche ainsi que par la *Österreichische Gesellschaft für Wirtschaftsraumforschung* à l'Université Economique de Vienne.

Der Druck dieser Schriftenreihe wird dankenswerterweise unterstützt durch das Bundesministerium für Wissenschaft und Forschung und die Österreichische Gesellschaft für Wirtschaftsraumforschung an der Wirtschaftsuniversität Wien (Hochschule für Welthandel).

The editor of this series also gratefully acknowledges the receipt of the grant towards covering the printing costs by the International Geographical Union.

L'éditeur de cette série remercie en outre l'Union Géographique Internationale de sa contribution à la couverture des frais d'impression.

Der Herausgeber dieser Schriftenreihe dankt ferner der Internationalen Geographischen Union für einen Zuschuß zur Deckung der Druckkosten.

ISBN 3 7019 5139 X

Filmsatz und Offsetdruck: Ferdinand Berger & Söhne OHG,
3580 Horn, Niederösterreich

Contents

Sommaire

Inhaltsverzeichnis

SUMMARIES

RÉSUMÉS

ZUSAMMENFASSUNGEN

Summaries in English

Recreation in the mountains

KARL A. SINNHUBER, Vienna, Austria

A mountain environment is an ideal terrain for recreation, or to avoid this elusive concept, outdoor leisure activities. There are some for which this environment is an essential precondition, like downhill skiing, some which in the mountains acquire distinctive characteristics like canoeing in rapid mountain streams and those for which this environment merely provides an added interest, like sailing in Alpine lakes. Historically the earliest of these pursuits and still going strong was stalking the deer and the chamois. In fact, in many areas, especially in the German Alps, the forests are now so overstocked that environmental dangers ensue. In other pursuits, mountaineering and skiing, it is the mass of people partaking which damage the environment for instance through the waste and litter problem and the building boom especially for second homes. Thus the Alpine societies which were the pioneers in opening up the Alps for visitors by building chalets and constructing paths have now come out against any further development of tourism in areas not yet opened up.

Sailing on the lakes as far as yachts and dinghies are concerned has also come near to saturation point; it is different in the case of windsurfing as these craft do not need fixed shore installations. This is part of the reason for the current boom of this kind of sailing.

Mountains are finally also a terrain for engine-less flying of which the newest is hang-gliding. Although no doubt a thrilling experience and although many successful descents have been made in the Alps from peaks of more than 3000 metres the accident rate has been so high that in the high mountains it should – if at all – only be done by the very best and highly experienced. On the whole in this craft without proper controls a flyer cannot react quickly enough against unexpected and strong air currents and it should thus be flown where these are rare in fine weather, viz. the foothills. On the other hand, glider flying in the high mountains offers perhaps the ultimate man can experience in a sport and yet does not involve undue risks. There is a twofold relationship between glider flying and geography: on the one hand to fly successfully i. e. for long distances, high altitudes and long duration a glider pilot needs to have a detailed knowledge of the terrain and the air currents to be expected in certain weather conditions at different periods of the day above slopes of different aspect, geology and vegetation cover; on the other hand although the actual numbers of the gliding fraternity are small compared for instance with skiers they must of necessity be of more than average financial substance. They also often bring their families and provide a point of interest to non-flyers so that in a number of places which have no other attraction except an airfield from which there is a good chance for long distance and/or high altitude flights, glider flying does promote a significant tourist trade.

Since the number of gliders that can be started at the optimum time of day is naturally small there would still be the possibility – since this is also a growing sport – with a modest investment to bring the economic benefits to some more places which have no income from tourism so far.

The place of Geography of Tourism and Recreation in the system of geography and in the field of leisure research

Z. TED MIECZKOWSKI, Winnipeg, Canada

The paper examines the new field of geography: Geography of Tourism and Recreation. An attempt is made to relate it to the other geographical branches and to determine the scope. The author presents his ideas on a model illustrating the areas of research interests for the Geography of Tourism and Recreation. He voices his opinion with respect to the discussion initiated by Professor RUPPERT (Munich) on the scope of Geography of Leisure and Geography of Tourism.

The place of Geography of Tourism and Recreation in the field of leisure research is discussed in the second part of the paper. The significance of these contributions is emphasized and future development outlined.

Recreation in perspective

ALICE COLEMAN, London, Great Britain

Recreational geographers have worked mainly on topics of leisure land and leisure activities, but have accepted social change leading to increased leisure time as given. The author questions whether such trends are, in fact, acceptable, and proposes the concept of *overleisure,* which can be destructive to the human personality. The growth of land for leisure in Britain has been so rapid and extensive that it is undermining essential activities such as food production and exceeding the capacity of public finance to repair the damage that it may cause. It is no longer sufficient to assume that problems can be resolved by more recreational provision, and a more integrated approach, which attacks overleisure at its source, is required.

The functional and spatial structure of public recreation in an urban environment

LISLE S. MITCHELL, Columbia, South Carolina, U.S.A.

This investigation has two primary concerns: First to categorize the units of a public recreation system into discrete functional classes and to identify their basic characteristics. The second to analyze the distribution of the system in terms of absolute and relative locational patterns.

Data pertaining to 172 public recreation sites in Columbia, South Carolina, were subjected to multiple dimensional scaling, Ward's grouping algorithm, and discriminate analysis. This procedure produced a five-class categorization scheme. The classes in the system differ more in degree rather than in kind of facilities and serve general recreation demands. The units are concentrated in densely populated urban areas and are proximate and accessible to residential communities.

The complex nature of the supply of public urban recreation opportunities may be best understood within the context of purpose, structure and distribution. The purpose of a particular recreation site determines the type of facilities, programs and activities established and the population attracted. These factors in turn influence the location of individual units or classes of recreation sites. It is concluded, therefore, public recreation places have an agglomerated spatial pattern because their purpose is to serve a densely concentrated population with general recreation facilities and activities.

Problems of the cartographic representation of tourism

PETER MARIOT, Bratislava, Czechoslovakia

The cartographic representation of tourism is a significant methodical aid to extend the body of information as to its preconditions, its localisation, intensity and structure.

The fundamental problems connected with the cartographic representation of tourism are determined by aims, contents, methods, scale and bases of the maps of tourism.

After the initial aim to document the outcomes of geographical research of tourism more exactly and visually more strikingly, the aim to support practical planning as well as contributing toward the formulation of a theory of geography of tourism was added.

Regarding their contents, maps of tourism can be classified by various aspects. One of these is the classification of maps of tourism according to criteria which qualitative facts of tourism are represented. From this aspect one can distinguish:

1. Maps representing the preconditions of tourism; within their group maps representing localization, selected preconditions and realized preconditions,
2. Maps representing the structural facts of tourism,
3. Maps representing the impact of tourism.

The making of such kinds of maps has been influenced in the recent past by the needs of planning and managing practice, which have contributed to extend the interest of geographers especially as to the problems of representing the potential of landscape, even out of intensively visited areas and to those of summarising interest regarding participation of resident population in tourism. From the point of view of development of theory a special significance is achieved by successively increasing the number of attempts to express synthetically various facts of tourism, which offer steps into a typification of resorts and a regionalization of tourism.

The problems of methods of cartographic representation of tourism are closely connected with the contents of maps. Especially the problems of selecting suitable criteria and of characteristics of the presented facts of tourism deserve special attention in this connection. Thus a trend can be noticed to move from the representation of specific indices to that of more complex, frequently combined characteristics. At the same time, particularly in the sphere of theory a need to coordinate closely the selection of represented indices manifests itself more and more strikingly, so that maps from different areas and by different authors may be comparable.

Both the scale and the contents of maps are also closely connected and together they correspond with the aims of using the map. Therefore the needs of practical application in particular have introduced more detailed maps of larger scales into the special literature, representing especially the local potentialities of tourism.

The cartographic basis is an important means to accentuate the relations of the represented characteristics of tourism to other elements of the landscape. These means have been used so far preliminary only in few cases. It is therefore necessary to leave the traditional topographical and administrative bases and to accentuate the basic situation, which is directly related to characteristics of tourism, as represented.

A look at the problems of cartographic representation of tourism shows that in the interest of further progress of geography of tourism, both for introducing the results of research into practical application as well as in the interest of constructing its theoretical basis, greater and more systematic attention should be devoted to the complex of problems of the cartographic representation of tourism.

In this connection it would be useful to direct the interests of geographers of tourism internationally to three important tasks:

1. to work out a thorough evaluation of the situations which characterize the problems of cartographic representation of tourism.

2. to devise the principles of selection and formation of these criteria and indices, which are most suitable to express cartographically the geographically significant aspects of tourism.

3. to extend cooperation in representing various aspects of tourism of definite territories by using a uniform method and uniform symbols.

Significant results in solving these tasks can be achieved especially through the support and on the basis of the Working Group of the Geography of Tourism and Recreation of the International Geographic Union (IGU).

Monuments of nature and tourism

JOSEF MATZNETTER, Frankfurt/Main, Federal Republic of Germany

Particularly characteristic natural features, as for instance larger water falls, striking rock formations or caves, but also special occurences of plants and animals, are in many countries protected against interference by legal measures as "monuments of nature". Amongst the sphere of human interests these are of threefold importance: firstly for scientific research, secondly as destinations for visits by tourists and thirdly, in a few cases, for economic utilisation. The opening-up of such a monument of nature for tourism demands various sets of measures to be taken, *viz.* those concerning access, the protection of visitors, explanatory notes, embodiment into the local tourism and additional ones depending on local circumstances.

According to the responsible opinion which in particular applies to caves, such opening-up for the public should be limited to relatively few objects. For those chosen the measures to be taken should be differentiated according to the local circumstances. The principal consideration must be to preserve the natural character of the monument and to bring this fact home to the visitor. One has to be particularly critical in attempts to enhance the aesthetic – artistic effect of a monument of nature. In this respect particular care has to be exercised in caves where the necessary provision of illumination can easily result in bad taste if too much is done in the way of shadow effects and coloured lighting. Concerning musical performances in caves a certain reserve is recommended. A visit to natural monuments should after all facilitate members of our civilisation to come once more closer to nature.

Geographical constraints on tourist development in small mid-sea islands

ALEXANDER MELAMID, New York, N. Y., U.S.A.

Geographical constraints on development in small mid-sea islands are related to problems of thresholds (minimum efficient sizes) of services. These include air and sea transportation, repair services, storage facilities,etc. Increasing tourist development to accommodate these threshhold requirements causes pressure on recreation and internal transportation facilities as well as on labor and fresh water supplies. These problems are aggravated by the increasing thresholds of transportation facilities. Examples are given from Bermuda, Cayman Islands, Seychelles, etc.

Predicting recreational highway traffic in Canada at a time of scarcity and high cost of motor fuel

ROY WOLFE, Downsview, Ontario, Canada

Within certain constraints having to do with adjacent land uses, the following simulation model works quite well in predicting recreational traffic on summer weekends on Ontario's highways:

$$R = 0.840 \frac{W_R}{W_T} + 3.410 \frac{D_T}{W_T} - 3.056 + 0.118 \left(\frac{W_R}{W_T}\right)^{1/2} \text{Log}^{-1} \left(\frac{W_R}{W_T}\right) \text{Log} \left(\frac{3.5D_T}{W_T} - 2.5\right)$$

where R = the ratio of weekend recreational traffic volume to average daily traffic volume in summer,

W_R = weekday recreational traffic volume,

W_T = average weekday traffic volume, and

D_T = average daily traffic volume, in summer.

What happens to the efficacy of this predictive model if new economic constraints are imposed upon weekend travel – specifically, in the form of unacceptably high prices for gasoline? At what point does the price become unacceptably high? For which economic, cultural and social strata of the population? In which regions? For what kinds of recreational activities? And at what distances between cities of origien and resorts of destination? Finally, what practical applications of the principle of substitutability can be devised for providing new activities, in new places, at costs differentially acceptable to different strata of society?

Can all these perturbations in the system be incorporated in a modified simulation model?

Skiing and winter resorts around the world

BERNARD BARBIER, Aix-en-Provence, France

Seventeen thousand five hundred ski-lifts, three thousand ski-resorts, thirty-seven million skiers, forty countries involved: such are the approximate figures of skiing in the world.

Nine countries, however, (six Alpine countries, the United States, Canada and Japan) possess nine out of ten ski-lifts and eight out of ten resorts.

These statistics show that the importance of skiing depends upon both the standard of living and the closeness to the mountain ranges. A closer analysis shows, however, that not all mountains are suitable for skiing and, especially that there are enormous differences between one Alpine country and the next: each one has its own particular kind of ski-resort and the impact of winter tourism on the economy of mountain regions varies from country to country.

Closer research, and more particularly comparative studies, should therefore be undertaken.

Cableways in Austria

A factor of tourism with considerable economic impact

FELIX JÜLG, Vienna, Austria

In Austria a fifth of the world's passenger cableways are operated. Both relevant authorities and scientific researchers have investigated for a number of years the impact of cableways and have found that the main consequences of the construction of cableways arise indirectly through their stimulation of the development of winter tourism.

In fact, only about 50 per cent. of Austria's cableway enterprises were able to make profits in 1975. Profitability depends largely on the technological system of construction. Heavy structures need for the same degree of profitability a greater number of users.

There is a strong connection between cableways and winter tourism. More than three quarters of all passengers are carried during the winter period and an investigation has shown that 85 per cent. of these are tourists. Today's Alpine skiing cannot be imagined without cableways. The effects of cableways can be seen in an increase of overnight stays in the winter period in communities where cableways were installed. In addition there is an impact on the whole local economy.

This economic impact is demonstrated on the example of three criteria in selected resorts:

1. An increase of population in regions, which in part were threatened by depopulation.

2. Building activities in mountain villages, which have had nearly the same number of houses for hundreds of years.

3. A high per-capita tax yield; in some major winter sport resorts higher than in communities with flourishing manufacturing industries.

There are three reasons why winter tourism is economically as successful:

1. A satisfactory utilization of capacity is achieved by a great number of tourist enterprises in a second season.

2. The average receipt per tourist is higher in the skiing season, because of additional expenditures for cableways, après-ski activities and so on.

3. Higher income groups participate in winter sport (at least in Austria).

In the development of cableways there are many problems, the most important of them are briefly pointed out:

1. There is a sort of "arms race" in the whole Alpine region, a strong competition between states, regions and resorts, partly promoted by over-optimistic estimates of growth in winter tourism.

2. There is a state of euphoria in the whole cableway-business, partly caused by this "arms race", partly by a false estimation of the economic situation. In this way many enterprises are established which may have to be subsidized in the future.

3. There is a danger of overdevelopment and concentration. Attractive skiing areas with a great number of cableways need large resorts in the valleys to utilize their capacity; the dimensions of these developments are no longer optimal for true recreation.

4. There is a detrimental influence on the natural beauty of landscape and new natural hazards like erosion and avalanches arise.

In Austria, cableways have been successful in increasing the share of winter tourism in total tourism since 1961 from 23 to 30 per cent. A remarkable part of its foreign currency receipts is based on cableways. They seem to be the most effective factor in the development of the regional economy in mountain regions suitable for winter sports.

Urbanisation and problems of tourism and recreation in Bulgaria

LJUBOMIR DINEV, Sofia, Bulgaria

Some basic problems in the development of tourism and recreation in the period of the socialist industrialization and urbanization will be interpreted.

The stages of the tourist occupance in the "middle mountains" *(Mittelgebirge)* by the industrial society of the Rhineland

GABRIEL WACKERMANN, Strasbourg, France.

With the development of tourism the industrial society has increased its needs for space. The "middle mountains" *(Mittelgebirge)* are subjected to a constantly increasing pressure of the towns nearby. The stages of their occupance shows the progressive hold gained by the upper classes contrary to the belief of a democratisation of tourism in *Mittelgebirge*. The traditional dialectic between towns and middle mountains is thus to be reconsidered. The Rhineland seems to offer itself for a very interesting model analysis of this development.

Ranges and catchment areas of selected recreation facilities in Bavaria

GÜNTER HEINRITZ, Munich, Federal Republic of Germany

On the example of indoor swimming pools, keep-fit paths and mini-golf courses, the hypothesis was tested whether specific ranges for such recreational facilities exist. The results showed that this is not possible owing to the large variance of ranges within each category. These variances, however, are smaller if facilities situated in comparable locations are considered. An important result of the investigation is that the various groups of users are not differentiated by the fact that they are prepared to cover different maximum distances in order to make use of these facilities but that with increasing distance between residence and the facilities the frequency of their use is differently reduced.

The impact of recreation on life styles of rural communities

A case study of Sleat, Isle of Skye

RICHARD W. BUTLER, London, Ontario, Canada

The paper discusses the impacts of recreation, particularly those of a social and cultural nature, upon the population of a rural insular area in Scotland. The residents of the parish of Sleat, Isle of Skye, were surveyed to obtain their opinions and attitudes about tourism, and the manner in which their life styles were affected, if at all, by tourism. These perceptions and attitudes are discussed and variations among sub-groups, according to location, language, amount of contact with tourists and involvement with tourists noted. Impacts are discussed in terms of benefits (employment, income, social intercourse and improvements in services) and disbenefits, (road traffic, second home development, increased stress, changes in social patterns and reduction in the amount of Gaelic spoken). The conclusions discuss the importance of considering local receptiveness and attitudes in planning for tourism in order to preserve the social environment of destination areas.

Planning for outdoor recreation at the local government level in Sweden

Some thoughts on the institutional framework of communal involvement

HANS ALDSKOGIUS, Uppsala, Sweden

At the local level planning for outdoor recreation is an activity in which a number of decision-making institutions are engaged. Local government authorities are of course of particular significance in this process, but special-interest groups, various types of private and public organizations, land owners, and entrepreneurs in the recreation sector are also involved and influence policy-making, planning, implementation and management in the outdoor recreation sector.

Fig. 1 illustrates, in a highly simplified manner, a local system of decision-making "actors" (institutions), some types of activities in which they are engaged, and the ways in which this creates situations of potential conflict or opportunities for cooperation between different groups of decision-makers.

Spatial patterns of facilities for outdoor recreation are the result not only of rational judgements about optimal or satisfactory locations, but also of land use competition and policy compromise in a system of decision-making institutions.

It is suggested that in studies of the development of recreational landscapes close attention should be paid to institutional factors. The local government area is of particular interest in this context, since this is where most decisions which regulate and coordinate land use are made, and where the complexities of the institutional structure become most obvious, because the full range of institutions is represented, from *ad hoc* special-interest groups to central government agencies.

Tourists and recreation facilities in the western United States – use and misuse

BURKHARD HOFMEISTER, Berlin (West)

The author investigated a number of National Parks, National Recreation Areas, National Forests and State Parks in the Western United States under the aspect to what extent the numbers of visitors which have increased rapidly during the 1950s and 1960s have resulted in overcrowding and ecological overuse and how the authorities responsible for these areas are tackling this problem. To begin with it could be demonstrated that this problem is more serious in some areas than in others, depending whether an area is provided with spectacular monuments of nature as for instance Grand Canyon and Yellowstone National Park or whether it lies relatively close to population agglomerations as for instance Lake Mead National Recreation Area in relationship to the metropolitan areas of California. In Yellowstone National Park the problem is more pronounced than in Yosemite Valley National Park since in the former visitors come mainly during the summer months whereas in the latter the number of visitors is more evenly distributed throughout the year.

The following problems are then discussed in greater detail: the multiple-use-concept of the U.S.Forest Service and its compatibility with the recreational function; the concept of further development of the "heavy-use" areas to the benefit of the extensive "backcountry" or "wilderness areas" visited merely by a few on foot or horseback; for the use of these areas the numbers of visitors have been kept under control by three different methods: in a few heavy-use areas by restriction of access by private cars and introduction of a shuttle bus service; by the freezing of the number of accommodation facilities in hotels, chalets and camp-sites (this is likely to lead to an increase in the number of motels outside the boundaries of the recreation areas proper); by the purchase of private land to provide access for the general public as for instance the purchase of extensive shore areas of Lake Tahoe by the State of California (to this should be added the consideration that the largest potential for augmenting recreation areas lies in the National Forests); and finally by commissioning of scientists to work out the carrying capacity of areas to have a sounder basis on which to make decisions in the future.

Recreation in the self-managing socialist society
Contemporary theory and practice in the Socialist Federal Republic of Yugoslavia

MOMČILO VUKIĆEVIĆ, Novi Sad, Yugoslavia

Under socialism conditions are being created in which the various needs of working people are gradually developed and covered, both quantitatively and qualitatively. Although this process does not move quite straight in all stages of the building of socialism i. e. in all countries, in the long run its trend is positive and it is connected directly with the building of the socialist community.

Similarly to other socialist countries, in Yugoslavia too the "trade-union" tourism has been developed. As a form of democratization of tourism it has been given special attention for a long time and was classified as one of the factors which determine advantageously the living standard of the working people. Yet, the "trade-union" tourism in our country was different from other national models. That difference has been increasing gradually and in the present stage of development these quantitative changes have resulted in a new quality: out of the "trade-union" tourism the "worker"-tourism has emerged, as a particular form in the current process of the democratization of tourism in the world.

Over-simplified by "worker"-tourism is meant the complex of the tourist-recreational activity of the workers in the place of their residence, as well as of the phenomena and relations resulting from their travel away from their place of residence.

Résumés en langue française

Montagne et loisirs

KARL A. SINNHUBER, Vienne, Autriche

La montagne est une zone récréative idéale ou, ce terme étant plutôt vague, un terrain idéal pour toute une série d'activités sportives. Certains sports ne peuvent être pratiqués que dans la montagne, comme le ski alpin, d'autres, comme p. ex. le canoéisme sur les eaux sauvages, y offrent des aspects tout à fait différents, tandis que pour d'autres encore, comme p. ex. la voile sur les lacs alpins, le paysage montagneux ne constitue qu'un attrait supplémentaire. Le sport le plus ancien pratiqué dans les Alpes est la chasse au chevreuil, au cerf et au chamois, sport qui, à quelques exceptions près, a été depuis toujours le privilège des classes supérieures. De nos jours, maintes parties des Alpes, notamment en République fédérale d'Allemagne, surabondent de gibier à tel point que l'environnement s'en trouve dégradé. Dans le cas d'autres sports, les randonnées en montagne et le ski, les dégâts (déchets ...) sont dus à la masse des visiteurs, mais c'est également le foisonnement de constructions, surtout de résidences secondaires, qui porte atteinte à l'environnement. De ce fait les clubs alpins, qui autrefois avaient fait oeuvre de pionnier en ouvrant les Alpes aux visiteurs par la construction de refuges et l'aménagement de sentiers, se sont prononcés contre la poursuite de la mise en valeur.

De même la voile, pour ce qui est des yachts et des yoles, ne connaîtra plus guère de développement important vu le nombre limité d'emplacements de stationnement. Ce problème ne se pose pas dans le cas du windsurfing ce qui explique en partie sa popularité croissante; il ne fait pas de doute cependant que, pour des raisons climatiques, les lacs des Alpes ne présentent pas le cadre idéal pour la pratique de ce sport.

Les montagnes sont finalement aussi un terrain pour le vol sans moteur, le deltaplane ayant pris un essor prodigieux au cours des dernières années. Le vol libre procure certes des sensations sans égal et a souvent été effectué avec succès à partir d'une altitude de 3000 mètres, pourtant les accidents, dont certains à issue fatale, étaient si nombreux qu' il y a lieu de conclure que seuls les excellents pilotes très expérimentés devraient voler en haute montagne, à moins qu'on ne préfère y renoncer totalement. Cet appareil sans gouvernails ne permet pas au pilote de réagir suffisamment vite contre des rafales latérales qui déséquilibrent le deltaplane. Il serait donc préférable de ne voler que dans les contreforts et les collines où ces courants atmosphériques sont rares par beau temps. Le vol à voile par contre comporte moins de risques et fait naître des sensations presque identiques. Il existe un double rapport entre le vol à voile et la géographie: pour pouvoir effectuer un long parcours à une grande altitude ou pour une longue durée, c'est-à-dire pour réussir son vol en montagne, le pilote d'une part doit avoir une connaissance approfondie du terrain et des courants aériens auxquels il faut s'attendre dans certaines conditions atmosphériques à certaines heures du jour au-dessus de versants d'une configuration, d'un type de rocher et d'une couverture végétale donnés. Il importe d'autre part de tenir compte des effets économiques découlant de la pratique du vol à voile. Même si le nombre des pratiquants du vol à voile est peu important par rapport à celui des skieurs, les premiers disposent nécessairement de revenus relativement plus élevés. Souvent ils sont accompagnés de leurs familles, et dans des localités sans attractions particulières par ailleurs, un terrain de vol à voile attire également d'autres visiteurs, fait qui peut favoriser un important développement du tourisme.

Du fait que le nombre des planeurs pouvant décoller à l'heure la plus favorable du jour est limité et que ce sport devient de plus en plus populaire, quelques lieux restés jusqu'ici à l'écart du mouvement et des recettes touristiques pourraient, sans investissements majeurs, bénéficier des avantages économiques du tourisme.

La position de la géographie du tourisme dans le cadre de la géographie et de la recherche sur le loisir

Z. TED MIECZKOWSKI, Winnipeg, Canada

Le but de cette dissertation est d'étudier un nouveau domaine en géographie: la Géographie du Tourisme et du Loisir. L'auteur a essayé de relier ce domaine aux autres branches de la géographie et d'en dégager son importance relative. Il a voulu exposer ses idées sur les domaines de recherches qui pourraient intéresser la Géographie du Tourisme et du Loisir. De plus l'auteur répond aux propos du Professeur RUPPERT de Munich, qui avait initié une discussion sur l'importance de cette nouvelle géographie.

Dans la deuxième partie de cette étude, l'auteur discute le rôle de la Géographie du Tourisme et du Loisir dans la recherche actuelle sur le loisir. L'auteur souligne l'importance de cette étude et expose dans ses lignes générales son prochain développement.

Réflexions sur le loisir

ALICE COLEMAN, Londres, Grande-Bretagne

Les géographes spécialistes des problèmes du loisir ont consacré la plupart de leurs études aux terrains et activités de loisirs, mais ils n'ont point mis en question le fait du changement social menant à l'augmentation des loisirs. L'auteur se demande si ces tendances sont acceptables, et propose le concept de *surloisir,* susceptible de détruire la personnalité de l'homme. En Grande-Bretagne, l'extension du terrain de récréation a été si rapide et vaste que des activités essentielles telles que l'agriculture sont mises en danger et la réparation des dommages causés dépasse la capacité des finances publiques. A l'avenir, l'on ne saurait plus se contenter de la supposition que les problèmes peuvent être résolus par l'augmentation des équipements récréatifs. Il faudra trouver une approche plus intégrée permettant d'attaquer à la source le problème du surloisir.

Structure fonctionelle et spatiale de la récréation publique dans un milieu urbain

LISLE S. MITCHELL, Columbia, Caroline du Sud, Etats-Unis

Cette enquête a deux aspects principaux. Le premier, de ranger les unités d'un système de récréation publique en classes fonctionnelles discrètes et d'identifier leurs caractéristiques de base. Le second, d'analyser la répartition du système du point de vue des modèles absolus et relatifs de localisation.

Les données se rapportant a 172 sites de récréation publique à Columbia (Caroline du Sud), ont été soumises a un tarage dimensionnel multiple, au groupement d'algorithme de Ward et à une analyse discriminante. Ce procédé a produit un système qui comprend cinq catégories. Les catégories de ce système diffèrent plutôt quant à leur degré que par leur genre de services, et répondent aux besoins généraux de la récréation. Ces unités sont concentrées dans les régions urbaines à population dense et sont proches et accessibles des quartiers résidentiels.

La nature complexe de l'offre en services récréatifs urbains se comprend mieux si l'on considère sa finalité, sa structure et sa répartition. La finalité d'un site de récréation précis détermine le type de services, de programmes et d'activités qui y sont implantés ainsi que la population qu'il attire. Ces facteurs, de leur côté, influencent la localisation de chaque unité et de chaque catégorie de sites récréatifs. En conclusion, les lieux de récréation publique se concentrent dans l'espace pour répondre aux besoins en activités et services récréatifs d'une population dense.

Problèmes de la représentation cartographique du tourisme

PETER MARIOT, Bratislava, Tchécoslovaquie

La représentation cartographique du tourisme est une méthode importante qui fournit des données supplémentaires quant aux bases, à la répartition géographique, l'intensité et la structure de celui-ci.

Les problèmes fondamentaux de la représentation cartographique du tourisme sont posés par l'objectif, le contenu, la méthode, l'échelle et la carte de base de représentations relatives au tourisme.

Aux objectifs initiaux, à savoir la représentation plus précise et plus illustrative des résultats de la recherche géographique, viennent s'ajouter des efforts visant à aider les planificateurs et à fournir des contributions aux théories de la géographie du tourisme.

En ce qui concerne leur contenu, les cartes de tourisme peuvent être divisées en différentes catégories. Une des méthodes de classification tient compte des caractéristiques qualitatives du tourisme. Peuvent être différenciées en plus les cartes représentant

1. les conditions (locales, sélectionnées, réalisables) du tourisme,
2. des caractéristiques structurales du tourisme,
3. l'impact du tourisme.

La forme de ces cartes a été influencée ces derniers temps par les besoins de la planification et de l'économie, fait qui a contribué à élargir l'horizon des géographes s'intéressant davantage à des problèmes tels que la représentation du potentiel d'accueil du paysage, également dans des régions moins fréquentées, ou la participation de la population résidante au tourisme. Au cours du développement de la théorie on a pu assister à une multiplication des efforts faits en vue de parvenir à la catégorisation des stations touristiques ainsi qu'à la régionalisation du tourisme, et ceci par la synthèse des différents faits du tourisme.

Les problèmes relatifs aux méthodes de la représentation cartographique du tourisme sont intimement liés au contenu des cartes. A cet égard, c'est la sélection de critères et caractéristiques valables pour les faits touristiques représentés qui mérite une attention particulière. La représentation de données isolées est de plus en plus abandonnée en faveur de facteurs complexes, souvent combinés. Les milieux scientifiques avant tout soulignent en même temps la nécessité d'une étroite coopération permettant de rendre comparables les cartes des différents régions et auteurs.

L'échelle et le contenu des cartes sont interdépendants et déterminés par l'utilisation à laquelle sont destinées ces dernières. De ce fait des cartes détaillées à grande échelle répondant aux besoins de la pratique ont été introduites dans la littérature spéciale, cartes qui représentent plus particulièrement le potentiel touristique local.

La carte de base est un outil important permettant de représenter les relations qui existent entre les différents facteurs du tourisme et les éléments du paysage; cependant cet outil n'a guère été utilisé jusqu'à présent. Il y aurait donc lieu d'abandonner la carte de base topographique ou administrative traditionnelle en faveur des facteurs liés directement aux caractéristiques touristiques représentées.

Cet inventaire des problèmes de la représentation cartographique du tourisme démontre que dans l'intérêt du progrès de la géographie du tourisme, non seulement en ce qui concerne l'application de ses résultats dans la pratique, mais aussi la définition de ses fondements théoriques, il faudrait étudier ces problèmes de façon approfondie et plus systématique.

Dans ce contexte il paraît essentiel d'attirer l'attention des spécialistes en matière de géographie du tourisme dans le monde entier sur trois tâches principales consistant à:

1. dresser un inventaire critique des problèmes de la représentation cartographique du tourisme,
2. élaborer des méthodes de sélection de critères et d'indices permettant de représenter les facteurs du tourisme géographiquement importants,
3. intensifier la collaboration en vue de la représentation de différents facteurs touristiques dans des régions définies au moyen de méthodes et symboles uniformes.

C'est surtout avec le concours du Groupe de travail Géographie du Tourisme et de la Récréation de l'UGI et à l'aide des travaux effectués au sein de ce groupe que l'on s'approchera de la solution de ces problèmes.

Monuments de la nature

JOSEF MATZNETTER, Francfort, République Fédérale d' Allemagne

Dans beaucoup de pays, des objets naturels très caractéristiques et impressionnants comme p. ex. des chutes d'eau importantes, des formations rocheuses singulières, des grottes, mais aussi des sites d'espèces végétales et animales particulières etc. sont classés curiosités naturelles et sauvegardés par la loi sur la protection de la nature.

Dans le champ des intérêts humains, de tels objets peuvent avoir une triple importance, à savoir à l'égard de la recherche scientifique, du tourisme et aussi, parfois, de l'utilisation économique. Leur mise en valeur pour le tourisme exige des mesures bien définies en ce qui concerne l'accessibilité, la sécurité des visiteurs, la conservation de l'objet, sa présentation, l'organisation des visites, l'intégration dans le tourisme régional et, finalement, des aménagements d'infrastructure supplémentaires.

Suivant une opinion qui fait autorité surtout en ce qui concerne les grottes, l'ouverture générale au public devrait rester limitée à relativement peu d'objets. Dans ces cas, les mesures à prendre varient selon les données individuelles. L'essentiel est que le caractère naturel soit maintenu et mis en évidence pour le visiteur.

Il faut juger dangereux les essais qui cherchent à relever l'effet esthétique d'une curiosité naturelle. Ce sont surtout les grottes qui risquent souvent d'être la proie du mauvais goût. Qu'on pense aux effets d'illumination (comme le jeu d'ombres et de couleurs) au-delà de l'éclairage nécessaire. Une certaine réserve paraît se justifier même vis-à-vis des manifestations comme p. ex. les concerts, car, en fin de compte, les visites de curiosités naturelles devraient avant tout contribuer à ramener les hommes de notre civilisation technique à une pensée plus proche de la nature.

Difficultés géographiques du développement du tourisme sur les petites îles situées dans l'océan

ALEXANDER MELAMID, New York, Etats-Unis

Des contraintes importantes résultent des quantités minimum (seuils critiques) dans le transport maritime. Dans les périodes de construction des hôtels etc. les quantités importées sont suffisamment grandes pour l'affrètement de navires. Normalement ces quantités ne sont pas suffisantes pour l'affrètement de navires sauf sur des routes régulières de transport maritime. Le problème de l'affrètement est devenu plus difficile par l'augmentation du tonnage des navires construits ces dernières années. Le développement du tourisme sur ces îles permettant l'affrètement des navires demande de grands investissements en hôtels, routes, terrains de golfe etc. ce qui peut réduire la valeur des plages, parcs nationaux etc. qui constituent l'attraction pour les touristes. Le coût du fret aérien étant très élevé, la plupart des biens destinés aux touristes et aux habitants des îles ne peuvent être importés par cette voie. Sont citées à titre d'exemple les îles Cook, Caimans, Bermudes et les Seychelles.

Prévision du volume du trafic sur les autoroutes canadiennes par des périodes de pénurie et d'un coût élevé du carburant

ROY WOLFE, Downsview, Ontario, Canada

Compte tenu de certaines restrictions relevant de l'utilisation des espaces adjacents, le modèle de simulation représenté ci-après se prête assez bien à l'établissement de prévisions sur le trafic de récréation des fins de semaine en été sur les autoroutes de l'Ontario:

$$R = 0{,}840 \frac{W_R}{W_T} + 3{,}410 \frac{D_T}{W_T} - 3{,}056 + 0{,}118 \left(\frac{W_R}{W_T}\right)^{1/2} \log^{-1}\left(\frac{W_R}{W_T}\right) \log\left(\frac{3{,}5D_T}{W_T} - 2{,}5\right)$$

R = indiquant le rapport entre le volume du trafic de récréation des fins de semaine et la moyenne journalière en été,
W_R = le volume du trafic de récréation des jours ouvrables,
W_T = la moyenne du volume du trafic des jours ouvrables
D_T = la moyenne du volume du trafic journalier en été.

Les questions qui se posent dans ce contexte sont les suivantes:

Dans quelle mesure la portée de ce modèle prévisionnel est-elle modifiée si le trafic de week-end est limité par de nouvelles charges économiques – surtout sous forme de prix d'essence jugés prohibitifs? A partir de quel niveau les prix sont-ils jugés inacceptables? Par quelles couches économiques, sociales et culturelles de la population? Et pour quelles distances entre lieux de départ et de destination? Finalement, quelles sont les applications pratiques du principe de substitution concevables en vue de la création de nouvelles activités, sur de nouveaux emplacements, à un coût différemment acceptable pour différentes couches de la société?

Tous ces facteurs de perturbation sont-ils susceptibles d'être intégrés dans un modèle de simulation modifié?

Ski et stations de sports d'hiver dans le monde

BERNARD BARBIER, Aix-en-Provence, France

17.500 remontées mécaniques, 3.000 stations, 37.000.000 de skieurs, 40 pays concernés: tels sont les chiffres approximatifs du ski dans le monde. Mais neuf pays (six pays alpins, Etats-Unis, Canada, Japon) possèdent les 9/10 des remontées mécaniques et les 8/10 des stations.

Ces données montrent que la pratique du ski dépend du niveau de vie et de la proximité de la montagne. Mais une analyse plus précise montre que toutes les montagnes ne sont pas aptes au ski et, surtout, qu'il y a de grandes différences entre les pays alpins: chacun a son style de station et l'insertion du tourisme d'hiver dans l'économie montagnarde varie selon ces pays.

Des recherches plus précises, et notamment, des études comparées doivent donc être menées.

Remontées mécaniques en Autriche, facteur du tourisme d'hiver avec une incidence importante sur l'économie

FELIX JÜLG, Vienne, Autriche

Actuellement, l'Autriche dispose d'un cinquième du nombre total des remontées mécaniques du monde. Les effets découlant de la mise en place de remontées mécaniques ont fait l'objet d'études effectuées par des services compétents et des chercheurs. Les changements majeurs – constatent-ils – sont dus indirectement au développement du tourisme d'hiver.

50% seulement des remontées mécaniques autrichiennes ont été exploitées avec profit en 1975. Leur rentabilité dépend dans une large mesure du système technique des installations. Les constructions lourdes ne sont rentables qu'à condition que le coëfficient d'utilisation soit plus élevé.

Il y a un rapport étroit entre remontées mécaniques et tourisme d'hiver. Plus des trois quarts de tous les utilisateurs des remontées mécaniques sont transportés en hiver, dont – comme on a pu constater – 85% sont des touristes. De nos jours, le ski alpin est inconcevable sans remontées mécaniques. L'augmentation du nombre de nuitées enregistrées en hiver dans les communes où de nouvelles remontées méchaniques avaient été ouvertes au public met en lumière les retombées de leur mise en place. Des effets secondaires peuvent être constatés pour l'ensemble de l'économie régionale.

Parmi la multitude des critères possibles, trois ont été choisis pour en fournir la preuve:

1. L'évolution démographique (on voit croître la population dans des régions menacées de l'exode rural il y a quelques années).
2. L'évolution du nombre de bâtiments (certains villages paysans de montagne, dont le nombre de bâtiments était à peu près stable pendant des siècles, connaissent un essor vigoureux de l'activité de construction).
3. L'évolution des recettes fiscales par habitant (les recettes par habitant provenant de la taxe communale sont plus élevées dans quelques grands centres de sports d'hiver que dans des localités à forte implantation industrielle).

Trois facteurs sont, pour l'essentiel, responsables du succès économique considérable du tourisme d'hiver:

1. Un coefficient d'utilisation des équipements touristiques élevé; la création d'une deuxième saison permet à un grand nombre d'établissements de franchir le seuil de rentabilité.
2. La moyenne des recettes par touriste est plus élevée en hiver qu'en été, fait qui est dû aux dépenses supplémentaires pour remontées mécaniques, écoles de ski, aprés-ski etc.
3. Les touristes visitant l'Autriche en hiver appartiennent à des couches sociales plus élevées que les estivants.

De nombreux problèmes vont de pair avec l'expansion des remontées mécaniques dont les plus importants seront brièvement évoqués par la suite.

1. La »course à l'équipement« dans les Alpes, due à la forte concurrence entre Etats, régions et stations de sports d'hiver, en partie également à des estimations par trop optimistes portant sur les taux d'accroissement dans le tourisme d'hiver.
2. D'une part ce sont les fausses estimations quant à la situation économique, d'autre part c'est la »course à l'équipement« mentionée plus haut, qui font vivre dans l'euphorie tout ce secteur. Par conséquent, l'on procède actuellement à la création d'un grand nombre d'entreprises qui, peut-être, devront être subventionnées à l'avenir.
3. Sur le plan régional existe le danger de surdéveloppement et d'une concentration trop poussée. Les domaines skiables attractifs, dotés d'une importante capacité de remontées mécaniques, ont besoin de grands centres touristiques pour pouvoir utiliser pleinement leur capacité. De ce fait, les centres dépassent de loin la taille considérée comme optimale pour un village de vacances.
4. La mise en place de remontées mécaniques implique une modification du paysage concerné, et ne porte pas seulement atteinte à sa beauté, mais augmente aussi certains dangers naturels, comme le risque d'avalanches et d'érosion.

Grâce aux remontées mécaniques, la part du tourisme d'hiver au tourisme a été portée en Autriche de 23% à 30% depuis l'année 1961. Les recettes touristiques en devises sont dues pour une part importante – et par voie indirecte – aux remontées mécaniques. Celles-ci semblent promouvoir le plus efficacement le développement économique dans les régions montagneuses qui se prêtent à la pratique des sports d'hiver.

L'urbanisation et les problèmes du tourisme et des loisirs en Bulgarie

LJUBOMIR DINEV, Sofia, Bulgarie

C'est au 19e siècle, avec les débuts du capitalisme, que commence à se développer et prendre forme le tourisme en tant que secteur de l'économie nationale. Le nombre croissant de touristes fait naître des centres et régions touristiques. Répondant au jeu de l'offre et de la demande, le tourisme se transforme progressivement en industrie touristique, branche spécifique de l'économie.

A cette époque, la Bulgarie tout comme le reste de l'Empire ottoman souffre d'un retard économique. Libéré du joug ottoman en 1878, la Bulgarie reste jusqu'à la Première guerre mondiale un pays agricole faiblement développé. Les conditions matérielles permettant le développement du tourisme ne sont pas encore réunies. L'essor économique dans l'entre-deux-guerres donne lieu à une urbanisation progressive et stimule le tourisme national bien que la base matérielle y nécessaire n'existe pas encore. Dans cette période se développe également le tourisme international.

C'est en 1895 que le tourisme organisé fait son apparition en Bulgarie; l'Union touristique bulgare (UTB), créée en cette année, jouera un rôle primordial dans le développement du tourisme jusqu'à la Seconde guerre mondiale. Dès l'adoption du système économique socialiste après la Seconde guerre mondiale, des changements radicaux ont bouleversé la structure socio-économique du pays. L'économie planifiée, l'industrialisation socialiste, la gestion coopérative de la terre et d'autres réformes révolutionnaires ont profondément changé la répartition de la population sur le territoire national. La part des personnes travaillant dans l'agriculture tomba de 82% en 1948 à 31% en 1975, la part de la population urbaine montant de 24% à 58%, le nombre des villes de 104 à 218.

L'urbanisation rapide du pays, la réorganisation socio-économique de celui-ci ainsi que la politique menée par le gouvernement constituaient des facteurs favorables au développement du tourisme. En peu de temps la Bulgarie devint un pays du tourisme tant national qu'international. La base matérielle qui jusque là faisait défaut put de même être créée, le tourisme se transforma en secteur spécifique de l'économie nationale.

Le tourisme actif international prit un essor extraordinaire et en 1976 quelque 4 millions de touristes sont venus visiter la Bulgarie, leur nombre ne s'élevant qu'à 8.500 en 1956. Au niveau du tourisme international il s'agit actuellement de développer non seulement le tourisme sur le littoral, mais également celui en montagne tout comme les activités balnéaires, le tourisme de congrès et culturel afin d'assurer une meilleure utilisation des capacités existantes et d'aller à l'encontre des fluctuations saisonnières.

Après la Seconde guerre mondiale l'essor du tourisme international allait de pair avec une intensification du tourisme national stimulé non en dernier lieu par l'Union touristique bulgare. Entre 1972 et 1977 28,5 millions de personnes ont participé aux activités organisées par l'UTB et ses différents bureaux. Les Unions syndicales jouent un rôle important dans le développement du tourisme social. Le tourisme dispose d'une base matérielle considérable: le Comité d'Etat de tourisme est propriétaire de 555 hôtels avec 91.550 lits. Dans les montagnes on compte 343 refuges avec 20.000 lits, les organisations du tourisme social disposent de 1.392 maisons de repos avec 90.700 lits.

L'apparition du tourisme de masse dans le cadre du tourisme national est due avant tout au processus d'urbanisation accéléré. La vie urbaine amène les citadins à chercher de nouvelles formes de tourisme et de récréation; par conséquent le tourisme de courte durée (week-end) a pris un essor particulièrement vigoureux. Une partie de la population urbaine cherche repos et détente dans les villas construites aux alentours des villes, une autre participe aux activités du tourisme individuel et collectif. Pendant ces dernières années le nombre de touristes-automobilistes s'est accru rapidement.

Les différentes formes du tourisme tendent de plus en plus à faire partie intégrante de la vie de la population. L'infrastructure existante ne satisfaisant plus les besoins du tourisme de masse, il s'agit actuellement d'augmenter le nombre d'hôtels, de refuges, de maisons de repos etc. L'aménagement de zones de récréation autour des villes constitue une des solutions possibles. Jouera un rôle important dans ce contexte la création de campings dans les montagnes utilisés en été ainsi que la création de refuges, non seulement à des endroits qui s'y prêtent de par leur nature, mais également à ceux rappelant d'importants événements historiques.

Les principales directives adoptées dans le cadre de l'aménagement du territoire et de l'urbanisme influeront de façon décisive sur le développement du tourisme de courte durée et du tourisme en général. Aux termes de ces directives, ce n'est pas au moyen de mesures isolées que l'on devrait chercher à résoudre les problèmes existants (infrastructure touristique, conditions économiques et sociales, qualité de la vie dans les villes et villages, migration et urbanisation ...), il faudrait, bien au contraire, recourir à un système complexe regroupant les mesures à prendre aux différents niveaux.

Les etapes de l'occupation touristique des montagnes moyennes par les sociétés industrielles. L'exemple rhénan

GABRIEL WACKERMANN, Strasbourg, France

La société industrielle intensifie sa consommation d'espace à travers l'économie touristique. Les montagnes moyennes sont soumises à une pression croissante des villes environnantes. Les étapes de l'occupation de leur sol marquent surtout l'emprise progressive de la bourgeoisie, sous l'apparence d'une popularisation des massifs forestiers. Aussi l'époque actuelle remet-elle en cause la dialectique traditionnelle entre les villes et la montagne moyenne. Le modèle rhénan se prête de façon intéressante à l'analyse de cette évolution.

Les rayons d'action et les zones d'attraction de quelques lieux de loisirs en Bavière

GÜNTER HEINRITZ, Munich, République Fédérale d'Allemagne

A l'exemple de piscines couvertes, de parcours d'entraînement sportif („Trimm-Pfade") et de golfs-miniatures il fut examiné s'il y a des rayons d'action spécifiques suivant le type de tels établissements. Le résultat obtenu n'est pas satisfaisant, car les différences des rayons d'action sont considérables. Mais la répartition des valeurs se réduit considérablement si l'on ne se réfère qu'à des établissements d'un emplacement comparable. Un résultat important des recherches est la constatation que les groupes de visiteurs ne diffèrent pas à l'égard de leur disposition à parcourir des distances maximales différentes, mais plutôt à l'égard d'une fréquentation diminuée suivant l'augmentation de la distance entre le lieu d'habitation et le lieu de loisir.

L'impact du tourisme sur les modes de vie de communautés rurales

Le cas de Sleat, Isle de Skye

RICHARD W. BUTLER, London, Ontario, Canada

Cette communication porte sur les impacts de la récréation, surtout ceux qui sont de nature sociale et culturelle, sur la population d'une région rurale insulaire en Ecosse. Une enquête a été effectuée chez les résidants de la paroisse de Sleat, Isle de Skye, pour obtenir leurs opinions et attitudes envers le tourisme. Ils ont aussi été questionnés sur les effets sur leurs propres genres de vie causés par le tourisme. La communication porte sur les perceptions et attitudes de différents groupes. Ces derniers sont identifiés selon les critères suivants: lieu de résidence, langue parlée, degré de contact avec les touristes et degré d'associations directes avec eux. Les impacts sont examinés du point de vue des bénéfices qu'ils causent et des problèmes qu'ils créent. Les bénéfices sont notés dans les emplois, les revenus personnels, les échanges sociaux et les améliorations dans les services. Les problèmes comprennent la congestion dans la circulation routière, le développement de résidences secondaires, les augmentations dans les tensions quotidiennes, les changements dans les associations sociales et la réduction de l'emploi de la langue gaélique. Les conclusions visent à souligner l'importance qui doit être attachée à la considération des attitudes locales envers le tourisme – surtout la rèception envisagée – dans l'aménagement de l'industrie. L'obet serait de préserver l'environnement social local des régions visitées par les touristes.

Planification au niveau communal des activités de plein air en Suède

Quelques réflexions sur l'importance des facteurs institutionnels

HANS ALDSKOGIUS, Uppsala, Suède

La commune constitue le niveau de base dans l'hiérarchie administrative de la Suède; actuellement il y en a 277, fortement différenciées quant au nombre d'habitants et à la superficie. Les communes ont le droit de déterminer la forme et l'ampleur de leur participation à la création d'équipements récréatifs. A cet égard, il y a des différences considérables entre les communes, dues non seulement aux différences de densité de la population, structure économique et milieu naturel, mais dépendant aussi dans une large mesure de l'existence d'activités politiques communales en matière de récréation.

Cette politique exige en premier lieu des décisions sur l'intérêt relatif de la »récréation en plein air« par rapport aux autres activités récréatives, l'importance des différentes formes de »récréation en plein air« et des intérêts de diverses couches de la population, ainsi que sur la fondation d'entreprises dans les communes ou l'aide à accorder à divers organismes compétents.

Il importe d'étudier le cadre institutionnel à l'intérieur duquel cette politique est conçue et administrée, c'est-à-dire la ligne de conduite adoptée par les groupements d'intérêt, par divers organismes (associations de sport, de jeunes), propriétaires fonciers, entrepreneurs de ce secteur et les autorités centrales et régionales de l'Etat, ainsi que leur mode de coopération ou de concurrence en ce qui concerne la mise en place d'équipements récréatifs, l'organisation d'activités de loisirs et l'information donnée à ce sujet, et finalement les règles d'accès aux ressources importantes pour les activités de plein air.

Il y a plusieurs motifs pour la prise en considération des facteurs institutionnels. De toute évidence, la création d'une »infrastructure pour les loisirs de plein air« est dans une large mesure le résultat de compromis politiques (problème des espaces nécessaires ...). L'étude de ce processus devrait mener à la connaissance approfondie du développement de l'organisation spatiale de »paysages de récréation«. La réalisation d'études comparées menées dans divers domaines pourrait fournir des résultats valables pour d'autres régions et de futures planifications.

Le niveau local se prête parfaitement à la réalisation d'une telle étude, de nombreuses institutions participant aux décisions y étant réunies, des groupements d'intérêt individuels jusqu'aux autorités de l'administration centrale. L'etude des facteurs institutionnels permet également de nouer de nouvelles relations fructueuses entre géographes et représentants d'autres disciplines (sciences politiques, sciences administratives).

Touristes et équipements récréatifs dans les Etats occidentaux des USA – Fréquentation et abus

BURKHARD HOFMEISTER, Berlin (Ouest)

L'enquête menée par l'auteur a porté sur plusieurs parcs nationaux, terrains nationaux de récréation, forêts nationales et parcs d'Etat dans les Etats occidentaux des USA; son but était de savoir dans quelle mesure la foule de visiteurs, devenus de plus en plus nombreux pendant les années cinquante et soixante, a mené à une saturation et à une surcharge écologique, ainsi que de connaître les réactions des autorités responsables de ces espaces. Il a été démontré que ce problème se pose de façon plus aigue pour certains espaces que pour d'autres, soit qu'ils offrent des curiosités naturelles spectaculaires comme p. ex. le Grand Canyon et le Yellowstone National Park, soit qu'ils se trouvent proches d'agglomérations urbaines, comme p. ex. Lake Mead National Recreation Area par rapport aux grandes villes de la Californie. La situation est plus grave dans le Yellowstone National Park que dans le Yosemite Valley National Park, étant donné que le premier est fréquenté surtout en été tandis que dans le second les touristes se répartissent de façon plus uniforme sur toute l'année.

Les points suivants sont discutés de façon plus précise: le concept »multiple-use« de l' »U.S. Forest Service« et sa compatibilité avec la fonction récréative;

le concept de la poursuite du développement des »heavy-use areas« utilisées jusqu'à présent de la façon la plus intensive, au profit des territoires plus éloignés et peu visités tant par les promeneurs que par les cavaliers (»back country« ou »wilderness areas«) pour lesquels les chiffres maximum de fréquentation touristique sont définis selon trois méthodes différentes; la limitation de la circulation automobile privée et l'introduction de transports alternants par autocars dans quelques »heavy-use areas«; le gel sur la base actuelle du nombre de chambres d'hôtel, de maisons d'accueil et du nombre de terrains de camping, ce qui devrait conduire ultérieurement à l'accroissement du nombre des motels en dehors des limites des parcs; l'achat de terrains privés pour la récréation publique, telle que l'acquisition de certaines zones de rivage au Lac Tahoe par l'Etat de Californie (il convient de compléter cette réflexion par le fait que le potentiel maximum d'élargissement des espaces de récréation se situe dans les forêts nationales); la signature de contrats avec des scientifiques qui seraient chargés d'effectuer des calculs de capacité touristique en vue d'une amélioration des possibilités de décision.

Le développement du tourisme dans une société autogestionnaire Théorie et pratique en Yougoslavie

MOMČILO VUKIĆEVIĆ, Novi Sad, Yougoslavie

L'analyse part du fait que, dans le socialisme, se créent les conditions permettant aux divers besoins des travailleurs de se développer qualitativement et quantitativement et d'être satisfaits. Quoique ce développement soit différent dans certaines phases de l'édification socialiste et qu'il ne se fasse pas toujours en ligne droite dans quelques Etats, cette orientation à long terme est positive et elle est liée au développement du système économique et socio-politique de la société socialiste.

Comme ce fut le cas dans tous les pays après la guerre, la Yougoslavie a développé à cette époque un tourisme »syndical«. Pendant plusieurs années, il eut un traitement spécial car il avait qualité de facteur de standard de vie des travailleurs, avec un effet positif. Toutefois, il différait des autres modèles nationaux. Cette différence augmenta graduellement pour devenir à l'étape actuelle une qualité nouvelle – du tourisme »syndical« naquit le tourisme »ouvrier«, comme forme spéciale du processus de démocratisation des activités touristico-récréatives des gens dans le monde.

Cette étape de fait a placé l'auteur devant la tâche complexe de dégager, à travers l'analyse, ce qu'on appelle la perspective historique de l'intégration des travailleurs de Yougoslavie dans le tourisme et d'éclairer les cadres économiques et socio-politiques du développement de leurs activités touristiques et récréatives ainsi que d'etablir la comparaison critique entre celui-ci et le tourisme »syndical« d'une part et le tourisme »social« de l'autre.

L'auteur donne des réponses aux trois questions, réponses de caractère théorique, fondées sur les résultats de l'analyse de l'expérience yougoslave.

Zusammenfassungen in deutscher Sprache

Die Bergwelt als Erholungsraum

KARL A. SINNHUBER, Wien, Österreich

Die Bergwelt ist ein ideales Gebiet für die Erholung und somit auch für eine Reihe sportlicher Tätigkeiten. Einige davon, wie der alpine Schilauf, können nur in den Bergen ausgeübt werden, andere gewinnen in den Bergen einen völlig anderen Charakter, wie Kajakfahren im Wildwasser, wieder anderen, wie zum Beispiel dem Segeln auf den Alpenseen, verleiht die Berglandschaft lediglich einen zusätzlichen Reiz. Der älteste Sport in den Alpen war die Jagd auf Reh, Hirsch und Gemse; sie war und ist mit wenigen Ausnahmen ein Sport der sozialen und finanziellen Oberschicht. Um genügend Tiere zur Jagd zur Verfügung zu haben, haben nun viele Teile der Alpen, besonders in der Bundesrepublik Deutschland, einen so großen Wildüberbesatz, daß Umweltschäden eintreten. Bei anderen Sportarten in den Bergen, dem Bergwandern und dem Schilauf, rufen die Besucher selbst infolge ihrer großen Zahl Umweltschäden hervor, besonders durch Müll, aber auch starke Bautätigkeit, vor allem Errichtung von Zweitwohnsitzen. Daher haben sich die Alpenvereine, einst Pioniere bei der Erschließung der Alpen für Besucher durch den Bau von Schutzhütten und Anlegen eines Wegnetzes, nun gegen eine weitere Erschließung ausgesprochen.

Auch im Segelsport, soweit es Jachten und Jollen betrifft, ist keine große weitere Entwicklung mehr zu erwarten, da es bereits heute sehr schwierig ist, noch einen Liegeplatz für ein Boot zu erhalten. Diese Schwierigkeit fällt beim Brettsegeln (Windsurfen) weg, und dies ist mit ein Grund für das rapide Zunehmen dieses Sportes, obwohl die Alpenseen aus klimatischen Gründen keineswegs dafür ideal sind.

Die Berge sind schließlich auch ein Gelände für den motorlosen Flug, wobei das Drachenfliegen in den letzten Jahren eine sprunghafte Entwicklung erlebte. Obwohl diese Art von Flug wohl den Höhepunkt des Fluggefühls überhaupt darstellt und schon zahlreiche Drachenflüge von Dreitausendern durchgeführt wurden, 1976 sogar von 7600 Metern im Hindukusch, so war die Zahl der Unfälle, auch der mit tödlichem Ausgang, so hoch, daß eigentlich nur besonders gute und sehr erfahrene Drachenflieger im Hochgebirge fliegen sollten. Mit diesem Gerät, ohne die bei einem Flugzeug vorhandenen Ruder, kann der Pilot einfach nicht schnell genug gegen einen unerwarteten, starken seitlichen Windstoß, der den Hängegleiter aus der sicheren Fluglage bringt, reagieren, und es sollte daher besser nur dort geflogen werden, wo solche Windströmungen bei gutem Wetter nicht zu erwarten sind, d. h. in den Vorbergen und Hügeln. Im Gegensatz dazu gibt der Segelflug die Möglichkeit, dieses Fluggefühl in fast gleicher Weise zu erleben, ohne übermäßige Risiken auf sich nehmen zu müssen. Zwischen dem Segelfliegen und der Geographie besteht eine doppelte Beziehung: Auf der einen Seite muß ein Pilot, um in den Bergen erfolgreich, das heißt über eine lange Strecke, in große Höhe oder auf lange Dauer fliegen zu können, eingehende Kenntnisse des Terrains und der Luftströmungen besitzen, die bei gewissen Wetterbedingungen zu bestimmten Tageszeiten über einem Gelände entsprechend seiner Neigung, seiner Felsart und seiner Pflanzendecke zu erwarten sind. Auf der anderen Seite sind auch die wirtschaftlichen Auswirkungen, die durch die Ausübung des Segelfliegens entstehen, zu beachten. Wenn auch, verglichen mit den Schiläufern, die Zahl der Segelflieger klein ist, so handelt es sich bei ihnen notwendigerweise durchwegs um Leute mit relativ hohem Einkommen. Sie bringen oft ihre Familienangehörigen mit, und der Segelflug bildet für Orte, die sonst über keine besonderen Attraktionen verfügen, auch einen Anziehungspunkt für andere Besucher, sodaß sich dadurch für einige Orte ein nicht unbedeutender Fremdenverkehr entwickeln kann.

Da die Zahl der Segelflugzeuge, die zur günstigsten Tageszeit gestartet werden können, nicht sehr groß ist und es sich um einen Sport handelt, der ständig neue Anhänger gewinnt, besteht hier noch die Möglichkeit, wirtschaftliche Vorteile des Fremdenverkehrs mit geringem Kapitalaufwand in einige Orte zu bringen, die bisher noch nicht daran teilhatten.

Die Stellung der Fremdenverkehrsgeographie im Rahmen der gesamten Geographie und der Freizeitforschung

Z. TED MIECZKOWSKI, Winnipeg, Kanada

Der Verfasser untersucht die Stellung der Geographie des Fremdenverkehrs und der Erholung zu anderen Disziplinen der Geographie und illustriert dies mit einem Modell. Er äußert seine Ansicht zur Diskussion über die Geographie des Fremdenverkehrs und die Geographie des Freizeitverhaltens, die von Professor RUPPERT (München) angeregt wurde.

Im zweiten Teil des Aufsatzes wird die Stellung der Geographie des Fremdenverkehrs und der Erholung im Rahmen der Freizeitforschung erörtert. Auf die Bedeutung bereits vorliegender Forschungsbeiträge und auf zukünftige Entwicklungsmöglichkeiten wird hingewiesen.

Die Erholung: Ein neuer Gesichtspunkt

ALICE COLEMAN, London, Großbritannien

In der Geographie des Erholungswesens hat man sich bisher hauptsächlich mit den Themen Erholungsraum und Freizeittätigkeiten beschäftigt, hat jedoch die soziale Umwälzung, die zu mehr Freizeit geführt hat, als gegebene Tatsache hingenommen. Die Autorin bezweifelt, ob eine solche Vorgangsweise gerechtfertigt erscheint und führt den Begriff der *Überfreizeit* ein, als einen Zustand, der auf die menschliche Persönlichkeit destruktiv wirken könnte. Der für Erholungszwecke gewidmete Raum ist in Großbritannien so schnell und umfangreich gewachsen, daß andere wesentliche Nutzungen wie die Versorgung mit Nahrungsmitteln bedroht erscheinen und die finanziellen Möglichkeiten der öffentlichen Hand, die Schäden, die durch dieses rapide Wachstum von Freizeitflächen entstehen, wieder gut zu machen, überfordert sind. Es ist daher nun nicht mehr gerechtfertigt, anzunehmen, daß Probleme dadurch gelöst werden können, daß man zunehmend mehr Erholungsmöglichkeiten bietet, sondern es ist notwendig, zu einer ganzheitlicheren Betrachtungsweise zu kommen, die die Überfreizeit von ihren Ursachen her sieht und bekämpft.

Die funktionelle und räumliche Struktur öffentlicher Anlagen für die Freizeitgestaltung in einer städtischen Umwelt

LISLE S. MITCHELL, Columbia, South Carolina, U.S.A.

Diese Untersuchung behandelt zwei Hauptfragen: Erstens die diskrete Kategorisierung von Einheiten eines Systems öffentlicher Spiel- und Sportplatzanlagen nach funktionellen Klassen und ihren grundlegenden Eigenschaften. Zweitens die Analyse der Verteilung der Anlagen in Form von absoluten und relativen örtlich festgelegten Schemata. Angaben, die 172 öffentliche Anlagen in Columbia, South Carolina, betreffen, wurden mehrdimensionalen Messungen, Ward-Algorithmen und einer Diskriminanz-Analyse unterworfen. Dieses Verfahren ergab ein fünfklassiges Kategorisierungsschema. Die Klassen in dem System unterscheiden sich mehr durch die Rangstufe als durch die Art der Einrichtungen, sie dienen der Nachfrage nach Erholung. Die Anlagen befinden sich in dicht bevölkerten, städtischen Gegenden angehäuft und sind Wohngebieten angeschlossen bzw. zugänglich.

Die komplexe Natur des Angebotes öffentlicher städtischer Anlagen zur Freizeitgestaltung kann am besten im Zusammenhang mit deren Zweck, Struktur und Verteilung verstanden werden. Der Zweck einer bestimmten Anlage bestimmt die Art der Einrichtungen, Programme und Freizeitbeschäftigungen, die angeboten werden, wie auch, welche Bevölkerung angesprochen wird. Diese Faktoren wiederum beeinflussen die örtliche Lage der einzelnen Anlagen oder Klassen von Spiel- und Sportplätzen. Daraus kann man schließen, daß öffentliche Spiel- und Sportplatzanlagen räumlich konzentriert sind, weil es ihr Zweck ist, der Bevölkerung in dicht besiedelten Gebieten mit Einrichtungen zur Freizeitgestaltung zu dienen.

Probleme der kartographischen Darstellung des Fremdenverkehrs

PETER MARIOT, Bratislava, ČSSR

Fremdenverkehrskarten sind eine wichtige Methode, die Kenntnisse über den Fremdenverkehr, seine Voraussetzungen, räumliche Verteilung, Intensität und Struktur, zu erweitern.

Grundlegende Probleme bei Fremdenverkehrskarten ergeben sich aus ihrer Zielsetzung, ihrem Inhalt, der angewandten Methode, dem gewählten Maßstab und der verwendeten Grundkarte.

Zu der ursprünglichen Zielsetzung, nämlich die Ergebnisse geographischer Forschung genauer und einprägsamer darzustellen, kommt nunmehr das Bestreben, die Planung zu unterstützen und Beiträge zu fremdenverkehrsgeographischen Theorien zu liefern.

Ihrem Inhalt nach können Fremdenverkehrskarten in verschiedene Gruppen eingeteilt werden. Eine davon befaßt sich mit qualitativen Merkmalen des Tourismus. Hier kann weiter unterschieden werden zwischen Karten, die

1. Voraussetzungen für den Fremdenverkehr erfassen (örtliche, besonders ausgewählte, realisierbare),

2. strukturelle Fremdenverkehrsmerkmale zum Inhalt haben,

3. den Einfluß des Fremdenverkehrs darstellen.

Die Gestaltung dieser Karten ist in letzter Zeit von Planung und Wirtschaft beeinflußt worden. Das hat dazu beigetragen, den Horizont der Geographen zu erweitern und ihre Aufmerksamkeit besonders auch auf Probleme wie die Aufnahmefähigkeit der Landschaft, auch in weniger stark frequentierten Gebieten, oder die Teilnahme der Wohnbevölkerung am Fremdenverkehr zu richten. Im Zuge der methodischen Weiterentwicklung ist eine Zunahme von Versuchen festzustellen, mit komplexen Inhalten einer Typisierung von Fremdenverkehrsorten und einer Regionalisierung des Fremdenverkehrs näher zu kommen.

Die Probleme bei der Wahl geeigneter Darstellungsmethoden hängen eng mit dem Inhalt von Fremdenverkehrskarten zusammen. Besonders die Auswahl geeigneter Kriterien und Charakteristika für die darzustellenden touristischen Sachverhalte verdient besondere Aufmerksamkeit. Hier kann ein Abgehen von Einzelangaben zugunsten von komplexen, oft kombinierten Faktoren festgestellt werden. Gleichzeitig wird vor allem von wissenschaftlicher Seite auf die Notwendigkeit einer intensiven Zusammenarbeit hingewiesen, um Karten von verschiedenen Gebieten und Autoren vergleichbar zu machen.

Maßstab und Inhalt von Karten sind voneinander abhängig, beide hängen wieder von dem Zweck ab, der mit der Karte verfolgt wird. Dadurch sind vor allem für die Praxis in der Fachliteratur großstäbige Detailkarten entstanden, welche besonders die örtlichen Voraussetzungen für den Fremdenverkehr zum Inhalt haben.

Die Grundkarte ist ein wichtiges Hilfsmittel, den Zusammenhang zwischen Fremdenverkehrsfaktoren und Elementen der Landschaft darzustellen, das bisher allerdings kaum genutzt worden ist. Es wäre daher an der Zeit, die herkömmliche topographische oder administrative Grundkarte aufzugeben und statt dessen jene Faktoren aufzunehmen, die einen direkten Zusammenhang mit den dargestellten Fremdenverkehrscharakteristiken haben.

Diese Bestandsaufnahme der Probleme der Gestaltung von Fremdenverkehrskarten zeigt, daß für den weiteren Fortschritt der Fremdenverkehrsgeographie, sowohl was die Anwendung ihrer Ergebnisse in der Praxis betrifft, als auch bei der wissenschaftlichen Erfassung der Grundlagen mehr Aufmerksamkeit der kartographischen Darstellung des Fremdenverkehrs zugewendet werden sollte.

In diesem Zusammenhang sollen alle Fremdenverkehrsgeographen auf drei Hauptaufgaben aufmerksam gemacht werden:

1. Kritische Bestandsaufnahme der Probleme der Fremdenverkehrskartographie.

2. Erarbeitung von Methoden zur Auswahl von Kriterien und Indikatoren, mit welchen die geographisch bedeutenden Faktoren des Fremdenverkehrs dargestellt werden können.

3. Intensivierung der Zusammenarbeit zur Darstellung von verschiedenen Fremdenverkehrsfaktoren in einzelnen Regionen durch Anwendung einer einheitlichen Darstellungsmethode und einheitlicher Symbole.

Fortschritte bei Bewältigung dieser Aufgaben sind besonders mit Unterstützung und im Rahmen der IGU-Arbeitsgruppe für Fremdenverkehr und Erholung zu erwarten.

Naturdenkmal und Tourismus

JOSEF MATZNETTER, Frankfurt/Main, Bundesrepublik Deutschland

Besonders charakteristische Gebilde der Natur, wie z. B. größere Wasserfälle, auffallende Felspartien oder Höhlen, aber auch spezielle Vorkommen von Pflanzen- und Tierarten u. a. werden in vielen Ländern als „Naturdenkmäler" vor zerstörenden Eingriffen rechtlich geschützt. Innerhalb des menschlichen Interessenfeldes kommt diesen eine dreifache Bedeutung zu, nämlich für die wissenschaftliche Forschung, dann für den Besichtigungstourismus und endlich – in einzelnen Fällen – auch zur wirtschaftlichen Nutzung. Die Erschließung eines solchen Naturdenkmales für den Touristenverkehr erfordert bestimmte Gruppen von Maßnahmen und zwar betreffend Zugänglichkeit, Sicherung der Besucher, Sicherung des Objektes, Darstellung des Denkmals, Besuchsorganisation, Eingliederung in den regionalen Tourismus, sowie zusätzliche Einrichtungen.

Einer namentlich für Höhlen maßgeblichen Meinung zufolge sollte sich eine derartige Öffnung für eine allgemeine Besichtigung auf relativ wenige Objekte beschränken. In diesem Falle sind dann die zu treffenden Maßnahmen nach den jeweiligen Gegebenheiten zu differenzieren. Entscheidend ist dabei, daß der naturhafte Charakter erhalten bleibt und dem Besucher verdeutlicht wird. Als besonders kritisch sind hier auch Versuche zu sehen, die ästhetisch-künstlerische Wirkung eines Naturdenkmales heben zu wollen. Besonders empfindlich sind diesbezüglich Höhlen, in denen die unerläßliche Beleuchtung durch gezielte Effekte – namentlich Schattenwirkung und Färbung – bis zur Verkitschung führen kann. Auch besondere Veranstaltungen, insbesondere Höhlenkonzerten gegenüber, erscheint eine gewisse Reserve geboten. Letzten Endes sollte gerade der Besuch von Naturdenkmälern dem Menschen unserer Zivilisation das Wiedererlangen naturnahen Denkens erleichtern.

Geographisch bedingte Schwierigkeiten für den Tourismus auf kleinen landentfernten Inseln

ALEXANDER MELAMID, New York, N. Y., U.S.A.

Schiffe legen an kleinen Inseln nur an, wenn genügend Fracht abgeladen werden kann, um die Entladung wirtschaftlich zu machen. Während der Bauperiode von Touristenhotels sind die Ladungen im allgemeinen groß genug, um ganze Schiffe zu füllen. Aber zu normalen Zeiten sind die Frachten, die kleine Inseln benötigen, nicht einmal groß genug, um auch nur Teilladungen von wirtschaftlicher Größe zu erreichen. Dieses Problem der Verfrachtung ist in den letzten Jahren durch die Zunahme der Tragfähigkeit der neuen Schiffe und die Erhöhung der Personalkosten noch schwieriger geworden. Luftfrachten sind aber für die meisten Güter, die von den Touristen und den Bewohnern dieser Inseln gebraucht werden, zu teuer. Passagierschiffe, die auf Kreuzfahrten diese Inseln anlaufen, können diese Frachten nicht befördern. Eine Lösung des Frachtproblemes wäre, weiterhin Hotels usw. zu bauen, um den Touristenverkehr so zu vergrößern, daß eine wirtschaftliche Belieferung möglich wird. Eine solche Vergrößerung des Tourismus könnte aber Strände, schöne Landschaften (National-Parks) usw. auf diesen kleinen Inseln derart überfüllen, daß dadurch die Attraktivität geringer wird. Beispiele dieser Entwicklung können bei den Seychellen, der Cook-Insel, der Osterinsel sowie den Cayman und Bermuda Inseln beobachtet werden.

Prognose des Verkehrsaufkommens der Autobahnen in Kanada in Zeiten von Treibstoffmangel und hohen Treibstoffkosten

ROY WOLFE, Downsview, Ontario, Canada

Mit gewissen Einschränkungen, welche sich aus der Landnutzung der angrenzenden Räume ergeben, kann das untenstehende Simulationsmodell ganz gut für die Verkehrsprognose des Erholungsverkehrs an Sommerwochenenden auf den Autobahnen im Staate Ontario verwendet werden:

$$R = 0{,}840 \frac{W_R}{W_T} + 3{,}410 \frac{D_T}{W_T} - 3{,}056 + 0{,}118 \left(\frac{W_R}{W_T}\right)^{1/2} \log^{-1}\left(\frac{W_R}{W_T}\right) \log\left(\frac{3{,}5 D_T}{W_{TT}} - 2{,}5\right)$$

wobei R das Verhältnis zwischen dem Verkehrsaufkommen des Wochenenderholungsverkehrs und dem täglichen Durchschnitt im Sommer angibt,
W_R = das Verkehrsaufkommen des Erholungsverkehrs an Werktagen,
W_T = das durchschnittliche tägliche Verkehrsaufkommen im Sommer.
D_T = das durchschnittliche tägliche Verkehrsaufkommen im Sommer.

Der Autor untersucht, wieweit sich die Aussagekraft dieses Prognosemodells ändert, wenn der Wochenendverkehr durch neue wirtschaftliche Belastungen eingeschränkt wird, besonders durch untragbar hohe Benzinpreise. Er versucht zu klären, ab welcher Höhe die Preise als unannehmbar empfunden werden und von welcher wirtschaftlichen, sozialen oder kulturellen Bevölkerungsschicht bzw. in welchen Regionen, für welche Arten der Erholung und für welche Entfernungen zwischen Wohn- und Erholungsort. Schließlich stellt er die Frage nach der Anwendbarkeit des Modells angesichts der Substitutionsmöglichkeiten von bestehenden touristischen Möglichkeiten durch solche an neuen Standorten, mit günstigeren Kosten, die von den einzelnen Gesellschaftsschichten in unterschiedlichem Maße angenommen werden können.

Ferner wird dargelegt, wieweit alle diese zusätzlichen Störfaktoren in ein modifiziertes Simulationsmodell eingebaut werden können.

Schifahren und Wintersportorte
Eine Weltübersicht

BERNARD BARBIER, Aix-en-Provence, Frankreich

17.500 Seilbahnen, 3.000 Wintersportorte und 37 Millionen Schifahrer in 40 Staaten, das sind die ungefähren Dimensionen des Schilaufes in der Welt. Aber in nur neun Staaten (sechs Alpenstaaten, die USA, Canada und Japan) befinden sich 90% der Seilbahnen und 80% der Wintersportorte.

Diese Angaben zeigen, daß die Ausübung des Schilaufes sowohl vom Lebensstandard als auch von der Erreichbarkeit von Gebirgen abhängig ist. Aber eine genaue Analyse bringt große Unterschiede, besonders auch in den Alpenstaaten, zu Tage. Nicht jedes Gebirge ist für den Schilauf geeignet, und der Einfluß des Wintertourismus auf die Wirtschaft in Gebirgsregionen ist von Land zu Land verschieden.

Weitere genauere Forschungen und besonders vergleichende Arbeiten über den Wintertourismus und dessen Verteilung sollten daher durchgeführt werden.

Seilbahnen in Österreich

Ein Faktor des Wintertourismus mit bedeutenden wirtschaftlichen Auswirkungen

FELIX JÜLG, Wien, Österreich

In Österreich verkehren heute ein Fünftel der Personenseilbahnen der Welt. Kompetente Stellen und wissenschaftliche Untersuchungen haben sich mit den Auswirkungen der Errichtung von Seilbahnen befaßt und festgestellt, daß die größten Veränderungen indirekt durch die Entwicklung des Winterfremdenverkehrs entstehen.

Nur 50% der österreichischen Seilbahnen konnten im Jahre 1975 Gewinne erzielen. Ihre Rentabilität hängt in einem großen Ausmaß vom technischen System der Seilbahnanlagen ab. Schwere Konstruktionen benötigen eine größere Kapazitätsauslastung, um rentabel betrieben werden zu können.

Zwischen den Seilbahnen und dem Winterfremdenverkehr besteht ein enger Zusammenhang. Mehr als drei Viertel aller Seilbahnfahrgäste werden im Winter befördert, und es konnte festgestellt werden, daß 85% von ihnen Touristen sind. Der alpine Schilauf wäre ohne Seilbahnen heute nicht möglich. Die Auswirkungen der Seilbahnen lassen sich an Hand der Steigerung der Winternächtigungszahlen in Gemeinden, in denen neue Anlagen eröffnet wurden, nachweisen. Im Zusammenhang damit sind Auswirkungen auf die gesamte regionale Wirtschaft feststellbar.

Diese Auswirkungen werden an Hand von drei der vielen möglichen Kriterien nachgewiesen:

1. Die Bevölkerungsentwicklung (in Gebieten, die vor Jahren noch von der Landflucht bedroht waren, ist eine Bevölkerungszunahme feststellbar).
2. Die Entwicklung des Baubestandes (Bergbauerndörfer, deren Häuserzahl durch Hunderte von Jahren annähernd gleich war, verzeichnen eine stürmische Bauentwicklung).
3. Die Entwicklung der Pro-Kopf-Steuereinnahmen (einige größere Wintersportzentren verzeichnen höhere Pro-Kopf-Einnahmen an Gemeindesteuern als Orte mit hohem Industriebesatz).

Für den großen wirtschaftlichen Erfolg des Winterfremdenverkehrs gibt es vor allem drei Gründe:

1. Eine hohe Kapazitätsausnützung der Fremdenverkehrseinrichtungen, welche durch die Schaffung einer zweiten Saison viele Betriebe über die Rentabilitätsschwelle hebt.
2. Die durchschnittlichen Einnahmen pro Besucher sind im Winter höher als im Sommer durch die zusätzlichen Ausgaben für Seilbahnen, Schischulen, Après-Ski u. ä.
3. Zumindest in Österreich stammen die Besucher im Winter aus höheren sozialen Schichten als im Sommer.

Mit der Entwicklung des Seilbahnwesens sind viele Probleme verbunden. Die wichtigsten davon sollen kurz erwähnt werden.

1. Ein Wettrüsten im gesamten Alpenraum bedingt durch die starke Konkurrenz der einzelnen Staaten, Regionen und Fremdenverkehrsorte untereinander, teilweise auch bedingt durch allzu optimistische Schätzungen von Zuwachsraten im Winterfremdenverkehr.
2. Der ganze Seilbahnsektor lebt in einer Euphorie, die teilweise durch eine falsche Einschätzung der wirtschaftlichen Situation bedingt ist, teilweise auch

durch das oben erwähnte Wettrüsten. Auf diese Weise werden derzeit eine Menge von Unternehmungen gegründet, die vielleicht in der Zukunft subventioniert werden müssen.

3. Regional besteht die Gefahr einer Überentwicklung und von zu starker Konzentration. Attraktive Schigebiete mit leistungsfähigen Seilbahnkapazitäten benötigen große Wintersportorte, um ihre Kapazität voll nutzen zu können. Damit wachsen die Talorte jedoch weit über jene Größe hinaus, die man für einen Urlaubsort als optimal bezeichnen könnte.

4. Mit der Erschließung der Seilbahnen sind wesentliche Eingriffe in die Landschaft verbunden, die nicht nur deren Schönheit beeinflußen, sondern auch verschiedene natürliche Gefahren erhöhen, wie die Lawinen- und Erosionsgefahr.

In Österreich war es durch Seilbahnen möglich, den Anteil des Winterfremdenverkehrs am Gesamtfremdenverkehr von 1961 an von 23% auf 30% zu erhöhen. Ein bedeutender Teil der Deviseneinnahmen aus dem Fremdenverkehr ist indirekt durch Seilbahnen bedingt. Es hat den Anschein, als ob die Seilbahnen der wirkungsvollste Faktor für die Wirtschaftsentwicklung in für den Wintersport geeigneten Berggebieten wären.

Wirtschaftsentwicklung und Probleme des Fremdenverkehrs und der Erholung in Bulgarien

LJUBOMIR DINEV, Sofia, Bulgarien

Der Fremdenverkehr begann in Bulgarien zur Zeit der Industrialisierung im 19. Jahrhundert wirtschaftliche Bedeutung zu erlangen. Fremdenverkehrsgebiete und -zentren entstanden auf Grund der touristischen Nachfrage. Diese Nachfrage und das daraus resultierende Angebot an touristischen Diensten machten den Fremdenverkehr zu einem Wirtschaftsfaktor mit eigenen Gesetzen und großen wirtschaftlichen Auswirkungen.

Bulgarien war in jener Periode ein in wirtschaftlicher Hinsicht stark zurückgebliebener Teil des Ottomanenreiches. Nach seiner Befreiung von türkischer Herrschaft im Jahre 1878 wurde das Land zu den schwach entwickelten Agrarländern gezählt. Damals waren die Grundvoraussetzungen für eine Fremdenverkehrsentwicklung noch nicht gegeben. In der Zwischenkriegszeit intensivierte sich in der Folge der wirtschaftlichen Entwicklung der Binnenfremdenverkehr. Auch der internationale Fremdenverkehr begann; es fehlte aber noch die notwendige Infrastruktur.

Bereits 1895 wurde als erste touristische Vereinigung der Bulgarische Touristische Verband (BTV) gegründet, der bis zum Zweiten Weltkrieg bei der Entwicklung des Binnentourismus eine große Rolle gespielt hat.

Mit der Einführung der sozialistischen Wirtschaftsform nach dem Zweiten Weltkrieg traten große Veränderungen in der Wirtschaftsstruktur des Landes ein. Planwirtschaft, Industrialisierung, Organisation der Landwirtschaft in Kooperativen und andere revolutionäre Veränderungen beschleunigten die Wirtschaftsentwicklung. Die Agrarquote sank von 82% (1944) auf 31% (1975). Der Anteil der städtischen Bevölkerung stieg in dieser Zeit von 24% auf 58%, die Zahl der Städte selbst erhöhte sich von 104 auf 218. Verstädterung und politische Maßnahmen der Regierung machten Bulgarien in kurzer Zeit zu einem Fremdenverkehrsland, sowohl für den Binnen- als auch für den internationalen Tourismus. Die notwendige Infrastruktur wurde geschaffen. Der Fremdenverkehr wurde ein eigener, wichtiger Zweig der Volkswirtschaft.

Der internationale Fremdenverkehr nach Bulgarien hat eine sehr günstige Entwicklung genommen. Im Jahre 1976 konnten bereits 4 Millionen ausländische Gäste gezählt werden (1956: 8.500). Neben dem Badetourismus an den Küsten versucht man jetzt auch den Tourismus im Gebirge, den Kur-, Kongreß- und Besichtigungsfremdenverkehr stärker zu fördern, um die Fremdenverkehrseinrichtungen auch außerhalb der Saison auslasten zu können.

Neben dem internationalen Tourismus konnte auch der Binnenfremdenverkehr seit dem Zweiten Weltkrieg große Erfolge verzeichnen, wobei sich der BTV große Verdienste erworben hat. Er veranstaltete in den Jahren 1972 bis 1977 315.000 Reisen mit rund 28,5 Millionen Teilnehmern. Die Bulgarischen Gewerkschaften haben einen großen Beitrag zur Entwicklung des Sozialtourismus geleistet. Die materielle Basis des Fremdenverkehrs ist bedeutend: Das staatliche Komitee für Fremdenverkehr verfügt über 555 Hotels mit 91.550 Betten. In den Gebirgsgegenden werden 343 Schutzhütten mit 20.000 Betten geführt. Dem Sozialtourismus dienen 1.392 Erholungsheime mit 90.700 Betten.

Im Binnenfremdenverkehr hängt die Entwicklung des Massentourismus mit der raschen Verstädterung Bulgariens zusammen. Die Lebensverhältnisse in den Städten veranlassen die Bewohner zu Urlaubsfahrten vielfacher Art. Besonders rasch entwickelten sich die Kurzurlaube (Weekendfahrten). Zum Teil werden die um die Städte entstandenen Zweithaussiedlungen aufgesucht. Zum anderen Teil werden Gruppen- oder Einzelfahrten durchgeführt. Die Zahl der Motortouristen hat sich in den letzten Jahren stark erhöht.

Die verschiedenen Formen des Tourismus werden immer mehr ein fester Bestandteil der Lebensweise der Bevölkerung. Für den Massenfremdenverkehr sind zahlreiche gute Einrichtungen notwendig. Hotels, Schutzhütten und Erholungsheime genügen hier nicht zur Lösung der Probleme. Ein Mittel dazu ist die Errichtung von Weekendhäusern um die Städte. Der Bau von Campingplätzen im Gebirge für die Sommermonate sowie die Einrichtung von Beherbergungsbetrieben an historisch wichtigen Stätten wären ein weiterer wichtiger Beitrag. Von besonders großer Bedeutung für die Lösung der Probleme des Fremdenverkehrs und der Kurzerholung werden die Konzepte zur weiteren Entwicklung der Regionen und Ortschaften Bulgariens sein, die den zukünftigen Ausbau der Ortschaften nach regionalen Systemen vorsehen. Darunter werden Ortschaften und ihre Einzugsbereiche verstanden, in denen wirtschaftliche und soziale Probleme – Wohnungswesen, Infrastruktur, soziale Dienste und Erholung, komplex gelöst werden sollen.

Die Entwicklung der Freizeitnutzung der Mittelgebirge durch die Industriegesellschaft im rheinischen Einzugsgebiet

GABRIEL WACKERMANN, Straßburg, Frankreich

Die Raumansprüche der Industriegesellschaft im Rahmen des Fremdenverkehrs steigen. Die Verstädterung übt einen immer stärkeren Druck auf die naheliegenden Mittelgebirge aus. Die verschiedenen Entwicklungsstadien der Bodennutzung zeigen wie sich die sozial höheren Bevölkerungsschichten allmählich Grundbesitz verschaffen, obwohl man allgemein an eine echte Demokratisierung des Tourismus in den Mittelgebirgen glaubt. So widerspricht die heutige

Entwicklung der traditionellen Dialektik zwischen Stadt und Gebirge. Das Rheingebiet bietet sich als besonders gutes Beispiel für eine solche Untersuchung an.

Reichweiten und Einzugsbereiche ausgewählter Freizeitfunktionsstandorte in Bayern

GÜNTER HEINRITZ, München, Bundesrepublik Deutschland

Am Beispiel von Hallenbädern, Trimm-Pfaden und Minigolfplätzen wurde geprüft, ob einrichtungsspezifische Reichweiten solcher Anlagen ermittelt werden können. Dabei ergab sich, daß angesichts der großen Streuung der Reichweiten innerhalb der einzelnen Kategorien dies nicht möglich zu sein scheint. Die Streuung der Werte wird freilich erheblich reduziert, wenn man sich nur auf Einrichtungen in vergleichbarer Lage bezieht. Ein wichtiges Ergebnis der Untersuchung ist die Feststellung, daß die einzelnen Besuchergruppen sich nicht darin unterscheiden, daß sie unterschiedliche maximale Entfernungen zurückzulegen bereit sind, sondern dadurch, daß mit zunehmender Distanz Wohnort - Funktionsstandort die Häufigkeit ihrer Besuche unterschiedlich stark zurückgeht.

Der Einfluß des Fremdenverkehrs auf die Lebensgewohnheiten von Fremdenverkehrsgemeinden, dargestellt am Beispiel der Gemeinde Sleat auf der Insel Skye

RICHARD W. BUTLER, London, Ontario, Kanada

Die Studie behandelt vor allem die Auswirkungen des Fremdenverkehrs sozialer und kultureller Art auf die Bevölkerung einer ländlichen Inselgemeinde in Schottland. Die Bewohner der Gemeinde Sleat, Insel Skye, wurden über ihre Meinung und Einstellung zum Fremdenverkehr befragt und auch wieweit, wenn überhaupt, ihre Lebensgewohnheiten vom Fremdenverkehr beeinflußt worden waren. Antworten und Stellungnahmen auf diese Befragung werden dargestellt und Unterschiede aufgezeigt, die sich aus Wohnort, Sprache, Kontakt mit Besuchern sowie Beschäftigung im Fremdenverkehr ergeben. Die Auswirkungen werden sowohl positiv (Arbeitsplätze, Einkommen, Kontakt mit der Außenwelt und Verbesserung der Infrastruktur), als auch negativ (Zunahme des Straßenverkehrs, Entstehung von Zweithäusern, mehr Streß, gesellschaftliche Veränderungen und Rückgang der gaelischen Sprache) empfunden. Die Schlußfolgerungen weisen auf die Notwendigkeit hin, bei Fremdenverkehrsplanungen die Beeinflußbarkeit und Haltung der örtlichen Bevölkerung zu berücksichtigen, um auf diese Weise das soziale Gleichgewicht in den Fremdenverkehrszielgebieten zu erhalten.

Kommunale Planung für die „Erholung im Freien" in Schweden.

Einige Gedanken über die Bedeutung von institutionellen Faktoren

HANS ALDSKOGIUS, Uppsala, Schweden

Auf dem untersten Rang der Hierarchie von Verwaltungsgebieten in Schweden gibt es heute 277 Gemeinden, unter denen bedeutende Unterschiede hinsichtlich der Größe und Zahl der Einwohner bestehen. Die Gemeinden können selbständig entscheiden, z. B. in welchem Umfang und in welchen Formen sie sich am Bau von Einrichtungen am Erholungssektor beteiligen wollen. In dieser Hinsicht gibt es zwischen den Gemeinden erhebliche Unterschiede, die nicht nur in ihrer unterschiedlichen Bevölkerungsdichte, wirtschaftlichen Struktur und ihren landschaftlichen Voraussetzungen begründet, sondern auch in hohem Maße vom Vorhandensein einer aktiven kommunalen Erholungspolitik abhängig sind.

Von besonderer Wichtigkeit für die kommunale Erholungspolitik sind Entscheidungen über die Bedeutung der „Erholung im Freien“ im Verhältnis zu anderen Teilen des Freizeitsektors, die Bedeutung der einzelnen Formen der „Erholung im Freien“ und auch der Interessen der verschiedenen Bevölkerungsschichten sowie schließlich über die Gründung eigener kommunaler Unternehmungen bzw. über die finanzielle Unterstützung verschiedener Organisationen, die sich mit Freizeitaktivitäten beschäftigen.

Es ist notwendig, den institutionellen Rahmen der kommunalen Erholungspolitik zu studieren. Von Bedeutung ist das Verhalten von Interessentengruppen, verschiedenen Organisationen (wie Sport- und Jugendverbänden), Grundbesitzern, Unternehmern auf dem Erholungssektor und den zentralen und regionalen staatlichen Behörden und auch die Art, wie sie zusammenarbeiten oder konkurrieren in Fragen wie der Errichtung von Erholungseinrichtungen, der Organisation von Freizeitaktivitäten und der Information darüber. Die Regelung des Zutrittes zu verschiedenen Erholungsflächen im Freien ist ebenfalls von Interesse.

Es gibt mehrere Gründe für die Berücksichtigung der institutionellen Faktoren. Offenbar ist der Aufbau einer „Infrastruktur der Erholung im Freien“ in hohem Grade das Ergebnis von Kompromißlösungen, auch wegen der Raumerfordernisse, die im politischen Rahmen ausgearbeitet werden. Ein Studium dieses Prozesses sollte tiefere Einsicht in die Entwicklung der räumlichen Organisation von Erholungslandschaften bringen. Vergleichende Untersuchungen auf verschiedenen Gebieten könnten Ergebnisse für andere Regionen und zukünftige Planungen bringen.

Für eine solche Untersuchung ist der lokale Rahmen sehr geeignet, denn dort findet man viele Instititionen, die mit dem Entscheidungsprozeß befaßt sind, von den einzelnen Interessentengruppen bis zu staatlichen Behörden in der Zentralbürokratie. Ein Studium von institutionellen Faktoren bietet auch Möglichkeiten, weitere und fruchtbare Kontakte zwischen Geographen und Vertretern anderer Disziplinen, wie Staatswissenschaft und Verwaltungswissenschaft, zu knüpfen.

Frequenzprobleme von Erholungseinrichtungen in den westlichen Staaten der USA

BURKHARD HOFMEISTER, Berlin (West)

Mehrere Nationalparks, Nationale Erholungsgebiete, Nationalforste und einzelstaatliche Parks in den Weststaaten der USA wurden daraufhin untersucht, wie weit die besonders während der 50er und 60er Jahre rasch gestiegenen Besucherzahlen zu Überfüllung und ökologischer Überbeanspruchung geführt haben und wie die verschiedenen Behörden, die für die Verwaltung dieser Gebiete verantwortlich sind, dieses Problem angehen. Es wird herausgearbeitet, daß dieses Problem in manchen Gebieten gravierender auftritt als in anderen, abhängig davon, ob besondere Naturdenkmäler geboten werden, wie z. B. im Grand Canyon und Yellowstone Park, oder auch von der Lage zu Bevölkerungsagglomerationen, wie z. B. der Lake Mead National Recreation Area zu den kalifornischen Großstädten. Im Yellowstone Park sind wegen der starken Konzentration des Besucherstromes auf die Sommermonate die Schwierigkeiten größer als im Yosemite Valley, wo sich der Besuch besser über das ganze Jahr verteilt.

Folgende Punkte werden genauer diskutiert: das Multiple-Use-Konzept des U.S. Forest Service und wieweit es der Erholungsfunktion entspricht; das Konzept der Weiterentwicklung der bisher bereits am intensivsten genutzten "Heavy-Use" areas zugunsten der weiten, nur von wenigen Wanderern und Reitern aufgesuchten mehr entlegenen Gebiete (backcountry oder wilderness areas), für deren Nutzung Höchstzahlen von Besuchern nach drei verschiedenen Methoden festgesetzt werden; die Einschränkung des privaten Kraftfahrzeugverkehrs und Einführung eines Pendelbusverkehrs in einigen "Heavy-Use" areas; das Einfrieren der Bettenzahl in Hotels, Blockhäusern und auf Campingplätzen auf den gegenwärtigen Stand, was künftig zu einer Erweiterung des Motelgewerbes außerhalb der Parkgrenzen führen dürfte; der Ankauf von Privatgrundstücken für die öffentliche Erholung, wie z. B. der Erwerb gewisser Uferzonen am Lake Tahoe durch den Staat Kalifornien (hierher gehört auch die Überlegung, daß das größte Potential für die Erweiterung von Erholungsräumen in den Nationalforsten liegt); die Vergabe von Aufträgen an Wissenschaftler für Kapazitätsberechnungen für eine künftige verbesserte Entscheidungsfindung.

Die Entwicklung des Fremdenverkehrs in einer sozialistischen Gesellschaft Theorie und Praxis in Jugoslawien

MOMČILO VUKIĆEVIĆ, Novi Sad, Jugoslawien

Ausgangspunkt der Analyse ist die Annahme, daß im sozialistischen Wirtschaftssystem Voraussetzungen für die Entwicklung und Befriedigung verschiedener Bedürfnisse der breiten Masse von Werktätigen nach Menge und Qualität sukzessive und allmählich geschaffen werden. Obwohl die einzelnen Phasen des sozialistischen Aufbaues nicht gleichmäßig und in den einzelnen Staaten verschieden verlaufen, ist ein langfristiger positiver Trend doch zu beobachten. Er ist unmittelbarer Bestandteil des politischen und wirtschaftlichen Aufbaues einer sozialistischen Gesellschaft.

Wie auch in den anderen sozialistischen Staaten entwickelte sich in Jugoslawien nach dem Krieg der „Gewerkschafts"-tourismus. Er wurde durch eine Reihe von Jahren wegen seiner großen Bedeutung für den Lebensstandard der arbeitenden Bevölkerung besonders stark gefördert, unterschied sich aber in Jugoslawien vom „Gewerkschafts"–Tourismus anderer sozialistischer Länder. Diese Unterschiede verstärkten sich im Lauf der Zeit und führten außer zu quantitativen auch zu qualitativen Veränderungen: Aus dem „Gewerkschafts"-Tourismus entwickelt sich der „Arbeiter"-Tourismus als besondere Form des weltweit zu beobachtenden, laufenden Demokratisierungsprozesses des Fremdenverkehrs.

Diese Tatsache stellt den Autor vor die schwierige Aufgabe, den zeitlichen Ablauf der Einbeziehung arbeitender Menschen in den Fremdenverkehr zu erforschen und im Rahmen der wirtschaftlichen und sozial-politischen Entwicklung ihre individuellen touristischen Aktivitäten zu analysieren. Andererseits war eine wissenschaftliche Analyse des „Arbeiter"-Tourismus und sein kritischer Vergleich mit dem „Gewerkschafts"-Tourismus und „Sozial"-Tourismus notwendig. Alle diese Fragen werden vom Autor auf Grund einer Analyse des jugoslawischen Fremdenverkehrs untersucht und kommentiert.

INTRODUCTION
EINFÜHRUNG

Editor's Preface

Ever since the foundation of the Working Group "Geography of Tourism and Recreation" of the International Geographical Union at the XXII. International Geographical Congress in Montreal it had been the plan of the Group eventually to hold one of its annual symposia in the United Kingdom. The fact that I was appointed president of Section E (Geography) of the British Association for the Advancement of Science (BA) for the year 1976/77 and the annual meeting of the British Association at the University of Aston in Birmingham and that, as president, one has traditionally a major say in making up the Section programme gave me the idea to suggest to both the Committee of Section E and the chairman JOSEF MATZNETTER and members of the Working Group to hold the 1977 symposium of the Working Group as a joint meeting of these two bodies. My suggestion was readily accepted by all concerned and at the symposium of the Working Group in Dombai, Caucasus, in July 1976, it was agreed that at the symposium in Birmingham the principal theme should be recreation, to emphasize the second part of the name of the Working Group which so far had not been the central subject of a symposium. At the business meeting of the Group in Dombai I also promised that the papers would be published in the *Wiener Geographische Schriften*. Papers were invited on this theme and by the deadline, which had to be mid-December 1976 to enable the secretariat of the British Association to make up the programme and print it, so many papers had arrived that it was absolutely impossible to fit them all in for reading in the two days of the joint meeting available for paper sessions i. e. Monday 5th and Tuesday 6th September. Thus a selection had to be made which papers should be put on the programme and the guiding criterion was whether, according to its title and brief summary, it dealt at least to a certain extent with recreation. The entire programme of the meeting included also a halfday tour – on Sunday 4th September – of recreational aspects of Birmingham where in particular the "leisure gardens" (a modern and aesthetically more pleasing form of allotments) at Cannon Hill Park and the annual Birmingham Show at Perry Park were visited.

There were, however, also other excursions laid on as for instance to the Black Country or to Coalbrookdale, the historic place where in 1709 Abraham Darby succeeded as the first person in producing pig iron by using coke; these too were available for the members of the Working Group. To give the members of the Working Group the opportunity to see a characteristic recreation area of Great Britain I had finally prepared a study tour of the Lake District, one of the National Parks, from Wednesday 7th to Saturday 10th September. The field trip terminated at Sheffield where the chairman and a few of the members of the Working Group took part in the 7th International Speleological Congress whose programme included a section on "Recreation and tourism in karst".

With the agreement of the secretary of the International Speleological Congress, HUBERT TRIMMEL, some of the papers of our members read there are also published in these two special volumes of the *Wiener Geographische Schriften*.

Before dealing with the central part of the meeting of the Working Group, the paper sessions in Birmingham, a few words about the field trip to the Lake District. The field study tour which was attended by 27 persons was based on the area of the picturesque village of Hawkshead, most members staying at Highfield House near the village, the rest a few miles away at Grizedale, the administrative centre of the national forest of that name. This forest, forestry in Britain in general and the problem of reconciling efficient forest management with the use of the forest for recreation for both the general public and people specially interested in various aspects of life in the forest was the first theme discussed and demonstrated. WILLIAM GRANT, the chief forester, a pioneer of this concept, was the ideal person to do this. It is impossible not to be carried away by his enthusiasm – a proof of it is the fact that almost everybody accepted his invitation for an "Observation Safari" of his forest in the very early hours of the morning.

Most of the second day was devoted to the study of problems of the National Park as a whole. This was done by way of a film and slide show and talks and discussions with officers of the National Park Commission and the Regional Tourist Board. The third day was used for a round trip through the National Park which gave the opportunity to gain an overview as well as discuss special problems on the spot like the use of the lakes as water reservoirs and for water sports, problems of re-afforestation, siting and sizes of camp and caravan sites, road improvement and construction of new trunk roads. The final day was rather spoiled by pouring rain and the short boat trip on Lake Windermere originally planned for the morning had to be omitted.

In addition to the impressive scenery what the participants will probably remember most is the generally negative attitude of the public and even authorities towards re-afforestation, the underlying reason being to preserve a man-made economically rather unproductive environment which, since destruction of the forests came much earlier than on the European Continent, is nevertheless felt to be a "natural landscape"; as regards use of these landscapes for tourism and recreation the lack of a body of even reasonably precise data regarding demand, supply and economic benefits which normally one would consider essential for planning a development which combines the optimum economic gains with the minimum of negative consequences for the region and its residents. It appears that the authorities rely basically on restrictions and are more interested in preservation of the landscape – construction of cable cars or chair lifts is quite out of the question – than in the development of tourism in order to realise the economic potential of the region which it without doubt has.

The paper sessions

As in any conference with a fairly large number of participants and especially at an international symposium – and our joint meeting was no exception – a number of the speakers for one reason or other were unable to be present.[1] In

[1] Apart from the British participants which in the case of a joint meeting included many not connected with the Working Group the following countries were represented by members of the group:

Austria	4	Finland	1
Bulgaria	1	France	2
Canada	4	Italy	2
Czechoslovakia	2	Poland	1
Federal Republic of Germany and West Berlin	8	Sweden	1
		United States of America	3
		Yugoslavia	3

our case, however, the number of members present ready and anxious to read a paper not on the programme almost exactly tallied with the number absent so that it was possible to have a full programme as planned and give everybody who was present and wished to read a paper the chance to do so. The paper session commenced with my presidential address which was given in a large lecture theatre and attracted many listeners also from other Sections.The session was then continued in a smaller lecture room but the attendance right to the end of the session was very satisfactory. The themes of the first papers related to Britain: COLEMAN'S Recreation in perspective, COPPOCK'S and DUFFIELD'S North Sea oil and leisure, COLLINS' geographical issues related to indoor sport centres and swimming pools, BUTLER'S case study of Sleat, Isle of Skye. They were followed by MIECZKOWSKI'S paper which raised principal issues of the place of geography of tourism and recreation, and a number of papers which though relating mostly to America also raised principal and methodological issues (HOFMEISTER, MELAMID, MITCHELL and WOLFE).

This was also the case with most of the other papers on themes taken from – politically speaking – Western Europe: ALDSKOGIUS (Sweden), HEINRITZ (West Germany), JÜLG (Austria), WACKERMANN (France). BARBIER'S paper, which like WACKERMANN'S was presented in French, gave a world-wide overview of wintersports. The programme on the last afternoon, which had been set aside for geographers from socialist countries, had to be changed beyond recognition as only three of the nine original speakers listed were present. The members who then actually read papers were: DINEV (Bulgaria), GOSAR, PEPEONIK and VUKIĆEVIĆ (Yugoslavia), SKVARČEKOVA (Czechoslovakia) and STALSKI (Poland).

The final item on the programme in Birmingham was a lively discussion that evening on problems of the cartographic representation of tourism which was introduced by a paper by MARIOT (Czechoslovakia) and where subsequently the difficulties of the application of internationally agreed methods, symbols and scales was demonstrated by means of sample maps.

Finally three social events should also be mentioned since they contributed towards cementing the Group and to making the Group known: The party of the president of Section E, the Dinner of the Section, and the Vice Chancellor's reception of the visitors from overseas.

Finally a word of explanation regarding this publication which consists of all papers submitted in time regardless whether read at the symposium or not.

Since the only official languages of the IGU are English and French and as these two special volumes are virtually the proceedings of the 1977 symposium of the Working Group it was after consultation decided to publish papers only in one of these languages (adding an abstract or resumé as the case may be to facilitate a wider comprehension). As, however, the *Wiener Geographische Schriften* are by tradition a German language publication with a largely German-speaking readership the editorial board decided to add to each paper also a *Zusammenfassung* as it was felt that this too would be beneficial in making the papers even more widely known.

The drawback in thus limiting the number of languages is that some of those authors who were not native English speakers found it difficult to express themselves in that language. As printing these papers exactly as they were submitted might have given rise to misunderstanding or at least to difficulties in comprehending their contents I have done more editorial work than is usual and tried as far as possible to "Anglicize" their English so that they should not only be without actual grammatical mistakes but, what is more important, be clear as to their meaning. I hope I have succeeded and I further hope that the authors concerned will not think I have done more than was necessary in this difficult task. Although I have in editing employed standard English spelling and vocabulary papers by American contributors were of course left with American spelling and expressions.

The choice which papers are included in the first volume and which in the second was first of all whether the paper was actually read, secondly whether the complete manuscript (including resumé and figures suitable for reproduction) arrived in time and finally whether it fitted in with the other papers of the first volume. We will publish the second volume as soon as possible and ask the authors of the papers of the second volume for their patience and understanding.

Last not least I wish to thank my colleagues who have assisted me in the task of preparing those volumes for publication, first of all the assistant editor FELIX JÜLG but also ELISABETH GLASER who retyped many of the papers and helped substantially in various ways and INGEBORG WIESLER who checked and in some cases translated the French resumés. Last not least I wish to thank my colleagues KARL SCHAPPELWEIN and NORBERT STANEK for their help with the illustrations.

Vienna, Spring 1978 Karl A. Sinnhuber

Préface de l'Editeur

Dès son institution à l'occasion du 22e Congrès International de Géographie à Montréal, le Groupe de travail »Géographie du Tourisme et de la Récréation« de l'Union Géographique Internationale avait eu l'intention d'organiser un de ses symposia annuels au Royaume-Uni. C'est en raison du fait que j'ai été nommé président de la Section E (Géographie) de la British Association for the Advancement of Science pour l'année 1976/77 et de la réunion annuelle de la British Association à l'université d'Aston/Birmingham et que le président influe de façon décisive sur l'élaboration du programme de la Section, que j'étais amené à suggérer et à la Commission de la Section E et au président, JOSEF MATZNETTER, et aux membres du Groupe de travail d'organiser en réunion commune des deux organismes le symposium 1977 de ce Groupe. Ma proposition fut acceptée d'emblée par tous les intéressés. Lors de la réunion du Groupe de travail en juillet 1977 à Dombai, Caucase, il fut convenu que la récréation constituerait le thème principal du colloque à Birmingham; ceci dans le but de mettre l'accent sur la deuxième partie du nom du Groupe de travail qui, jusqu'à ce moment, n'avait jamais été l'objet principal des débats. A l'occasion de la réunion de travail du Groupe à Dombai je me suis engagé en outre à faire paraître les exposés dans les *Wiener Geographische Schriften*. Par la suite, les spécialistes en la matière ont été invités à nous faire parvenir des exposés jusqu'à une date limite fixée pour la mi-décembre 1976, date qui permettrait au secrétariat de la British Association de mettre au point le programme et de le faire imprimer. Notre invitation ayant trouvé un écho extraordinaire, il s'est avéré absolument impossible de présenter tous les exposés lors de la réunion commune durant les deux jours réservés aux conférences, i. e. lundi 5 et mardi 6 septembre. C'est pourquoi nous étions forcés de faire une sélection; furent choisis les exposés qui, d'après leur titre et bref résumé, traitaient – du moins dans une certaine mesure – de la récréation. Le programme de la réunion prévoyait également, pour dimanche 4 septembre, un tour d'une demi-journée permettant aux participants de connaître les aspects récréatifs de Birmingham. Ce tour comportait plus particulièrement la visite des »leisure gardens« (des jardins ouvriers modernes et bien aménagés) situés dans le Cannon Hill Park et de l'annuelle Birmingham Show dans le Perry Park.

Il y avait également d'autres excursions auxquelles pouvaient prendre part les membres du Groupe de travail, comme p. ex. celle vers le Black Country ou une autre à Coalbrookdale, lieu historique où en 1709 Abraham Darby fut le premier à réussir la production de fonte brute à l'aide de coke. Enfin j'avais organisé (de mercredi 7 à samedi 10 septembre) un voyage d'études vers le Lake District, un des parcs nationaux, afin que les membres du Groupe de travail puissent voir une zone de récréation caractéristique de la Grande-Bretagne. Ce voyage a pris fin à Sheffield où le président et certains membres du Groupe de travail ont participé au 7e Congrès International de Spéléologie dont une partie du programme était consacrée au sujet »Loisir et tourisme dans le karst«.

Avec l'assentiment de HUBERT TRIMMEL, secrétaire du Congrès International de Spéléologie, quelques-unes des conférences données par nos membres à cette occasion sont également reproduites dans ces deux volumes spéciaux des *Wiener Geographische Schriften.*

Voilà encore quelques remarques au sujet du voyage d'études vers le Lake District avant que nous abordions la partie principale du symposium du Groupe de travail, à savoir les conférences faites à Birmingham. Pendant ce voyage auquel ont participé 27 personnes, nous avons étudié la région du pittoresque village de Hawkshead, la plupart des membres logeant près du village dans le Highfield House, les autres un peu plus loin à Grizedale, le centre administratif de la forêt nationale portant le même nom. Cette forêt, la sylviculture en Grande-Bretagne en général et le problème de l'harmonisation d'une exploitation rationnelle des forêts et de l'affectation de celles-ci à des fins récréatives profitant au grand public et aux personnes intéressées aux divers aspects de la vie forestière, voilà les thèmes sur lesquels portait – appuyée par la démonstration – la première discussion. Elle fut animée par WILLIAM GRANT, garde forestier en chef et pionnier de cette conception, partant le personnage le plus habilité à présenter la problématique. Passioné de son métier, il savait parfaitement nous enthousiasmer, nous aussi, ce qui a été prouvé par le fait que presque tous ont accepté son invitation à découvrir, de bon matin, sa forêt au cours d'un »Safari d'observation«.

La deuxième journée fut consacrée pour l'essentiel à l'étude des problèmes du Parc National dans son ensemble avec lesquels les participants pouvaient se familiariser lors de séances cinématographiques (films et diapositives) ainsi que dans des discussions et échanges de vues avec les fonctionnaires de la Commission pour les Parcs Nationaux et de l'Office Régional du Tourisme. Une excursion à travers le parc national, organisée le troisième jour, nous a permis de gagner une vue d'ensemble et de discuter sur place les problèmes spécifiques tels que l'utilisation des lacs comme réservoir d'eau ainsi que pour les sports nautiques, les problèmes du reboisement, du choix de l'emplacement et de la dimension de terrains de camping, l'amélioration des routes et la construction de nouvelles routes nationales. Le dernier jour – plutôt gâché par une pluie tombant à torrents – il fallait renoncer à la courte promenade en bâteau sur le Lac Windermere prévue initialement pour le matin.

Ce qui a probablement frappé le plus les participants, c'était – outre le paysage fort impressionnant – l'attitude généralement négative du public et même des autorités à l'égard du reboisement, la raison profonde en étant le souci de sauvegarder un environnement aménagé par l'homme, plutôt improductif du point de vue économique, mais qui est néanmoins considéré comme »paysage naturel«, la destruction des forêts étant intervenue à une époque bien plus lointaine que sur le Continent Européen; en ce qui concerne la mise en valeur de ces paysages à des fins touristiques et de récréation, c'était le manque de données suffisamment précises relatives à la demande, l'offre et les avantages économiques, qui normalement constitueraient un facteur essentiel pour la planification d'un développement associant un optimum de bénéfices économiques et un minimum de conséquences défavorables pour la région et ses habitants. Les autorités semblent s'en tenir pour l'essentiel à des restrictions et s'intéresser plutôt à la sauvegarde du paysage – la construction de funiculaires ou de télésièges est pratiquement hors de question – qu'à la promotion du tourisme permettant de mettre en valeur le potentiel économique dont la région dispose sans aucun doute.

Les séances de conférences

Comme c'est le cas pour toutes les réunions et notamment pour des colloques internationaux avec un nombre assez important de participants – notre réunion commune ne fit pas exception à cette règle – certains conférenciers ne pouvaient pas honorer l'assemblée de leur présence.[1] Toujours est-il que, lors de notre symposium, le nombre de participants présents et prêts à faire une communication ne figurant pas sur le programme était presque égal au nombre de ceux absents de sorte que nous pouvions présenter un programme complet comme prévu tout en donnant à chacun des participants présents et désireux de lire un papier la possibilité de le faire. En tant que président j'ai ouvert la séance de communications par une allocution qui, prononcée dans une grande salle de conférences, attira bon nombre d'auditeurs venant également d'autres Sections. Cette séance fut poursuivie dans une salle plus petite et jouit jusqu'à sa fin d'une assistance très satisfaisante. Les thèmes des premières communications concernaient la Grande-Bretagne: Réflexions sur le loisir par COLEMAN, Pétrole de la Mer du Nord et Loisirs par COPPOCK et DUFFIELD, Géographie et centres de sport couverts et piscines par COLLINS, Sleat, Ile de Skye, présentée dans une étude de cas par BUTLER. Suivirent ces communications l'exposé de MIECZKOWSKI traitant des aspects fondamentaux de la position de la géographie du tourisme et de la récréation, et de nombreux papiers qui, tout en se référant principalement à l'Amérique, soulevèrent également des problèmes de principe et de méthode (HOFMEISTER, MELAMID, MITCHELL et WOLFE).

Il en était de même pour la quasi-totalité des autres communications sur des thèmes concernant – politiquement parlant – l'Europe de l'Ouest: ALDSKOGIUS (Suède), HEINRITZ (République fédérale d'Allemagne), JÜLG (Autriche), WACKERMANN (France). Le rapport de BARBIER, présenté comme celui de WACKERMANN en langue française, a fait le tour d'horizon des sports d'hiver dans le monde entier. Le programme du dernier après-midi, réservé aux géographes venant de pays socialistes, a dû être totalement changé, étant donné que seulement trois des neuf rapporteurs inscrits à l'origine étaient présents. Les membres qui finalement ont donné lecture de leurs communications furent les suivants: DINEV (Bulgarie), GOSAR, PEPEONIK et VUKIĆEVIĆ (Yugoslavie), SKVARČEKOVA (Tchécoslovaquie) et STALSKI (Pologne).

Vint clôturer le programme de cette journée à Birmingham une discussion animée sur les problèmes de la représentation cartographique du tourisme soulevée par l'exposé de MARIOT (Tchéchoslovaquie) qui, moyennant cartes-échantillons, démontra les difficultés surgissant lors de l'application de méthodes, symboles et échelles approuvés sur un plan international.

Finalement trois événements sociaux méritent encore d'être mentionnés, puisqu'ils ont largement contribué à consolider le groupe et à le rendre connu: la party organisée par le président de la Section E, le dîner offert par la Section et

[1] Mise à part la délégation britannique qui dans le cas de réunions communes comprit également beaucoup de participants n'appartenant pas au Groupe de travail, les pays suivants furent représentés par des membres du Groupe:

Autriche	4	Finlande	1
Bulgarie	1	France	2
Canada	4	Italie	2
Tchécoslovaquie	2	Pologne	1
RFA et Berlin-Ouest	8	Suède	1
Etats-Unis	3	Yougoslavie	3

la réception donnée par le Vice-chancelier en l'honneur des participants d'outre-mer.

Avant de terminer mon rapport, je tiens à donner quelques explications relatives à cette publication qui réunit tous les exposés présentés à temps, indépendamment de la question de savoir si lecture en a été donnée ou non lors du congrès.

Vu le fait que l'anglais et le français sont les langues officielles de l'UGI et que ces deux volumes spéciaux contiennent de fait les travaux menés par le Groupe de travail lors du symposium 1977, nous sommes convenus de ne publier ces dossiers qu'en une seule langue (en annexant un résumé ou condensé selon le cas afin d'en faciliter la compréhension). Comme d'autre part la publication des *Wiener Geographische Schriften* se fait traditionnellement en langue allemande et que les lecteurs en sont aussi, pour la plupart, de langue allemande, le comité de rédaction a décidé d'ajouter à chaque exposé également un *Zusammenfassung* qui, à notre avis, permettrait une plus large diffusion.

Cette limitation du nombre des langues comporte évidemment l'inconvénient que certains des auteurs n'ayant pas l'anglais comme langue maternelle ont eu de la difficulté à rédiger leur exposé en cette langue. Les textes imprimés tels quels auraient pu provoquer maints malentendus, du moins rendre la compréhension du contenu plus difficile; je me suis donc permis de faire plus de travail rédactionnel que l'on ne fait d'habitude en essayant d'»angliciser« tant que possible l'anglais des exposés afin de supprimer toute faute grammaticale et – ce qui est plus important – de les rendre clairs et compréhensibles. J'espère avoir réussi cette tâche et j'espère en plus que les auteurs concernés ne penseront pas que j'ai fait plus qu'il ne fallait. En tant qu'éditeur j'ai utilisé l'orthographe et le vocabulaire standard de l'anglais, les contributions américaines par contre sont reproduites telles quelles sans modification ni de l'orthographe ni des expressions.

Le choix des exposés publiés dans le premier volume et de ceux destinés à paraître dans le deuxième fut arrêté selon trois critères, le premier en étant la question de savoir si les papiers étaient réellement lus, le deuxième si le manuscrit complet (y compris résumé et schémas pouvant être reproduits) était arrivé à temps, et le troisième si le papier s'harmonisait avec les autres sélectionnés pour le premier volume. Nous publierons le deuxième volume aussitôt que possible et nous nous permettons de demander patience et compréhension aux auteurs des exposés qui seront rassemblés dans celui-ci.

Enfin et surtout je tiens à remercier mes collègues qui ont contribué à la préparation de la publication des deux volumes, tout d'abord le rédacteur en chef adjoint, FELIX JÜLG, mais aussi ELISABETH GLASER qui nous a apporté son aide précieuse et a retapé bon nombre de ces textes, et INGEBORG WIESLER qui a bien voulu relire et dans quelques cas traduire les résumés français, ainsique KARL SCHAPPELWEIN et NORBERT STANEK, qui ont contribué à la réalisation graphique de ce volume.

Vienne, printemps 1978 Karl A. Sinnhuber, Editeur

Vorwort des Herausgebers

Dieser und der nächste Doppelband der *Wiener Geographischen Schriften* erscheinen ausnahmsweise mit Beiträgen in englicher und französischer Sprache. Es handelt sich dabei um die Veröffentlichung von Vorträgen, die mit weltweiter Beteiligung im Rahmen der Jahrestagung der *British Association for the Advancement of Science (BA)* im September 1977 gehalten wurden. Als dem für 1977 gewählten Präsidenten der Sektion E (Geographie) dieser Gesellschaft war es mir möglich, auch die Mitglieder der Arbeitsgruppe für *Tourismus und Erholung der Internationalen Geographischen Union (IGU)* mit ihrem Vorsitzenden, JOSEF MATZNETTER, nach Birmingham einzuladen und eine gemeinsame Sitzung zu organisieren. Als Leitthema war *„Erholung in der Industriegesellschaft“* gewählt worden.

Es ist mir eine besondere Freude, als Präsident der *Österreichischen Gesellschaft für Wirtschaftsraumforschung* diese Vorträge in den *Wiener Geographischen Schriften* veröffentlichen zu können. Ich nehme an, daß viele der behandelten Themen gerade den Leserkreis dieser Schriftenreihe, die sich ihrer wissenschaftlichen Zielsetzung nach auch mit Problemen der Fremdenverkehrsgeographie befassen muß, interessieren werden. Die Vorträge werden – wie erwähnt – in den von der IGU allein zugelassenen Sprachen Englisch und Französisch abgedruckt. Zusammenfassungen in deutscher, englischer und französischer Sprache sollen den Inhalt einem weiten Leserkreis zugänglich machen.

Im Anschluß an die Veranstaltung in Birmingham konnte ich viele Teilnehmer im Rahmen einer *Exkursion in den Lake District* führen. Daran schloß eine weitere Vortragsserie im Rahmen des *Internationalen Speläologischen Kongresses* in Sheffield, an der auch einige Mitglieder der IGU-Arbeitsgruppe teilnahmen. Mit Zustimmung des Sekretärs dieses Kongresses, HUBERT TRIMMEL, konnten auch einige der dort gehaltenen Referate in die Veröffentlichung der Vorträge der Arbeitsgruppe aufgenommen werden.

In Birmingham waren außer zahlreichen Teilnehmern aus Großbritannien Vertreter folgender Staaten anwesend: Bulgarien (1), Bundesrepublik Deutschland und West Berlin (8), Finnland (1), Frankreich (2), Italien (2), Jugoslawien (3), Kanada (4), Österreich (4), Polen (1), Schweden (1), Tschechoslowakei (2), USA (3). Die Vortragsserie begann mit der traditionellen “Presidential Address”, für die ich das Thema: „Die Bergwelt als Erholungsraum“ gewählt hatte und die auch von zahlreichen Mitgliedern anderer Sektionen der BA besucht wurde. Dann folgte eine Reihe von Beiträgen aus Großbritannien, so ALICE M. COLEMAN'S Referat über „Die Erholung: Ein neuer Gesichtspunkt“, das von JOHN T. COPPOCK und BRIAN S. DUFFIELD über „Fremdenverkehr und Nordsee-Öl“, MICHAEL COLLINS geographische Aspekte von Sportzentren und Hallenbädern, und schließlich RICHARD W. BUTLER'S Fallstudie über Sleat auf der Insel Skye. Mit grundsätzlichen Fragen beschäftigte sich das Referat von Z. TED MIECZSKOWSKI: „Die Stellung der Fremdenverkehrsgeographie im Rahmen der gesamten Geographie und der Freizeitforschung“. Auch weitere Vorträge behandelten wichtige methodische Aspekte und bezogen sich meistens auf Nord-Amerika; es waren dies die Referate von BURKHARD HOFMEISTER, ALEXANDER MELAMID, LISLE S. MITCHELL und ROY WOLFE.

Die Referate aus – politisch gesehen – anderen westeuropäischen Ländern befaßten sich ebenfalls mit der Methodik: HANS ALDSKOGIUS (Schweden), GÜNTER HEINRITZ (Bundesrepublik Deutschland), FELIX JÜLG (Österreich), GABRIEL WACKERMANN (Frankreich). Der Beitrag des zweiten Teilnehmers aus Frankreich, BERNARD BARBIER, gab einen weltweiten Überblick über den Wintersport. Das Programm des letzten Nachmittags war Vortragenden aus den sozialistischen Staaten vorbehalten. Es mußte vollkommen geändert werden, weil von den neun vorgesehenen Vortragenden nur drei erschienen waren. Einige der ausgefallenen Referate erscheinen im 2. Doppelband. Gehalten wurden schließlich Vorträge von LJUBOMIR DINEV (Bulgarien), ANTON GOSAR, ZLATKO PEPEONIK und MOMČILO VUKIĆEVIĆ (Jugoslawien), GABRIELA SKVARČEKOVA (Tschechoslowakei) und MICHAŁ STALSKI (Polen).

Am letzten Abend fand dann eine anregende Diskussion über Probleme der kartographischen Darstellung des Fremdenverkehrs statt. Nach einführenden Worten von PETER MARIOT (Tschechoslowakei) wurden die Schwierigkeiten, die bei der Anwendung international einheitlicher Methoden, Symbole und Maßstäbe entstehen, an Hand von Testkarten aufgezeigt.

Für die Aufnahme eines Beitrages in den ersten oder zweiten Doppelband war in erster Linie maßgebend, ob der Vortrag tatsächlich in Birmingham gehalten worden war. Ferner war die zeitgerechte Vorlage des druckfertigen Manuskripts (mit Zusammenfassungen in drei Sprachen und Darstellungen) sowie ein gewisser inhaltlicher Zusammenhang mit den anderen aufgenommenen Beiträgen von Bedeutung. Der zweite Band soll sobald wie möglich erscheinen. Wir bitten die Autoren, deren Beiträge in diesem Band nicht mehr Platz fanden, um Geduld und Verständnis.

Schließlich möchte ich meinen Kollegen, die mich bei der Vorbereitung der Texte für den Druck unterstützt haben, für ihre Bemühungen danken: FELIX JÜLG, der die Schriftleitung besorgte, und ELISABETH GLASER, die zahlreiche Beiträge nochmals umschrieb und auch sonst bei vielen Anlässen wertvolle Hilfe geleistet hat. Mein Dank gilt ferner INGEBORG WIESLER, welche die Korrektur und teilweise auch die Übersetzung der französischen Texte besorgte, sowie meinen Mitarbeitern KARL SCHAPPELWEIN und NORBERT STANEK für ihre Mithilfe bei der graphischen Gestaltung der beiden Bände.

Wien, im Frühling 1978 Karl A. Sinnhuber

Recreation in the mountains

KARL A. SINNHUBER, Vienna, Austria *

To say mountains and recreation go very well together is a truism that does not need proof. What I would like to discuss in this paper is various aspects of the relationship of mountains and recreation, especially the question which recreational activities can be pursued and to which degree of intensity so that they benefit their practitioners without harming the mountain environment. Before going into *medias res* I would like to remark briefly on the key words of the title of this paper "Recreation" and "Mountains".

Recreation, or in German *Erholung* or *Rekreation,* might be defined as "the renewal of the strength of body and mind to keep fit for the demands of work and life". However, as RUPPERT remarked in a paper in a previous meeting of the ICU Working Group, Geography of Tourism and Recreation, even the medical profession is still far from unanimous whether and if so to what extent the activities commonly understood by "recreation" really do "recreate" as defined above. A particular activity, say downhill skiing, that even without preparatory training is of recreational value to a healthy person, beyond a critical point of exertion may well turn into the opposite and may instead of "recreating" cause serious damage to his or her health. The state of fitness is thus a vital point whether an activity is in fact recreation or not and some pursuits, although they might well be included amongst the recreational activities, mainly since they are pursued in one's spare time, are so demanding that even for the fittest they cannot be considered recreation. Taking part in an international championship should not cause damage to health to the participants but is a far cry from recreation. I think it is therefore better to use a more neutral term like "leisure time pursuits" which covers all these activities. Most of these will potentially be also recreation but need not be so in every instance. Although in the mountains there are some enjoyable ways of spending leisure time indoors, like passing a pleasant evening in a mountain hut in congenial company, the mountain environment, in contrast to an urban environment, is essentially a field for outdoor activities. I would, however, like to add, that the Geography of Recreation does include many indoor leisure activities too. The difficulty is where to draw the line and there may well be differences of opinion. That the locational aspects of all sports which have to be carried out indoors only at certain times, mainly for reasons of climate or weather, like swimming, skating, athletics, horse riding or various ball games are clearly within our field of study there can be no doubt, in the case of other indoor leisure time activities, say dancing or card playing one may well come to the conclusion that they are not our concern.

---

* Dr. KARL A. SINNHUBER, Professor, Department of Geography, University of Economics, Vienna, Austria.

This paper is a slightly modified version of the paper read as presidential address of Section E (Geography) of the British Association for the Advancement of Science at the 139th Meeting of the BA at the University of Aston in Birmingham on 5th September 1977.

The second key word I would like to remark upon is *mountains*. Although all mountains have much in common with each other I will confine myself on the whole to the Alps, and in particular the Austrian Alps. Although the valleys are naturally also part of these, emphasis is laid on the heights and the peaks since they offer the possibilities for the most typical and most exciting pursuits in this environment. It is, however, interesting to note that the peaks which as scenery, as targets for an ascent or as terminals for cableways are now the most valuable assets – note for instance the high fees that have to be paid to the Nepal government for permission to climb a Himalayan peak – not so long ago they were economically the least important part of a mountain system. This is demonstrated in the German language area of the Alps in a number of cases by earlier uses of the word *Berg* which one would normally translate as "mountain" or "peak". Historically this word was not used for the peaks since these were virtually useless, except in some instances for making it possible to tell the time in relation to the position of the sun as the name *Elfer Kogel* (eleven o'clock peak) indicates. *Berg* was employed to refer to the useful part of the mountain environment: the passes, the summer pastures, or those parts where mineral resources occurred. Thus the most important *Berge* of Tyrol were formerly the Brenner, the Reschen and the Arlberg, i. e. mountain passes[1]. However to add the word "pass" to them as is frequently done on maps is in two respects, as regards local usage as well as historically, wrong. I wonder how many visitors have as a result vainly tried to find a peak of that name in the Arlberg region as I did on my first visit. Even more frequently is the word *Berg* used in combination with the name of a village to denote the area of its summer pastures. These seasonal chalet settlements have in many cases eventually become permanent villages in their own right. To demonstrate this point again with an example from Tyrol: the village "Wattenberg" was originally the temporary settlement on the summer pastures of the village of Wattens near Innsbruck down in the Inn Valley.

Probably as early as the natural mountain meadows were used for summer pastures, the mountains attracted man for another reason: their mineral resources. Mountain formation, the uplift of rocks to lofty heights, is followed by accelerated erosion, so that in mountains mineral resources become exposed or at least more easily reached; a mine in German is a *Bergwerk* and a *Bergmann* is by no means one who climbs mountains but a miner.

In addition to these two uses, pasture and mining, the mountains had traditionally two more, the cutting of timber and the hunt for augmenting the food supply, but quite early also as a sport. Areas where none of these uses were possible were considered useless waste and this was with notable exceptions the general attitude towards the mountains. Even modern landuse maps usually classify this area as *Ödland,* i. e. waste. With the growth of mass tourism just those parts of the mountains became one of the most valuable assets of the Alpine states *per se,* Austria and Switzerland. Apart from their value in attracting tourists one must not forget their value as sources of inexhaustible energy stored in the glaciers.

---

[1] Indicative of this usage is for instance the fact that in the map of Tyrol by LAZIUS, 1561, the mountain passes have to their name the word *mons* added.

Cf. KINZL, H.: Der Brenner im Kartenbild. Beiträge zur geschichtlichen Landeskunde Tirols. Festschrift für H. HUTER. *Schlern Schriften,* 207, Innsbruck 1959, p. 169 f.

Looking at mountains from the aspect of an environment for outdoor activities one has to distinguish those which can only be carried out in such an environment, like downhill skiing or rock climbing, those which become very different compared with carrying them out away from mountains like canoeing in wild mountain streams, and those which are essentially identical regardless whether they are pursued within or outside the mountains, but for which the mountain environment provides an added interest. These include walking, game shooting, fishing, sailing. It is clearly impossible to consider all these activities comprehensively. I will therefore briefly review a few of these and then turn to one sport which very few may think of as a characteristic mountain pursuit, glider flying or more specifically Alpine soaring. One reason for having chosen this, to be quite honest considering the relatively small numbers involved, "elitist activity", is that to my knowledge geographers have so far paid hardly any attention to it. J. A. PATMORE[2] in his book "Land and leisure" devotes less than half a page to it, in I. G. SIMMONS' book "Rural recreation in the industrial world"[3] it is merely included in a diagram showing the growth rates of various sports, and in the collective volume "Recreational geography" (edited by PATRICK LAWERY)[4] it is not even mentioned, although a no less elitist activity, game shooting, is included. Even my distinguished predecessor as president of Section E in 1975, Prof. E. CAMPBELL, in her presidential address on "Cartography and outdoor sports" had omitted maps related to gliding for shortage of time, as she told me afterwards. There is another reason for going into more detail with this sport: since I am a keen glider pilot myself I can draw on some personal experience in my attempt "to put it on the map". This and hang-gliding are, however, the most modern leisure activities in the Alps; thus before considering their geographical aspects I would like to let others pass review in a roughly chronological sequence.

The earliest outdoor pursuit in the Alps, which for some was a leisure activity, was beyond doubt *hunting;* the principal game being red and roe deer and in the High Alps the chamois. Hunting as a sport was a privilege of the nobility. Anyone who has been in the Tyrolese Inn valley will remember the rock precipice a few miles west of Innsbruck called the Martinswand. To this rock face is attached the legend of how the Holy Roman Emperor Maximilian in stalking a chamois had lost his way and was unable to move forward or backward, and would-be rescuers could not reach him either. He had given up hope of being rescued but an angel came and guided him safely down the mountains. Stalking the chamois, to come nearer to the present, was the favourite pastime of the Austrian Emperor Francis Joseph who for that purpose spent the summer months at Bad Ischl in the Salzkammergut. Pictures showing him in his green hunting suit were very popular and can still be seen in some mountain inns. Today hunting is no longer restricted to the titled classes, but apart from those owners of large farms who have hunting rights attached, the huntsmen belong overwhelmingly to the social upper crust and have their normal domicile outside the Alps. To most of them hunting is beyond doubt a status symbol. The principal game, according to numbers, is the deer – roe deer and red deer – but in order to be assured of a

[2] PATMORE, J. A.: Land and leisure. In: HALL, P. (ed.): *Geography and environmental studies.* Harmondsworth 1972, p. 213

[3] SIMMONS, J. G.: *Rural recreation in the industrial world.* London 1975, p. 46

[4] LAWERY, P. (ed.): *Recreational geography.* London 1971

successful hunt the hunting fraternity has insisted for a long time on overstocking with game so that it can no longer support itself naturally from the environment but needs additional winter feed. The noble huntsmen of the last century through systematically eradicating the larger predatory animals, wolf, bear and lynx started a development which resulted in a radical disturbance of the biological balance. The absence of natural enemies combined with this winter feeding practice resulted in a tremendous increase in numbers of red and roe deer: within a hundred years in the German Alpine area it was a five-fold one. Where formerly the smaller number of deer had found winter feed in the foreland now closed to them they now proceed to eat up anything in the forest which they find edible in order to supplement the unbalanced winter feed provided. The result is the disappearance of the mixed forest with rich undergrowth, the habitat of many smaller animals, and the spread of stands of fir which because of their shallow roots are less resistant to storms and avalanches, so that eventually distruction of the mountain forest may result and may in its wake bring about a serious hydrological deterioration. Small mountain streams then turn into uncontrollable torrents and pastures, paths and settlements become overwhelmed by masses of mud, debris or the packed snow of avalanches. According to the German Alpine Institute of Environmental Research at Munich, there is a danger, if the present development continues, that at least in the German Alps mountain forests above 1400 m will disappear over the next century or century and a half. F. FLIRI, in his inaugural address as Vice Chancellor of Innsbruck University, stated that damage by game on the forest amounted in the single year 1976 in Tyrol to AS 5,5 million (that is more than £ 3 per head of agricultural population) and also stressed that winter feeding of game emphasizes the disturbance of the ecological balance[5].

Other users of the Alps for leisure purposes contribute of course their share towards the deterioration of the mountain environment, in this case mainly by their sheer numbers. When around the middle of the 19th century visiting the Alps for *mountaineering*, or simply for having a restful holiday, ceased to be something for the few and increasing numbers of visitors came, often from far afield, it was then beyond doubt of immeasurable benefit to the region, halting the depopulation of Alpine valleys. The Alpine societies of Austria, Germany and Switzerland which were founded around that period (the *Österreichische Alpenverein* in 1862, the *Deutsche Alpenverein* in 1869, joined in 1873 as *Deutscher und Österreichischer Alpenverein;* now they are separate again) were an indication of the broadening of the appeal of the Alps for the middle classes. These societies by building, marking and maintaining numerous foot paths and constructing mountain chalets for their members and others were instrumental in systematically opening up the Alps for visitors. The first mountain hut was opened in 1865 in Kaprun, Salzburg; today there are about 700 chalets in the Austrian Alps though not all belonging to the Alpine societies. It is no overstatement to say that no other organisation did as much to promote tourism in the Austrian Alps as the *Deutsche und Österreichische Alpenverein.* Despite the substantial numbers, up to

---

[5] FLIRI, F.: Über Landschaft, Bauerntum und Universität. *Innsbrucker Universitätsreden,* 12, Innsbruck 1977, p. 23
For a more detailed discussion *viz.:* MEISTER, G.: Wald und Wild, Forstwirt – Jäger. In: WICHMANN, H.: *Die Zukunft der Alpenregion.* München 1972, pp. 116–123

World War I the number of visitors compared with present-day figures was still rather modest.

Numbers began to increase substantially when after World War I *skiing* became a popular sport. Reasons for this were that many Austrians and Germans had received a basic instruction in skiing while serving with the mountain troups, lots of ex-army skis were available cheaply and the experience gained during the war in constructing cable cars was put to peaceful use to serve tourists. Mainly where there were cable cars, the first genuine winter sport resorts came into being, best known amongst them St. Anton on the Arlberg and Kitzbühel both in regions of well-rounded grassy mountains. F. JÜLG[6] has made special studies of the importance of cableways for tourism and this topic is well illustrated in his paper in this volume, thus this brief mention will suffice. Compared with the number of people who began to spend their winter holidays in the Alps after World War II, the number of visitors in the inter-war period was still of manageable size. The increase from about 1950 onwards was a veritable explosion, surpassing all expectations. In the winter season 1976/77 Austria counted ca 34 million overnight stays, more than two thirds by visitors from abroad.

That this tremendous increase in numbers had to have serious consequences was to be expected, but because of the speed of its happening measures of guiding the concomitant development in providing accommodation and places of entertainment as well as preparing ski runs were often inadequate and came too late to prevent serious damage. A new feature, hardly known before World War II and certainly no problem then, resulted from the increasing affluence but probably also from the desire to invest safely; this new feature is the *second home.* This is of course not unique for the Alps but it is perhaps there particularly serious. In some well-known Alpine resorts of Bavaria 60–70 per cent. of the dwellings are second homes and the Austrian government became so alarmed of the number of Germans buying property in Austria that it has put a stop to the purchase of property in Austria by non-Austrians. That does not solve the problem of more and more Austrian city dwellers buying or building a second home in the mountains[7]. Perhaps the fear that with all this bulding activity the concrete covered areas in the Alps from Geneva to Vienna and from Upper Bavaria to Upper Italy might soon merge to form one huge "Alpinopolis" is unfounded but the seasonal increase in settlement density in some parts of the Alps is reason for concern. In some of the most popular Alpine valleys there is a seasonal population concentration of 1.300 people per square km, a settlement density of urban dimensions and the exhaust fumes of motor cars in an Alpine health resort like Bad Tölz, Bavaria, produce at times concentrations of carbon monoxide which are rarely exceeded even in industrial centres of the Ruhr region.

The situation is hardly better on the ski runs of those places that have been thorougly developed. Except when new snow has fallen there is no natural winter landscape to be seen; instead of the white snow cover of days past there is a dirty surface of snow mixed with suncream and the soot from the exhausts of the diesel engines of the rollers which turn the natural ski

---

[6] JÜLG, F.: Die Seilbahnen Österreichs und ihre Auswirkungen auf die Wirtschaft. *Veröffentlichungen des Österreichischen Instituts für Raumplanung,* 29, Wien 1966

[7] There is a sizeable literature on this topic; for a summary discussion by a geographer *cf.* the paper by K. GANSER:

GANSER, K.: Zweitwohnungen: Konflikt: Individuum – Gemeinwesen. In: WICHMANN, H. (ed.): *Die Zukunft der Alpenregion,* München 1972, pp. 124–136 runs into ski "motorways", and it is "decorated" with orange peel, cigarette packers, beverage cans and many other items of our throw-away society. Whether in this sort of environment, after having endured traffic jams to reach it and having waited impatiently to get on a cableway – all activities which promote aggression – genuine "recreation" is still possible, is more than doubtful. These overdeveloped places are especially in danger of losing their function as recreation areas for good. A decline in the number of overnight stays of up to 7 per cent. in such well-known resorts like Garmisch or Mittenwald (both in Bavaria) are unmistakable danger signs. The consequences of preparing the ski runs, a necessity because of the masses who use them, are usually also detrimental to the environment. In the first place preparation usually involves some clearing of woodland. For the preparation of ski runs in the Austrian provinces of Salzburg and Tyrol more than 1.000 ha forest areas disappeared in the period 1964–75[8]. If then the soil, after levelling, is not suitably prepared by adding topsoil, manuring and establishing a suitable herbaceous vegetation, the consequences can be disastrous. The water storage capacity is reduced to a fraction of what it was before, plants that do establish themselves cannot withstand periods of drought, and heavy downpours cause serious soil erosion; values of 10 t/ha have been measured. Even more dangerous is the establishment of a prepared ski run above the natural forest limit. There, once the precarious balance is disturbed, it may be impossible to re-establish a vegetation cover at all[9]. If ski runs are prepared on agriculturally used land the result is a considerable reduction in yield, more serious than is generally realized. The main reason is that as a result of compressing the snow by the heavy rollers the growing period is shortened by 1–2 weeks and as a result of also impeding the "breathing" of the soil, most of the better fodder plants die off. At some spots of maximum wear, e. g. turning points of a run, the steel edges of the skis erase the plants and on these spots there is no yield at all. There exists further the danger of injury to livestock through items lost or thrown away. True, compensation is usually paid, sometimes generously, but this does not alter the fact that the environment has been damaged[10].

An increasing number of skiers become bored with going down the prepared slopes, partly because of their overcrowding. There are rarely the 800 m² open space per skier available which according to the Innsbruck psychologist LÜCKE[11] are necessary to create the feeling of well-being. If they then ski through plantations of young trees the sharp steel edges often damage trees to such extent that they die off. Leaving the prepared run does, however, have other dangers, in this case for the skiers themselves, the danger of death in an avalanche. In the winter season 1976/77 seventeen people were killed in avalanches, thirteen of these because they were on their way off a prepared ski run. Altogether 84 persons were involved in these avalanches which in most instances they had triggered off themselves in ignorance or through carelessness. Most of these were "Sunday skiers", technically probably very capable but without sufficient experience of the mountains. Much time and money is spent in the resorts to minimize the danger –

[8] Bundesministerium für Verkehr (ed.): *Österreichisches Seilbahnkonzept.* Teil II: Grundlagen, Wien 1978, p. 222

[9] HEMBERGER, M. Th.: Skilauf – Die weiße Droge Österreichs. *Die Presse,* Wien 1978, Jan. 31st

[10] PIFFNER, A.: *Landschaftsschäden und Entschädigungspraxis in Zusammenhang mit dem Schisport.* Undergraduate dissertation. Schweiz. Landwirtschaftliches Technikum, Weisstannen 1976

[11] HEMBERGER, M. Th.: Skilauf – Die weiße Droge Österreichs. *Die Presse,* Wien 1978, Jan. 26th

but it helps little if a closure notice of a run put up by the local "avalanche commission" is ignored[12].

Deaths in skiing are not only due to avalanches, they occur also as a result of skiing accidents – the principal reason of all such accidents is loss of control because of excessive speed. A contributory factor is the hard, often icy surface of the prepared run. Compared with the total number of skiers – in the whole world an estimated 35 million, in Austria 1,3 mill, i. e. 4 per cent. of the world's skiers – the number of deaths is fortunately still small but the accident risk is higher than in most other sports. The number of injured needing hospital treatment in ski accidents in Austria for 1976/77 was approaching 30.000, about half the number of those involved in traffic accidents in an entire year. The direct and indirect costs (medical treatment, loss of work time, losses to the national economy), are estimated at AS 420 millions; against this there are a number of items on the credit side which for the national economy makes it still worthwhile to be a country of skiers. There were 34 million overnight stays counted in the skiing season 1976/77 – two thirds of these by visitors from abroad and they left AS 21.600 million in currency in the country. Apart from the large number of those employed in the catering trade there are the operators and attendants of the cableways and – the dream job of many boys in the Alps – about 7.000 ski instructors who find well-paid employment. There are in addition the earnings of the Austrian ski manufactures who employ 4.600 people, who produced, in 1976, 1,6 million pairs of skis of which about 70 per cent. were exported. A third of all skis used in the world were produced in Austria! To this must be added the earnings from exporting cableways and ski tows so that, excluding what the Austrians themselves spend on equipment, skiing contributes to the Austrian national economy *in toto* about AS 26.000 million (nearly £ 1.000 million)[13].

A potential and locally important source of income is a new kind of skiing which, however, is deplored by those circles which neither practise it nor benefit from it financially; it is the so-called "heli-skiing".

By heli-skiing one understands the transport of skiers by helicopter to high altitude glaciers or mountain tops so that they save the walk up and have an opportunity to ski down in virgin snow. Not having to walk up gives a competent and fit skier the chance to have downhill runs of up to 10,000 metres altitudinal difference in a single day. Heli-skiing, aptly described by its practitioners as "a new dimension of skiing" or sometimes somewhat snobbishly as "skiing for gentlemen", by its antagonists, however, called "an insult to the peaks" and "audio pollution of the mountains which spoils the enjoyment for those who make for the heights by their own effort" began in the 1950s in Switzerland and spread in Europe to France, Italy and also Austria. In the mid 1960s it began also in the Rocky Mountains of the USA and Canada.

There can be no doubt that it must be very pleasurable to reach the top of a ski run without effort, to enjoy watching the scenery from the air, survey the run to be taken and then, well rested, ski down behind a local ski instructor. Alas, this kind of skiing is not without drawbacks and dangers. Reaching these high altitudes so rapidly and without physical effort one's

[12] *viz.:* RONGE, Ch.: Land der Berge – Land der Lawinen. *Die Presse.* Wien 1978, Febr. 28th, March 2nd and 7th

[13] HEMBERGER, M. Th.: Skilauf – Die weiße Droge Österreichs. *Die Presse,* Wien 1978, Jan. 27th

Plate 1:

Hang-gliders assembled and ready for take off at the top of the chair lift in Kössen, Tyrol, Austria. This place, long established as a skiing resort, can claim to be the cradle of hang-gliding in Austria. The first Hang-gliding World Championship was held there in 1976.

In their appearance hang-gliders have something in common with windsurfers since in both cases the sails are multicoloured and in both cases excellent fitness and mastery over one's body are essential since steering these craft is affected not by rudders or similar controls but by shifting one's body weight.

Plate 2:

Of the various Austrian airfields the one at Innsbruck, Tyrol, is amongst those which are particularly popular with visiting glider pilots, especially to those from Germany as this picture demonstrates since all the 'planes on which identification marks can be made out show a "D", the mark for Germany *(Deutschland).* There are two main reasons for this attractiveness. Firstly Innsbruck airfield is particularly easily accessible since it lies close to the Austrian motorway from the Brenner Paß which continues down the Inn valley to the German border and from there on to Munich whence motorways lead northward and westward. Thus there is no place in West Germany from where it would not be possible to reach Innsbruck in a day's drive even towing a trailer with a dismantled 'plane inside. Secondly it is the good chances offered for long distance and high altitude flights by the locational qualities of Innsbruck airfield; for the former it is its location in the great longitudinal valley trough, for the latter it is for being in an area where the *Föhn* blows particularly strongly and thus gives rise to a good wave air current (see fig. 15). Thus when the weather conditions are favourable many glider pilots take a few days leave and converge at Innsbruck airfield in the hope of achieving their life's flying ambition, the golden "C" award or even the diamond supplement to it.

This photograph was taken some years ago when even high performance sail 'planes were still built of plywood and/or canvas over a steel frame.

Plate 1

Plate 1:

Photograph through the courtesy of Dr. W. LENOTTI, editor in chief of *Austroflug*, Vienna

Plate 2:

Photograph by SIEBLER, Innsbruck, through the courtesy of Dr. W. LENOTTI, editor in chief of *Austroflug*, Vienna

Plates 3 and 4:

Photographs by UWE VAN HUSEN, Vienna, through the courtesy of UL VAN HUSEN, head of the Flying School, Niederöblarn, Styria, Austria

Plate 2

Plate 3

Plate 4

Plates 3 and 4:

In the great longitudinal valley troughs of the Inn, Salzach and Enns rivers in the north and the Drau and Mur-Mürz rivers in the south of Austria optimum conditions are found during the right kind of weather for long distance flights and for achieving altitudes of several thousand metres. In these valleys lie the gliding fields which have become justly famous: Lienz and Timmersdorf in the south and Innsbruck (plate 2), Zell am See and Niederöblarn in the north (cf. map). The pictures 3 and 4 were taken near Niederöblarn. Plate 3 shows the 'plane close to a precipice within the Northern Limestone Alps, in plate 4 it glides above the centre of the Enns valley with the Central Alps visible to the south. The cloud formation above the crest of the Central Alps indicates *Föhn* weather, ideal conditions for soaring – but only for the experienced pilot. The 'plane, a West German model, built of plastic material, is characteristic of the latest generation of gliders. There is very little similarity with the gliders of the early twenties which looked like contraptions made of broomsticks, covered with canvas, glued together and tied up with string. However, even with the most modern high performance 'planes, the flying skill of the pilot and his knowledge of the conditions of the ground and air currents to be expected are paramount if a flight is to be successful.

organism has little chance to adjust. Unless one is very fit this can result in a mild attack of mountain sickness, a symptom of this is dizziness, and in being in far less than top form for a run which certainly requires much more effort than one on the prepared "piste". Having said that one has to add that this is, however, only different in degree but not principally, from going up to a high peak like the top of the Marmolata (3.342 m) by cableway. Secondly skiing down these wide open slopes without having made the ascent on the ground and been able to judge the conditions optimally, the danger of starting and getting caught in an avalanche is much greater. This is, however, no serious argument against heli-skiing since a local ski instructor should be able to judge whether there are conditions of avalanche danger, and skiers do unfortunately get killed by avalanches in other kinds of skiing also. Many arguments once advanced against building cableways are now advanced against heli-skiing. "Spoiling the mountain scenery": this applies certainly less, if at all, to the sight of a helicopter (or any other small 'plane) which in any case may be on its way to a mountain rescue or to bring supplies to a mountain chalet. "Something for the rich only": True, it is not exactly cheap but since the cost of flights starts at AS 350,– (ca. £ 12,–. The flight to the top of the Monte Rosa was in 1977 SF 150,– and to the top of Mt. Blanc FF 300,– – FF 400,–), it is manageable for an appreciable number of people. A single après-ski evening can easily cost as much. The noise aspect, spoiling the quiet enjoyment for the true ski tourist who seeks solitude, is a more serious aspect as is possibly also the annoyance to a skier who after some hours of climbing and being tired out, is then met by a few skiers jumping out of a helicopter as fresh as a daisy. But all these negative aspects of heli-skiing are, in my opinion, no valid reason for forbidding it altogether but merely for limiting it in time and space: perhaps not have flights at weekends and leaving enough good touring areas free of helicopter landing spots. This is what has happened in Austria and Switzerland. In Austria, in 1977, seven ski resorts offered heli-skiing services and there were about thirty well-defined landing spots permitted though only a few services were able to operate at weekends or public holidays. In Switzerland 19 resorts offered these services and 48 landing spots were permitted and there is a regulation that every group must be accompanied by a qualified ski instructor or mountain guide; in the French Alps only five resorts offer heli-services but more than a hundred destinations are available including the top of Mt. Blanc, from which it is possible to have the longest ski run in the world. In Italy only the resort of Courmayeur offered heli-skiing in the 1976/77 season. Further reasons for not stopping these services altogether is that a certain well-to-do clientele will now only go to places where these services are available, and that these helicopters are also used for important supply flights and rescue flights and in the precautionary releasing of avalanches. The four helicopters of Air Zermatt are used ca. 60 per cent. for supply flights, 18 per cent. for rescue flights and hardly more than 20 per cent. for heli-skiing. It is likely that without the more remunerative business of heli-skiing the number of helicopters available would be much reduced.

The *El Dorado* for heli-skiing is, however, the American Mountains. There, where a gigantic area, because of nature protection measures, is closed to road and cableway construction, it is the only possibility of skiing at all. As it does not disturb anybody else no reasonable objections can be raised. An increasing number of skiers go every year for a skiing holiday from Austria and Germany to the Canadian Rockies. Package tours for a fortnight are offered for £ 800 – £ 900. However, the danger is there too – in the skiing season 1976/77 about a dozen skiers were killed by avalanches. Downhill skiing is, of course, not the only winter activity but it is the only one of mass tourism. Other winter sports are ski bob sleighing, tobogganning, curling and skating on natural ice surfaces but in comparison the numbers involved are small; very often opportunities for these sports are offered as supplementary activities in skiing resorts.

There have also been developments in skiing to supplement the usual downhill skiing in winter. Over the past ten years or so a change in skiing has started and cross-country skiing, the original type of skiing as it had developed in Scandinavia, has been gaining increased popularity. This has given smaller resorts without spectacular runs and cableways also a benefit from winter tourism. Another – contrary – development in skiing since the middle of the 1960s has been the development of a few centres to all the year round skiing resorts. One of the best known and most recent ones in Austria lies in the Stubaital in Tyrol. Opening up this area by a road, a high capacity cableway, 4 ski tows and ski runs prepared by rollers, it has changed its character thoroughly to the regret of many. There is however no doubt that a demand for this kind of skiing existed – in 1975 there were over 350.000 visitors – and that by spreading the season and increasing the use of the available accommodation, villages up to more than 50 kms distance away have benefited. A detailed investigation carried out by the Innsbruck geographer P. HAIMAYER[14] has not only demonstrated this fact but also that the fears that the skiers would ruin the solitude of an extensive area, were unjustified. Serious and not yet solved problems are, however, refuse disposal and protection of the access road against avalanches.

From summer skiing I turn to what in the Alps are normally *summer activities*. Although now that all Alpine peaks have been conquered even over the most difficult routes the challenge in serious rock climbing is to attempt difficult ascents in winter, this involves hardly more than a handful of devotees, thus does not affect the classification of mountaineering as a summer activity. Something has already been said about the increasing interest in the Alps, the foundation of the various Alpine mountaineering societies and the great merits they had in opening up the Alps to visitors, by no means all mountaineers. An indication of the increasing popularity of visiting the Alps in summer for mountain walking or climbing has been the growth in the number of members of the various Alpine societies. At the turn of the century the *Deutsche und Österreichische Alpenverein* had 30.000 members in 214 local branches, by 1914 the membership had risen to over 100.000. In 1939 the *Deutsche Alpenverein* (German Alpine Society), as it was then called, had about 200.000 members in 456 local branches. The German part of this society, of which only the Austrian branch continued without a break after 1945, was refounded again in 1950 and has now ca 320.000 members in 290 local branches whereas the Austrian part has now over 200.000 members in 160 branches. After 1945 the former local branches of the *Deutsche und Österreichische Alpenverein* in South Tyrol, which had been unable to operate during the Mussolini regime, reformed and the *Südtiroler Alpenverein*

[14] HAIMAYER, P.: Zur Frage der Ganzjahresschigebiete: Das Beispiel Hochstubai/Tirol. *Berichte zur Raumforschung und Raumplanung,* Wien 1977, p. 5–13

was founded which now has 17.000 members. Including other associations with interest in the mountains, there are now well over 650.000 members in the various mountaineering societies of Austria, Germany and South Tyrol whose interest centres on the Eastern Alps. They are the solid stock of visitors to the mountain huts and users of foot paths and regular climbs. Because of the various activities in the branches, like lectures about the dangers of the Alps, techniques of mountain climbing and the equipment required, these visitors come quite well prepared; alas, there is the great mass of other visitors who without any experience and proper equipment, in particular suitable boots, go up to some place in a cableway, venture away from the secured paths and become accident victims. In the entire Alps up to the end of July there were in 1977 139 deaths, and 400 tourists were injured, some very seriously (not counting skiing accidents). The director of the Innsbruck Mountaineering School is convinced that 80 per cent. of the accidents could have been avoided as they were due to carelessness arising from ignorance. The best precaution for somebody not really experienced is to take part in a climbing course in one of the many mountaineering schools (there are ca 20 in Tyrol and 5 in Salzburg) or join a group under a qualified mountain guide (they number 400 in Tyrol, 50 in Salzburg). Suitably prepared, mountaineering is an activity for all healthy men and women which can be carried on into a ripe age, is genuine recreation, and even has preventative medical value; this was a conclusion reached in a symposium of the Austrian, German and South Tyrol Alpine societies held in Innsbruck in June 1977.

From mountaineering, an activity confined to mountains – if one excludes climbing practice in quarries or rock outcrops or up the façade of a College! – I briefly turn to sports which, when carried out in the mountains, acquire a different aspect or even a new dimension. These are various water sports: rafting, canoeing in swift mountain streams, water skiing, sailing and windsurfing on the Alpine lakes. *Rafting* was of course traditionally not a leisure activity but a means of transporting logs and goods economically, especially in areas not yet opened up by road and rail. As this sort of means of transport it has virtually ceased at least in the Eastern Alps, a major reason has been the construction of numerous dams to harness the rivers for the generation of electricity. There are, however, still people left with the skill to steer a raft down a swift stream like the Isar, or Loisach, Bavaria, and raft trips are laid on on these as tourist attraction. (Such trips are also possible on the Dunajec river in the Beskid Mountains in Poland). For the participants it is a fairly passive but pleasurable, if sometimes wet, experience. A very active sport is in contrast *wild water canoeing* which has received a great boost from the development of the light weight, reasonably priced and yet sturdy fibre glass craft to replace the fragile craft made of a wooden frame and covered by a skin of some sort. While canoeing on still water or large, slowly flowing rivers is something any fit person (who can also swim) should be able to master, canoeing on wild waters is something for the experts and can be quite dangerous. As in rock climbing, even experts meet their fate in this pursuit. In Austria there are a number of people active in this sport and in the World Championship held in Carinthia (Austria) in 1977 the Austrian competitors featured prominently.

Fairly small, but for different reasons, is the number of *water skiers.* There is in the first place the financial aspect: unless one joins a club one requires a powerful motor boat (which is expensive to buy and to run) for towing and the Alpine lakes are not very suitable for water skiing owing to their low water temperature. On most of these lakes the use of motor boats except the slow, noiseless, electrically propelled ones, is no longer allowed during the months of July and August.

Again fairly small, but very much larger than even a few years ago, is the number of people who have learned to *sail* and have their own craft. Sailing schools and sailing clubs have multiplied since the 1950s on all lakes, although the Alpine ones are not exactly ideal as sailing waters. Because of their sheltered position and relatively small size good winds are rare. However, what is lacking in wind conditions, is made up by the beauty of the scenery which one can enjoy while becalmed. As far as numbers go at least for yachts which need a jetty or an ancorage, the limits of expansion have been nearly reached. Unless one finds a private owner of a stretch of beach who will allow one to keep a boat on his jetty or one joins a sailing club which, however, is again not easy since most have no spare capacity for additional boats, to buy one's own craft, unless it can be transported on top of a car or is trailable and easily launched by means of a launching trolley, is not a sound investment.

These difficulties facing would-be helmsmen as to where to put their boat were certainly at least a contributory factor for the explosive growth in the number of *windsurfers* now found on the lakes. In the summer of 1975 I saw the first one on the Traunsee, Salzkammergut; now the lake is full of them and they have a windsurfing school, a surfing club and surfing regattas there. The great advantage of windsurfers is that they are easily transported and launched and further do not require a substantial capital investment like a yacht or even a sailing dinghy. Provided one is fit and can swim, one can handle this sailcraft after about 5 hours instruction and practice and there are no particular dangers except of course catching a chill in the cool breeze or from a ducking in unpleasantly cold water. Thus the chilly, glacier-fed mountain lakes are anything but ideal for this sport, the usually light winds, on the other hand, are an advantage compared with larger sailing craft. Nevertheless they attract many windsurfers who guard against the cold in a so-called "wet suit" of neoprene. Windsurfing appears to have an affinity to skiing as it is a similar balancing act. A survey by the German Ski Club in 1977 found that 80 per cent. of windsurfers are also skiers. Here, in my opinion is a sport, no environmentalist can seriously object to: it is noiseless, does not cause any pollution since not even an auxiliary engine can be fitted and can hardly cause an injury even in a collision. Alas, in confined waters windsurfers do become a nuisance to swimmers and sailing boats and the first restrictions on where they can be launched and when used have been issued. As to their visual appearance I think their multicoloured sails add an additional point of interest to a "lakescape".

Many skiers are attracted to yet another sport where the cost of the apparatus is within reach of many: *hang-gliding* or sky sailing, in German *Drachenfliegen*. This (apart from ballooning) is the earliest and the latest form of taking to the air.

However, even if after suitable training and responsibly done it is not as dangerous as it looks, it is certainly one of the riskier pastimes, especially when carried out in high mountains with their strong air currents in which a hang-glider which has no controls like a 'plane is much more difficult to master. Although one can experience in high mountains the ultimate elation and although many successful flights have been made from high mountain peaks – in the Alps the Ortler (South Tyrol) 3859 m, the Großvenediger (Salzburg) 3674 m, the Zuckerhütl (Tyrol) 3607 m, outside Europe from the Kilimanjaro (Kenya) 5895 m, from a peak of the Hindu Kush as high as 7600 m and as additional achievement of the Austrian Mt. Everest expedition of 1978 to climb this peak without taking an oxygen supply, a flight from a ridge at 6000 m to base camp, and many other high mountains, the risks are so high that it should better be relegated to the hills of the foreland with predictable air currents. Because of the many fatal accidents hang-gliding has already been dubbed "kamikaze" flying. Up to September 1976 out of the then approximately 400 hang-glider pilots in Austria 20 had fatal accidents. In 1976 alone there occurred in Austria 19 serious accidents, true out of over 100.000 flights. The first world championship in hang-gliding took place in September 1976 in Kössen, Tyrol (plate 1). The world champions in the 3 different classes were an Austrian, a New Zealander and an Australian respectively. 150 pilots from 25 states took part. This competition was completed without serious accidents. The Austrian championship of 1977 was, however, cancelled after two fatal accidents during the official training. As a result of these various accidents hang-gliding has in Austria been brought under very strict control. To watch a hang-glider come down is no doubt an interesting sight but even this fragile kite is liable to endanger people. If anyone does cause damage, a fine of up to £ 10.000 or 6 weeks imprisonment may await him. But even if he does not cause damage, to fly outside the area of a hang-gliding school can cost him a fine of £ 80 if he cannot produce his pilot's licence. For this he has to take a course in one of the 6 hang-gliding schools or with a club with qualified instructors (there are about 20 such facilities in Austria) and has to have carried out a minimum of 50 practice flights and then to have passed a practical and theoretical test. It is to be hoped that proper training and further improvements in the gliders will substantially reduce the accident rate.

Hang-gliding is in a way a rediscovery of the early stages of flying at the turn of the century. In fact the first engine-less flight in Austria took place in 1906 in something one could describe as a hang-glider. The distance covered was only 250 m. In 1911, at the Semmering Pass, even a gliding competition was held, but here the longest distance flown was merely 170 m. *Glider flying* as we understand it today, began in Austria, as in Germany, in the early 1920s arising out of the situation that under the articles of the peace treaties motor flying was initially forbidden to them. Austrians went to learn gliding in the cradles of this sport in Germany, the Rhön Mts. and the sand dunes of Rositten on the Kurische Nehrung (now in the USSR). One of the Austrians who went there, in 1927, was ROBERT KRONFELD who three years later became holder of world records in altitude (3.500 m) and distance (164,5 kms). A few years earlier some gliding descents had been made from some of the marginal hills (rather than mountains) of the Austrian Alps, e. g. the Schöckl near Graz in Styria. The conquest of the Alps, the flight from the mountains proper, started around 1930 still from peaks near the foreland: The Gaisberg in Salzburg, by HANS WOLF, (where in 1935 Austria's first glider flying school began to teach its pupils), the Rax in Lower Austria by KRONFELD, the Zugspitze by ERNST UDET, and from the Rigi by some Swiss glider pilots. True the Zugspitze is a peak of nearly

3000 m altitude, but like these other mountains it is situated near the edge of the Alps so that one could glide to the foreland and touch down there. The day which can properly be considered the birthday of High Alpine flying is 10th June 1931, the day the German GÜNTHER GROENHOFF flew from the Jungfraujoch to Interlaken (Switzerland). This first flight nearly ended in disaster. Because of a starting mishap the 'plane, instead of being catapulted into the air, merely slid down the glacier, broke through a snow cornice, loosing half the elevator in the process, and then hardly manoeuverable, plunged downwards. After first deciding to bale out GROENHOFF changed his mind and managed to land after a flight of just under one hour on a meadow near Interlaken.

Not put off he repeated the attempt two days later; this time all went well and he landed again on the same spot as before. A few days later he accepted the invitation to attempt to fly as far as Berne and land there on the airfield – as a special feature of an air rally – and succeeded splendidly. Still in the same year a Swiss, WILLI FARNER, also took off from the Jungfraujoch; he flew southward; the distance covered was 56 kms.

In the summer months of 1932 and 1934 "gliding camps" were held in the German Alpine Foreland – at Chiemsee and Garmisch Partenkirchen – and flights into the Fore-Alps and the Northern Limestone Alps were carried out.

The first High Alpine glider competition was organized by the Swiss glider pilots in 1935; the place for launching the gliders was again the Jungfraujoch. 15 pilots took part – Swiss, Austrians, Germans and Jugoslavs. The longest distance covered on this occasion was 108 kms. Independently of the competition the Swiss pilot HERMANN SCHREIBER had himself brought by aero-tow from Interlaken to the Jungfrau Massif. After soaring there for two hours he succeded as the first glider pilot to cross the Alps from North to South and landed in Bellinzona in the Ticino (Switzerland). The years 1936 and 1937 saw further developments in the sense that gliders were aerotowed in the Northern Alpine Foreland merely to moderate heights, about 500 m, and then using thermals to gain height some pilots managed to cross the Alps. Particularly spectacular was the success of the International Glider Meeting in May 1937 in Salzburg when 6 German pilots succeeded in crossing the Alps. Amongst them was the by now almost "legendary" Captain HANNA REITSCH, now well into her sixties and still going strong. (In 1977 she achieved 2 German women's distance records, a declared destination with return of 644 kms, and with 680 kms the best achievement of a German woman so far. This year [3rd June 1978] taking off from the same place as the previous year, Timmersdorf in Styria, she broke the women's world record in declared destination return flights with a flight to St. Anton am Arlberg, Tyrol, and back, 720 kms total distance).

In those days, Alpine crossing by glider was truly a pioneering achievement. One knew by then a great deal about air currents above the plains or the *Mittelgebirge* or even the Fore-Alps. Very little was yet known, however, about the meteorological conditions of the High Alps: how would the great contrasts in temperature and air pressure, the mighty rock walls which reached 3.000 to 4.000 metres up, the contrast of bare rock and *firn* act on thermal activity? The flights were all carefully evaluated meteorologically and it is thanks to these early attempts that it is now possible for lesser mortals (say like me) after suitable experience to hope to attempt Alpine distance flights on well-tested routes.

These Alpine flights were carried out by utilising hill or ridge lift (air being forced up by a slope – fig. 1 and 2) and also thermals (fig. 3, 4 and 5), but completely new possibilities were opened up by making use of the so-called "wave lift" of the *Föhn* wind. Wave lift had already been discovered in 1933 on the northern side of the Giant Mountains. The director of a meteorological observatory in Silesia had pointed out to the well known German glider pioneer WOLF HIRTH, that in conditions of southerly wind above Hirschberg (now Zilona Gora in Poland) there appeared at 3.000 to 4.000 m a strong eliptical stationary cloud, which the locals called "*Moazagotl*". It was soon realized that a mountain obstruction sets up a wave system, not dissimilar to that created in water downstream of an obstruction. The altitudes achieved through use of the *Moazagotl* increased from about 1.500 m in 1933 to over 7.000 m in 1937. Wave lift in Britain was used for the first time in 1939 and I am happy to report that one of our elders and betters, Prof. GORDON MANLEY had a hand in it. NOEL McLEAN had discussed the possibilities of soaring in a local wind of the Cross Fell in the Pennines, the "Helm Wind", with him, because GORDON MANLEY had by then become not merely a meteorologist of repute but knew the area well. McLEAN, after take off, found initially some very turbulent air but then got into an uplift exceeding 20 ft/sec. and reached at first 9.000 feet and in a second wave 11.140 feet. The main difficulty was then for him getting the glider down again as the uplift was so great that even diving, side slipping and spinning was hardly sufficient to lose height.

Fig. 1 and 2: The influence of slope profiles on anabatic air currents

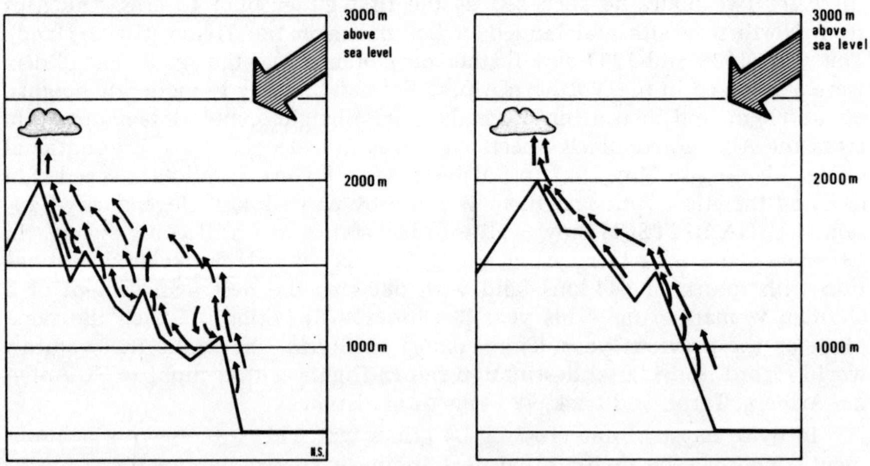

The smoother a slope the greater the heat gain of the rising air and the stronger and more regular the thermal lift.

Source: v. KALCKREUTH, J.: *Segeln über den Alpen. Erlebnis und Technik des Hochgebirgsfluges.* Zug und Stuttgart 1976, p. 123

Fig. 3, 4 and 5: The interference between thermal and orographic air currents

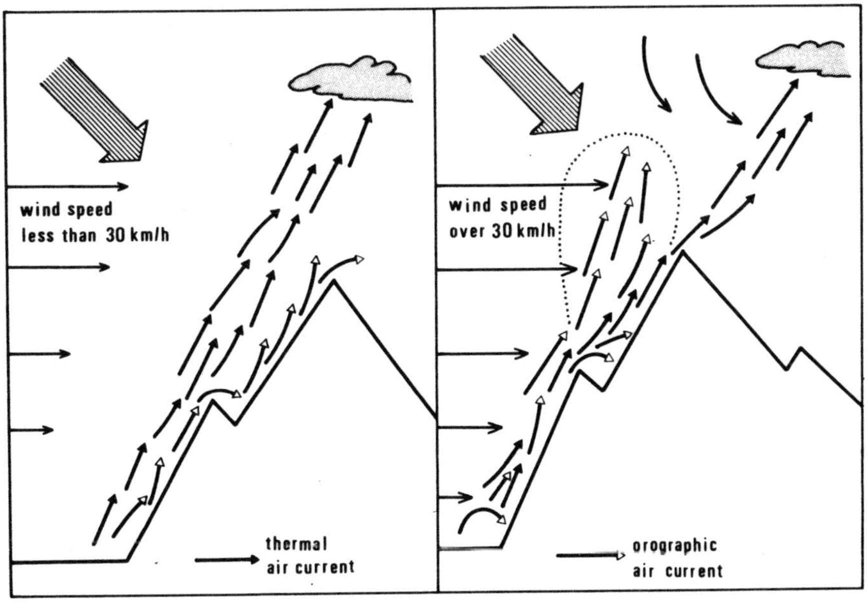

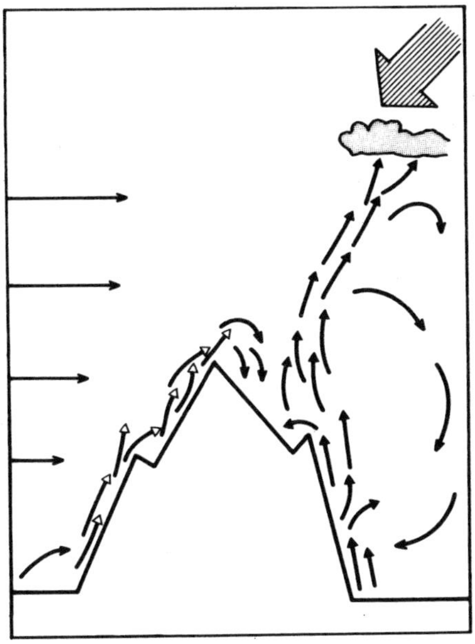

In mountains air may rise for orographic and thermal reasons. When both causes are present simultaneously the resulting uplift depends mainly on wind direction and wind speed. When the wind acts in the same direction the two air streams stay virtually separate if its speed is low; maximum uplift is present in the thermal air current somewhat before the slope (fig. 3). When the wind speed is higher then the air currents at the lower and middle reaches become intermingled, reinforce each other and give rise to maximum uplift close to the slope. Above the top, however, two separate uplift zones exist (fig. 4). When wind and insolation are of opposite directions ridge lift ceases at the top. There the wind causes turbulence and a diversion of the termal air stream (fig. 5).

Source: v. KALCKREUTH, J.: *Segeln über den Alpen. Erlebnis und Technik des Hochgebirgsfluges.* Zug und Stuttgart 1976, pp. 125 and 126

Fig. 6, 7, 8 and 9: The development of the valley (anabatic) and mountain (katabatic) wind system in a mountain valley running approximately in a direction from north to south during a period of fine weather in summer

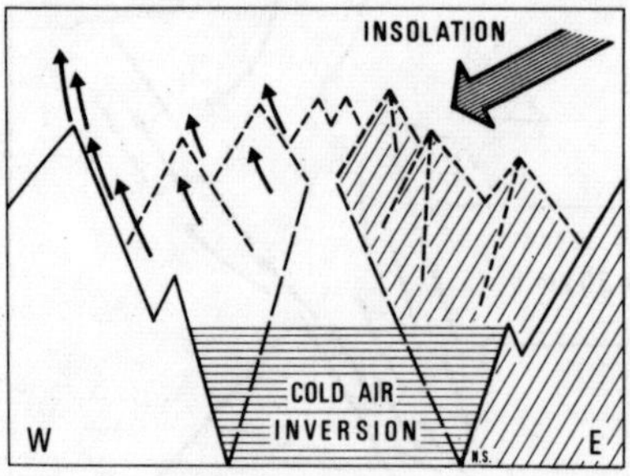

situation ca 08.00 hours

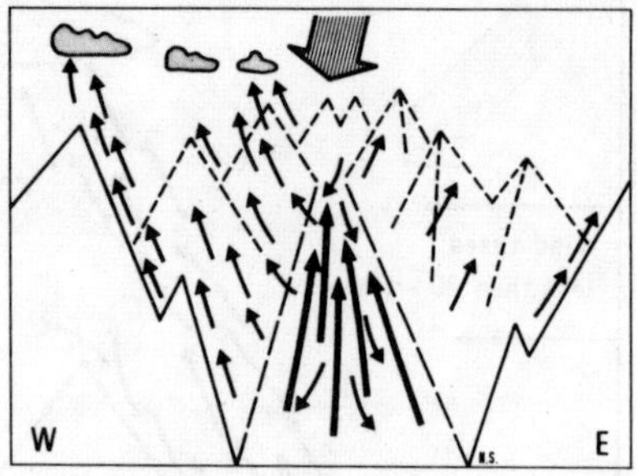

situation ca noon

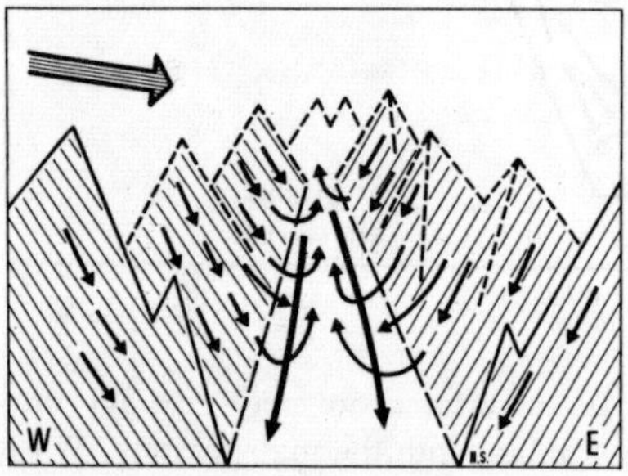

situation ca 16.00 hours

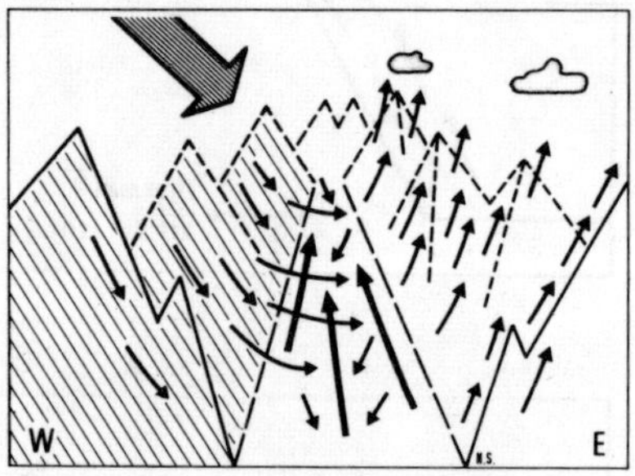

situation at late evening

Insolation during the day, air drainage starting in the late afternoon and going on until sunrise produce in mountains a local wind system. This phenomenon has to be taken into consideration already in the planning stage of a long distance flight by sail 'plane.

Source: v. KALCKREUTH, J.: *Segeln über den Alpen. Erlebnis und Technik des Hochgebirgsfluges.* Zug und Stuttgart 1976, p. 118

In the same year a systematic investigation of the Alpine *Föhn* and the lift conditions associated with it was started from Bavarian Airfields. It was the crowning of the life's work of WALTER GEORGII, the creator of the meteorology of soaring. In October 1941 ERICH KLÖCKNER in an ascent by means of the *Föhn* waves reached a height of 11.460 m, the border of the stratosphere (fig. 15).

After World War II wave systems were discovered and used in New Zealand where nearly 36.000 feet and in California where over 46.000 feet were reached.

But back to the Alps:

World War II soon called a halt to Alpine glider flying for pleasure, except in Switzerland, where Samedan in the Upper Engadin became a centre of High Alpine soaring and the Swiss national gliding championships were held there in 1943.

After World War II – unlike after World War I – Germany and also Austria were initially not allowed any aviation, not even gliding or model flying, until the 1950s. The first remarkable post-war Alpine gliding achievement was accomplished by a Swiss, SIGHART MAURER, in April 1948, who was the first to cross the entire Alpine chain from South to North – from Locarno to Basle (fig. 16).

In the same year the first International Gliding Competition after World War II was held at Samedan, Switzerland. (Later these competitions were upgraded to World Championships). Eight nations with 28 pilots (including six from Britain) took part. The British participants, as the WELCHS[15] wrote in their history of gliding, had "apprehensions over how to learn to soar in the high mountains – obviously quite a different task to floating above the rolling downlands of England." Unfortunately these apprehensions proved to have been correct: two of the British pilots had fatal accidents – one probably as a result of his glider being sucked into a cloud and thus losing control, the other by hitting an unmarked steel cable when flying close to the flank of a mountain and having a wing cut off. (The many cables on the mountain side – electric cables, cables of cableways – those for bringing down hay or taking supplies to mountain huts and those of the numerous commercial cableways – are serious dangers in high mountain gliding, and a pilot setting out for a distance flight is well advised to study closely large scale maps of his proposed route). The championship was won by a Swedish pilot, PER AXEL PERSON, with a declared destination flight to Geneva (293 kms). This, incidentally, was one of the longest flights in these years, now it would not even warrant a line in a gliding journal so much has the standard risen since then. From the middle of the 1950s onward when after the conclusion of the Austrian State Treaty and the end of the occupation regime (both in 1955) the restrictions on flying in Austria had come to an end, young Austrian glider pilots set new standards in High Alpine flying with the achievement of distances exceeding 300 kms and 500 kms thus fulfilling the distance flight requirements for the highest international soaring distinctions of the *Fédération Aéronautique Internationale* (FAI) the golden "C" and the "Diamond Supplement" respectively. (The other requirements for the golden "C" are a flight of 5 hours duration – which one also has to achieve already for the silver "C" and an altitude gain of 3.000 m; there are two other diamond supplements possible: a declared destination of at least 300 kms and an altitude gain of 5.000 m. In 1977 155 Austrian glider pilots – amongst them one woman – out of a total of about 5.000 were holders of the golden "C" with all three diamond supplements). Almost at the same time as in Austria restrictions on gliding were dropped by the Allies in Germany and pilots from West Germany came quickly to the fore once again in Alpine soaring. Since the early 1960s regional and national competitions in the Alps gave an increasing number of pilots the chance of gaining experience in the High Alps, and more and more glider pilots from outside the Alps come to Austrian gliding centres in the Alps, usually bringing their own glider along or chartering one (which is possible in a few centres) or taking part in an High Alpine soaring course in one of the gliding schools in the Alps (in Aus-

[15] WELCH, A. and L.: *The story of gliding.* London 1965

Fig. 10, 11, 12 and 13: The development of rising air currents during fine weather in summer in a major valley running roughly southwest to northeast

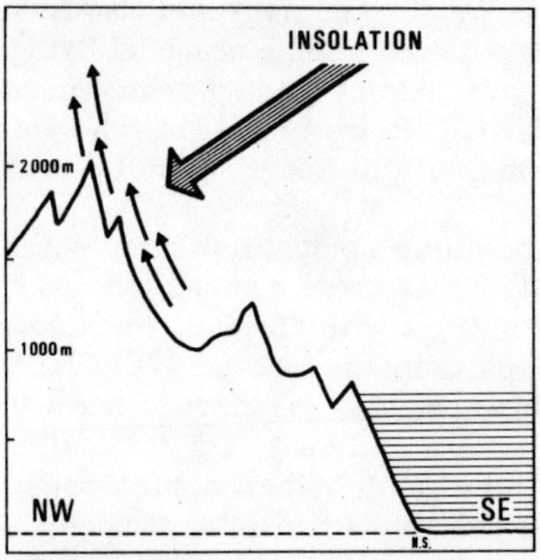

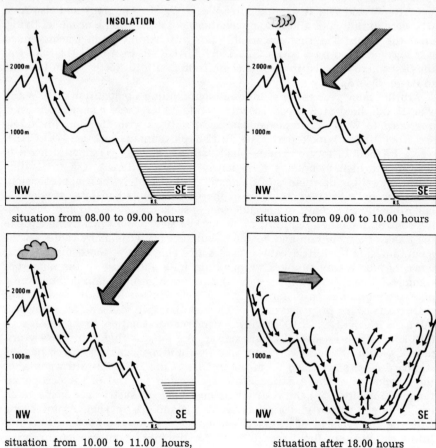

situation from 08.00 to 09.00 hours

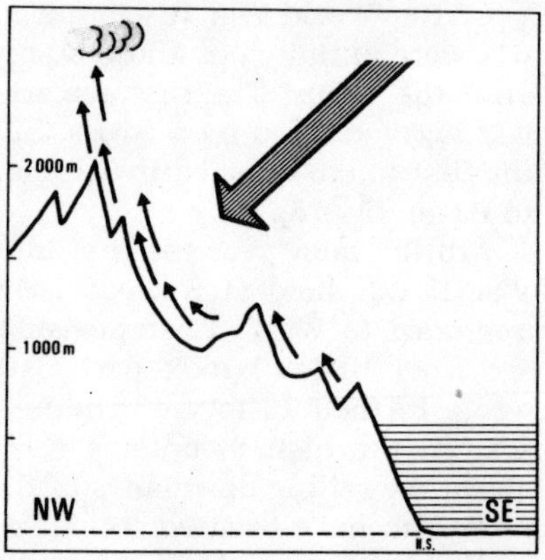

situation from 09.00 to 10.00 hours

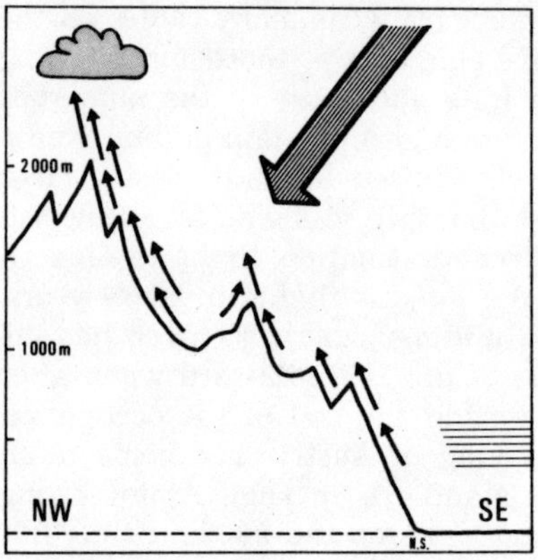

situation from 10.00 to 11.00 hours, maximum thermals ca from 12.00 to 16.00 hours

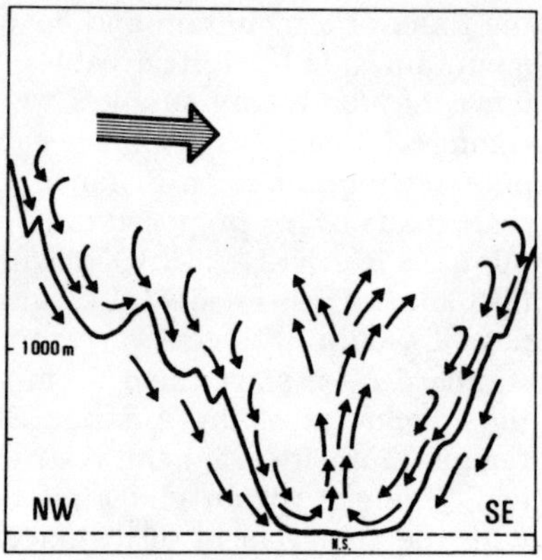

situation after 18.00 hours

Source: v. KALCKREUTH, J.: *Segeln über den Alpen. Erlebnis und Technik des Hochgebirgsfluges.* Zug und Stuttgart 1976, pp. 117 and 125

Fig. 10–14:

Most important for soaring in high mountains are thermals, and a sound knowledge where to expect them at certain periods of the day is an essential precondition for successful long distance flights by sail 'plane. After sunrise the first parts of a mountain where air begins to ascend are the uppermost east facing slopes. By about 8 to 9 a. m. the lift should be strong enough to be utilized by an experienced pilot to start a long distance flight; it does, however, necessitate an aero-tow fairly high up and thus expensive. Another drawback is that at this early stage of development of thermals the zone of maximum lift is not yet indicated by the formation of cumulus clouds (fig. 10). As the sun rises higher increasingly larger parts of the slopes are heated and the zone of thermals expands down to the lower slopes (fig. 11, 12). Gradually more and more cumulus clouds develop, an indication that thermal convection is very strong. Simul-

Fig. 14: The utilization of the „valley wind" for an ascent

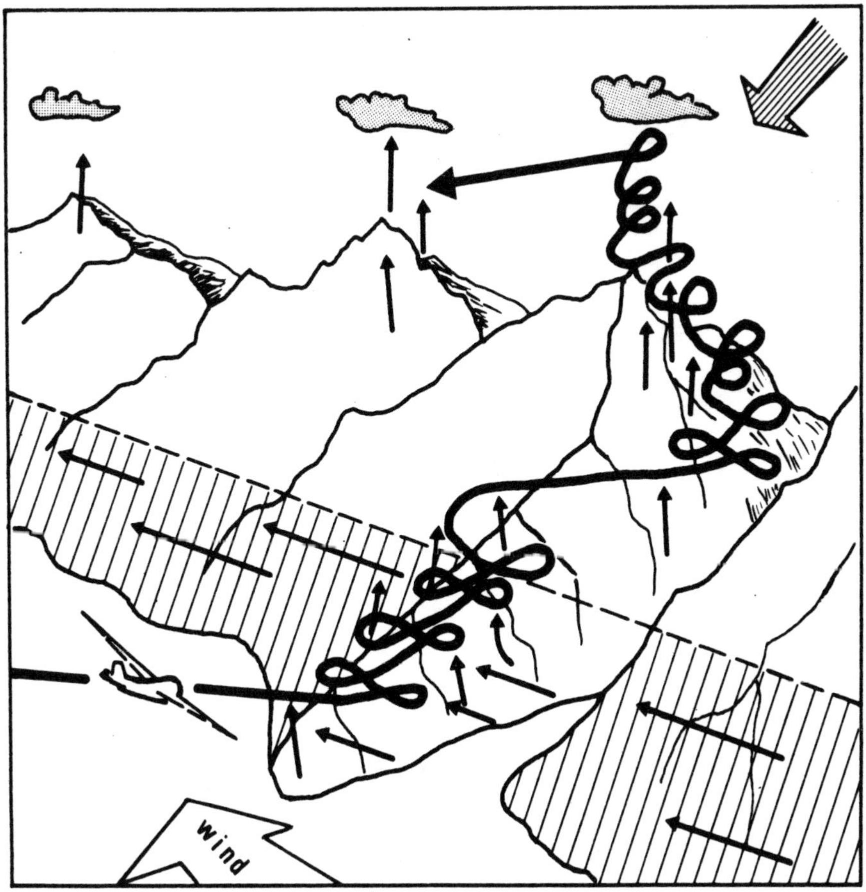

Source: v. KALCKREUTH, J.: *Segeln über den Alpen. Erlebnis und Technik des Hochgebirgsfluges.* Zug und Stuttgart 1976, p. 158

taneously the valley wind sets in (cf. fig. 7). Where it is forced up by an obstruction like the down-valley facing side of a tributary valley, a good orographic lift develops. This facilitates the lower part of the ascent of a sail 'plane from an aero-tow of merely a few hundred metres or even from a winch take-off, or the regaining of height should a 'plane have had to come down from the mountain tops. Once above the lower valley side (marked by parallel lines) mountain thermals should make the further ascent to the zone of maximum lift above the crest possible (fig. 14). In the later afternoon starting high up on the east facing slopes, air drainage sets in (cf. fig. 8). Eventually there are katabatic air streams on both valley sides and by the early evening they reach down to the valley bottom. As they converge there from opposite sides they absorb heat stored during the day in this usually damp zone and a gentle upward air movement results (fig. 13). This would usually not be strong enough for a glider to gain height but it facilitates at the onset of dusk the completion of a long distance flight in a very gentle "stretched" glide thus adding a few more miles or in case of a declared destination return flight reaching the "home" airfield.

Fig. 15: The use of rotor and wave air currents to achieve a high altitude ascent in *Föhn* conditions in an Alpine valley running roughly from west to east

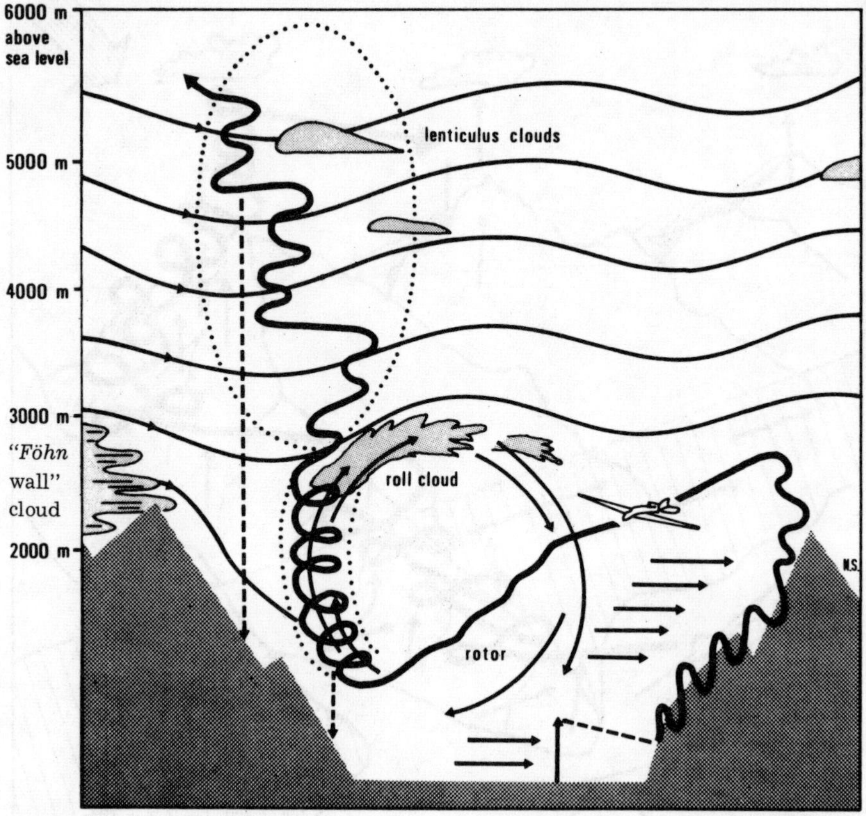

Optimum conditions for reaching high altitudes with a sail 'plane exist during *Föhn* weather and it is during such a meteorological situation when after take off at Zell am See, Salzburg, Austria, the height record of 11.400 metres was achieved in 1941. During *Föhn* weather three kinds of lift exist: Firstly orographic lift on south facing slopes and somewhat above them; secondly lift in that part of a vertically rotating air current, the rotor, which is closest to the lee of the main chain, in case of Zell am See the Hohe Tauern, and which is situated approximately vertically above the foot of its northern flank; thirdly wave lift high above and at varying distance to the north of the crest of the principal chain, its existence and position being indicated by lentil-shaped clouds. To reach a high altitude a pilot, after take off usually by aero-tow, would first ascend in the ridge lift of a south facing slope flying figures of eight, then, after a glide at high speed, attempt to gain height in the narrow upwind zone of the rotor by flying tight circles – a very buffeting experience – and if he was sucessful ascend smoothly in the "wave" air current. For such a flight it is of course necessary to use oxygen breathing apparatus and be dressed as to be able to withstand the extreme cold up there.

Source: v. KALCKREUTH, J.: *Segeln über den Alpen. Erlebnis und Technik des Hochgebirgsfluges.* Zug und Stuttgart 1976, pp. 143

Fig. 16: The crossing of mountain chains using orographic and thermal anabatic air currents

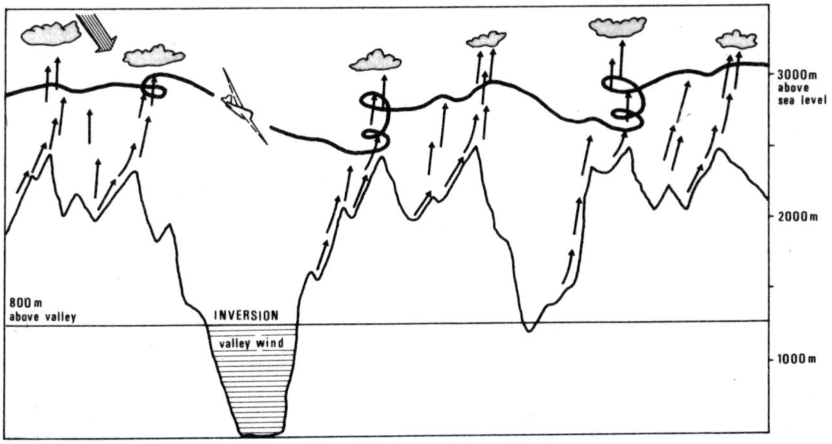

When, as for instance in crossing the Alps from north to south or *vice versa,* instead of soaring in the same direction as the mountain chains they have to be crossed it is important to know that height can and must be gained above the crests whereas larger valleys must be crossed at high speed to minimize loss of height.

Source: v. KALCKREUTH, J.: *Segeln über den Alpen. Erlebnis und Technik des Hochgebirgsfluges.* Zug und Stuttgart 1976, p. 141.

tria they are at Zell am See, Salzburg, and Niederöblarn, Styria, but at other places like Scharnstein, in the Upper Austrian Lake District flying clubs provide training for visitors). Gradually the entire Alpine chain from Geneva to Vienna became explored systematically for the possibilities of moving quickly over long distances, using conditions related to relief and vegetation cover as well as to the meteorological situation throughout the year. By recording these experiences and freely passing them on to other pilots the knowledge of the physiographic and meteorological characteristics and their bearing on soaring to cover large distances or climb to great heights is being constantly perfected.

The outstanding publication in this respect which no pilot wishing to soar in the Alps can afford to ignore is that by JOCHEN VON KALCKREUTH[16] *Segeln über den Alpen* (Soaring above the Alps) and I have also found this publication invaluable in the preparation of this section of my paper. Since in the first part of the book this pilot who has flown over 70.000 kms in the Alps and holds many records, relates the story of Alpine soaring and also personal experiences of his flights most vividly and since at is also beautifully illustrated, it is a book not only for glider pilots but for everybody with an interest in mountains.

In the 1970s the achievements in High Alpine flying rose to heights one would not have thought possible just after World War II. True the German

---

[16] v. KALCKREUTH, J.: *Segeln über den Alpen: Erlebnis und Technik des Hochgebirgsfluges.* Zug and Stuttgart 1976

ERICH KLÖCKNER in 1941, using the wave of the *Föhn* of the Hohe Tauern, had reached the phantastic altitude of 11.460 m, but this was an achievement standing quite on its own. In the 1970s altitudinal gains of over 3.000 m by means of the *Föhn* wave, have become nothing very special any more and even the 1.000 kms distance flight in the Alps will probably soon be achieved.

This tremendous progress in the exploits of engine-less flights in the Alps was on the one hand made possible by the perfection of 'planes and equipment: this involved using new materials like fibre glass, improving the aerodynamic qualities, development of highly sophisticated instruments and employing techniques like taking on water ballast which increases the 'plane's speed when thermals are very good but improves the gliding angle when it is dumped after the up-currents have become weak. On the other hand, and this is one of the links of High Alpine soaring with geography, it was only made possible on the basis of the cumulative knowledge gained of the physiographic and meteorological conditions of the Alps and the application of this knowledge to flying. Especially to succeed in a long distance flight a pilot has to have a thorough knowledge of the basic topography, the pattern of valleys and mountain ranges and also possible landing sites in the mountains; furthermore he must know the essentials what the ground cover consists of since in case of barren ground the potential uplift – if any – is closely connected with the type of rock; he has to know in advance the location of the glacier-covered areas or snow fields as their reflection is so great that no heat is stored and no thermals develop above them. Similarly a knowledge of the vegetation cover is important since different vegetation stores heat differently – e. g. a dark coniferous cover does it much better than a cover of broadleaf trees. A pilot has also to have a good knowledge of the Alpine wind systems: *Föhn* conditions, mountain and valley wind as it develops in the course of a day during high pressure weather and its special forms where valleys meet so that it blows in the opposite direction as the one expected. As KALCKREUTH states no one observes the Alps as carefully as a glider pilot – and as the great geographer FERDINAND VON RICHTHOFEN once said "Observation is the basis of geography" – a statement in my opinion still true today.

There is a second, no less important link between High Alpine soaring and geography – in this case economic geography, in particular the geography of tourism: it is the impact of this outdoor pursuit on the local economy of the places where the glider airfields are, and somewhat more removed, the work created in building and serviceing the apparatus needed in this activity: 'planes, instruments, trailers, etc.

Let it be said that despite the relatively large and growing number of glider pilots now soaring in the Alps, this sport will mainly, because of the great proficiency required, remain a rather elitist pursuit and numbers involved will never emulate those of the Alpine activities in which masses participate like skiing or mountain climbing of the general kind. The numbers are perhaps comparable to those of the rock climbers but could become larger since, happily, if one retains good health, soaring, even in High Alpine conditions, can be continued well into one's sixties (as HANNA REITSCH has shown) whereas climbing rock faces has to cease long before that.

Nevertheless, in some places in the Alps the economic consequence of the presence of air fields for gliding and the attraction they provide for active flyers, their families or just visitors who like to watch them, is appreciable. I have carried out a survey of all Austrian airfields for general aviation and gliding (there are 42 airfields in all, for a country like Austria quite a satisfactory number) and although the questionnaires have not been returned from all of them it is nevertheless clear that some attract a good number of visiting pilots from abroad, the number being governed by the available space and the need to get the 'planes airborne by aero-tow within the span of say 1–2 hours in the morning, to have the optimum chance of a long distance or duration flight. The airfields, which because of their location in longitudinal valleys and closeness to high peaks, offer the best chances for long distance flights are of course those in greatest demand. With about hundred gliders brought there by visitors during a single season both the airfield of the Alpine Gliding School at Zell am See, Salzburg, to which pilots from Britain regularly come, in the northern longitudinal trough, and the airfield at Timmersdorf, Styria, in the southern longitudinal trough, tie for first place followed by Lienz in Eastern Tyrol, also in the southern trough, with 50 to 80, and Scharnstein in the Austrian Lake District with 30 to 50 visiting pilots a year.

Although for gliding one does by no means have to be a millionaire since most 'planes are owned by a club or a "syndicate" one cannot be exactly poor either since aero-tows are quite expensive e. g. up to 1.000 metres ca. £ 15. In the holiday spirit there is usually – in addition to satisfying the basic necessities of life, board and lodging – a bit of money left over to trickle into the local economy, which for small places like Timmersdorf, Niederöblarn and Scharnstein does make a difference. To individual visitors or visiting flying clubs with their own planes must be added those people who come to attend a gliding course or charter gliders. The cost for a three week course for gaining the glider pilot's licence is about £ 300. Chartering a glider costs about £ 10 per hour, for a glider with auxiliary engine about £ 20 per hour. To the Alpine Gliding School in Niederöblarn there came altogether in 1976 over 600 people either with their own planes or attending a course.

Since the beginning of the 1970s establishing new airfields or expansion of existing ones has met with increasing resistance from the environmental lobby and has also led to restrictions in flying activity. Sail planes themselves make no noise but the usual way of launching them is by aero-tow, which does. However, except for training, a glider is usually launched only once or twice in one day and then stays up, thus the noise nuisance is of short duration, a small fraction of that caused by cars and especially small, two-stroke motorcycles.

At the gliding centres one has done a lot to meet these objections by fitting noise suppressors on the towing planes and keeping the lunch hours clear of starts (the early morning is automatically kept clear since conditions for soaring only develop at the earliest after 8 a. m. but more generally from about 10 a. m. onwards). But to those short-sighted people who would like to have glider flying banned altogether the answer has to be a clear: "Never".

In our time with its many strains and stresses gliding and even more so soaring in the High Alps has much to offer as a counterbalance, and for refreshing body and mind. There is hardly any other activity with a similar subtle challenge to use natural force to fulfil the ancient dream of mankind to overcome gravity. There are many steps from the first solo glide of a few minutes until one is capable of soaring, of staying up for some hours, of gaining heights of some 1.000 metres and flying distances of 50 kms and more. When beginning one thinks anyone who holds the silver "C" certificate must be a pilot capable of almost anything in soaring; once one has achieved this oneself, although one is naturally proud, one realizes how much there is still to learn to be able to use the potentialities offered for soaring in the High Alps even reasonably well. But although still only in these initial stages I am at least in a position to realize how right HANNA REITSCH was, who must have had a more varied flying career than any other pilot in the world, when she said that in her life as a pilot nothing came up in beauty to soaring in the Alps, and that an engine-less flight across the Alps is one of the most beautiful experiences man can have. It is to be hoped that regulations and regimentation will not develop to such extent that the joy is taken out of this sport, one of the last great adventures of our time, and let it be said, a sport that to the geographer gives an added perspective to what in my view is still his principle field of study: the landscape.

References

Bundesministerium für Verkehr (ed.): *Österreichisches Seilbahnkonzept.* Wien 1978

CARRIER, R.: *The complete book of sky sailing.* New York, London, Toronto 1974

Compress Verlags-Ges.m.b.H. (ed.): *Handbuch der österreichischen Flugfelder.* Wien 1975

COOKE, R. U. – ROBSON, B. T.: Geography in the United Kingdom 1972–1976, *Geographical Journal,* 142, London 1976, pp. 81–100

DEGLMANN-SCHWARZ, R.: Helicopter skiing made in Europe, *Ski,* 11, München 1977, pp. 84–88

Deutscher Skiverband (ed.): *Ski Atlas 1977/78,* Stuttgart 1977

FLIRI, F.: Über Landschaft, Bauerntum und Universität. *Innsbrucker Universitätsreden,* 12, Innsbruck 1977, pp. 17–27

GANSER, K.: Zweitwohnungen. Konflikt: Individuum – Gemeinwesen. In WICHMANN, H.: *Die Zukunft der Alpenregion,* München 1972, pp. 124–136

GEORGII, W.: *Meteorologische Navigation des Segelfluges.* Braunschweig 1971

GRUMM, R.: *Der Beitrag des Alpenvereins für die Entwicklung des Fremdenverkehrs* (pp. 13) (cyclostyled) Paper delivered at the Symposium of the *Österreichische, Deutsche und Südtiroler Alpenverein.* Bergsteigen als Lebensform und Lebenshilfe. Innsbruck 1977

HAIMAYER, P.: Zur Frage der Ganzjahresschigebiete: Das Beispiel Hochstubai/Tirol, *Berichte zur Raumforschung und Raumplanung,* 21, Wien 1977, pp. 5–13

— : *Gedanken zur Frage der Belastbarkeit touristischer Landschaften* (pp. 15) (cyclostyled) Paper delivered at the meeting of the Tourism Committee of the Bundeskammer der gewerblichen Wirtschaft in Wien 1977

HEMBERGER, M. Th.: Skilauf – Die weiße Droge Österreichs. A series of 6 articles in *Die Presse,* Wien 1978, Jan. 26th, 27th, 28th, 30th, 31st and Febr. 1st

BUBU HIMAMOVA (= BUNNELL, F., BUNNELL, P., BUCKINGHAM, S., HILBORN, R., MARGREITER, G., MOSER, W., WALTER, C.): *Das Modell Obergurgl. Ein Mikrokosmos: Wirtschaftswachstum im begrenzten Raum* (Title of the original edition: *The Obergurgl model. A microcosm of economic growth in relation to limited ecological resources).* International Institute for Applied System Analysis, Laxenburg 1974

JÜLG, F.: Die Seilbahnen Österreichs und ihre Auswirkungen auf die Wirtschaft. *Veröffentlichungen des Österreichischen Instituts für Raumplanung,* 29, Wien 1966

v. KALCKREUTH, J.: *Segeln über den Alpen. Erlebnis und Technik des Hochgebirgsfluges.* Zug and Stuttgart 1976

KINZL, H.: Der Brenner im Kartenbild. Beiträge zur geschichtlichen Landeskunde Tirols, Festschrift für H. Huter, *Schlern Schriften,* 207, Innsbruck 1959, pp. 163–180

KRANS, O.: Massentourismus. Konflikt: Erholung – Landschaft. In: WICHMANN, H. (ed.): *Die Zukunft der Alpenregion,* München 1972, pp. 108–115

LAVERY, P. (ed.): *Recreational geography,* Newton Abbot and London 1971

LEIDLMAIR, A.: Tirol auf dem Wege von der Agrar- zur Erholungslandschaft. *Mitteilungen der Österr. Geogr. Gesellschaft,* Wien 1978, pp. 38–53

MAIER, J. – RUPPERT, K.: Der Zweitwohnsitz im Freizeitraum. Raumrelevanter Teilaspekt einer Geographie des Freizeitverhaltens. *Informationen,* 21, Bad Godesberg 1971, pp. 135–157

MEISTER, G.: Wald und Wild. Forstwirt – Jäger, In: WICHMANN, H. (ed.): *Die Zukunft der Alpenregion,* München 1972, pp. 116–123

MORGAN, A.: *Airborne for pleasure,* Newton Abbot and London 1975

PATMORE, J. A.: Land and leisure, In: HALL, P. (ed.): *Geography and environmental studies,* Harmondsworth 1972

— : Recreation and leisure. *Progress in Human Geography 1,* London 1977, pp. 111–117

PIFFNER, A.: *Landschaftsschäden und Entschädigungspraxis im Zusammenhang mit dem Skisport.* Undergraduate dissertation, Landwirtschaftliches Technikum, Weisstannen 1976

POOLE, B.: Hang-gliding. *Country Landowner,* 28, London 1977, p. 28

REICHMANN, H.: *Strecken-Segelflug,* Stuttgart 1975

RONGE, Ch.: Land der Berge – Land der Lawinen. A series of 3 articles in *Die Presse,* Wien 1978, Feb. 28th, March 2nd and 7th

SCHWARZENBACH, F. H.: *Grenzen der Belastbarkeit touristischer Regionen* (pp. 8) (cyclostyled) Paper to introduce a discussion on the above topic delivered at the Symposium of the *Österreichische, Deutsche und Südtiroler Alpenverein,* Bergsteigen als Lebensform und Lebenshilfe, Innsbruck 1977

SIMMONS, J. G.: *Rural recreation in the industrial world.* London 1975

WELCH, A. and L.: *The story of gliding.* London 1965

ZECHMANN, H.: *Bergsteigen – auch morgen?* Graz, Stuttgart 1977

Deutschlands Alpen in Gefahr. *Der Spiegel,* Hamburg 1977, pp. 62–79

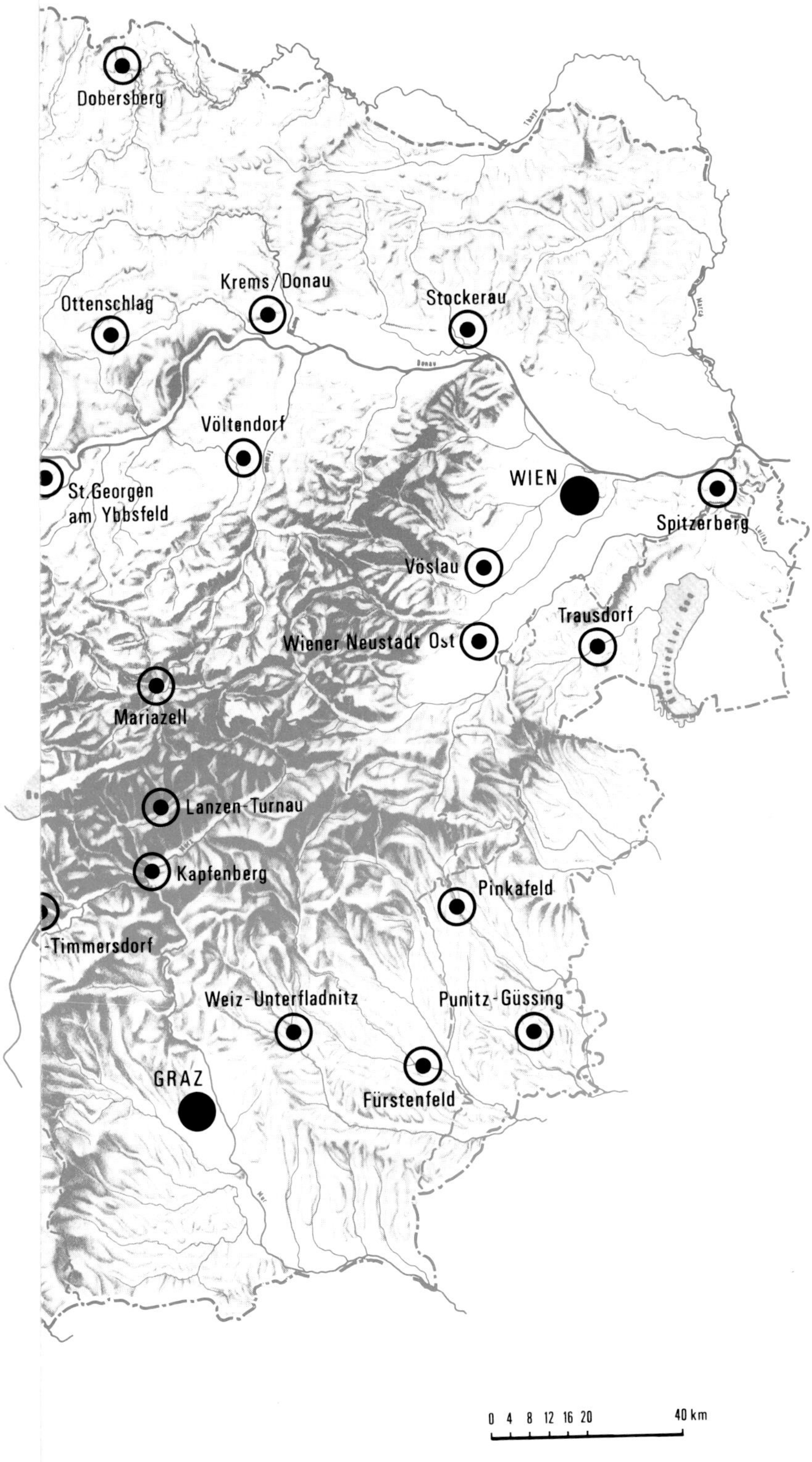
Dobersberg
Krems/Donau
Ottenschlag
Stockerau
Völtendorf
St.Georgen
am Ybbsfeld
WIEN
Spitzerberg
Vöslau
Trausdorf
Wiener Neustadt Ost
Mariazell
Lanzen-Turnau
Kapfenberg
Pinkafeld
-Timmersdorf
Weiz-Unterfladnitz
Punitz-Güssing
GRAZ
Fürstenfeld
0 4 8 12 16 20 40 km

STUDIES OF THE GEOGRAPHY OF TOURISM AND RECREATION IN GENERAL

ÉTUDES GÉNÉRALES

BEITRÄGE ZUR ALLGEMEINEN FREMDENVERKEHRSGEOGRAPHIE

The place of geography of tourism and recreation in the system of geography and in the field of leisure research

Z. TED MIECZKOWSKI, Winnipeg, Canada*

1. Geography of tourism and recreation – a latecomer in the field of leisure research

According to the recent trends in the natural and social sciences the traditional impregnable walls, the distinct division lines between various research fields tend to disappear, strict boundaries change to broad frontier zones. The complexity of tasks to be solved dictates this overlapping or even blending process and implies close cooperation between various specialists. Such is certainly the case in leisure research which has acquired a definite interdisciplinary character: economists, geographers, psychologists, sociologists, lawyers, medical doctors, biologists, ecologists, foresters, zoologists etc. are contributing to the research without losing their identity, enriching the field with their ideas and approaches.

The discussion of research achievements in the field of leisure research and particularly of tourism and recreation[1] lies beyond the scope of this paper.[2] What is important to note here is the fact that this is a very recent history and that geographers were not the pioneers. According to OGILVIE "The scientific study of tourist problems may perhaps be said to have begun first in Italy, in 1899, with an article: Sul movimento dei forestieri in Italia e sul denaro che vi spendono (Giornale degli Economisti, 1899, 54–61) by BODIO, Director of the Italian Statistical Office".[3]

However, only since the interwar period and more strictly since the 1930's is it possible to speak of a fullfledged development of the field. The pioneers were the economists, later joined by business administrators, sociologists, psychologists, and medical specialists who became aware of the relationship between their disciplines and tourism and recreation and wanted to devote their work towards better understanding and correct solutions in this burgeoning field of human activity. Apart from some exceptions[4] it is interesting to note that geo-

---

* Dr. Z. TED MIECZKOWSKI, Associate Professor, Department of Geography, University of Manitoba, Winnipeg, Canada

[1] For discussion on the relationships between leisure, tourism and recreation see MIECZKOWSKI, Z. T.: Geography of leisure, geography of tourism and geography of urban recreation. *Proceedings of the Canadian Association of Geographers,* Winnipeg 1970

[2] See WOLFE, R.: Perspective on outdoor recreation. A bibliographical survey. *Geographical Review,* New York 1964, pp. 203–238

GEIGANT, F.: Der Urlaubs- und Ferienverkehr als Objekt wissenschaftlicher Forschungen. *Jahrbuch für Fremdenverkehr,* München 1962, pp. 39–49

RUNGALDIER, R.: Fremdenverkehr und Geographie. *Der Österreichische Betriebswirt,* Wien 1960, 2, pp. 85–92

McMURRY, K. C.: *Recreational Geography. American Geography: Inventory and prospect.* Syracuse 1954, pp. 251–257

CLAWSON, M., KNETSCH, J.: *Economics of outdoor recreation,* Baltimore 1966

[3] OGILVIE, F. W.: *The Tourist Movement. An economic Study.* London 1933, p. 8

[4] For U.S. see: McMURRY, K. C.: *Recreational Geography. American Geography inventory and prospect.* Syracuse 1954, pp. 251–257. An European example was POSER, H.: Geographische Studien zum Fremdenverkehr im Riesengebirge. *Abhandlungen der Gesellschaft der Wissenschaft zu Göttingen, math.-phys. Klasse,* 3. Klasse, 3. Folge, Heft 20, Göttingen 1939

graphers showed relatively little interest in the new research field. For many years the relationship between geography and tourism was ambiguous: they sort of "coexisted" side by side: tourism receiving from geography some crumbs of descriptive information but actually no real assistance in the solution of important scientific, planning and management problems. One has almost an impression that geographers were ashamed to regard tourism as a legitimate field of scholarly endeavor. A change of attitude appeared only relatively recently. Geographers started to order the chaos of empirical material into an integrated scholarly system only after the Second World War. Yet RITTER[5] criticized some fundamental works in geography published after World War II for either completely omitting or giving only slight attention to the phenomena of tourism and recreation so conspicuous in the contemporary landscape.

With respect to some particular questions let us take an example of population geography. The traditional maps of population distribution, even large scale maps, do not reflect the high mobility of our "dynamic society". These maps should not only show the distribution according to the domicile (night distribution) but also work (day distribution) and free time (weekend, vacation distribution) and spatial dynamics of tourist flows.

We have to confront the questions: Why did geographers show an interest in tourism and recreation so late? Why this apparent underestimation of the field even now? The first reason is the "frivolity" – an alleged lack of seriousness of the subject. WOLFE claims that one of the reasons why very few geographers are engaged in solving the problems of outdoor recreation is that they don't find the subject challenging enough.[6] The geographers are preoccupied with other subjects, expecially connected with production which they feel are more important and where the data are more easily to come by. DEACY and GRIESS stress the lack of facts in reaction from which to form hypotheses.[7] "The reasons may stem from the subject which is heterogeneous and multi-facted; its highly decentralized control; its former lack of professional respectability; its youthfulness; and its omission until recently from academic and governmental institutions."[8]

2. *The place of geography of tourism and recreation in the system of geography*

The recent trends of specialization in teaching and particularly in research have naturally been reflected in the development of geography. The field expanded its frontiers thus embracing various spatial aspects of reality, aspects to a large degree connected with the nature- society interaction. These scholarly interests also started to take up some relatively new phenomena in socio-economic development such as leisure; a new specialized field of geography appeared under many names: "geography of leisure", "geography of tourism", "geography of recreation" (or "recreational geography"), "geography of recreational activity", "geography of outdoor recreation", "geography of recreational land use" to name a few. Undoubtedly, geographers have achieved many suc-

---

[5] RITTER, W.: *Fremdenverkehr in Europa: Eine wirtschafts- und sozialgeographische Untersuchung über Reise und Urlaubsaufenthalte der Bewohner Europas.* Leiden 1966, p. 41

[6] WOLFE, R.: Perspective on outdoor recreation. A bibliographical survey. *Geographical Review,* New York 1964, p. 277

[7] DEASY, G. F., GRIESS, P. R.: Impact of a tourist facility on its hinterland. *Annals of the Association of American Geographers,* Lawrence, K., 1966, p. 290

[8] *Ibid.*

cesses in this field during the recent decades, especially since the end of the Second World War.

Quite rightly the emphasis in the field of tourism and recreation has been put on concrete empirical research (this attitude is especially characteristic for North America). However, despite undeniable achievements the young discipline has encountered many problems resulting from very rapid recent development. Methodology concerning the scope of the discipline and its relationship with other geographical and non-geographical fields of research are still somewhat vague and lack general acceptance. There is a fair amount of confusion with respect to terminology, basic notions and definitions. We are plagued by ambiguous definitions introduced without an effort do define them.

All these problems and associated discussions are understandable "symptoms of transitional periods in the evolution of science".[9] Geography of tourism and recreation is no exception. Especially notable are the results of work on general methodology and terminology achieved by the IGU Working Group on Geography of Tourism and Recreation. The 1974 Crakow, Poland, meeting of the group serves as a good example of such a contribution. The Working Group constitutes an important forum of international cooperation between the three major regions of the world, namely North America, Western Europe and the Socialist countries, where much of the research in the geography of tourism and recreation is at present conducted. The creation of the group made it possible to establish the so sorely missing links between these regions, the dissemination of knowledge about research conducted and problems encountered. The author of this paper hopes to make another contribution towards better understanding of some basic methodology of the new discipline: the geography of tourism and recreation. Thus the present paper discusses two questions:

1. The place of *geography of tourism and recreation in the system of geographical sciences.*

2. The place of *geography of tourism and recreation in the broad field of leisure research.*

It is very difficult to assign the geography of tourism and recreation a specific place in the system of geography. The first problem is that geographers themselves represent various views about the subdivision of their discipline. Secondly, the multifaceted and heterogenous subjects make the decision complicated.

Many East European geographers regard the geography of tourism and recreation as part of economic geography.[10] In Western Europe, despite a different understanding of scope of economic geography, similar views are common[11] because the authors feel that economic aspects prevail with respect to tourism and recreation.

This "economic" approach to geography of tourism and recreation is reflected in the definition proposed by JACOB: "The geography of tourism examines the spatial structure of tourism, the conditions and peculiarities of its development in individual countries, regions and centers" or more succinctly "the geography

---

[9] HAGGET, F.: *Geography. A modern synthesis.* London 1975, p. 20

[10] JACOB, G.: Modell zur regionalen Geographie des Fremdenverkehrs, *Wissenschaftliche Zeitschrift der Hochschule für Verkehrswesen „F. List“*, Dresden 1968, p. 267
Ungarisches Fremdenverkehrsamt (ed.): *III. Fremdenverkehrskolloquium.* Nov. 22–24, 1966, Budapest 1966, pp. 108–109

[11] CHRISTALLER, W.: Beiträge zu einer Geographie des Fremdenverkehrs. *Erdkunde,* Bonn 1955, p. 1
JÜLG, F.: Praktische Hinweise für wissenschaftliche Arbeiten in der Fremdenverkehrsgeographie, in Festschrift L. G. SCHEIDL zum 60. Geburtstag, *Wiener Geogr. Schriften,* 18–23, Wien 1965, p. 56

of tourism examines tourism as a factor of territorial production-complexes (economic areas of regions)."[12]

McMURRY in *American Geography: inventory and prospect* also regards recreational geography as a subdivision of economic geography. However, he predicts that "if fully developed . . . , it may well emerge as a distinct topical field."[13] More than 20 years have passed since these words were written and this prediction came fully true: geography of tourism and recreation today constitutes an independent fullfledged geographical field, having gained acceptance all over the world – even in the Soviet Union, where this branch of geography is very new.[14] Its place in the "system of geographical sciences" is separate, but interaction with economic, population, physical and medical geography is emphasized by very close links with a new branch in the Soviet geographical spectrum–geography of services.[15] The appreciation of heterogeneity of the subject is shared by most North American geographers. MURPHY has stated that "geographical research in outdoor recreation includes aspects of nearly every major division of systematic geography".[16] This fact indicates that it is a separate field beyond the scope of any traditional division.

This writer shares the views of MURPHY and KOVALEV about the independent place of geography of tourism and recreation in the system of geography. In fact, he thinks that because of its multifaceted spatial and environmental links it is *most infrageographical* of all branches of geography. In order to demonstrate the relationship between geography of tourism and recreation and various subdivisions of geography the following table has been devised.

The table merits some comments and explanations:

Table 1: Relationship between geography of tourism and recreation and various subdivisions of geography

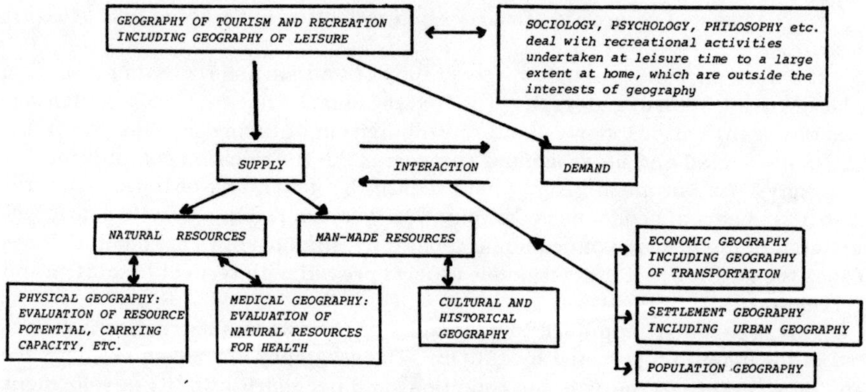

[12] JACOB, G.: Modell zur regionalen Geographie des Fremdenverkehrs. *Wissenschaftliche Zeitschrift der Hochschule für Verkehrswesen „F. List"*, Dresden 1968.

[13] McMURRY, K. C.: Recreational Geography. *American Geography: Inventory and prospect*. Syracuse 1954, pp. 251–257

[14] PREOBRAZHENSKIY, V. S., VEDENIN, Y. A.: Geografia i otdykh. *Znanie*, Moscow 1971, 48 pp

[15] KOVALEV, S. A.: O geograficheskom izuchenii sfery obsluzhivaniya. *Vestnik Moskovskogo Universiteta*, 1973, 6, Moscow, p. 8

[16] MURPHY, R. E.: Geography and outdoor recreation: An opportunity and an obligation. *Professional Geographer*, New York 1963, pp. 33–34

1. In this table the term leisure is understood in its practical meaning as discretionary (free) time and not in the philosophical sense (free time well spent).

2. *Geography of leisure* and *geography of tourism and recreation* are very close in their scope. However, the latter has a wider meaning than the former: Geography of tourism and recreation encompasses the geography of leisure. The scope of leisure is very close to that of recreation (recreation means activity undertaken during leisure time, recreation is the content or part of the content of leisure). However, the term tourism overlaps only with leisure (as well as with recreation):

a) The following belongs to tourism and is outside leisure – recreation: business, professional (including congress), educational, religious, health and personal travel. Although there might be certain elements of recreation involved – essentially the non-recreational components prevail.

b) The following belongs to leisure – recreation and is outside tourism: urban and suburban recreation by residents.[17]

c) There is a significant overlap between tourism and recreation: pleasure of recreational travel is mainly but not exclusively associated – see point a) – with travel and overnight stay of non-residents (or travel of more than 24 hours outside the domicile).

3. Some geographers try to introduce such terms as *geography of leisure or geography of leisure behaviour* to designate the whole field including *geography of tourism.*[18] Others, notably the Soviet geographers, insist that tourism is a variety of recreation, therefore the *geography of tourism* should be subordinated *to recreational geography.*[19] In view of the difficulties in establishing an all-encompassing one-word term, this author casts his vote for *geography of tourism and recreation* as defining the whole discipline in the most appropriate way.

3. The scope and place of geography of tourism and recreation in the field of leisure research

With respect to geography's contributions in the field of tourism and recreation three areas can be distinguished:

a) travel literature
b) scholarly research
c) planning

Although we concentrate in this discussion on research we shall briefly mention also the two other fields.

Travel literature

Travel has played a focal role in geography since antiquity. Travel descriptions take an important part in the geographical literature in the past and today regional geographies contain information used by travelling geographers. Modern tourism and recreation as mass phenomena are centered on travel, this seasonal migration which leaves such a conspicuous imprint on contemporary landscapes.

---

[17] The German terms: *Naherholung* or *Kurzzeiterholung* illustrate the space – time component characteristic for this type of recreation

[18] RUPPERT, K.: Zur Stellung und Gliederung einer Allgemeinen Geographie des Freizeitverhaltens. *Geographische Rundschau,* Braunschweig 1975, pp. 1–6. Zur Diskussion gestellt. *Geographische Rundschau,* Braunschweig 1975, pp. 518–525

KNIRCH, R.: Fremdenverkehrsgeographie oder Geographie des Freizeitverhaltens, oder? *Zeitschrift für Wirtschaftsgeographie,* Hagen 1976, pp. 248–249

[19] LIKHANOV, B. V. (ed.): *Geographicheskiye problemy organizatsii tourizma i otdykha.* Akademia Nauk, SSSR, Moscow 1975, Vyp. I, p. 5

The contribution of geography to these spatial aspects of tourism and recreation seems to be most appropriate although unfortunately largely inadequate in view of the fact that contemporary travel literature seems to concentrate on history of arts and pays little attention to landscape and human problems in their regional aspect.

Research

The geography of tourism and recreation focusses its attention on a specific group of spatial and environmental phenomena related mainly to leisure. This sphere of interest determines its position among other disciplines dealing with this field and constitutes an important contribution for the development of leisure research as a whole: Geography of tourism and recreation concentrates on spatial interaction between society and natural environment (man-environment system), patterns of distribution (static element) and movement (displacement-dynamic element) related mainly to leisure time activities. In other words geography of tourism and recreation is concerned with "areal differentiation", territory, location. These locational aspects of tourism and recreation are the focus of attention of geographers working in this field. One could argue that all phenomena occur in space, but certainly in this field space, distance, size, direction and seasonal variations of tourist flows, area travel patterns, tourist regions and their spatial arrangement play a basic role.

The spatial interaction between society and physical environment necessitates an integrated research. This interaction is evident and conspicuous in the landscape in its relation to tourism and recreation.[20] The contribution of geography, integrating the social and natural sciences, is indispensible. The interdisciplinary character of the research in the field of tourism and recreation is especially suited to geography, which is regarded by many as an "interdisciplinary study, involving the acquisition of data of physical, economic, social and arts type, and synthesising them within an areal , systematic of thematic idiom".[21] Geographers understanding both the society and its environment are certainly well qualified to research this "industry without smokestacks" in an overall integrated, "synoptic" way. Economists and politicians tend to overemphasise economic development, biologists and ecologists – conservation of the environment. Geographers, being aware of the laws governing both society and its environment can express a really balanced view in these matters. They certainly are in a unique position to play a major – in some instances even leading – role. WOLFE agrees that "it is the geographer who should be expected to take the best rounded view"[22] but adds that this occurs only rarely for various reasons, one of them being the resource orientation of most geographers working in the field of tourism and recreation.

With respect to their research subjects geographers both in West and East have tended to overemphasise the supply side of tourism and recreation.[23] This involved, first of all, physical geographers engaged in evaluation of natural re-

---

[20] "The geographer describes what he sees, and outdoor recreation is highly visible". WOLFE, R. I.: The Geography of outdoor recreation: A dynamic approach. *British Columbia Geographical Series,* Vancouver 1967, 8, pp. 7–12

[21] NOWAK, W. S.: On the interdisciplinary approach to geography, *Journal of Geography,* Oak Park, Jll., 1976, p. 402

[22] WOLFE, R.: The geography of outdoor recreation: A dynamic approach. *British Columbia Geographical Series,* Vancouver 1967, 8, p. 9

[23] ANANYEV, M. A.: Sdvigi v razvitii geografii mezhdunarodnogo turizma, *Izvestiya, Akademiya Nauk SSSR, seriya geografiya,* Moscow 1967, 2, pp. 37–49

Ungarisches Fremdenverkehrsamt (ed.): *III. Fremdenverkehrskolloquium.* Nov. 22–24, 1966, Budapest 1966, pp. 108–109.

sources for recreation (resource potential) in assessing the impact of tourism and recreation on the landscape and its structure, determining its carrying capacity (the impact of use on the resources and on the landscape as a whole). The human geographers have concentrated their attention on historical and cultural resources (attractions), on the economic evaluation of the whole resource spectrum as a part of costbenefit analysis, on the impact of tourism and recreation on the economy of the area and its population.

However, the best analysis of the tourism-recreation regions and their natural and human resources, although very useful especially with respect to smaller areas, constitutes a limited approach. Only additional research into the demand side of the equation may render a full picture. On the demand side lies a large research field for human geographers: spatial analysis of segmented markets, areal distribution of prerequisites of demand, of the need and demand for various recreational activities, etc. This type of research has gained ground conspicuously in recent years.

A final step in geographical research of tourism and recreation is the establishment of an interrelationship between supply and demand areas. Here certainly lies the central focus of the geographer's interest, here all the elements can be integrated and examined in their mutual interrelationships and spatial patterns established. Mobility of population and its relationship to transportation, distance between market and tourist regions, intra-urban and extra-urban travel patterns; volume, structure, distance and direction of tourist flows – these are some of the research aspects contributing to the conceptual framework explaining tourist movement and helping in differentiation of types of tourist-recreation regions and their location.

On the subject of research into tourism and recreation geographers agree among themselves only in very broad approximation on both the subjects of their research and on the methodology.[24] Here is an openended list:

1. Environmental research:
Evaluation of natural and human resources. Interaction between tourism and environment (incl. impact and carrying capacity studies).

2. Tourist flows: size, direction, variations in time.

3. Spatial patterns (incl. typology): resorts, urban areas, integrations (e. g. lake-forest, maritime, alpine), regions, zones (usually regions or elongated or concentric shape e. g. coastal zone, zone along transportation route, suburban zone), parks, tourist infrastructure (incl. capacity).

---

[24] WOLFE, R.: Recreation Geography, Chapter 5 in: *Practical Geography.* JACKSON, J. N. and FORESTER, J., Toronto 1974, pp. 70–90
JACOB, G.: Probleme der Geographie des Fremdenverkehrs, *Wiss. Abhandlungen d. Geographie Gesellsch. d. DDR,* Leipzig 1968, pp. 17–20
JACOB, G.: Modell zur regionalen Geographie des Fremdenverkehrs, *Wissenschaftliche Zeitschrift der Hochschule für Verkehrswesen „F. List", Dresden 1968, pp. 267–271*
MERCER, D. C.: The Geography of leisure – A contemporary growth point, *Geography,* Sheffield 1970, pp. 262–273
HOCHHOLZER, H.: Weltfremdenverkehr und Massentourismus. *Zeitschrift für Wirtschaftsgeographie,* Hagen 1973, pp. 65–71
GINIER, J.: *Les touristes étrangers en France pendant l'été.* Paris 1969
PATMORE, J. A.: Recreation, in: *Evaluating the Human Environment. Essays in Applied Geography.* London 1973
NAZAREVSKIY, O. R., ZORIN, I. V.: Sovremennaya postanovka problem geografii otdykha i turisma, *Razvitie Industrii Turisma v SSSR,* Moscow 1968
TVERDOKHLIBOV, I. T., MIRONENKO, M. S.: Rekreatsionnaya geografiya – novaya otrasl ekonomicheskoy geografii, *Ekon. geografia Mizhvid nauk,* Moscow 1972, pp. 167–175
PREOBRAZHENSKIY, V. S., VEDENIN, A.: Geografiya i otdykh, *Znanie,* Moscow 1971, 48 pp.
FAYBUSOVICH, E. L., CHECHETOVA, L. V.: Problemy geografii turisma, in: *Kraevedenie i turism,* Moscow 1972, p. 3–16

4. Socio-economic research: tourism and recreation as tools correcting economic imbalances between regions including economic impact studies. Spatial interrelationship between tourism and recreation and other branches of economy. Social and cultural impact of tourism.

The differences in emphasis emerge with respect to certain subjects. The Soviet geographers focus on regionalization, territorial integrations of resources and infrastructure;[25] the Western geographers, after a long period of concentration in the field of supply have in recent years started to pay more attention to spatial patterns of demand (including study of perception regarded as too subjective by Soviet geographers). Some American geographers think that too much emphasis has been put on outdoor or non-urban recreation.[26] They suggest that more research endeavours should be concentrated in the field of urban recreation.[27]

Planning

The practical results of geographical research may be implemented in planning which is "primary a means for putting known facts together, evaluating them and coming up with a proposed line of action."[28] Especially important are the contributions of regional planning so indispensable in our modern society with limited resources, with the necessity for clear delimitation, management und preservation of recreational, living and working spaces.

[25] For example: *Study of the territorial-recreational system of the Caucasus.* Stavropol 1976
Current problems of recreational geography. *XXII International Geographical Congress.* Moscow 1976
Teoreticheskiye osnovy rekreatsyonnoy geografii, *Izdatelstvo „Nauka"*, Moscow 1975
Rekreatsyonnaya geografia, *Moskovskiy filial geograficheskogo obshchestva SSSR,* Moscow 1976

[26] MIECZKOWSKI, Z. T.: Geography of leisure, geography of tourism and geography of urban recreation. *Proceedings of the Canadian Association of Geographers,* Winnipeg 1972

[27] McMURRY, K. C.: Recreational Geography. *American Geography: Inventory and prospect.* Syracuse 1954, pp. 251–257
MITCHELL, L. L.: Recreational Geography, Evolution and research needs. *Professional Geographer,* New York 1969, pp. 117–119

[28] CLAWSON, M., KNETSCH, J.: *Economics of Outdoor Recreation,* Baltimore 1976, p. 292

Recreation in perspective

ALICE COLEMAN, London, Great Britain*

Recreation is like motherhood, in that it has always appeared to be an absolute good. However, in a world of severe over-population, motherhood has lost this unqualified approval and there are signs that recreation may be following suit.

Recreation is also like sugar. In Man's natural, pre-civilised diet sweet substances were rare and a genetic hankering for them was a dietary asset, but in modern life, where sugar is all too common, that same genetic hankering can lead to overdoses which are hazardous to our health. Similarly, it seems that our sweet tooth for recreation, which was a safeguard in the struggle for survival, may also have led to overdoses in today's conditions of more assured existence.

1. *Purposefulness in leisure*

Genetically, Man is a purposeful animal. Children's play is essentially functional; exercising the body and brain as a means of development; exploring the nature of the habitat as a means of understanding and survival; interacting with other people as a means of acquiring social skills; and simulating the adult world as a means of preparation for joining it. The most successful toys are those that aid these functional activities.

The adult counterpart of play is leisure, which may or may not be seen as functional. It may include exercise for the sedentary worker or respite from exercise for the manual worker; mental exercise such as reading, puzzle solving or other hobbies; exploration of the wider habitat through travel; the exercise of social skills on social occasions; and creative simulation of the future, as in entrepreneurial imagination. All these things parallel the play of children in an adult way; they are all functional and legitimate.

A quite different way of generalising leisure pursuits is simply to regard them as the opposite of work – as desirable idleness – and it is in this context that the danger of an overdose arises. A certain amount of idleness is rest and relaxation but an excessive amount can be destructive to the personality. For example, S. ALBURY suggests that the 8-hour cycle of the heroin addict is a means of providing a framework of activity to fill otherwise unstructured time, and P. LAURIE comments, "A working-class Victorian boy, of the personality type that would now become an addict, would not have to use drugs because he would work from dawn to dark. He would have no agonising decisions to make about what he should do . . ."[1]

The boredom of the idle rich has been known for at least 2000 years, and now that social security guarantees life support, the boredom of the idle poor has also been unmasked. The idleness of unemployment is demoralising and so, too, is the

---

* ALICE COLEMAN, Reader in Geography, King's College, London, Great Britain.

[1] ALBURY, S.: *The integration and control of Heroin, Marijuana and L.S.D. in the U.S. and Britain.* M. A. Thesis, University of Sussex, 1968

LAURIE, P.: *Drugs: Medical, psychological and social facts.* Pelican Burmaster, La., 1974, p. 46

under-employment of many housewives. The long and empty leisure hours of the young are increasingly recognised as a factor in vandalism and crime, while the enforced leisure of retirement is attracting attention as a possible cause of premature death.

This is a strange age in which some of us are grossly overworked, while others are grossly overleisured. Of the two extremes it is usually the overworked who find life more satisfying, because they have a sense of purpose and achievement, of which the overleisured are deprived.

2. *The land and leisure causational chain*

Recreational geographers have recognised four links in a causational chain, to which, as yet, they have given very unequal attention (fig. 1.). They started, naturally enough, with the end product, or fourth link, *land use*. Land uses are identifiable and quantifiable, and lend themselves readily to critical analysis, in the study of land misuse.

Working back along the causational chain to the third link, we find the *leisure activities* that generate the demand for land uses. The second link is the *leisure time* that generates the demand for leisure activities, and the first link is the *social change* that generates the supply of leisure time.

Fig. 1: The land and leisure causational chain

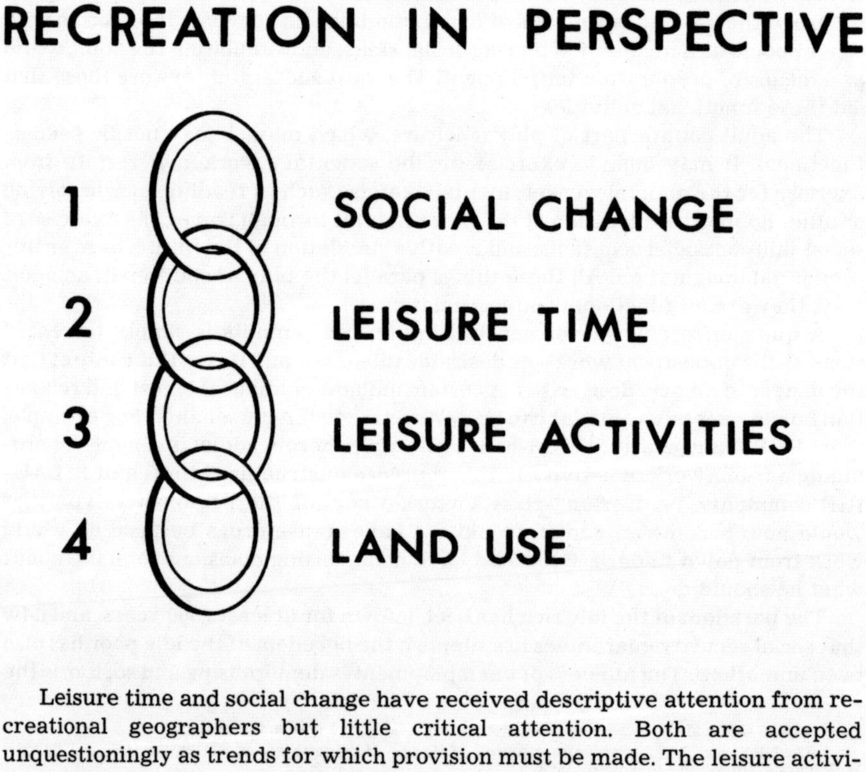

Leisure time and social change have received descriptive attention from recreational geographers but little critical attention. Both are accepted unquestioningly as trends for which provision must be made. The leisure activities of the third link are used as guidelines for the type of provision, and the land uses of the fourth link as the means of implementation. Yet recreational land-use problems are widely recognised and there is a continuing call for increased spending to repair the damage that recreation causes.[2] In these circumstances, more recreational land, more damage and more spending sound like the ingredients of a vicious circle.

3. *Growth and limits to growth*

It is well established that recreational land use is a growth phenomenon, and the scale of growth may be illustrated by two land-use surveys,[3] made a decade apart, of 850 km² in south-east England (fig. 2). At the beginning of the decade this area was characterised by a shortage of housing and an abundance of recreational land; both tended open space and woodland occupied above the national average proportion of the land. One would expect, therefore, a more rapid growth in housing than in recreational land, especially as the area contained two new towns, Basildon and Thamesmead.

Fig. 2: The Thames Estuary area, surveyed in 1962 and resurveyed in 1972
"Scapes and Fringes" are shown for the end of the decade

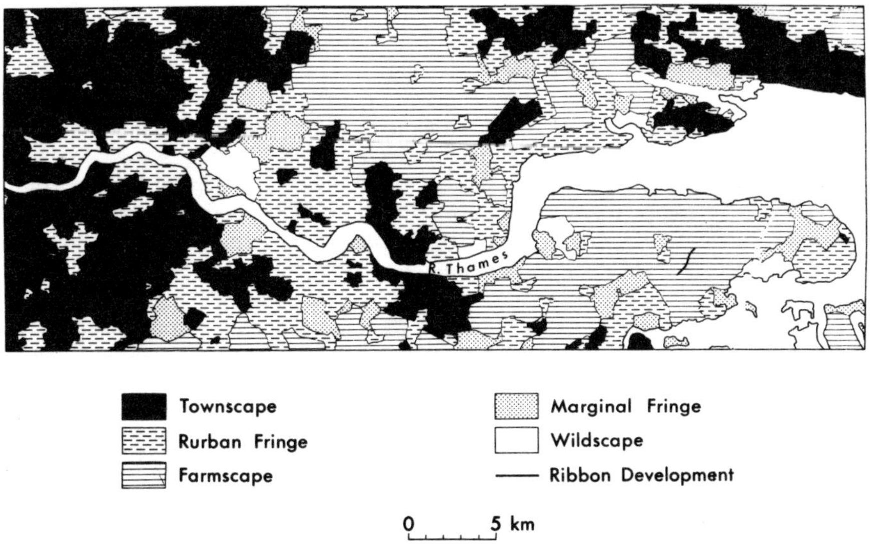

In actuality the reverse was true. Table 1 shows that 16 per cent. of the area had changed in use during the ten years, and that while residential land had gained 18.5 km², it had also lost, through demolition, 18 km², giving a net gain in housing of only half a square kilometre. The net growth of tended open space was fifteen times as great; no less than 600 ha of sorely-needed housing were demolished to contribute part of this new leisure-land. But this is not the total provision. Outdoor recreation also takes place on abandoned farmland, and indeed is often the cause of farmland abandonment. The planners may refer to such land euphemistically as green wedges but the Second Land Utilisation

---

[2] HALL, A.: Management in the urban fringe. *Countryside Recreation Review,* London 1976, pp. 8–13
[3] COLEMAN, A.: Is planning really necessary? *Geographical Journal,* London 1976, pp. 411–437

Survey of Britain maps it more prosaically as waste land. In the decade between the two surveys the net gain in waste land was no less than 61 times as great as the net gain in housing, and thus, taking tended and untended open space together, recreational land grew 76 times as fast as residential land. However, this does not include horticulture, which is concealed under the heading of farmland rotations; nor does it include urban or coastal recreational provision. Altogether there seems little reason to doubt that recreational land may be growing up to one hundred times as rapidly as land for housing.

Is this the right order or priority? Is recreation really one hundred times more important than shelter? Or is it a form of land-use in which growth has become runaway growth? In a time when all kinds of growth are being subjected to very close scrutiny, and limits to growth are being very seriously debated, should we not at least review the possibility of limits to growth in recreation?

4. *Some possible criteria*

I would like to mention a few possible criteria that might be taken into account. The first is: *Can we afford the land?* Britain is only about half self-sufficient in food and is therefore extremely vulnerable in an era of world food shortage, yet we are using up our improved farmland at a rate which is heading towards complete extinction within 200 years. In 1974 we produced food for two million fewer people than in 1973, and in 1975 production remained equally low. In the drought year of 1976 there was a 10 per cent. reduction in output,[4] while 1977's rain has caused much fallow land and a difficult, expensive harvest. The ancient Romans had the option of bread and circuses; with us it will be bread *or* circuses, and at present we are choosing circuses.

A second criterion might be: *Can we afford the environmental deterioration?* When the carrying capacity of one area after another is being exceeded by the influx of the human animal, are we right to regard the expansion of outdoor leisure as a basic axiom of recreational geography?

Can we afford the money? In a recent land-use survey two city parks had to be mapped as waste land because the borough could not afford to maintain them. Yet the same borough was spending money on the creation of new open spaces, which presumably it could not guarantee to maintain either.

Can we afford the energy that is consumed in transporting urban populations to rural playgrounds? Limits to energy growth have attracted serious concern, and if energy shortage should approach the severity experienced during World War II, then resources for recreational travel may well be among the first sacrifices.

Can we afford the vandalism that goes with over-leisure, not only in recreational resorts but also on home territory? *Can we afford to cling to the belief that education can solve recreational problems, when for thirty years its failure rate appears to have exceeded its success rate?*

Can we afford the demoralisation that stems from under-employment – the loss of self-value that is intensified rather than assuaged by panacea proposals for yet more recreational provision?

To all the questions the answer is beginning to be "NO". In one quarter after another it is being recognised that useful activity is even more essential to human welfare than leisure activity.

---

[4] Ministry of Agriculture, Fisheries and Food: *Annual review of agriculture*, London 1977

Table 1: Land-use changes in the Thames Estuary Area

	Settlement						Farmland				Vegetation						Total losses (sq km)
	R	I	E	D	T	O	O	H	A	G	Wd	S	Wa	H	M	Wr	
Settlement																	
Residential		1			4	6		2	1	½		2	1½				18
Industry					1½	½							2				4
Extractive	½			4½		½				1			5				11½
Derelict					1							½	½				2
Transport	1	½										½	1				3
Open space	2				1½			1½	1	2	½	1				½	10
Farmland																	
Orchards	1												1				2
Horticulture	1½	½	½		½	1½			Rotations				2½				7
Arable	2½		1½		½	3			90½				7				14
Improved Grass	5	2½	1½	1	1	2½						½	18				32½
Vegetation																	
Woodland					½	½	½	1				1½	1				5
Scrub	½		½		½	½				½	½		3½				6½
Waste	4½	2½	2	1		2½				2		1					15½
Heath													½				½
Marsh													1½				1½
Water			½							½			½				1½
Total gains	18½	7	6½	6½	11	17½	½	4½	2	6½	1	7	46	—	—	1	134½

5. *An approach to new solutions*

At the headquarters of the Second Land Utilisation Survey, we see many straws in the wind of change. For example, Leeds has decided that its land supply for recreation far exceeds the foreseeable financial resources to convert it into recreation use, and consequently only a five-year supply will be retained while the rest will be released for other purposes. Or there is the recent agreement reached between conservation interests and the government that tourism shall no longer take precedence in areas of severe environmental concern. And when even an organisation called Fair Play for Children opines that pure play is less desirable than purposeful activity that integrates children into adult society, it seems that a sharp change of direction is in process.

This change will not undermine existing forms of leisure activity that I have described as functional and legitimate; it will be primarily an attack upon what has been thought of as desirable idleness and is now coming to be regarded as undesirable idleness. It will include frontal attacks on overleisure, such as Britain's Job Creation Programme and President Carter's programme for work in exchange for welfare payments. It may include more homework for children, and more serious education in place of the play way, and it may expand service to the community instead of leisure time in prison.

What is the message for recreational geography? I believe it will become less specialist and more integrated into the fabric of geography as a whole. The recreational needs of Man will no longer be looked at in isolation but seen as an integral part of the total pattern of purposeful activity. Let me conclude with an example of the new type of integrated solution that is being proposed.

A. PATMORE[5] has emphasised the quantitative importance of gardening as a form of recreation. Yet for the last 30 years there has been a systematic policy of depriving people of gardens by building council flats rather than houses. In Tower Hamlets at least three-quarters of the population is deprived in this way (fig. 3), and the garden land of which they have been deprived has been converted into tended open space that is not actively used but is nevertheless a continuing charge upon the public purse for its maintenance. If urban design had been based upon the traditional British house and garden, possibly some or all of the following benefits might have accrued.

1. More people would have enjoyed a popular form of recreation.
2. They would have enjoyed it at home, thus conserving energy that would otherwise have been consumed in making recreational trips.
3. Fewer trips by car would also mean a reduction in air pollution, noise pollution and accident injuries.
4. There would be less urban pressure upon rural areas. Even a 10 per cent. respite would be welcome, both ecologically and agriculturally.
5. There would be less vandalism, which is notoriously more associated with council flats, because of their maximisation of the density of children and minimisation of scope for home recreation of any purposeful kind.[6]
6. There would be less apathy and demoralisation. Children would be reared with a model of parental achievement in the management of the domestic territory. Decisions would be taken to improve the garden or the house, and action would follow, in a freedom of choice that is totally forbidden to tenants of council flats.

---

[5] PATMORE, J. A.: *Land and leisure in England and Wales,* Newton Abbot 1970

[6] WILSON S. and STURMAN, A.: Vandalism research aimed at specific remedies. *Municipal Engineering,* London 1976, pp. 705–707.

Fig. 3: Residential areas in Tower Hamlets (inner London)
There is approximately three times as much land under flats as under houses with gardens. Surveyed in 1977

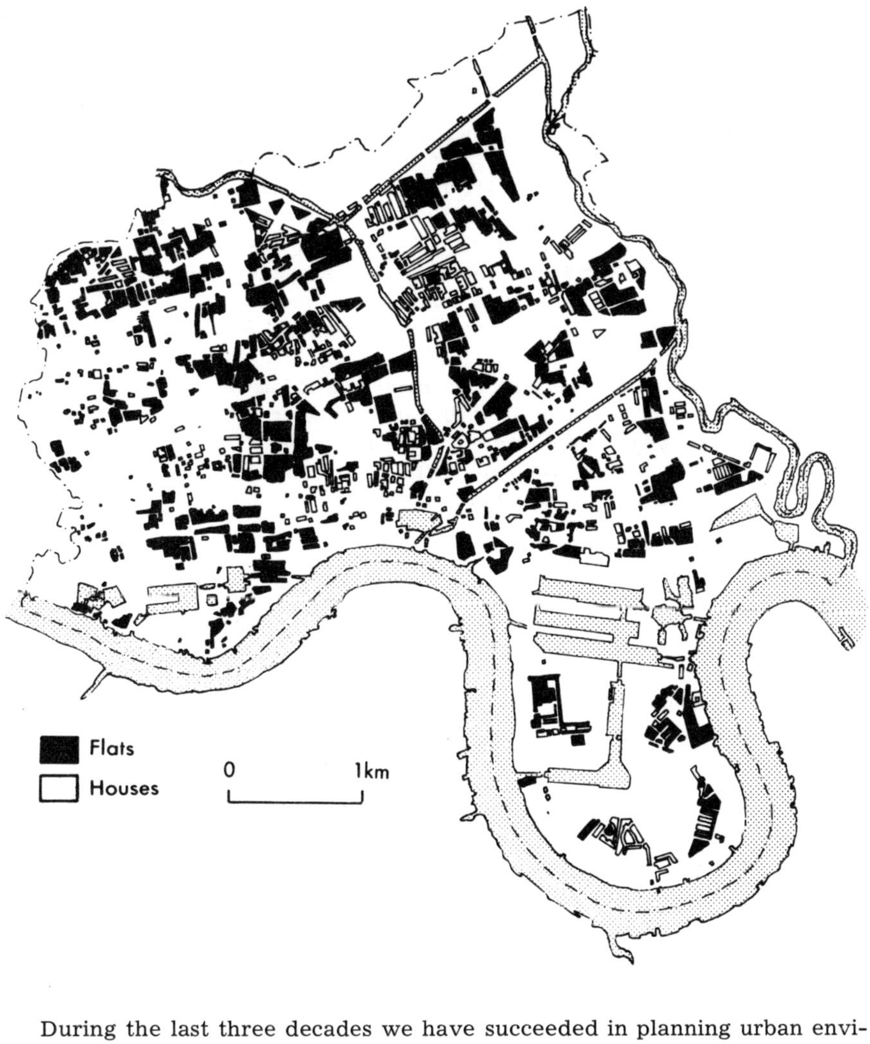

During the last three decades we have succeeded in planning urban environments that look good on paper, but that people desparately want to escape from, if they are to enjoy their recreation. Living and leisure have been artificially divorced. The future beckons toward a reintegration through purposeful activity, and a widening of vision and opportunity in the field of recreational geography. The objective should be to replace problem solving by problem prevention.

The functional and spatial structure of public recreation in an urban environment

LISLE S. MITCHELL, Columbia, South Carolina, U.S.A.*

Marion CLAWSON stated that "recreation research is almost unknown at the city level".[1] This statement has been reiterated by others since then (MITCHELL, STANDFIELD and RICKERT, MONCRIEF, HODGES and VAN DOREN and GUNDERSON).[2] Some general synthesizing and fundamental research on public urban recreation systems has been carried out as witnessed by the Outdoor Recreation Resources Review Commission Reports, SHIVER and HJELTE and GOLD.[3]

In order to add to these efforts this investigation has two primary concerns. The first is to categorize the units of the public urban recreation systems of Columbia, South Carolina into discrete functional classes and compare their basic characteristics. The second is to analyze the distributions of the systems in terms of absolute and relative locational patterns.

1. *Research design*

Study Area. The Standard Metropolitan Statistical Area (SMSA) of Columbia, South Carolina, was the empirical work area for this investigation. The SMSA centers on Columbia, the State Capital, and encompasses Richland and Lexington Counties. The two counties cover approximately the same area: Richland 758 and Lexington 767 square miles. Richland County, where Columbia is located, is predominately urban in character with a population density of 303 persons per square mile and a relatively large proportion of blacks, thirty-one percent.[4] The County is the major source of employment for the SMSA and its economy is dominated by government, finance, education, real estate, wholesale services, and retail trade. Manufacturing is also an important basic economic activity but in a relative sense it is not as significant as other activities. Lexington County, on the

---

* Dr. LISLE S. MITCHELL, Professor, Department of Geography, University of South Carolina, Columbia, South Carolina, USA

[1] CLAWSON, M.: *Land and water for recreation.* Chicago, III., 1963, p. 95

[2] GUNDERSON, P.: Spatial indicators to determine outdoor recreation needs in Detroit. *Metropolitan America: Geographic perspectives and teaching strategies.* Bloomington, Ill., 1972, p. 241

HOOGES, L. and VAN DOREN, C. S.: Synagraphic mapping as a tool in locating and evaluating the spatial distribution of municipal recreation facilities. *The journal of leisure research.* Washington, D.C., 1972, p. 342

MITCHELL, L. S.: Recreational geography: evolution and research needs. *The professional geographer.* New York 1969, p. 118

STANFIELD, C. A. and RICKERT, J. E.: The recreational business district. *The journal of leisure research.* Washington, D. C., 1970, p. 213

VAN DOREN, C. S.: Urban recreation and park standards in the United States. *Proceedings of the Association of American Geographers.* Washington, D.C., 1973, p. 266

[3] GOLD, S. M.: *Urban recreation planning.* Philadelphia, Penn., 1973, pp. 92–93.

Outdoor recreation resources review commission Study Report 21: *The study of outdoor recreation in metropolitan regions of the United States,* Washington, D. C., 1962

SHIVERS, J. S. and HJELTE, G.: *Planning recreational places.* Teaneck, N. J., 1971, p. 221

[4] U. S. Department of Commerce, Bureau of Census: *United States Census of Population and Housing: 1970.* Final report PHC (1)–48, census tracts, Columbia, S. C. Standardized Metropolitan Area. Washington, D. C., 1970.

other hand, is principally rural and suburban in character with a density of only 124 individuals per square mile and black population of only twelve percent.[5] The county is growing rapidly as a source of employment in manufacturing and craft industries, but because more than one-half of the total labor force is employed outside the county it serves as a bedroom for Richland County.

The counties are similar in their physical makeup with both divided by the "fall line" which separates the Piedmont plateau on the west from the Sandhills portion of the inner coastal plain on the east. The local relief rarely exceeds 200 feet and most of the area consists of a dendritic pattern of gently to moderately sloping ridges with maximum elevation of 350 to 500 feet. The only significant physiographic difference between the counties is the concentration of poorly drained swamp land in the southeast portion of Richland County and the location of Lake Murray in the northwest section of Lexington County.

The SMSA is not typical of many urban regions because it circumscribes a state capital; is located in a non-industrial state, although that condition is rapidly changing; and centers on a small central city (117,000) with a relatively low population density. Thus the findings of this study may not be applicable to a large number of other urban regions. However, the cultural and physical characteristics cited here are comparable to other urban areas of the South and are not dissimilar to some in mid-western states and to a majority of those in the plains and mountain states. Therefore, the results of the research may be more universal than first suspected.

Data. The data used in this investigation were taken from one basic source: Recreation and open space for the Central Midlands Region.[6] The data were updated and field checked for accuracy in the spring of 1976. Public recreation areas were defined as parcels of land and/or water having definite boundaries, being owned by or function under the authority of a public agency, possessing or not possessing permanent facilities and buildings, regions where formal and informal recreation activities and programs are conducted as either a primary or secondary function. These areas are intensively used both temporally and spatially and are open to the general public.[7] There are 172 sites which fit this definition including both parks and school playgrounds.

The 172 public sites offer thirty-nine different recreation facilities or activities. The data consist of nominal numbers (i. e., the presence or absence of a facility or an activity). Nonmetric data can be of significant use in geographic research but when input into analytical algorithms the results may appear misleading or contradictory. Therefore, a statistical technique was employed to transform the data into a form which will minimize errors or misinterpretations.

Procedures. The first procedure employed in this study was the use of multidimensional scaling[8] to translate the nonmetric (i. e., nominal) data to metric distance measures suitable for input into a categorization procedure. The scale values were then classified using a single linkage method known as Ward's group-

[5] U. S. Department of Commerce, Bureau of Census: *United States Census of Population and Housing. 1970* Final report PHC (1)–48, Census tracts, Columbia, S. C. Standardized Metropolitan Area. Washington, D. C., 1970.

[6] Central Midlands Regional Planning Council and Department of Housing and Urban Development: *Recreation and open space for the central midlands region.* Columbia, S. C., 1972

[7] MITCHELL, L. S. and LOVINGOOD, P. E.: Public urban recreation: An investigation of spatial relationships. *The journal of leisure research.* Washington, D.C., 1976, p. 7

[8] GOLLEDGE, R. G. and RUSHTON, G.: Multidimensional scaling: Review and geographical applications. *Annals of the Association of American Geographers.* Lawrence, K., 1972, pp. 72–73.

[9] WARD, J. H.: Hierarchical grouping to optimize an objective function. *Journal of the American statistical Association.* Washington, D.C., 1963, pp. 236–243

ing algorithm.[9] The resulting classes were subjected to discriminate analysis to determine if any of the sites were misclassified. Each class was then named and described by the percentage of activities found in each.

The second procedure involved the use of a nearest neighbor technique[10] to describe the locations of the two recreational systems. The spatial similarities and differences within and between the classification schemes were identified along with the relationships of the distributions to physical and cultural factors by the use of cartographic analysis.

2. *Categorization of facility types*

Public recreation was investigated by subjecting the data to multidimensional scaling analysis. To assist in finding an appropriately dimensioned solution, the analysis was carried out in eight dimensions and the relationship between stress and dimensionality was plotted. A noticeable "elbow" in the curve indicated five to be the appropriate number of dimensions and the coordinates of this configuration were used as input into the classification scheme. Ward's grouping algorithm produced five functional (i. e., defined by recreational facilities and activities) classes of recreational sites. Grouping procedures such as this have been used successfully in the formulation of regions but these methods have had a major problem of neighbor definition. In functional classification, however, contiguity questions may be ignored because they are irrelevant. The five classes were then subjected to discriminant analysis and it was determined that only ten of the 172 sites were incorrectly classified. These sites were placed in the proper classes to complete the taxonomy.

The identification and characterization of the classes were arbitrary although a standardized procedure was followed. Each class was compared with all others, facility by facility, and the facilities which ranked first or second in each class were noted. For example Archery was only found in Class I, while Baseball Fields is first in Class I (7.07 per cent.) and second in Class V (5.96 per cent.). This process was continued through the entire list of thirty-nine activities and the number of first and second rankings was compiled for each class (table 1).

Based on this procedure, Class I was identified as *Organized Sports*. This class ranks first in seventeen facilities and the most dominant are: Outdoor Basketball Courts, Tennis Courts, Baseball Fields, Softball Fields, and Football Fields. Other complementary, functional and spectator facilities are related to these sport facilities: Bleachers, Lighted Facilities, and Concession Stands. These eight facilities account for almost two-thirds of the total and because the emphasis is focused on organized sport activities the name given seems appropriate.

Class II ranks first in six and second in seven facilities. The first-ranking facilities which give character to the class are Picnic Tables and Benches and Grills. The second-ranking and related facilities include Tires, Climbing Apparatus, Outdoor Basketball Courts, Tether Ball Poles, Volley Ball Courts, Open Fields, and Softball Fields. The second-ranking facilities make up more than eighty percent of the total found in the class. The name assigned is *Family Elementary Activities* because the class has facilities indicating activities which center around the family (i. e., picnicing) and relatively unorganized games played by elementary school children.

---

[10] CLARK, P. J. and EVANS, F. C.: Distance to nearest neighbor as a measure of spatial relationship in populations. *Ecology*. Durham, N.C., 1954, pp. 445–453.

Table 1: Percentage of public recreational activities by class

Facilities	Classes				
	I	II	III	IV	V
1. Archery	1.31				
2. Baseball Fields	7.07	0.24		1.49	5.86
3. Basketball, Indoor				0.21	0.56
4. Basketball, Outdoor	12.17	11.08	3.87	3.64	2.45
5. Benches or Chairs	5.26	3.89	16.53	2.56	15.50
6. Camping Sites			15.50		
7. Chinning Bars	4.93	4.75			
8. Climbing Apparatus	3.94	14.12	6.84	12.41	2.64
9. Fishing Areas	0.16				
10. Football Fields	4.11				0.75
11. Grills		4.26	2.32	2.14	2.45
12. Hard-surface Areas	0.98	1.46	1.67	0.42	0.18
13. Horseshoe Courts			3.10	0.42	0.94
14. Merry-go-rounds		0.12	2.32	2.35	2.45
15. Open Fields	3.94	3.89	0.25	3.85	1.32
16. Picnic Tables & Benches	2.79	11.81	6.97	9.85	7.75
17. Pipe Tunnels	0.49	1.46	1.67	2.35	2.83
18. Sand Boxes		0.73	1.29	0.21	0.94
19. Shelter Houses	0.98	0.48	3.22	1.92	2.83
20. Slides	0.32	1.09	3.22	4.06	3.59
21. Soccer Fields	0.82			0.21	
22. Softball Fields	5.26	3.16	1.16	2.14	2.45
23. Swimming Pools, Indoor					0.18
24. Swimming Pools, Outdoor		0.32	0.12	0.12	0.37
25. Swing Sets		0.73	12.01	23.98	9.26
26. Teeter-Totter, See-Saw	0.32	0.97	6.45	2.35	3.59
27. Tennis Courts	7.89	0.12	1.29	3.64	4.53
28. Tether Ball Poles	0.32	10.23	2.71	0.64	0.37
29. Tracks	0.83				0.18
30. Volleyball Courts	2.30	7.55	1.29	0.21	0.56
31. Wading & Spray Pools		0.12	1.93	0.85	0.75
32. Balancing Bars	0.98	0.85	0.38	0.64	0.18
33. Bleachers	17.92	0.48	0.64	5.13	10.77
34. Concession Stands	2.46	0.12	0.12	0.42	1.32
35. Spring Animals		0.12	1.03	5.56	5.48
36. Tires	2.30	15.83	0.12	1.49	
37. Lighted Facilities	9.37	0.12	0.51	1.92	6.80
38. Golf Courses	0.16				
39. Riding Stables	0.16				
Total Percentage	99.85	99.90	99.82	99.84	99.83
Class Size	58	48	21	30	15

Source: Compiled by authors.

Class III was designed as the *Family Mixed Activities Class.* The term Family was justified on the basis of Benches or Chairs, Camping Sites, Picnic Tables and Benches, Shelter Houses, and Grills as these facilities symbolize many passive family and adult activities. Mixed Activities was selected as a portion of the class name because facilities which provide activities for all age groups are present: Shelter Houses, Benches or Chairs, and Horseshoes for adults and Swings, Teeter-Totters, Tether Ball Poles, Wading and/or Spray Pools, and Sand Boxes for children.

Class IV was labeled *Family Tot Lots.* Similar to Classes II and III the Family designation pertains to Picnic Tables and Benches and Grills. The term Tot Lot was deemed appropriate due to the high percentage of facilities with first or second ranking in the class (i. e., 51.56 per cent.) and which are most suitable for younger children: Swing Sets, Climbing Apparatus, Spring Animals, Slides and others. This type of recreation site seems to provide the kind of recreational facilities and activities which best serves families with young children.

Class V was the most difficult to name because of the small percentages of the facilities in which it ranked first (10.74 per cent. for six facilities) and because it ranked second in thirteen facilities. The six leading facilities are a heterogeneous group: Indoor Basketball Courts and Swimming Pools, Outdoor Swimming Pools, Spring Animals, Pipe Tunnels and Merry-Go-Rounds. The class ranked second in a number of organized sports (i. e., Baseball Fields and Tennis Courts), in facilities related to organized sport (i. e. Benches or Chairs, Bleachers, Lighted Facilities, Concession Stands), in facilities pertaining to family activities (i. e., Picnic Tables and Benches, Grills, Shelter Houses), and in facilities for young children (i. e., Slides, Teeter-Totters, Sand Boxes). No pattern is apparent in this mixture of facilities and therefore the class was identified as the *Miscellaneous Activities and Sport Class.*

Class I is oriented toward active sports activities and provision of related spectator facilities. Classes II, III, and IV are similar because of their orientation toward family related activities. Their differences are based upon activities geared toward very young children (i. e., tots), elementary school children, or a mixture of children and adults and thus the basic distinguishing characteristics are a matter of degree not kind. Class V, Miscellaneous Activities and Sports, is a transition class between Class I and the other three.

3. *Distribution of facility types*

The spatial structure of the 172 units of the public recreation system has an agglomerated pattern (map 1 and table 2). About sixty-two percent, 106 units, are located within the legal limits of one of the incorporated places. An additional twenty percent, thirty-five units, are situated within one mile of a corporate boundary. Therefore, approximately eighty-two percent of the public sites are found either in or within one mile of an urban place (map 1). This pattern reflects the concentrated nature of the public agencies which provide recreational opportunities for a relatively dense population.

The agglomerated distribution of each of the five classes logically follows from the total spatial pattern and is explained by the fact that the purpose of each class is to offer a particular combination of facilities and activities to a slightly different segment of the urban population. In order to achieve this purpose sites need to be both proximate and accessible to a population having a concentrated pattern. In addition, the spatial organization is not effected by physical site requirements as any site can be altered to fit the needs of public recreation units. The only physical differentiation is in terms of area or size.

Table 2: Nearest neighbor analysis public recreational classes

Class	Number	Nearest neighbor ratio
All	172	0.631
I	58	0.558
II	48	0.717
III	21	0.463
IV	30	0.806
V	15	0.675

A nearest neighbor ratio of 0.000 denotes a perfectly concentrated distribution, 1.000 indicates a random pattern and 2.150 connotes a perfectly uniform arrangement.

All of the values in this table are statistically different from 1.000 at the 01 significance level and thus tend to be concentrated.

4. *Summary*

The two objectives of this study have been achieved. First, the 172 public recreation sites examined were grouped into five functional classes based upon the presence or absence of 39 recreation facilities or activities. The classes of the public system tend to serve general recreational needs. Three of the five classes meet the desires of individual families and their members by providing common recreational facilities and activities and account for almost 58 per cent. of the units in the system. One class serves the specialized needs of the athletically inclined by providing facilities for organized sports and games. Another class attempts to meet both needs: those of individual family units and those individual with a competitive nature.

The classes which comprise the public recreation system differ more in degree than in kind because the facilities and activities which are present overlap to a large extent. They, therefore, have no specific focus, no principal facility or activity, and no single compelling attraction and as a total system they seem to be meeting general recreation desires. In addition, because they provide many similar functions, they serve an extremely heterogeneous population.

Second, the recreation units which comprise the public system were found to have a concentrated pattern. All 172 sites and each of the five functional classes tend to be clustered. The agglomerated nature of the distributions is not unexpected in light of the overlapping character of the facilities and activities provided by each of the classes. The spatial organization is most influenced by the distribution of the population and is little effected by physical site requirements.

5. *Conclusions*

The complex nature of the supply of public urban recreation opportunities may be best understood in the context of purpose, structure and distribution.

Purpose. The objective of any recreation program is to supply the goods and services demanded by that portion of the population which has a particular re-

Map 1: Distribution of public recreational units by class
LEXINGTON AND RICHLAND COUNTIES, SOUTH CAROLINA

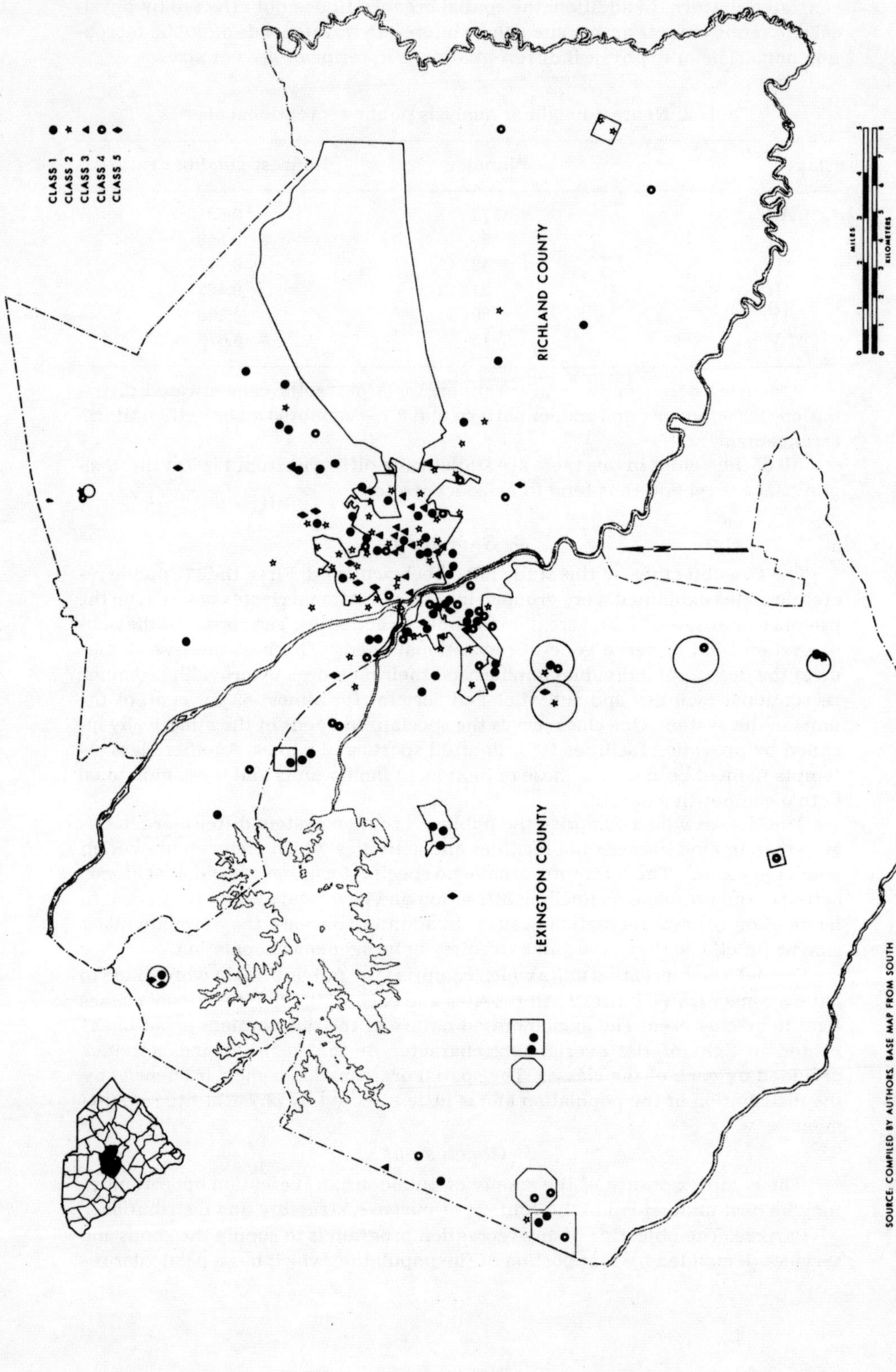

creational need or want. This goal is achieved through the provision of facilities, programs, and activities at various locations. The specific aim of the public urban system is to provide general recreation opportunities for the entire urban population as close to their residences as possible.

Structure. The operational framework for the supply of recreational experiences is based on the classification of the recreation units which comprise the public system. These sites provide universal kinds of facilities and activities, at little or no cost to the user, which require little or no equipment for participation, to individuals in the low to middle socio-economic groups. This system is created, maintained and controlled by an administrative process which functions within the general political system. The organization of supply, therefore, results from the type of recreation opportunity provided; and the social, political, and/or economic costs of the experiences; and the socio-economic group being served.

Distribution. The distribution of the units and classes which comprise the public recreation system reflects the differences in their purpose and structure. The purpose determines the type of facilities, programs and activities established and the population attracted. These factors in turn influence the location of particular types or classes of recreation sites. Therefore, public recreation places have an agglomerated spatial pattern because their purpose is to serve a densely concentrated population with general recreation facilities and activities.

Problems of the cartographic representation of tourism

PETER MARIOT, Bratislava, Czechoslovakia*

1. Significance of the cartographic representation of tourism

The general development of tourism and especially the constantly more intensive manifestations of its presence in the landscape have become a stimulus for extending the number of attempts to represent it cartographically. Just as in the cartographic representation of other phenomena, for which the differences in distribution, intensity and structure are characteristic, so have arisen also in case of the cartographic representation of tourism model representations, which make it possible to characterize more exactly, more relevantly and more obviously especially the spatial aspects of different facets of tourism.

The cartographic representation is thus a significant methodical aid to extend the body of information about its preconditions, its localisation, and its intensity and structure. In connection with this fact this approach plays a particularly significant role:

1. as a means of expressing partial results of the research and to synthesize these;
2. as a basis for discovering fundamental relations between tourism and different landscape elements;
3. as a starting point for formulating general principles in the theory of tourism;
4. even as important means for preparing a basis for a planned development of tourism of specific areas.

The basic problems connected with the cartographic representation of tourism may be divided into five thematic groups, the significance and influences of which are in a close interrelationship. They are thematic units which characterize the aim, contents, methods, scale and basis of the maps of tourism.

2. Aim of the cartographic representation of tourism

In the early attempts to represent tourism cartographically, the sole aim was to document more exactly and visually more strikingly outcomes of the research of distribution, intensity and structure of tourism. Such maps may be found in many papers by geographers published in the 1950s and 1960s.

Parallel with the increasing pressure of the need of planned development of tourism, the papers begin to be published from the 1960s onward, in which the cartographic contents aimed toward supporting planning measures. Therefore their contents – as distinct from purely documentary cartographical bases – is clearer cut and especially in the key a terminology similar to the language of professional planners is used. The subsequent increase of the interest of planning agencies in the geographical aspects of tourism contributed to a proliferation of these kinds of maps of tourism at the beginning of the 1970s.

---

* Dr. PETER MARIOT, Slovak Academy of Science, Department of Geography, Bratislava, Czechoslovakia.

There is, however, yet another item, towards which the cartographic representation of tourism should be aimed. It is formed by a complex of questions concerned with the endeavour to formulate the theory of tourism, i. e. to determine the general principles of the origin, forms, manifestations and influences of tourism. Although the attempts, as far as the theoretical papers go, are at the moment still sporadic, it is indisputable that in formulating the principles of a theory of tourism the cartographic interpretation will play a significant role also. Of the series of maps representing various facets of tourism those in particular may be placed to this group which represent and do justice to the sphere of interrelationships of tourism in the country, or also those, which in a larger territory represent variability of the effects present and in this way they call attention also to its broader spatial links. They are above all the maps which cover the entire territories of states in national atlases.

3. *Contents of the cartographic representation of tourism*

The growth in the number of papers devoted to the geography of tourism has contributed both to an increase of the number and also a broadening of the contents of cartographic presentation of their results. In spite of the fact that the interpretation of some bases are found in many papers, the scale of the elements represented is broad enough to provide the possibility of classification by contents from several points of view.

One can distinguish a group of cartographic illustrations which represent primary characteristics of tourism (e. g. number of guests, origin of guests, number of over-night stays and so on), or also indirect characteristics of tourism (e. g. age of establishments, accessibility by public transport etc.).

Another criterion to classify the cartographic illustrations of papers devoted to the study of tourism may be determined by the nature of elements represented. In this way, one can distinguish maps representing characteristics of natural elements which have a bearing on tourism (e. g. the suitability of snow cover for winter sports or ruggedness of relief from the viewpoint of tourism), or also socio-geographical characteristics which have a bearing influence on tourism (e. g. tourist-expenditure of the population, utilization of transport facilities by tourists).

Further similar approaches in classifying cartographic illustrations of papers on tourism allow to become acquainted with the interest of the individual authors. Mostly, however, a proper systematic and more detailed view of thematic peculiarities of the content of these bases, when judged by their relation of tourism, is missing in them. From this point of view, in other words, according to which qualitative characteristics of tourism are found within the contents of maps, three main groups of the maps of tourism can be distinguished:

1. maps representing the bases of preconditions of tourism,
2. maps representing the structural facts of tourism,
3. maps representing the impact of tourism.

To 1: *Maps representing the preconditions of tourism*

They are important bases, which help to explain the causes of the different spatial distribution and intensity of tourism. In view of the large size of the complex of preconditions of tourism, one can distinguish maps representing:

1.1. Preconditions for localisation
1.2. Selected preconditions of tourism
1.3. Realized preconditions of tourism

To 1.1.: Maps representing the preconditions for localisation of tourism were introduced into the special literature above all by the endeavour of authors to present the conditions which led to the formation and development of tourism in areas which are mostly visited intensively already. Among such maps the representations of the suitability of relief, climate, hydrology, vegetation, or cultural-historical features for recreation activities dominate. The range of criteria characterizing these presuppositions is relatively broad. As to the later papers, there is a typical tendency to use fewer indices, but those of a synthetizing character viz. types of relief, dynamic climate, carrying capacity of forest areas, degree of attraction of cultural-historical objects and so on.

The needs of practical application, however, influenced the work of authors in such a way that they began to devote greater attention representing preconditions of tourism also in areas where no intensive tourism had developed so far. The importance of these areas in the planning practice is, however, extraordinarily great, especially with respect to the constantly increasing need for extending places for recreation. In response to this trend maps expressing the potential of local preconditions of tourism have come into the special literature, having formed an important connection between geography of tourism and practice. In addition, they offer important bases for understanding general regularities and localisation principles of tourism, which are the basic starting point for formulating statements of a theoretical nature.

To 1.2.: Maps representing selected preconditions of tourism are found in the special literature considerably less frequently than maps of localisation of realisation of preconditions of tourism. They relate above all to the nature and place of the concentration of the selected preconditions of tourism, which most intensively occur above all in areas where tourism is not a dominating factor and which therefore are mostly of little interest to the geographers of tourism. More systematically and in a more complex way the selective preconditions began to be studied only under the influence of practical needs determined especially by the endeavour to sum up the interest of the population in participating in tourism.

Just as in the case of the research of the localisation of preconditions, so were also in analyses of the selective preconditions of tourism in the first stage of research, maps were used, which were adapted as cartographic monuments from other special geographical research, chiefly from population and settlement geography. Only later these results began to be applied more concretely and were specially modified in the interest of a more relevant representation of their relationships to tourism. In this way these maps arose, which represent various aspects of the population in its participation in tourism: by social group, by income, by ownership or means of transport, by its interest as a whole in participating in tourism and so on.

Although these preconditions, the criteria used in them as well as the results derived from them have a substantially more limited regional validity and are more difficult to generalize than the results of the study of conditions of localisation, this group of maps has acquired a place of significant and sought-out bases especially in the planning practice.

With respect to a lesser frequence of such kinds of research there are, however, large potentialities to a further broadening of both the number and contents of such maps. In addition to their use in practical application, such maps have also real importance for broadening significantly the starting basis to provide a useful foundation for finding regularities of the mechanism of tourism, its spatial dynamics and thus also in forming its theory.

To 1.3.: Maps representing realized preconditions of tourism are numerous. They are in the most cases found in the special literature and generally they were the first attempts to represent the problems of tourism cartographically. In these are shown chiefly characteristics of the material-technical basis of tourism monitored by official statistics such as the capacity and performance of various establishments. Less frequent are maps which represent the relationships rising from the location of a place or an area as regards communication lines, but this aspect is usually dealt with in the text in almost every regionally orientated paper.

In some papers a trend to present the realization of preconditions as found as a result of research by maps is very clearly discernable. This is due to their ability to illustrate both quantitative and qualitative differences as to the spatial distribution of the manifestations of tourism, as well as the differences of the use of various parts of the territory. In fact, however, this pattern is above all a reflection of a properly or improperly orientated investment policy, which led to the construction of establishments so that it is not relevant to the total potential of a territory. This aspect has a special role in particular in the planning practice, for which the maps of the realization of preconditions of tourism offer the possibility of summing up the existing state of the material-technical basis, but its comparison to actual needs or to the potential of the territory under observation is only possible, when combined with other bases.

The interest of practice has broadened the sphere of attention also to such kinds of facilities which do not relate directly to catering for visitors but in spite of this fact play a significant role in tourism like the sale of souvenirs, tobacco, petrol and so on. In this way, the contents of the maps of realized preconditions of tourism has been enriched by other elements, whose influences are not only to be found but which are also taken into consideration when studying the regularities which determine the main features of the participation of the population in tourism.

To 2: *Maps representing the structural facts of tourism*

They are maps, whose contents are derived above all from various data from the statistics of tourism, or data acquired in another way: by inquiries, observation etc. By a combination of these quantitative bases, by a formation of indices, relative values, conversions related to the values of other elements and so on, an ample set of indices has arisen, which makes it possible to characterize the structural marks of tourism from different points of view.

Characteristics of performance of the material-technical basis of tourism, the number of overnight stays, frequency and income of the establishments of tourism and so on belong to the subjects most frequently represented on these maps, offering in the spatial projection suitable bases especially for considerations regarding territorial differences in their economic sphere. Increasingly more frequent, however, are also maps which represent and characterize more specific aspects of the structure of tourism e. g. the length of the stay of guests, the normal residence of visitors, seasonality of tourism and so on. These bases are of great significance for the practice and theory of tourism, because they enable one to draw and follow in more detail the relationships, which influence the differences in distribution, intensity and structure of tourism.

The attempts to characterize various visited places in a more complex way led the authors not only to a more profound way in devising methods of a classification of resorts, but they represent also the first steps in the search for more complex indices of the structure of tourism. By cartographic representation of them maps of tourism arose, which offer a more complex view of spatial differences in the structure of tourism. Their most general expression are so far the infrequently found and methodically not yet satisfactory maps which represent the results of regionalization of tourism, which is the synthetic culmination of endeavours to represent the structural characteristic of tourism.

To 3: *Maps representing the impact of tourism*

The widening of the aspect from the viewpoint of geographers regarding tourism has shown hat its long-term presence has strikingly influenced the areas where tourism has acquired its greatest intensity. In this connection, approximately since the 1960s, papers were also published, which are devoted to studying the influences of tourism upon the landscape. Their *raison d'être* has been fortified by the rapid development of environmental studies which are characteristic especially for last decade. Within this body of research tourism emerges as an important factor, the presence of which gives rise to significant and far-reaching changes in the physiognomy and also in the functional structure of the landscape and by this fact also to the environment of Man. In connection with this trend, true, so far in a small number only, maps occur, which represent the influences of tourism upon selected elements of the landscape and their number is increasing.

Above all a complex of problems related to the negative consequences of a high visit rate as to the physio-geographical landscape elements in recreation areas, especially vegetation, belongs to the most remarkable influences of this kind. Visually clearly striking are also extensive changes within the sphere of the construction of visiting centres and areas, where the tourism gives rise to building activities, changes in the function of buildings, construction of new communication lines and so on. These problems when represented on maps in development projects make it possible to draw exactly and study various stages of the process of transforming the landscape under influence of tourism. In this connection such maps are of a special significance not only for the practical directing and managing the development of tourism, but also for finding general principles of the development of its links with the landscape, this being one of fundamental bases in the formation of the theory of tourism.

Another group of the impact of tourism concerns the demographic and economic spheres of resorts and tourist regions. Only minimal attention has been paid to studying them up and maps which represent these aspects are also sporadic. In spite of this fact, extensive and interesting possibilities from many points of view to represent, for instance, the changes in using soil resources, changes in the social structure of the population, in its income and so on would be possible within this sphere.

A general view of the development of maps of tourism according to contents allow one to state that the original, analytical maps expressing above all basic characteristics of tourism have been joined increasingly by more complex, synthetizing maps whose authors endeavour to represent the significantly broader sphere of problems as far as conditionality and impact of tourism.

4. *Methods of the cartographic representation of tourism*

The problems concerning the methods of the cartographic representation of tourism are closely connected with the contents of maps. Arising from the thematic heterogeneity the criteria for expressing the contents are also very different. The individual aspects of tourism have different units of measurement, so that almost every characteristic acquires another index. In spite of this fact, one can say that in each of the above mentioned groups of maps of tourism, the use of two to three cartographic methods for expressing the special contents prevail.

In the maps of localization of preconditions of tourism methods of representation are by choropleths and isolines. The selective and realized preconditions of tourism are mostly expressed either by the symbol or dot method, only some characteristics by choropleths. The maps representing structural aspects of tourism use above all advantage of exactness by choosing a symbol, which allows accentuating the link of data represented to individual localities. On the maps illustrating the influences of tourism the symbol method is combined most frequently with the choropleth one.

A specially interesting range of problems, in view of the cartographic methods in expressing contents of the maps of tourism, is formed by the question of criteria and indices used in expressing the individual characteristics of tourism. In this brief contribution this broad sphere of problems cannot be discussed in detail. When mentioned, however, one should at least state two facts:

There is above all a striking trend to move from the former analytical, special indices towards the use of more complex, frequently differently combined indices, which provide information on several aspects of tourism on the same map. The second fact arises from the great benefit the study of tourism gains, when different territories are represented by the identical method. In connection with this fact, there appears a need to coordinate closely the selection of indices to be represented so that maps of different territories and by different authors may be comparable. To accomplish this task, it is inevitable to analyze in detail various criteria and indices, to make a selection among them and to suggest those characterizing the element to be represented most relevantly.

5. *Scales of the maps of tourism*

The contents and scales of maps of tourism are closely correlated, thus with an increasing scale of a map the generalization of its content decreases. There is also a close relationship between the scale and the aim of a map. Especially for practical needs maps of large scales down to 1:50.000 are required, their contents aimed at summarizing the potentialities of further development of tourism. In most papers, however, the maps of median scales 1:100.000 to 1:500.000 prevail which in intensively used areas of tourism allow expressing the existing spatial differences especially from the viewpoint of selected and realized potentialities of tourism, or its structural characteristics. In spite of this fact, the influences of tourism upon the landscape are usually represented on large scale maps.

Among experts of tourism recently an initiative to use identical scales on maps representing the results of research in different areas and countries took place. This step together with the use of identical criteria could doubtless contribute to improve facilities for comparing situations in different territories, to extend the bases for organizing international cooperation and to enlarge the stock of materials required to form a theoretical basis of a science of tourism.

6. *Basis of the maps of tourism*

The basis of the maps of tourism is an important way to accentuate the relationships of the characteristics of tourism represented to other landscape elements. Within this field, much still needs to be done. Authors have concentrated their attention almost entirely to express a special content and in consequence the information value of maps was in many cases lessened, especially from the aspect of the relations between tourism and environment, where its characteristic features come to the fore. Thus only few maps – mostly technically more elaboratedly prepared ones in various atlases – utilize suitably the informative value of the basis of a map.

Although this situation is due to some extent to the use of black and white only a method very sensitive to overcrowding of a map, it is nevertheless necessary to emphasize the need to demonstrate close links between the special contents and the basis of map. To accomplish this it will in many cases be necessary to leave aside the traditionally used basis represented by the fundamental topographic situation, or the administrative division of the territory studied and to replace it by a simpler base map which complements the special content more relevantly.

As to concrete examples of such constructive fusion between the special content and the base map, they are preliminarily only few. It is thus even more urgent to introduce new criteria concerning base maps and, for instance, in representing mountainous recreation areas use the hypsographic situation in illustrating recreation hinterland of large towns to put isochores, isochrones or similar data into the base maps. This approach will beyond doubt contribute to a clearer expression and a better understanding of the relationships between tourism and landscape.

7. *Conclusions*

The brief summary of problems which characterize the cartographic representation of tourism is one of the first attempts to summarize these questions. Therefore its aim is first and foremost to call attention to this series of problems and to their significance for theory and practice. It offers secondly also incentive for a desirable orientation of papers within the orbit of cartographic representation of tourism in the future. It may in conclusion be stated that while up to now these problems were at the fringe of the interest of geographers of tourism, the development of the situation shows that for its further progress, for introducing its outcomes into practice as well as for the construction of its theoretical conception it will be necessary to shift this complex of problems nearer to the centre of attention.

In this connection it appears to be desirable to divert the interests of geographers of tourism within broader international limits especially to three important tasks:

1. to work out a thorough evaluation of the situation which characterizes the problems of cartographic representation of tourism,

2. to devise the principles of selection and formation of these criteria and indices, which are most suitable to express cartographically the geographically significant aspects of tourism.

3. to extend cooperation in representing various aspects of tourism of definite territories by using a uniform method and uniform symbols.

Significant results in solving these tasks can be achieved especially through the support and on the base of the Working Group of the Geography of Tourism and Recreation of the International Geographical Union (IGU).

Monuments of nature and tourism

JOSEF MATZNETTER, Frankfurt/Main,
Federal Republic of Germany*

The expression "monument of nature", a term coined by ALEXANDER VON HUMBOLDT, is used to denote remarkable creations of nature such as striking rock formations, waterfalls, significant springs, exits of karst rivers and caves but also a solitary rare tree or groups of them or other plants, or possibly even a very localised occurence of particular animals. In many countries of the world such natural phenomena are protected by those laws which have the protection of nature or areas of outstanding beauty as their basic objective; in Germany for instance they are the *Naturschutzgesetz* or in Britain the *Countryside Act.* Simultaneously these *monuments of nature* are thus declared *national monuments* and their care is in the hands of central or provincial authorities. In this paper monuments of nature are to be understood simply as remarkable local natural phenomena regardless of their legal status, and special attention will be accorded to caves. Such natural phenomena do occur rather frequently within nature parks, national parks or nature preserves, but this is by no means always the case; they can be situated in isolation or occasionally very close to a built-up area.

Such monuments of nature as striking, not man-made, features of the environment have acted as stimuli of the imagination and left their mark in poetry, religion or superstition. In their relation to man these features are essentially of threefold interest: for scientific investigation, for sightseeing and lastly – even in a rather limited way – for a possible economic use. In every case scientific investigation and demonstration must take absolute precedence which means that their natural character should never be impeded to a high degree so as not to prejudice their scientific investigation which in many cases requires to be undertaken again under new aspects.

As far as sightseeing is concerned, both that originating in greater distances but also the local one has to be considered under the same heading. The possibility of economic use exists only in rare cases as for instance in the case of waterfalls for electricity generation, the case of hot springs and very rarely also in the case of caves with phosphate deposits which can be used to produce fertilizers.

Concerning the utilisation of a monument of nature for Tourism the following measures need to be considered:

1. establishing access
2. securing a sufficient number of visitors
3. protective measures for the object itself
4. presentation
   a) to enhance the aesthetic-artistic effect
   b) to explain to and teach the visitors
5. organisation for visiting

---

* Dr. Josef MATZNETTER, Professor, Head of Department of Economic Geography, Johann-Wolfgang-Goethe-Universität, Frankfurt/Main, Federal Republic of Germany

6. considering it as a part of the regional tourism
7. additional measures

The question whether a particular monument of nature should be opened up for a larger number of tourists is one of principle, as there are two aspects largely opposed to each other which have to be considered: on the one hand the preservation of this particular monument of nature without damage or impairment of its natural character; on the other hand the aim to show it to the greatest possible number of visitors under the following aspects:

1. promotion of general education in the widest sense
2. providing the possibility for our industrial society, far removed from nature, to experience nature in a striking way
3. to cover the costs arising from the opening up, the maintainance, the organisation set up for making the visits possible, and advertising
4. the desire of regional tourism to offer particular attraction

In general when attempting to answer these questions one has to agree with H. TRIMMEL who suggests in the case of caves to limit their opening up to a relatively small number. There may of course be exceptions to this rule as will be shown later in this paper. This problem whether to utilize a monument of nature for tourism or not does not of course arise when either it is *a priori* easily accessible and can be visited and viewed without difficulty or causing a threat or when on the contrary it lies to such an extent out of the way and access to it is so difficult that making it accessible would require unproportionately great efforts and high costs. Apart from these cases it is principally essential to consider this question very carefully; decisive factors are likely to be whether similar monuments of nature occur fairly frequently within the same region or administrative unit or what the general situation in the respective area is like. If the decision is positive, i. e. that it should be utilized for tourism, then the various measures to be undertaken must be modified according to local conditions and requirements; under no circumstances should one proceed according to a standard model. When going over the list of measures in detail, a process where in respect of the above mentioned measures 1–3 there is a close interdependence, the following elements may in detail be of importance or even decisive: The provision of access may be seen in three ways: access by a major line of communication as far as that point, from where a walk to the site is not an unreasonable request; access to the immediate vicinity of the monument of nature so that depending on its nature it may be viewed from a certain distance; in certain cases and always in the case of caves access into the monument of nature itself. In each of these cases the number of visitors that may be expected and the maximum capacity of the object in accomodating visitors will be of prime importance. In respect of the general accessibility the kind of access provided by the nearest existing main line of communication as well as the distance between it and the monument of nature and the character of the terrain to be crossed will be decisive. According to these conditions the decision will be taken whether cableways, roads of a certain category or even a railway branch line are to be built. In connection with this question whether direct access to the monument of nature should be provided may be answered in some cases. Essential are well secured foot paths of merely moderate gradients; they must either be sufficiently wide to make walking in both directions possible or better still be separate paths for entrance and exit respectively. In addition viewing platforms of sufficient size should be provided so that visitors who are particularly interested may halt a while and one is not forced merely to walk past in a continuous file. Direct access into the object itself, which applies primarily in the case of caves, must be constructed only after carefully considering the safety of the visitors, protecting the object from damage and strictly observing the legal provisions. In some cases access may have to be limited and certain groups of people like children or the infirm may have to be excluded.

In spite of what has been said it nevertheless appears necessary to provide a certain minimum access also for those monuments of nature which are not intended to be opened up for the general public. One purpose of this in particular is to facilitate demonstration of their features to study groups, not merely experts and students but also amateurs like groups of mountaineering clubs or associations of popular science. In these cases the people involved are of a kind capable of a somewhat greater effort. Measures which secure the safety of visitors are regulated by laws, at least in developed countries. The case is similar regarding the protection of the object. The measures needed in case of a monument of nature are not unlike those necessary in a museum, a zoo or an open air exhibition. One always has to reckon with the thoughtlessness or even recklessness of some visitors *vis-à-vis* whom the natural character of the monument has to be protected at all costs. In consequence it is advisable to keep more or less large parts – depending on the situation – of the natural monument for visitors out of bounds. This is normally quite easily done in the case of caves but is also carried out in the case of such large objects as the national parks of the United States.

A group of very important measures are those which have the presentation of the natural monument to the visitors as their objective. If a visit to it is to be meaningful the natural character and the fact that it stands for other similar ones has to be emphasized and this the more the fewer objects of its kind have been opened up for viewing by the general public in the respective region. These measures must be considered carefully and in particular should not be excessive. This applies in particular to measures which aim to enhance the aesthetic-artistic effect; these are in many cases overdone. Where natural monuments are on the surface, buildings or structures which spoil their appearance should normally be removed; exceptions are for instance where buildings of architectural merit blend with the monument of nature and achieve a particularly pleasing effect. An example is the juxtaposition of the conglomerate precipices and ancient buildings in the "olden city" of Salzburg. It goes without saying that vestiges of past human civilization within the precincts of a monument of nature should be preserved; where a direct connection between both exists this should even be emphasized. The most usual means of enhancing the effect of a monument of nature is its illumination. In caves and on the surface by night this is an *a priori* requirement. Much thought must, however, be given to the degree of illumination whether it is to be a total one or whether it should only light up parts; whether it should be single or multicoloured, or whether, in the latter case, the colours should be used simultaneously or in sequence. The use of multicoloured light brings always the danger that the object may be falsified or even become a piece of *kitsch*. A warning example for many are the illuminations of the Niagara Falls where the entertainment places in the near vicinity emphasize the unfavourable impression. Illumination is overdone also in a number of caves. This coincides with the tendency to give single objects within them, like stalagmites or stalagtites, niches, grottos or also ice figurations the names of figures of legends or fairy tales. It is true that this stimulates the imagination of the visitors and makes it easier for them to remember selected objects. However when some caves or large parts of them have been turned into veritable fairytale forests, this is nevertheless questionable and even more if this should set an example for imitation. One has conclusively to consider how far one can safely go with illumination without endangering the natural character of the object; the old rule "less is often more" applies. This kind of presentation may possibly be all right in artificial caves as for instance the disused gypsum mine "Seegrotte" near Mödling (about 10 miles from Vienna) now open to visitors. In the case of natural caves a presentation of the kind described is in bad taste and should be avoided. Incredible though it seems there have been cases where figures of gnomes were put into caves to make them more interesting for the tourists. In this context the question may be put to what extent performances of various kinds should be allowed in caves, in particular where large domes exist; permission for performances has been and is being given in a number of cases. There are certainly no objections to performing religious services in caves or in the immediate vicinity of other monuments of nature since the unusual environment may contribute to an enhancement of the depth of the experience. In the case of concerts the special acoustics should not be the sole reason for holding them there; if musical performances are given there the programme and the instruments should be chosen to suit this environment.

Great care must also be used in the preparation of the scientific interpretations to be presented to the visitors. This applies equally to the training of the guides, the preparation of guide books or tapes, or the erection of explanatory boards and maps. These tasks must be carried out by experts in the respective field. Whenever possible a small museum should be near the monument of nature and it should be furnished in such a way as to be a teaching aid. In the exhibition therein the place of the respective monument of nature within the group of phenomena to which it belongs should be demonstrated, the history of its discovery, and there should be accounts of important persons and special phenomena connected with it.

The organisation for visiting should be arranged according to the local conditions, the number of visitors to be expected; it must conform to local byelaws and should be set up in agreement with the local and regional tourist organisations. The monument of nature should similarly be made a part of regional tourism. It should nevertheless be stressed that the institution in whose care a monument of nature lies may have to take a firm stand *vis-à-vis* demands of a tourist organisation if these might lessen the natural character of the object. Service buildings are normally to be put up at the end of the access route or at the entrance to the immediate vicinity of the object. These buildings are box offices, waiting and refreshment rooms, lavatories etc. as well as the museum mentioned and finally souvenir shops – of the latter as few as possible. Everything else should be kept well away from a monument of nature and all attempts to turn it into a sort of fairground with swings and roundabouts should be nipped in the bud.

The problem "Monument of nature and tourism" can only be solved in such a way that people of our present civilisation, many of whom have little understanding of nature, are shown how to think once again in harmony with nature.

Geographical constraints on tourist development in small midsea islands

ALEXANDER MELAMID, New York, N. Y., U.S.A.*

Ever since the publication of the adventures of Robinson Crusoe, many youngsters and oldsters have dreamt of spending their lives – or at least a vacation – on a small mid-sea island far from the cares of their regular activities in developed societies. Today with the availability of air services, it is relatively easy to realize these dreams and many mid-sea islands have accomodated to this tourist interest. As virtually all these islands are part of the developing world, and usually these islands have no other economic alternatives, tourism is in fact the only means these areas have to advance their standard of living.

Due to this dependence on tourism for economic betterment, all these islands suffer from a contrast between the affluence of the tourists and their own poverty. However, this contrast is shared by mainland and other tourist areas in the developing world, and I will therefore concentrate my attention on a geographical problem which is characteristic of mid-sea islands and which defines them: how to get supplies both for the tourist and the resident population to these areas. As these islands are, by definition, located far from mainlands, supplies cannot be transported there by barges or small ships. Instead, relatively large ships are required, which implies large tonnages of deliveries – preferably, today, by container ships. Thus minimum sizes or thresholds are substantial and shipping economists regard vessels of under 10.000 tons as no longer economical for this purpose. These minimum sizes can be expected to increase further with the changing technology of ocean transportation. In contrast, as recently as 1950, ships could be induced to call at some of these islands to deliver cargoes as small as 200 tons. Although air transportation can be used for some tourist and other supplies, it is only economical for some high value products[1] and certainly not for such heavy requirements as basic food, furniture, kitchen materials, pianos, etc., as well as for almost all supplies for the local population. However, air transportation will bring the tourists and will also serve the personal transportation needs of the inhabitants.

A good case study to investigate this problem of supplies are the Seychelles Islands which are located in the Indian Ocean over 1.000 miles east of Mombasa, Kenya and 2.000 miles west of Bombay, India. Described in 1881 as a "Garden of Eden" by General Gordon – later of Khartoum fame – this archipelago has a total land surface of 107 square miles divided among 86 islands located mainly in about 400.000 square miles of ocean. With an oceanic equatorial climate, beautiful beaches, bays and steep granitic mountains and a French speaking population, mainly of African origin, of about 60.000, the islands definitely qualify as a desirable mid-sea tourist area.

---

* Dr. ALEXANDER MELAMID, Professor of Economics, New York University, N. Y., USA

[1] MELAMID, A.: Thünen's Theories in geographical analysis of economic growth. *Proceedings, 20th International Geographical Congress,* London 1964

Significant tourist development began only in 1971 after the construction of an airport, the first in the island group, suitable for use by large aircraft.[2] Simultaneously with the construction of the airport, hotels – together with the required infrastructure of roads, sewers, water reservoirs – were also built and services such as banks, car and yacht rentals, etc., as well as better telecommunication connections, were provided. During this period the local port was also improved to handle vessels up to 20.000 tons. Today 1.700 tourist beds, mainly in luxury and first class hotels are available and several direct daily air services bring visitors from Europe and the Middle East. Almost daily direct air service is available from the Far East and on three days a week good connecting services via Mauritius provide transportation with South Africa and Australia. The number of tourists increased from about 4.000 in 1971[3] to over 45.000 in 1976. Tourist and other development is concentrated on the island of Mahé, largest of the island group which contains almost 50 per cent. of the total land area and 85 per cent. of the population. Here, the airport was built. As a result of this development, per capita income on the islands increased to $ 411 in 1975, having probably more than quadrupled since 1968 when construction of the airport, hotels, etc., began.

Most of the labor required for this construction boom was available locally, reinforced by Seychelles nationals expelled from East Africa after independence and Africanization in the 1960s, who had been working there mainly in the building and allied trades, some of them for three generations. During the peak of the construction period (to the end of 1973), about 25 percent of the working population was engaged in this activity. Supplies for most construction activities as well as most other imports were shipped to Mahé by charter vessels as the quantities then required were large enough to warrant such transportation both from Europe and other points of origin. Additional supplies from Europe could also be relatively easily obtained as the closing of the Suez Canal (1967–1976) permitted diversion of liners en route to Western India, Pakistan, and the Persian Gulf to Mahé.

During 1974–1976, the construction boom came gradually to a halt. By today, import requirements are no longer large enough to warrant charter of whole ships. Shared ship charters are difficult to arrange, as other likely destinations (mainly Red Sea or East African ports), are badly congested and cause delay (as, for example, a three to four month delay recently at Jidda in Saudi Arabia). The problem is aggravated by the geographically diverse origin of imports: industrial products come mainly from Europe or the Far East and less significantly from South Africa and Australia, whilst agricultural products come mainly from Australia as well as South and East Africa. Use of cruise ships, mainly from South Africa, has proven not very satisfactory due to the small quantities carried by such vessels and occasional difficulties in unloading. Small tankers bring petroleum products regularly from East Africa, as well as on occasion from other western Indian Ocean refineries, but these ships cannot normally be used for other cargoes.

During 1976, the old-established and heavily subsidized British liner service, Bombay-Mombasa, was terminated for an overall lack of cargoes. This service had supplied the Seychelles since the middle of the 19th century and during most

---

[2] For military purposes a weekly sea-plane service from Mombasa had existed since 1963 which had no effect on tourist development.

[3] No statistics are available before 1971. All statistics quoted here are from government of the Seychelles: *A review of the economy,* Victoria, 1976.

of this period had been the islands' only regular link to the outside world. Although an Indian Government line has promised to call at Mahé, no arrangements for a service schedule have yet been made and the islands will thus have to rely on charter vessels or air cargo for its supplies. Exports – mainly cinnamon, copra and, more recently, tea – provide only small cargoes and thus no attraction for shipping services.

A factor seriously aggravating the shipping problem is local manufacturing. Formerly, beer and soda were imported in bottles which occupied a significant amount of cargo space. Today these beverages are produced locally (by one firm having rights to a number of name brands); bottles are recirculated and imports are significantly reduced. Some furniture and appliances are also now locally assembled, which similarly reduces space requirements of imports. Location of these manufacturing plants in the Seychelles, all on Mahé, is economical as the industrial processes utilized are weight or volume gaining, which in accordance with Weber's model,[4] made production at the market attractive in addition to providing local employment opportunities.

Under these circumstances, there remain several alternatives to keep tourism, the main and really only motor of the local economy, going.

1. Greater use of air freight to bring in supplies. As the Seychelles are distant from most points of origin for its imports and aircraft cannot complete turn-arounds in one day (as in Bermuda of Carribean islands), air freight is very expensive and cannot be used for most tourist and other requirements. Use of ship transportation to East Africa and air transportation from there has proven unsatisfactory. However, the availability of relatively cheap air transportation from East Africa has already induced a growing volume of imports from there – mainly meat and other agricultural products from European properties in Kenya – which has thus become the second most important supplier of the Seychelles.[5]

2. Provision of more storage facilities to handle more imports over a longer period of time. Such provision is rather expensive, both in financing and construction, and is regarded as unsuitable for some tourist requirements. There is no doubt that the islands now require more storage facilities and the government will have to aid in the financing process. However, even this financing will not resolve the islands' tourist supply problem.

3. Calculation by government and consulting economists has shown that increasing the number of tourist beds from the present 1.700 to 3.500 would raise shipping requirements to about threshold levels of modern vessels. An expansion of this magnitude necessitates doubling the capacities of the local road system (very expensive on granitic islands with a heavy equatorial rainfall), adding to water reservoir capacities (which would terminate agricultural activities in several inland valleys) and costly sewers, provision of more golf courses (which would use up much coastal agricultural land), and greater, if not excess, utilization of the extra-ordinarily beautiful beaches which, limited in number and size, are the greatest tourist asset of the islands. Thus, the doubling of the number of tourist beds is very expensive and most the costs would have to be borne by the public purse. Further, such an expansion would significantly decrease the islands' main tourist and agricultural assets.

4. The opposite move would be to cut back the number of tourists to those using only luxury accomodations. This would limit the number of tourist beds to

[4] FRIEDRICH, C. J. (ed.): *Alfred Weber's theory of location of industries*. Chicago 1929.

[5] Including petroleum products. Great Britain is the foremost supplier. The third-ranking supplier is now Holland.

about 800. Higher prices for these tourists would permit more air imports but would increase the supply problems of the local population besides increasing unemployment. A similar tourist policy is now considered in East Africa where the large number of visitors in recent years have significantly reduced the wildlife amenities in national parks.

5. Diversion of imports to South Africa would permit use of charter vessels although not all imports could be obtained from this source. For foreign exchange reasons, it would also entail accepting more tourists from South Africa, who are already now increasing in numbers. Despite the expulsion of its nationals from East Africa, the Seychelles Republic is a member of the Union of African States and such economic arrangements may not be acceptable to its largely black, if French speaking, population.

6. Subsidization of a Seychelles shipping line; several governments, especially in Latin America, have resorted to this device, although not always for this reason. Subsidization is extremely expensive and total costs cannot be forecast with any accuracy. In view of the limited revenue of the islands, adoption of this alternative is unlikely.

So far, the government of the now independent Seychelles has not yet decided on any of these alternatives, hoping that its development will survive with occasional ship charters and help from other governments. However, the alternatives faced by this government clearly describe the difficulties faced by tourism in mid-sea islands.

The other islands of the Seychelles group suffer from the same problems in an extreme form: their cargo requirements are far too limited to warrant any shipping services. Most of these islands can only be reached by private arrangements and only the main islands are connected to Mahé by limited ferry or air services. Despite the attractions of these islands, tourist development is very limited and no plans have been formulated for their enlargement.

Another example is tourist development on Easter Island which lies in the Pacific over 2.000 miles east of Chile. Here an airport, together with a 120 bed hotel, is supposed to supply tourist revenues to the (about 2.000) inhabitants. Supplies are brought to the island twice a year by a steamer as well as by a weekly air service. Obviously heavy subsidies are required to keep this tourist development going – at present less than 25 per cent utilized. Similar considerations stopped tourist development on several small outer islands of the Fiji group, although these islands – like the Seychelles – have all the attributes of Robinson Crusoe's island. However, several tourist developments on small French Pacific islands are apparently kept going by means of heavy subsidies from metropolitan France.[6] For supply reasons, attempts to develop tourism on the Cook Islands (New Zealand) are being delayed, although a 103-room luxury hotel was completed there in April 1977. Similarly, nothing is being done to develop tourism on the Falkland Islands despite general recommendations of the Lord Shackleton mission.[7]

The contrast with the Cayman Islands (100 square miles, population about 12.000 in 1975), located in the Caribbean Sea, is significant. These islands are located closer to the mainlands of Florida, Jamaica, Central America and Cuba (although the latter is not used for supplies at present), than any of the islands described above. Thus, barges and small ships can make deliveries. Even trailer

---

[6] No statistical data were made available to the author

[7] LORD SHACKLETON: "Prospect of the Falkland Islands", *The Geographical Journal*, London 1977, p. 1–13

trucks are used for direct deliveries from inland points in the United States to destinations inland on the two main islands, and increasing sizes of ocean-going vessels have not affected the development of tourism there.[8]

Despite its more marked mid-sea location, Bermuda (30 square miles) shares some of the tourist development characteristics of the Cayman Islands. Relatively small ships can make the journey from North America. In addition, the affluent population of about 60.000, together with the very large number of tourists (411.783 in 1975),[9] permits regular imports by larger and more economical vessels.

In conclusion, we can observe that the tourist potential of small mid-sea islands, despite their intrinsic and sentimental attractions, is limited due to geographical constraints of size and location. Only those islands where the constraints do not fully operate – as in the Cayman Islands or Bermuda – can expect tourist development in an age of increasing size of ships.

---

[8] MELAMID, A.: Development in the Cayman Islands. *Geographical Review,* New York 1975, pp. 107–109

[9] Selected tourism statistics of Bermuda 1971–1975. Bermuda Department of Tourism, 1976

Predicting recreational highway traffic in Canada at a time of scarcity and high cost of motor fuel

ROY WOLFE, Downsview, Ontario, Canada*

The present paper is the outgrowth of findings made during a year of sabbatical research in Europe in 1975–1976. The purpose of the sabbatical research was to compare the recreational landscapes in Europe with those earlier examined in North America, to discover which kinds were most vulnerable to damage should international and internal traffic become increasingly difficult through growing scarcity and higher cost of motor fuel. It was tentatively found that the resorts most resistant to damage were those consisting of individually- owned second homes that were within the primary recreational field of the cities where the owners lived. Cars would be less used for work trips during the week so that there would be gasoline available for the weekend trip to the cottage.

This finding led to the question: what would be the situation in Canada if stringent fuel rationing were introduced (with absolute priority being given to utilitarian trips) or if the price per gallon of gasoline were raised past a certain critical point? An analogy to the phase rule presents itself: what fuel cost would correspond to the critical temperature at which a chemical compound under constant pressure shifts from the liquid to the solid phase? The hypothesis was formulated that, at all levels of scarcity and price below the critical point, most car owners will cut back much further on utilitarian trips than on recreational trips, where possible making greater use of mass public transit and car pools, but keeping the private car for weekend use inviolate. At some critical point, which would be different for different segments of the population (by the phase-rule analogy, pressures would be different), this situation would change, and the stubbornly-adhered-to recreational trips would at last have to be given up. Canadians would find such a condition traumatic. For many reasons, it would be advisable to search for indicators well in advance of the critical point's being reached, so that adequate policy can be implemented in good time, and suitable substitutes to recreational travel – if such exist – be employed. The possibilities may be stated in the form of the following hypothesis:

In times of scarcity and high cost of fuel, the volume of recreational highway traffic decreases less than that of utilitarian traffic.

In 1967 it was theorized that all highways could be characterized in terms of their seven-day traffic profiles.[1] In fig. 1 are presented the ideal seven-day profiles for summer traffic of nine types of highways, from the commuter road at one extreme to the tourist arterial at the other. The hypothesis stated above may now be reformulated in technical terms:

In times of stress, occasioned by scarcity and high cost of motor fuel, there is a shift in the seven day profile of a given stretch of highway in a direction away from

---

* Dr. ROY WOLFE, Professor, Department of Geography, York University, Downsview, Ontario, Canada

[1] WOLFE, R.: *A theory of recreational highway traffic.* D. H. O. Report No. RR 128, Department of Highways, Ontario 1967, 53 pp.

the profile characteristic of a commuter route and towards that of a tourist arterial.

Each of the profiles in fig. 1 is completely described by the value of the variable *R* found below it.[2] For the "ideal" commuter highway the value is 0.71, and for the "ideal" tourist arterial it is 1.31. Thus our original hypothesis may be given this final shape:

In times of stress, occasioned by scarcity and high cost of motor fuel, the value of "R" for a given highway increases.

Figure 1: Ideal figures of summer traffic

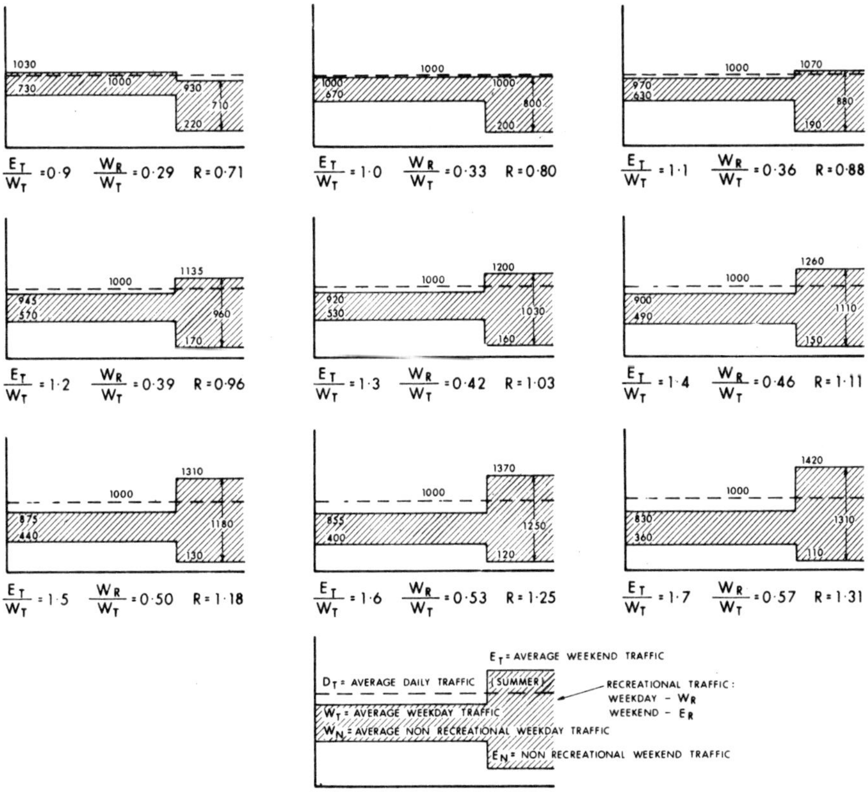

Source: WOLFE, R.: *A theory of recreational highway traffic.* D. H. O. Report No. RR 128, Department of Highways, Ontario, Toronto 1967

---

[2] R is defined as "the ratio of weekend recreational traffic volume to average daily traffic volume in summer". Empirical values for R on Ontario highways may be derived from the following predictive model (WOLFE, *op.cit.*, p. 17):

$$R = 0.840\,\frac{W_R}{W_T} + 3.410\,\frac{D_T}{W_T} - 3.056 + 0.118\left(\frac{W_R}{W_T}\right)^{1/2} \log^{-1}\left(\frac{W_R}{W_T}\right) \log\left(\frac{3.5D_T}{W_T} - 2.5\right)$$

W_R = weekday recreational traffic volume,

W_T = average weekday traffic volume, and

D_T = average daily traffic volume, in summer.

To quantify the expected increase in "R" it will be necessary to devise what might be called a "distress" factor. Possibly the resulting formulation will resemble the following:

$$R_s = kR_n e^{d(R_n - 1)}$$

in which R is as defined above, with value R_n in normal times and R_s in times of stress; k is an empirically determined constant; and d may turn out to be the desired "distress" factor.

A formulation of this kind may prove, on application, to be insufficiently flexible, in which case it may be better to adopt a kind of formulation patterned on the technique initiated in the construction of the inertia model.[3] Here distance was made a function of distance (a rubric appropriated by J. BEAMAN[4] for use in the title of his paper on recreational travel models). This is a feedback mechanism to allow the perception of distance to influence the effect that distance has on a given activity. In general terms, a variable is made its own parameter, and parameters are no longer exclusively constants, as before. In a similar way, a formulation might be sought in which the distress factor becomes a function of itself. This procedure could conceivably turn it into its opposite: a "stubborness factor", and would thus help explain the seeming paradox that, the greater the external stresses are, the more obligatory does an activity that is usually thought of as discretionary become: in appearance, the weekend trip to the cottage becomes, not a disposable luxury, but a need, taking precedence (in expenditure of energy resources) over trips that really are obligatory, the trips to work.

Proportion of city dwellers owning their own homes who also own vacation homes[5]

Province	per cent.
Newfoundland	7.8
Prince Edward Island	11.0
Nova Scotia	12.0
New Brunswick	13.6
Quebec	13.1
Ontario	10.3
Manitoba	10.0
Saskatchewan	8.5
Alberta	4.7
British Columbia	4.7
Yukon and N. W. T.	7.3
Canada	9.8

[3] WOLFE, R.: The inertia model. *Journal of leisure research.* Washington, D. C., 1972, pp. 73–76

[4] BEAMAN, J.: Distance and the reaction to distance as a function of distance. *Journal of leisure research,* Washington, D. C., 1974, pp. 220–231

[5] WOLFE, R.: Vacation homes as social indicators: Some preliminary findings and suggestions for future research. *Leisure Science.* New York 1977, pp. 21–35

It may be necessary to insert an additional factor into the predictive model, one that will take into account the differing travel habits in different parts of the country. For example, the United States and Canada are alike in exhibiting great regional disparities in the propensity to own vacation homes. In the United States the pattern is complex, but it is remarkably simple in Canada: as can be seen from the following table, the propensity to own vacation homes is highest in the eastern und central part of the country and lowest in the west.

Since it has been established that travel to vacation homes is especially sensitive to the friction of distance, this factor should be given special consideration in the modified prediction model.[6]

A *distress factor* could serve a function in predictive models similar to that of the interest rate in cost-benefit analysis. It would therefore help solve the extremely difficult problem of quantifying the concept of *substitutability:* one activity or site or road will act as a substitute for another if the sum of its computed distress factors is no greater than that of the one to be substituted for. The method is of course not infallible; there are occasions when no substitute will do; but in a fallible world, we must grasp at any consolation we can, and for the quantifier of substitutability the distress factor may well be such.

[6] WOLFE, R.: Parameters of recreational travel in Ontario. *Proceedings,* Canadian Good Roads Association, Ottawa 1965, pp. 235–261

Ski et stations de sports d'hiver dans le monde

BERNARD BARBIER, Aix-en-Provence, France*

17.500 remontées mécaniques, trois mille stations et centres de sports d'hiver, 37.000.000 de skieurs, une quarantaine de pays concernés. Ces chiffres, qui fixent un ordre de grandeur plus qu'ils ne prétendent enfermer la réalité, montrent bien la place que tient le ski dans le monde à notre époque. Le ski, moyen de transport historique de certains pays, est devenu, depuis quelque vingt ans, un sport d'agrément dont la clientèle s'étend chaque année, encore que son prix en limite la croissance.

Il s'agit donc d'un phénomène important, qui n'est plus le privilège de quelques stations célèbres d'avant 1939. Il convient donc de l'examiner. Or, si les études partielles abondent, les synthèses sont pratiquement absentes. Cet article veut donc faire une analyse géographique du ski et des stations de sports d'hiver dans le monde. Pour cela, il convient de faire un inventaire, afin de localiser et de chiffrer skieurs, remontées mécaniques, stations etc. Il est nécessaire aussi de caractériser ces centres de sports d'hiver, à travers leurs équipements sportifs, leurs hébergements, leurs relations avec le milieu physique, l'influence qu'elles reçoivent du milieu socio-économique etc. Bien sûr, il faudra aussi tenter d'expliquer tout cela.

Disons tout de suite que, malgré son extension à plus du quart des pays de la planète, le ski n'en concerne, de façon profonde, qu'un nombre encore limité: les six pays alpins et les deux de l'Amérique du Nord anglo-saxonne détiennent 80% des remontées mécaniques et 70% des stations. Cependant, la place tenue par le ski dans des pays aussi différents des précédents (ou entre eux) que la Finlande, le Japon ou la Tchécoslovaquie, ainsi que l'existence de stations au Chili, au Liban, en Iran, ou en U.R.S.S., justifient une étude menée à l'échelle mondiale.

Nous commencerons par la présentation des méthodes utilisées pour le recueil de la documentation et par l'exposé de données chiffrées. Nous chercherons ensuite à avancer des explications ou des hypothèses sur cette nouvelle activité touristique.

1. *La recherche de documents et l'inventaire*

1.1. *Les sources de la documentation*

Si les articles, voire même les livres, consacrés à l'étude des sports d'hiver sont très nombreux, il est à noter que ceux-ci se limitent à leur examen dans un pays ou une région, ou bien ne concernent qu'un aspect de la question. Une vue globale manque. Toutefois, la lecture de ces publications est indispensable pour formuler des explications et celle-ci, de même que la connaissance que nous avons de nombreuses stations en Europe de l'Ouest, en Scandinavie ou dans les pays socialistes, nous a permis une approche »sensible« du phénomène, mais sans fournir la base chiffrée indispensable à une étude d'ensemble.

Nous avons donc écrit à tous les Offices Nationaux du Tourisme, à Paris tout d'abord, mais bien souvent aussi dans le pays d'origine. Nous avons reçu une

* Dr. BERNARD BARBIER, Professeur, Institut de Géographie, Université d'Aix-Marseille, France

abondante documentation publicitaire, qui nous a donné une multitude de précisions. Ceci a été complété par le recours à des annuaires statistiques, ou à des brochures spécialisées faisant le point dans un pays.[1]

Une fois de plus, nous avons constaté que le même souci de recherche pouvait animer plusieurs personnes. En même temps que nous menions ce travail, nous avons découvert quelques inventaires dressés récemment à propos des remontées mécaniques et des stations de ski, notamment dans les revues »Aménagement et montagne« et »Economie et Prospective de la montagne« (cf. bibliographie). Nous avons utilisé toutes ces précisions chiffrées, en particulier l'enquête lourde sur les remontées mécaniques.

1.2. Les difficultés et les limites de l'enquête

Si le récolement de toutes les données est un problème difficile mais non insurmontable, leur exploitation se heurte à des difficultés considérables pour lesquelles aucune solution vraiment satisfaisante n'est possible.

Tout d'abord l'absence de réponses précises, même dans des pays où l'appareil statistique existe, ne permet pas de remplir convenablement toutes les colonnes des tableaux: les U.S.A. et l'U.R.S.S., par exemple, n'ont pas fourni les données nécessaires. Lorsque la réponse exíste, elle indique surtout ce qui est important et néglige les petits centres de sports d'hiver, qu'il faut recenser autrement. Si plusieurs relevés minutieux et sérieux ont été dressés pour le même phénomène, on constate des différences notables d'une source à l'autre; même en France, établir la liste des stations de ski avec leurs équipements sportifs et leur capacité d'hébergement relève de la quadrature du cercle et il faut se contenter d'un ordre de grandeur. (cf. Annexes: Tableaux 7a et 7b).

Mais il y a aussi un problème de vocabulaire. Qu'appelle-t-on station ou centre de sports d'hiver? Si le Québec et l'Autriche publient des brochures qui contiennent des listes exhaustives en y incluant les plus petits centres, d'autres pays signalent d'abord ce qui compte pour le tourisme international et il faut poser de nouvelles questions pur être à peu près renseigné. En Scandinavie, la pratique du ski de fond ne nécessite aucun engin de remontée et il suffit de pistes balisées avec de petits hébergements pour constituer un centre de ski; dans certains cas, là où c'est possible, des pistes de slalom s'ajoutent, mais elles ne constituent pas l'élément important. Qu'est-ce qu'une remontée mécanique? Nous n'avons retenu que celles qui sont fixes en éliminant les téléskis mobiles; ceux-ci, qui sont environ 2.500, n'ont peut-être pas été mis à part dans certaines statistiques sans qu'il soit possible de le savoir. Il n'est pas toujours facile non plus d'éliminer les remontées qui mènent à des belvédères, sans jamais être empruntées par des skieurs. Dans le domaine de la capacité d'accueil, la difficulté est encore plus grande. Selon les cas, on a affaire, sans que cela soit toujours explicité, soit aux seuls lits hôteliers, soit aux lits „utiles" (hôtels et locations de qualité), soit à la capacité totale réellement calculée (avec dortoirs, colonies de jeunes, auberges de jeunesse etc.).

Comme il est nécessaire d'aboutir à des résultats, nous avons préféré publier les données recueillies, malgré leur marge d'incertitude. Cela permet de se faire une idée approximative de la réalité et de raisonner. Cela permet aussi de provoquer des réponses et des corrections, que nous souhaitons nombreuses, afin d'arriver à une connaissance meilleure du ski dans le monde.

---

[1] Le dépouillement de cette documentation a été en grande partie effectué par des chercheurs de l'Institut de Géographie d'Aix-en-Provence en constituant les dossiers exigés pour le „C2 Tourisme" ou dans le cadre de leur maitrise, Nous tenous à remercier tres vivement à cet effet Mlle F. CHARLET et M. M. ANTONELLI (depouillement genéral), Mmes F. MUCKENSTURM et L. LACROIX (arc alpin), Mlle I. BROUSSE (Norvege), Mme LARUELLE (Pologne). Mlles A. FIORANI et R. JIMENEZ (Tchécoslovaquie).

1.3. Données chiffrées globales
(cf. Annexes, Tableaux 1 à 7)

Plusieurs tableaux sont donnés. Nous rappelons que les chiffres ne sont qu'indicatifs et doivent être considérés avec prudence.

Les remontées mécaniques (R. M.)

Le nombre des remontées mécaniques (tableau 1) est sans doute un des moins inexacts: 17.329 engins, dont 12.424 téléskis (71,7%) et 4.905 engins téléporteurs (28,3%[2]); si l'on y ajoute quelque 2.500 remontées démontables (500 en France, 500 en Suisse), on arrive à un total de 20.000 engins pour hisser les skieurs au sommet des pistes. Leur répartition souligne une forte concentration au profit de quelques pays: 11.245 (64,9%) an Europe occidentale (Scandinavie exclue), dont 10.481 (60,5%) dans les six pays alpins (Yougoslavie incluse); 3.307 aux Etats-Unis et Canada; 1.159 (6,7%) au Japon; ainsi, neuf pays totalisent 14.947 remontées, soit 86,3% de celles du monde. Le restant, soit 2.382 (13,7%), est réparti entre une trentaine d'autres pays; si l'on excepte les pays scandinaves (610 R.M. = 3,5%) et les pays socialistes d'Europe (1.242 R.M. = 7,2%), il reste 530 engins (3,1%) qui s'éparpillent entre une vingtaine de pays.

Si l'on rapporte ce nombre des remontées à celui des habitants (tableau 2), la place des deux petits pays que sont l'Autriche et la Suisse est vigoureusement soulignée, avec une remontée mécanique pour moins de cinq mille habitants, Tchécoslovaquie, France, Suède, Canada, Italie, Norvège, ont une R.M. pour 20.000–35.000 personnes. Puis, la densité diminue: si l'on n'arrive pas à 100.000 h. pour un engin avec la R.F.A., la Finlande, les U.S.A., la Nouvelle Zélande et le Japon, on dépasse ce rapport pour plusieurs pays et l'on atteint même le ratio d'un million ou plus pour une R.M.!

La progression des R.M. est récente et s'est effectuée surtout à partir des années soixante. L'Autriche a doublé sont parc entre 1965 et 1975; la Suisse a quadruplé le sien entre 1961 et 1975; la Slovaquie est passée de 49 engins à 357 de 1964 à 1975, soit une multiplication par sept; en France, entre 1970 et 1975 seulement, la progression a été de 40%. Aux Etats-Unis et au Canada, le nombre de remontées mécaniques mises en service annuellement a été de 100 à 200 et n'a diminué qu'avec la crise née en 1973.

Quels types de remonte-pente ont été mis en place? Le téléski a partout triomphé (12.424, soit 71,7%); son pourcentage dans le monde comme dans presque tous les pays est le plus fort et ne cesse de s'élever (76,5% en Autriche en 1965 et 84,8% en 1975; 77% en Slovaquie en 1964 et 94% en 1976). Le télésiège, rapide, de bon débit, pas trop onéreux, est aussi en progression, mais il vient partout loin après les téléskis. Le téléphérique, qui faisait l'orgueil des stations internationales, mais qui est d'un coût très élevé, est encore construit, soit dans les grands centres de ski comme élément de prestige (les dix premières stations françaises en ont chacune de un à trois, et Chamonix en dispose de sept), soit parce que la forte pente l'exige. Le funiculaire est très peu utilisé, mais a gardé une certaine faveur en Autriche.

D'un pays à l'autre, les proportions varient, mais oscillent autour de la moyenne. Deux pays font exception: le Japon, avec 97,4% d'engins téléporteurs, à cause des réglements de sécurité, et les Etats-Unis, avec 55,1%, sans doute parce qu'ils en ont les moyens.

[2] Il s'agit des télésièges, télébennes, télécabines et téléphériques; les funiculaires ne sont pas pris en compte.

Les stations et centres de ski

Le nombre des stations et centres de ski est très aléatoire et le tableau 1 avance plusieurs chiffres suivis d'un point d'interrogation, parce que les définitions et les relevés sont trés variables, d'un pays à l'autre et à l'intérieur d'un même pays (cf. tableau 7b). Le nombre de 3.000 est probable, sans plus.

La localisation de ces villes et villages consacrés au ski est, évidemment, celle des remontées mécaniques. Les neuf pays alpins, nord-américains et japonais, qui détenaient 86,3% des R.M., disposent de 79,5% des stations; la différence entre les deux pourcentages provient de ce que leurs stations sont mieux équipées.

Il y a de grandes disparités entre ces centres de ski. Leur altitude est très variable. Si Narvik, au delà du cercle polaire, est au niveau de la mer, les moyennes montagnes d'Europe localisent leurs stations à généralement moins de 1.000 m, alors que cette altitude est souvent dépassée dans les Alpes (32% des cas en Autriche; 88% des cas en France, où la base de certaines stations est au dessus de 2.000 m); dans les Andes, les altitudes sont beaucoup plus fortes, avec 2.800 m pour Portillo (Chili) et, record du monde, 5.300 pour Nevado del Ruiz, l'unique station colombienne, mais à quelques degrés seulement au nord de l'Equateur. Les dénivellations sont aussi d'une grande diversité; celles des centres scandinaves ou du Québec sont au grand maximum de quelques centaines de mètres, mais les grandes stations alpines offrent de 800 à 1.000 m, et quelquefois davantage.

Toutefois, c'est par leurs équipements et leur capacité d'accueil que les stations se différencient. Les centres disposant de moins de 10 R.M. et d'au plus quelques milliers de lits sont les seuls existant dans la plupart des pays et constituent l'énorme majorité, même dans les grands pays de sports d'hiver. Ceux-ci, toutefois, offrent à leur clientèle quelques très grands centres. Ainsi, les pays alpins (cf. tableaux 3, 4 et 5) disposent de 126 stations qui ont chacune plus de quinze remontées mécaniques et dont la capacité d'hébergement doit aller de 5–10.000 lits jusqu'à environ 25.000; il s'agit alors de véritables villes qui, le dimanche, sont encore plus peuplées si l'on tient compte des skieurs venus pour la journée. Mais, là encore, les différences se dessinent. L'Autriche, qui est le premier pays mondial du ski, est restée fidèle à la station petite ou moyenne, avec au plus quinze R.M., et n'offre que dix centres en ayant plus de quinze (2,8% du total); la Suisse lui ressemble, avec seulement onze grandes stations (5,4%), mais la France se distingue avec cinquante-six grandes localités de sports d'hiver (21,5% du total), suivie par l'Italie (32 = 10,7%). La comparaison entre la France et la Suisse quant au nombre de lits des stations (tableau 5) est éloquente: 21 stations (8,1% du total) ont plus de 10.000 lits touristiques pour notre pays et 7 (3,4%) pour notre voisin helvétique! Il est possible que les chiffres de remontées et de lits soient à réviser, mais cela ne changerait en rien le sens des comparaisons.

Autres données

L'on ne dispose que de peu de données pour évaluer le domaine skiable, c'est-à-dire la superficie sur laquelle les skieurs peuvent évoluer. Parmi les pays alpins, la France aurait les plus vastes champs de ski (1.900 km^2), suivie de la Suisse, de l'Italie (1.350, km^2), de l'Autriche (1.050 km^2) et de l'Allemagne (450 km^2), mais Suisse et Autriche ont déjà fortement entamé leur capital, ce qui laisse un bel avenir à la France et à l'Italie. Cependant, les Alpes, bien avant la fin du siècle, ne suffiraient pas à la demande, estime-t-on couramment, et il faudrait alors aller plus loin.

Les statistiques montrent que le nombre de skieurs est faible: 37 millions en 1970, soit même pas 1% de la population mondiale (cf. tableau 6). Le Japon (9 millions) et l'Amérique du Nord (7 millions) tiennent la tête, suivis des pays européens dont tous ne sont pas des pays de montagne. Mais, si l'on rapporte le chiffre des skieurs à celui de la population, les nations montagnardes et alpines sont au premiere rang; il faut notamment souligner les forts pourcentages de la Suisse (31%), de l'Autriche (28%) et de la Scandinavie (17,7%), certains pays sont inattendus dans ce classement, comme la Bulgarie (11,5%) ou la Tchécoslovaquie (6,8%), ou encore la Belgique (3,1%). On attend une croissance de l'effectif des skieurs qui passerait à 56 millions en 1982.

Les données concernant la fréquentation sont les plus aléatoires de toutes. En se limitant aux statistiques des flux internationaux (1976), précisons que 90% des skieurs restent dans leur pays (cf. tableau 8). Ceux qui se rendent à l'étranger (3.600.000) proviennent surtout d'Allemagne (2.000.000) et, pour une part plus faible, de quelques autres pays: Belgique (300.000), Royaume-Uni (250.000), France (200.000). Les grands bénéficiaires de ces flux sont l'Autriche (1.200.000, dont 760.000 Allemands), la Suisse (960.000 dont 500.000 Allemands); la France, malgré ses progrès, ne reçoit que 360.000 skieurs (dont 140.000 Allemands), mais voudrait doubler ce chiffre dans les années à venir. Il est à souligner que certains skieurs n'hésitent pas à franchir d'énormes distances pour chercher d'autres neiges: 100.000 Américains et autant de Japonais franchissent chaque année leurs frontières et viennent skier ailleurs, essentiellement dans les Alpes et, là encore, surtout au profit de l'Autriche et de la Suisse, mais ils ne sont que 5,5% du total.

Toutes ces données concernant le ski dans le monde ont permis, malgré les réserves qu'il faut toujours rappeler, de se faire une idée de la réalité, mais il convient de les expliquer géographiquement.

2. *Le commentaire des données*

La lecture de tout ce qui vient d'être présenté fait venir immédiatement à l'esprit un certain nombre d'explications; il est certain que la proximité de montagnes enneigées et l'existence de pays à haut revenu individuel permettent de comprendre beaucoup de la pratique du ski, mais ce ne sont pas les seules raisons et il y a beaucoup de nuances à apporter.

Il faut classer les facteurs explicatifs. On serait tenté de mettre en premier les données naturelles, mais nous pensons que l'apparition d'une demande croissante est un élément encore plus notable.

2.1. *Le rôle de la demande*

Le ski, malgré quelques efforts de démocratisation, reste un sport cher, et ne peuvent s'y livrer que ceux dont le revenu est suffisant. Il est donc normal que les skieurs proviennent à 94% de dix-sept pays à haut niveau de vie individuel, que les stations s'y trouvent concentrées à 90% et les remontées mécaniques à 91%. Ces pourcentages fort élevés s'accroîtront encore dans les années qui viennent, puisque les dix-huit millions de nouveaux skieurs attendus pour 1982 seront originaires presque uniquement de ces pays.

Comme le ski a connu dans ces pays un développement considérable depuis la guerre, le niveau moyen des skieurs s'est remarquablement élevé et les exigences de ceux-ci se sont accrues d'autant. Les clients, surtout s'ils sont jeunes, ne se contentent plus de stations faiblement équipées et à faibles dénivellations; ils veulent des domaines skiables vastes, variés, aux différences d'altitude de 800 m ou plus. Cela a entraîné une modification dans la répartition des centres de ski alpins. Les stations »historiques« des Préalpes françaises du Nord, qui avaient reçu les premiers skieurs parisiens, lyonnais et grenoblois, se sont trouvé dépassées dans les années soixante; quelques-unes seulement ont pu établir de nouvelles remontées mécaniques plus hautes, comme Morzine, mais le succès est allé aux jeunes stations des grandes Alpes internes du Nord (Tignes, Val d'Isère). Le skieur marseillais se suffisait de la montagne de Lure ou de celle de Ceüse (près de Gap), mais les cinq remontées de chacune et lurs quelques centaines de mètres de dénivellation ne peuvent rivaliser actuellement avec les 26 engins de Vars ou les 46 de Serre-Chevalier qui toutes deux offrent des pistes de 1.000 mètres de descente! Les stations se relient entre elles pour étendre le champ d'action des sportifs; en 1977, de nouvelles remontées ont uni Pra-Loup et la Foux d'Allos qui totalisent ainsi 42 remonte-pentes. La haute-montagne a des avantages certains.

Toutefois, certains correctifs doivent être apportés à ce rôle essentiel du niveau de vie. Les pays scandinaves sont certainement parmi les plus riches d'Europe mais, s'ils ont proportionnellement beaucoup plus de skieurs que les Allemands, cela ne tient qu'en partie à leur richesse, puisqu'ils pratiquent un ski de fond peu onéreux et qu'ils ont seulement de courtes pistes de slalom. La tradition du ski dans un pays aux longs hivers enneigés tient une place essentielle. Il en est de même pour certains pays de l'Europe de l'Est (Tchécoslovaquie, par exemple) dont les revenus individuels ne sont pas encore très élevés.

La politique sociale de certains Etats peut compléter des revenus qui, quoiqu'en progrès, ne seraient pas suffisants. C'est le cas de plusieurs pays socialistes, comme la Tchécoslovaquie et la Bulgarie, mais les efforts n'en sont qu'à leurs débuts dans d'autres, comme la Pologne ou l'U.R.S.S.

Comme les skieurs laissent beaucoup d'argent dans les stations, certains Etats cherchent à les attirer chez eux pour gagner de précieuses devises.

Quelques pays riches et montagnards s'en sont fait une spécialité: 40% des clients des stations autrichiennes sont étrangers et 33% en Suisse; la France, qui n'en a que 13%, voudrait porter ce taux à 16% en 1982! Tout ceci renforce la position des grands pays où les sports d'hiver sont traditionnellement implantés, mais ceux-ci ne sont pas les seuls à vouloir recueillir la manne et de nouveaux Etats, entrent dans la concurrence, cherchent des bénéfices en séduisant les skieurs par de nouvelles stations: la Yougoslavie a déjà une bonne réputation dans ce domaine, la Tchécoslovaquie a fait un énorme effort et voudrait obtenir le déroulement des Jeux Olympiques dans les Tatras pour se faire mieux connaître, Chypre a créé deux petites stations et l'U.R.S.S. a planifié l'aménagement de son Caucase pour accueillir des Occidentaux.

Cependant, ces tentatives restent limitées par le problème de la distance.

2.2. Le rôle de la distance

Pour le skieur, comme pour n'importe quel touriste, la distance est une question de temps et d'argent. Il faut donc ne pas aller trop loin. Cela explique que les montagnes équipées soient proches des pays riches: les Alpes, entourées de régions et villes »émettrices« de skieurs, disposent donc tout naturellement de 60% des remontées mécaniques du monde et de 45% des stations. La clientèle est celle des pays alpins, mais aussi celle de pays voisins ou pas trop éloignés: plus des trois-quarts des skieurs du Bénélux fréquentent les Alpes et 60% des skieurs britanniques s'y rendent; on y voit aussi des Scandinaves.

A contrario, si l'éloignement est trop grand, les skieurs ne viennent pas: que n'a-t-on pas dit des Américains qui étaient plus près des Alpes que des Rocheuses? Seulement 1,4% des leurs franchissent l'Atlantique pour se rendre en Europe et leurs pratiquants fréquenten ces Rocheuses ou les moyennes montagnes du Nord-Est. Même l'Angleterre conserve presque la moitié de ses skieurs. Ce besoin de faire du ski, tempéré par la distance, amène la création de centres de sports d'hiver partout où la nature la permet à peu près, s'il y a une clientèle aisée proche. Ainsi, l'Angleterre a quelques stations et la Belgique dispose de la sienne; le Maroc et l'Algérie conservent les leurs du temps de la colonisation; des centres apparaissent en Turquie, en Iran, dans l'Amérique andine etc. Même dans les pays alpins, de nouvelles stations apparaissent hors des Alpes. En France, avantagée par ses nombreuses montagnes, 39% des stations se trouvent dans le Pyrénées (28 centres), les Vosges (27), le Jura (22), le Massif Central (22) et la Corse (3), et disposent de 31% des remontées mécaniques. Les petites montagnes de l'Allemagne moyenne abritent 64,5% des stations et 53,7% des remontées. En Italie, les téléskis apparaissent dans les Apennins et jusqu'en Sicile et même en Sardaigne, représentant 14% du parc italien.

Un cas particulier est posé par les skieurs de week-end; s'ils habitent Nice, Innsbruck ou Grenoble, ils ne perdent aucun temps pour aller skier. C'est déjà un peu moins simple de Marseille, de Lyon ou de Milan, mais que dire des Parisiens ou des Romains! Ce mouvement de fins de semaine favorise les stations les plus proches des agglomérations, si elles sont bien équipées en engins mécaniques; l'on a même cherché à développer en France des »stades de neige«, ayant peu d'hébergements et beaucoup de remonte-pentes, mais cela ne permet pas quand même d'admettre l'opposition que l'on a voulu établir entre stations de séjour et stations de fins de semaine: les qualités des grands domaines skiables séduiront toujours les citadins qui veulent aller en montagne pour le week-end.

2.3. Le rôle des données naturelles

S'il y a une clientèle, on équipera la montagne. Mais il faut que celle-ci présente des caractéristiques convenables; n'oublions pas que le domaine skiable reconnu bon ne couvre que 6.000 km² dans tout l'arc alpin, soit l'équivalent d'un département français!

Il faut d'abord un bon enneigement, qui tienne au moins quatre mois, pour assurer la rentabilité des investissements. Cela favorise les hautes montagnes tempérées et les pays de haute latitude; la moyenne montagne européene doit se contenter de centres de ski modestes; dans les montagnes subtropicales et tropicales, il faut s'élever haut: l'Oukaimeden (Maroc) est à 2.650 m, Portillo (Chili) à 2.800 et deux stations andines atteignent ou dépassent les 5.000 m. A l'intérieur de la chaîne alpine, la recherche d'une quantité suffisante de neige a poussé les promoteurs à s'élever jusqu'à 1.800–2.000 m, bien au-dessus de l'habitat traditionnel, alors que l'Autriche a développé ses stations à basse altitude à partir de ses villages traditionnels. La qualité de la neige intervient aussi pour l'implantation des centres de ski: il faut éviter les zones trop ventées où la neige est vite »tôlée« et, dans les monagnes déjà un peu ensoleilées, les versants que regardent vers le sud. Enfin, n'oublions pas que le ski se pratique l'hiver, c'est-à-dire la nuit aux hautes latitudes. La plupart des pistes de slalom et beaucoup de pistes de fond sont illuminées en Scandinavie: 80% des stations finnoises sont éclairées; 8 des 18 principaux centres japonais de ski le sont aussi; le cas se retrouve en Allemagne, dans 21 stations, et jusque dans le Jura français.

La neige ne suffit pas. Il faut des pentes. Même dans les pays scandinaves où le ski de fond est roi, les skieurs en recherchent pour le slalom: Norvégiens et Suédois ont équipé leurs montagnes, là où une pente satisfaisante s'offrait, comme à Geilo (Hardangervidda); les Finlandais n'hésitent pas à se rendre dans leurs montagnes au delà du cercle polaire et ils ont même installé, tout au Sud, quelques remonte-pentes sur le rebord intérieur de la Salpaüsselka! Mais, pour le ski alpin, qui est celui de la descente ou de la randonnée en montagne, il faut des pentes de plus en plus longues, variées en difficultés, très nombreuses, et qui soient à l'abri des avalanches. Ces exigences ne sont pas satisfaisantes partout, pour des raisons structurales et lithologiques: les zones charriées des Alpes françaises conviennent mieux que les Massifs Centraux dont les flancs d'auge cristallins sont trop raides. S'il n'est pas toujours aisé de trouver un bon domaine skiable pour la descente, il l'est encore moins d'offrir, dans les Alpes, des itinéraires satisfaisants pour le ski de fond dont la vogue récente est certaine: les stations s'y essaient, mais combien, en dehors de quelques-unes comme celles du Vercors du Nord, peuvent réussir?

Ainsi un enneigement satisfaisant et des pentes convenables créent les beaux domaines skiables; ceux-ci, quand ils totalisent 10 ou 20 km², atteignent des dimensions peu courantes. C'est pourquoi, les très grands sites étant rares ou déjà aménagés, on cherche la jonction entre les champs de ski voisins; il ne s'agit pas de relier par des cars des centres plus ou moins proches, mais d'implanter des remontées pour que le skieur, sans déchausser, puisse se rendre d'un champ de neige à un autre; la récente jonction Pra-Loup – La Foux d'Allos offre 16 km² aux skieurs. Vars, qui disposait déjà d'un des plus beaux domaines skiables des Alpes Françaises, vient, depuis l'hiver 1977, de se relier à Risoul, donnant à ses clients une surface de 32 km² pour évoluer.

Les causes générales, comme les hauts revenus des pays développés, les impératifs de la distance ou les données naturelles n'expliquent pas tout. Il faut aussi tenir compte d'autres éléments moins évidents mais qu'il convient de souligner.

2.4. *L'âge des stations et les particularités nationales*

Toutes ces stations n'ont pas été construites en même temps et chacune a pu profiter de l'expérience des précédentes pour établir un nouveau modèle qu'elle pourrait croire meilleur. Ainsi la localisation, tant en altitude qu'à l'intérieur des massifs, diffère: il faut tenir compte des nouvelles exigences du client en matière de domaine skiable, tout en étant obligé de se rabattre sur les derniers sites disponibles! Les remontées mécaniques seront plus nombreuses, à base d'une gamme importante de téléskis et de plusieurs télésièges. L'ancien village sera souvent noyé sous une avalanche brutale de constructions nouvelles, parfois discutables, quand il n'est pas totalement laissé à l'écart. Le problème d'un bon accès routier sera le premier résolu. Ainsi, dans sa localisation, dans sa structure, dans son utilisation du milieu naturel, la station change de type pour s'adapter à l'évolution de la demande. Un bon exemple est fourni par les »quatre âges« des stations françaises: le premier âge, qui date de l'avant-guerre et qui offre ses vieux villages et son manque d'organisation; le deuxième âge, dans les années cinquante, avec l'appui des Conseils Généraux et les débuts d'aménagement rationnel; le troisième âge, celui des années soixante, qui voit le triomphe de la

»station intégrée«, située en haute altitude, de grandes dimensions, où tout a été conçu et réalisé par un même promoteur; actuellement, on s'achemine vers un quatrième âge, qui proposera des centres de ski plus nombreux et moins vastes, tenant mieux compte des nécessités de l'environnement physique et humain de la montagne, et dont le ski de descente ne sera plus l'unique et totale préoccupation.

Cet exemple français souligne une autre donnée qui est parfois mal perçue et qu' une étude à l'échelle mondiale montre à l'évidence: il s'agit des particularités nationales. Chaque pays a son tempérament propre, ses traditions, sa manière d'être en relation avec le milieu montagnard; quand le tourisme d'hiver a abordé ses montagnes, la situation économique et les possibilites humaines de celles-ci lui étaient spécifiques et différentes de celles des voisines.

Ainsi, on s'explique facilement les nombreuses petites et moyennes stations de l'Autriche, modérément grandies à partir de villages vivants et pittoresques. Ce pays, dont les hautes et belles montagnes constituent l'essentiel du territoire et qui ne peut que bien connaître ce qu'est une montagne, dispose en outre d'un enneigement de qualité, qui tient de longs mois et au niveau même des villages. Il possédait donc de remarquables aptitudes naturelles, face à la croissance constante d'une demande allemande et européenne, qui ne trouvait pas satisfaction chez elle. Or, dans l'entre-deux-guerres, alors que le tourisme d'hiver prenait naissance, la nouvelle Autriche du traité de St. Germain, très réduite en superficie et devant vivre avec une capitale disproportionnée et surpeuplée, n'a pas pu connaître l'exode rural qui ailleurs vidait les villages alpins. Les habitants du Tyrol et des contrées voisines, à la recherche de nouvelles ressources, se tournèrent vers le ski, tout en continuant leur élevage; grâce à cette double activité, ils restèrent dans leurs villages bien enneigés, agrandissant ceux-ci et les équipant de remontées, gardant le contrôle de leurs propres communes, sachant respecter le milieu naturel, apprenant à vivre en harmonie avec leurs visiteurs. Cela a abouti à la multiplication de centres de ski qui ont su éviter le gigantesque et garder une dimension humaine. La réputation de l'Autriche a été ainsi bien établie et une habile publicité a su utiliser ce nouvel atout: n'est-ce pas ce petit pays qui reçoit le plus grand nombre de skieurs? Il est compréhensible que le vieux pays conquérant des Habsbourg soit devenu la très pacifique première nation du monde pour les sports d'hiver.

A l'autre bout de la chaîne alpine, la France offre un contraste éclatant. Nettement mieux doué que l'Autriche par l'étendue de son domaine skiable, disposant d'un très bon enneigement et, en outre, d'un meilleur ensoleillement, notre pays reçoit à peine le tiers du nombre des skieurs étrangers de l'Autriche et le total de ceux qui, nationaux ou non, fréquentent ses stations (2.700.000) est inférieur à celui des clients des centres de ski autrichiens (3.100.000). En outre, les caractères, déjà cités, de ses grandes stations lui donnent une place originale dans l'arc alpin.

Pourquoi? A la différence des Autrichiens ou des Suisses, les Français vivent dans des plaines, pensent à partir de Paris, disposent d'une gamme de ressources étendues; ils ont ignoré la montagne alpine, marginale et éloignée. Quand la révolution industrielle a débuté, au milieu du XIX⁰, l'exode rural a vidé les montagnes, leur enlevant leurs jeunes et leur dynamisme; les Alpes du Nord ont été moins touchées, mais la houille blanche et ses industries ont profité essentiellement aux basses vallées sans intéresser la haute ou moyenne montagne, et le tourisme d'hiver n'y a début que très modérément dans l'entre-deux-guerres. Lorsque, au lendemain du deuxième conflit mondial, il a fallu créer des stations pour répondre à une demande nouvelle et en brutale croissance, l'on se trouvait en face de remarquables domaines skiables vierges et, surtout, la haute montagne était à peu près vide d'hommes et sans possibilités financières. Après les tâtonnements et les peu nombreux exemples des stations du deuxième âge, la multiplication des grandes stations intégrées du troisième âge a été soudaine, utilisant un vide que les promoteurs ont rempli avec allégresse et dans l'ignorance ou le mépris du milieu humain et physique montagnard. Un homme a joué un rôle déterminant dans ces années soixante: M. MICHAUD, responsable du Service des Etudes à la Commission Interministérielle pour l'Aménagement Touristique de la Montagne est devenu le „dictateur de la neige" par la fonction qu'il occupait et l'autorité qu'il avait. Mettant à profit son expérience de constructeur de Courchevel et voulant exploiter le capital skiable français pour y attirer une clientèle riche, nationale ou étrangère, il a édifié une „doctrine", qui recommandait notamment la création de ces grands ensembles de haute altitude, entièrement neufs et artificiels, ayant une unité de conception et véritables „usines à ski"; imposant ses vues et encourageant les promoteurs à venir investir en montagne, il a marqué les aménagements alpestres de ses idées. S'il a aussi soutenu les stations moyennes et pensé aux „stades de neige", M. MICHAUD n'en a pas moins été un de ceux qui ont façonné le visage de nos nouvelles stations montagnardes. Ce »troisième âge« est fini; s'il partait souvent d'idées justes et saines, il a succombé à ses excès et à l'oubli de certaines réalités humaines. Un »quatrième âge« a commencé il y a quelques années, que la politique vient d'officialiser (discours de Vallouise, août 1977) et qui modifiera l'aspect de la montagne d'hiver française.

Les attitudes française et autrichienne sont opposées et chaque station alpine pourrait être plus ou moins proche de l'une des deux. Il y a beaucoup d'autres spécificités nationales. La Suisse, se rapproche beaucoup de l'Autriche, mais n'a pas tout à fait atteint son niveau international et n'a pas réalisé ce mariage élevage-tourisme. L'Italie est plus proche de la France. Hors des Alpes, les Tchécoslovaques, qui ont toujours beaucoup skié, pratiquent moins la descente et se consacrent davantage à la randonnée; en exceptant leurs six grandes stations des Hautes-Tatras et des Monts des Géants, ils disposent de centres de ski plus modestes mais nombreux; ils ont même la particularité, qui n'est pas inconnue ailleurs mais que le Français récusent, de dissocier l'habitat des skieurs et leur domaine skiable dans leurs grands centres de ski carpatiques. En Scandinavie, le goût de la nature des habitants, leur besoin de longues randonnées en forêt, l'espace dont ils disposent, leur ôtent toute idée d'une station »à la française« et leurs centres de ski les plus réputés font figure à nos yeux de stations moyennes.

Malgré la similitude apparente des conditions qui président à la naissance des stations de ski, malgré les problèmes communs de rentabilité, malgré l'impression d'unité que laisse l'emploi de certains critères dans l'étude que nous avons menée (nombre de lits ou de remontées mécaniques, question de distance etc.), l'examen comparé des centres de sports d'hiver révèle une profonde diversité et permet de mieux comprendre chaque cas national que l'on a trop tendance à isoler et à partir duquel beaucoup d'études veulent généraliser. S'il existe un classement typologique qui permet de distinguer la station alpine du centre de ski scandinave, la nouvelle station des pays de l'Est de celle des pays du Tiers Monde, la diversité est beaucoup plus grande.

Il est à souhaiter que, pour les sports d'hiver comme pour les autres activités touristiques, de nombreuses études synthétiques et de comparaison soient menées afin de mieux saisir la réalité à l'échelle mondiale et de mieux comprendre chaque cas national.

Tableau 1: Stations de ski et remontées mécaniques dans le monde (1975 ou 1976)

Pays	Nombre de stations	Remontées mécaniques Total	dont téléskis		dont engins téléporteurs	
France	260	2.247	1.851	(82,4%)	396	(17,6%)
R.F.A.	166	1.624	1.500	(92.4%)	124	(7,6%)
Suisse	205	1.503	1.095	(72.9%)	408	(27,1%)
Autriche	355	3.035	2.573	(84,8%)	462	(15,2%)
Italie	300	1.942	1.486	(76,5%)	456	(23,5%)
Yougoslavie	54	130	90	(69,2%)	40	(30,8%)
Andorre		25	23		2	
Belgique	1	1	1		–	
Grèce	7	22	16		6	
Royaume-Uni	7	33	15		8	
Portugal	1	5	4		1	
Espagne	26	191	128	(67 %)	03	(33 %)
Norvège	95	156	123	(78,8%)	33	(21,2%)
Suède	150?	348	313	(89,9%)	35	(10,1%)
Finlande	60	38	80		8	
Islande	8	18	5		3	
Tchécoslov.	120?	801	764	(95,4%)	37	(4,6%)
Bulgarie	7	34	25		9	
Roumanie	8	24	12		12	
Pologne	22	76	60		16	
R.D.A.	15?	97	80		17	
U.R.S.S.	70?	210	200	(95,2%)	10	(4,8%)
Algérie	3	6	5		1	
Maroc	3	17	15		2	
Canada	300?	853	665	(78 %)	188	(22 %)
Etats-Unis	500?	2.454	1.101	(44,9%)	1.358	(55,1%)
Argentine	12?	31	15		16	
Bolivie	1	1	1		–	
Brésil	?	?				
Chili	75	25	20		5	
Colombie	1	2	2			
Japon	200?	1.159	30	(2,6%)	1.129	(97,4%)
Inde	2	7	5		2	
Iran	8	26	21		5	
Liban	5	21	17		4	
Turquie	6	19	6		13	
Chypre	2	6	3		3	
Australie	8?	58	49		9	
Nouvelle-Zélande	4?	27	22		5	
Monde	3.000?	17.329	14.424	(71,7%)	4.905	(28,3%)

Tableau 2: Nombre d'habitants par remontée mécanique

Pays	1 remontée mécanique pour habitants
Autriche	2.400
Suisse	4.250
Tchécoslovaquie	18.000
France	23.000
Suède	23.000
Norvège	26.000
Canada	27.000
Italie	29.000
R.F.A.	38.000
Finlande	53.000
U.S.A.	86.000
Japon	95.000
Nouvelle-Zélande	115.000
Yougoslavie	165.000
R.D.A.	175.000
Espagne	185.000
Bulgarie	260.000
Chili	410.000
Pologne	450.000
Roumanie	880.000
U.R.S.S.	1.200.000
Iran	1.250.000

Tableau 3: Nombre de remontées mécaniques par station pour quelques pays

Pays	Nombre de stations			
	de 1 à 15 R.M.		de 16 à 30 R.M.	+ de 30 R.M.
France	204	(78,5%)	43	13
Suisse	194	(94,6%)	8	3
Autriche	345	(97,2%)	10	–
Allemagne	156	(94 %)	8	2
Italie	268	(85,3%)	29	3
Japon		?	5	2

Tableau 4: Capacité d'hébergement des stations des pays alpins (uniquement lits hôteliers; enquête de 1972)

Pays	Nombre de stations ayant		
	1.000–2.000 lits	2.000–2.500	+ de 5.000
France	8	8	–
Suisse	15	10	8
Autriche	97	21	9
Italie	19	8	1
Allemagne	6	3	3
Yougoslavie	1	2	–

Tableau 6: Les skieurs dans le monde

Pays	Nombre de skieurs (Millions)	% de skieurs par rapport au nombre d'habitants
Japon	9 M	8 %
USA-Canada	7 M	3,0 %
Allemagne	5 M	8 %
Scandinavie	8 M	17,7 %
France	2,5 M	4,7 %
Italie	2 M	3,6 %
Autriche	2 M	28 %
Suisse	2 M	31 %
Espagne	1 M	2,8 %
Tchécoslovaquie	1 M	6,8 %
Bulgarie	1 M	11,5 %
Australie	0,4 M	3,0 %
Royaume-Uni	0,4 M	0,7 %
Belgique	0,3 M	3,1 %
Yougoslavie	0,15 M	0,7 %
Pays-Bas	0,1 M	0,7 %
Argentine	0,1 M	0,4 %
U.R.S.S.	0,05 M	0,02%
Chili	0,02 M	0,02%
Total	37 M	

Tableau 5: Capacité d'hébergement des stations de deux pays
(Capacité totale: lits hôteliers et autres hébergements)

Pays	Nombre de stations ayant							
	– de 2.000 lits		2.000–5.000		5.000–10.000		+ de 10.000	
France	187	(71,9%)	30	(11,5%)	22	(8,5%)	21	(8,1%)
Suisse	164	(80 %)	25	(12,2%)	9	(4,4%)	7	(3,4%)

Total: France 260
Suisse 205

Tableau 7: Différences entre les statistiques
a) Remontées mécaniques des stations françaises

Stations ayant	D'après »Aménagement et Montagne«			D'après enquête d'Aix-en-Provence		
plus de 41 R.M.	7	Deux Alpes	60	6	La Plagne	51
		Courchevel	59		Val d'Isère	49
		Val d'Isère	59		Courchevel	49
		Morzine-Avoriaz	58		Serre-Chevalier	46
		Tignes	57		Deux-Alpes	43
		La Plagne	52		Tignes	41
		Alpe d'Huez	44		+ Morzine	21
					Avoriaz	20
de 31 à 40 R.M.	9	Les Arcs	39	7	Chamonix	37
		Mégève	37		Les Rousses	37
		Serre-Chevalier	37		Alpe d'Huez	34
		Les Rousses	39		Villard de Lans	32
		Chamonix	36		Méribel	31
		Méribel	35		La Clusaz	31
		Métabief	34ù		Mégève	31
		La Clusaz	32			
		St. Gervais	32			
	18	Villard de Lans	27	23	Les Arcs	27
					St. Gervais	26
					Métabief	23
de 16 à 20 R.M.	15			20		
moins de 16 R.M.	–			204		

b) Capacité d'hébergement des stations françaises

Stations ayant:		D'après »Aménagement et Montagne«		selon R. BALSEINTE		Enquête d'Aix-en Provence
Plus de 20.000 lits	2	Courchevel 25.400 Chamonix 25.000	3	Chamonix 24.700 Mégève 24.000 Morzine Avoriaz 20.500	2	Chamonix 25.250 Mégève 24.000 + Morzine 12.800 Avoriaz 7.800 20.600
10–20.000 lits	5	Orcières- Merlette 16.150 La Clusaz 16.150 Deux Alpes 15.770 Tignes 15.240 Serre- Chevalier 15.000	5	Courchevel 19.700 La Plagne 17.000 Orcière Merlette 15.800 Alpe d'Huez 15.100	4	Courchevel 19.400 Orcières- Merlette 15.200 Alpe d'Huez 15.150 La Clusaz 15.000
10–15.000 lits	10	Morzine- Avoriaz 14.600 Mégève 14.500 La Plagne 11.420	9	La Clusaz 14.800 Tignes 14.500 Serre- Chevalier 12.400	16	Tignes 14.500 Deux Alpes 13.650 Serre- Chevalier 12.400 La Plagne 11.000
5–10.000	23	Alpe d'Huez 9.000	31		22	
total (plus de 5.000 lits)	40		48		44	

Tableau 8b: Flux internationaux de skieurs (1976)

Pays	Nombre de skieurs étrangers venant en		
Allemagne	760.000	500.000	140.000
Belgique	40.000	100.000	60.000
Royaume-Uni	100.000	90.000	40.000
France	70.000	80.000	–
Italie	15.000	50.000	40.000
Pays-Bas	55.000	35.000	7.000
Scandinavie	35.000	15.000	10.000
Autriche	–	40.000	10.000
Suisse	50.000	–	20.000
USA-Canada	35.000	30.000	18.000
Japon	50.000	20.000	10.000
Tchécoslovaquie	30.000	–	–
Yougoslavie	10.000	–	–
Espagne	2.000	2.000	4.000
Total	1.200.000	960.000	360.000

Tableau 8a: Flux internationaux de skieurs
(1976)

Pays	Nombre de skieurs nationaux	dont se rendant à l'étranger
Allemagne	5.000.000	2.000.000
Belgique	300.000	300.000
Royaume-Uni	400.000	250.000
France	2.500.000	200.000
Italie	2.000.000	150.000
Pays-Bas	100.000	100.000
Scandinavie	3.000.000	100.000
Autriche	2.000.000	100.000
Suisse	2.000.000	100.000
USA-Canada	7.000.000	100.000
Japon	9.000.000	100.000
Tchécoslovaquie	1.000.000	50.000
Yougoslavie	150.000	30.000
Espagne	1.000.000	10.000
Total	37.000.000	3.610.000

Bibliographie

A côté des sources évoquées dans l'article, il convient de citer certaines études qui nous ont fourni une documentation précise.

HIRIGOYEN, J.: Plus de 15.802 appareils sur cinq continents, premier essai de statistiques à l'échelle mondiale. *Economie et prospective de la montagne.* No. 42. Voiron 1976. p. 12–24. Cette étude constitue, par son inventaire précis et serieux, une base essentielle: l'auteur a publié dans les numeros suivants une série de mises au point partielles à propos de l'Amérique du Nord, de l'Autriche, de la France (cf. No. 45) etc. . . .

QUINTRIE – LA MOTHE, T.: A publié trois articles récents très utiles dans la même revue *(Economie et prospective de la montagne):*
1965–1975, Bilan sur les sports d'hiver. No. 43, Voiron 1976, p. 18–20.
Le marché international de la neige. No. 46, Voiron 1977, p. 32–40.
Les marchés réceptifs de l'arc alpin. No. 47, Voiron 1977, p. 15–18.
Ces études contiennent beaucoup de données statistiques recueillies dans des annuaires où élaborées par l'auteur; nous les avons utilisées (nombre de skieurs, flux internationaux, prévisions, domaines skiables etc.).
Radioscopie de 90 stations de sports d'hiver. *Aménagement et Montagne,* No. 8, Grenoble 1977, p. 20–26. L'étude fournit une mise au point chiffree de 90 stations françaises, à jour pour l'hiver 1976-7 (remontées mecaniques, capacité d'hébergement, pistes, nouveaux equipements).

BALSEINTE, R.: »Le nouveau classement typologique des stations de sports d'hiver françaises.« *Aménagement et Montagne,* No. 8, Grenoble 1977, p. 32–38.
Ce classement, suivi de critiques et d'une réponse (cf. No. 9, même revue, p. 52–54), toute une intéressante typologie de 96 stations, fournit en même temps beaucoup de caractéristiques sur chacun des centres retenus.

STUDIES OF THE GEOGRAPHY OF TOURISM AND RECREATION WITH REFERENCE TO PARTICULAR COUNTRIES

ÉTUDES RÉGIONALES

BEITRÄGE ZUR FREMDENVERKEHRSGEOGRAPHIE AUS EINZELNEN STAATEN

Cableways in Austria

A factor of tourism with considerable economic impact

FELIX JÜLG, Vienna, Austria*

In mountain tourist regions, suitable for winter sports, cableways appear to be the most important factor of regional development. This is the result of investigations in Austria, where approximately one fifth of world's passenger cableways are operated.[1] The authorities responsible and scientific researchers have investigated the impact of cableways for a number of years. This report presents some results of this work which I have contributed to.[2]

The direct impact of cableways, for example, the creation of new jobs, on the cableways themselves, *is not nearly as important as the indirect consequences on the regional economy,* as a result of the accelerated development of winter tourism. These indirect effects are very complex; their dependence on cableways is often not easily proveable.

Passenger cableways in Austria have been of importance since the moment they had become perfected technically. A first period of cableway construction after World War I was discontinued by the world wide economic depression and World War II.

After the signature of the Austrian State Treaty in 1955, when normal conditions for the development of tourism were initiated, *a boom of cableway construction* has taken place. As early as 1966, a study published by the Austrian Institute of Regional Planning pointed out that the further opening up of areas by cableways should be slower and more cautious to prevent an excessive development with all its unfavourable consequences. Now, after 11 years, we must conclude that the boom is still going on. A large number of cableways are under planning or construction, many of these of considerable scale and boldness, and the whole sector of cableways seems to be in a state of euphoria. This is surprising, considering the fact that in 1975 only about 50 per cent. of the cableway businesses were able to achieve profits. In previous years with poor snow conditions the economic situation of cableways was even worse.

The profitability of cableways, however, depends to a large degree on the *system of technical construction.* The following types, in use in Austria, are to be distinguished.

---

* Dr. FELIX JÜLG, Senior Lecturer, Dept. of Geography, University of Economics, Vienna, Austria

[1] SCHMOLL, H. D.: *Versuch einer internationalen Statistik über Seilbahnanlagen.* Vortrag am 4. Internationalen Seilbahnkongreß in Wien, vervielfältigtes Manuskript, Wien 1975

[2] Österreichisches Institut für Raumplanung: *Studie über Auswirkungen der Seilbahnen auf die Wirtschaft.* Verfaßt im Auftrage des Bundesministeriums für Verkehr und Elektrizitätswirtschaft, Wien 1962

JÜLG, F.: *Die Bedeutung der Bergbahnen für den Fremdenverkehr in Österreich.* Diss. Hochschule für Welthandel, Wien 1964

Österreichisches Institut für Raumplanung: Die Seilbahnen Österreichs und ihre Auswirkungen auf die Wirtschaft. *Veröffentlichungen des Österreichischen Instituts für Raumplanung* Nr. 29, Wien 1966

Österreichisches Institut für Raumplanung: *Entwurf für ein Österreichisches Seilbahnkonzept.* Im Auftrag des Bundesministeriums für Verkehr. Vervielfältigter Entwurf, Wien 1977,

and others.

1. Funicular-railways on rails and hauled by a traction cable. This is the oldest cableway system but some of them were constructed only within the last few years. This system operates in a pendular way, which means that while one carriage goes up the other comes down.

2. Bi-cable systems, which have both a suspension and a traction cable. These are equipped with large cabins to hold up to 120 passengers or small gondolas up to six passengers and are operated either in a pendular or circulating manner, the latter case, the gondolas are detachable.

3. Mono-cable systems which use the same one cable for suspension und traction. These systems are usually operated in a circulating manner. The carriages may be detachable and closed, i. e. gondolas, or undetachable and open, i. e. chairs.

4. Most of the Austrian cableways however are ski-tows constructed in various ways. In this context I should also mention the so-called "combi-lifts" which are operated as ski-tows during the skiing season and as mono-chairlifts with small loads during the rest of the year. These "combi-lifts" are very economic for small resorts which are just in the initial stages of winter tourist development.

Table 1: Development of cableways by types of technical construction in Austria (1955–1975)

Types of technical construction	1955	1960	1965	1970	1975
Funicular-railways	6	9	14	17	22
Aerial tramways					
Bi-cable systems pendular	26	46	56	69	70
circulating	8	9	10	10	13
Mono-cable systems					
Gondola-cableways	—	1	1	1	12
Triple chairlifts	—	—	—	—	1
Double chairlifts	4	8	13	52	132
Single chairlifts	66	101	163	219	218
Ski-tows	273*	380	826	1.970	2.729
Combi-lifts	—	—	2	9	13
Cableways altogether		554	1.085	2.347	3.210

* By 31. 12. 1956

Source: Bundesministerium für Verkehr (ed.): *Amtliche Eisenbahnstatistik der Republik Österreich,* Wien, annually.

These types of cableways according to technical construction were built in Austria with different degrees of intensity. Depending on technological progress, the preference for particular systems changed during the periods shown on table 1.

Generally the technical system chosen depends on the kind of the terrain, the obtainable haulage capacity, and the available capital. Often the choice of a particular technical system is affected by prestige and local competition. The actual function of the cableways, however, was for a long time not an important factor in the choice of a technical system.

The *obtainable haulage* is given in persons per hour in one direction. But for geographical research and tourist planning, the so-called *"transport-capacity"* is much more important. "Transport-capacity" means persons per hour in one direction multiplied by meters of altitude; this gives an answer to the question of how many skiing visitors going uphill several times on a day can be managed by the cableway. "Transport-capacity" is a suitable basis for harmonising ski-lift capacity with other touristic installations, such as the number of beds, or the seating capacity of restaurants.

The obtainable haulage, however, is limited by technical conditions and security regulations imposed by the supervising authorities. The limits imposed in Austria at present are shown in table 2.

Table 2: Hauling capacity, speed limit and interval between carriers by types of technical construction

Types of technical construction	Hauling capacity pers/h in one direction	Speed limit m/sec	Intervals of carriers sec
Funicular-railways	1.540	5 (in exceptional cases 10)	—
Aerial tramways			
Bi-cable systems			
pendular	900	10	—
circulating	1.400	3,5	15
Mono-cable systems			
Gondola-cableways	1.400	3,5	12
Triple chairlifts	1.800	2,0	6
Double chairlifts	1.440	2,0 (in exceptional cases 2,5)	6
Single chairlifts	900	2,0 (in exceptional cases 2,5)	4
Ski-tows	1.440	2,0 (in exceptional cases 5,0)	6

Source: Bundesministerium für Verkehr, Vienna

Of course capital expenditure is less for a simple ski-tow than for a heavy funicular. The following Table 3 points out the large variation in expenditure related to the haulage of one person per hour for a standardised distance.

Table 3: Investment and fixed expenditures for cableways by types of technical construction

Types of technical construction	*Investment Expenditures* per person hauling capacity per hour in Austrian Shillings*	index (ski-tow = 1)	*Fixed Expenditures* index (ski-tow = 1)
Funicular-railways Aerial tramways Bi-cable systems pendular circulating	42.000 to 50.000	12,5 to 15,0	7,0 to 7,5
Mono-cable systems			
Gondola-cableways	23.000	7	3,75
Triple chairlifts	8.000	2,5	1,8
Double chairlifts	10.000	3,0	2,0
Single chairlifts	13.300	4,0	2,5
Ski-tows	3.300	1,0	1,0

* By 31. 12. 1976.

Source: Gröbner, H.: *Sicherheit und Rationalisierung im Seilbahnbau.* Vortrag bei der Österreichischen Seilbahntagung in Baden bei Wien 1976, Manuskript. Author's own calculations.

That means that, depending on technical construction, it might cost up to fifteen times as much to lift a human being over the same distance. Therefore the heavy technical systems are charged with high fixed expenditures, resulting in high rates of depreciation and personal expenses. Hence, these systems would need for the same degree of profitability a higher employment capacity and higher fares than a ski-tow. In fact this difference in cost is not covered by higher demand to any satisfactory degree.

For the impact on the regional economy, however, the matter of profitability in the cableways business is not so essential. Of greater importance are the *functions which are met by the cableways.* These are only to a very small degree functions for general transportation. That is the case where cableways serve mountain farmers in out-of-the-way places, but today this function is performed more profitably and appropriately by roads.

Of *dominant importance* are the functions for tourism and amongst them the *functions for winter sports.* Here two sub-functions can be mentioned: a function for ski-runs and a feeder-function. With respect to the ski-function, the main purpose of a cableway is to haul the passengers to the start of one ore more runs or slopes. A cableway, performing the feeder-function, opens up a whole skiing area in a high altitude. In this case, at least a part of the passengers will use the cableway also downhill in the evening, returning to their accomodation in the valley.

But apart from the winter sport-functions, cableways can perform other recreational functions, most of them important all through the year. For instance, to reach look-outs or starting points of mountain trails.

In the course of my work on an Austrian cableway-plan, I have tried to classify cableways according to their functions, as far as corresponding statistical data were obtainable. Ski-tows, of course, were not classified; their function to serve ski-runs is obvious.

Table 4: Functional types of Austrian cableways
(Ski-tows excluded)

Function	In Percent of Cableways	
Wintersport function exclusively		
Ski-runs	21,0	
Mixed (ski-runs/feeder)	1,2	23,1
Feeder	0,9	
Wintersport function predominant		
Ski-runs	23,0	
Mixed (ski-runs/feeder)	4,6	28,8
Feeder	1,2	
Wintersport function prevailing but also other recreational functions		
Ski-runs	19,5	
Mixed (ski-runs/feeder)	7,1	31,7
Feeder	5,1	
Other recreational functions prevailing but also wintersport function		8,3
Other recreational functions predominant		
with particular additional functions	4,4	7,3
without particular additional functions	2,9	
General transportation function		0,8
410 Cableways classified	=	100,0

Source: Classification based upon data from the Official Statistics of Railways. Bundesministerium für Verkehr (ed.): *Amtliche Eisenbahnstatistik der Republik Österreich 1975,* Wien 1976

The results of this classification are shown on Table 4. Even for cableway experts, the dominance of wintersport functions was surprising. 84 per cent. of passengers of cableways (ski-tows excluded) are registered during the winter period. The function for winter sport is also demonstrated by the fact that there are many more downhill passengers in summer than in winter, as can be seen on Table 5. The number of passengers per operating day is on the average higher in winter than in summer.

Table 5: Passengers on Austrian cableways 1975
(Ski-tows excluded)

	1975 altogether	Winter	Summer
	in millions of passengers		
Passengers carried	98,2	76,9	21,3
uphill	80,7	68,1	12,6
downhill	17,5	8,2	9,3

Source: Bundesministerium für Verkehr (ed.): *Amtliche Eisenbahnstatistik der Republik Österreich 1975*, Wien 1976

I further attempted to analyse to what extent the various functions are met by the different technical systems of cableways. The result was that the technical systems are spread over nearly all functions.

The consequence is that *a cheap ski-tow can have nearly the same economic impact as an expensive heavy aerial tram.* And in fact, there are a lot of skiing resorts which started their winter season development with a small ski-tow. Some of them have achieved an outstanding development by the establishment of simple ski-tows and chairlifts only.

Proof of the importance of cableways for tourism is the fact that an inquiry has shown that *85 per cent. of cableway passengers are tourists.* Only 15 per cent. are inhabitants of the community in which the cableway station is situated or from the area nearby. One third of the 85 per cent. tourists mentioned are excursionists or persons on short stays. Depending on the particular cableway, the structure of passengers is quite different; it is obvious that a cableway situated in Innsbruck will have a greater share of residential users than a cableway in a winter resort.

The connection between cableways and winter sports is emphasized by the fact that alpine skiing cannot be imagined without "lifts" today. There are only very few people willing to climb for hours for one beautiful run. In the years after World War II, when only a few cableways were operating and people had to queue possibly for hours, climbing was an alternative to waiting. Today, if one should have to wait for a longer time, one would go on to another cableway situated in the neighbourhood. The curriculum of a modern ski school would not be possible without lifts. To-day's regular skiing equipment does not allow for long ascents.

In Austria, based upon research in individual resorts, an estimated *two-thirds of all tourists* registered *in winter are active skiers.* The connection between cableways and winter tourism is therefore evident. It can be verified that in many tourist communities there was *a boom in the number of overnight stays* in winter *after the establishment of a cableway.* In graph 1, several communities were selected in which most cableways were constructed after 1965. This enables a comparison to be made with the Austrian average, and thereby an exposition of the impact of the cableways. For most Austrian skiing resorts a comparison like this needs to be done for a longer period because many cableways which had an influence on the development of winter tourism, were established years before.

Graph 1: Winter overnight-stays in selected resorts 1974/75

Resort	P.	Cableways excl. tows 1965	Cableways excl. tows 1975	Cableways total 1975
Ischgl	T.	1	5	15
Neustift	T.	–	3	18
Tux	T.	3	6	17
Fügen	T.	–	3	11
St. Jakob	T.	–	3	11
Leogang	S.	–	2	14
Kaprun	S.	3	6	18
Heiligenblut	C.	–	3	11
Bad Klein-kirchheim	C.	2	4	20
Pichl-Preunegg	St.	–	2	10
Schladming	St.	1	4	12
Gaming	L.	1	2	9

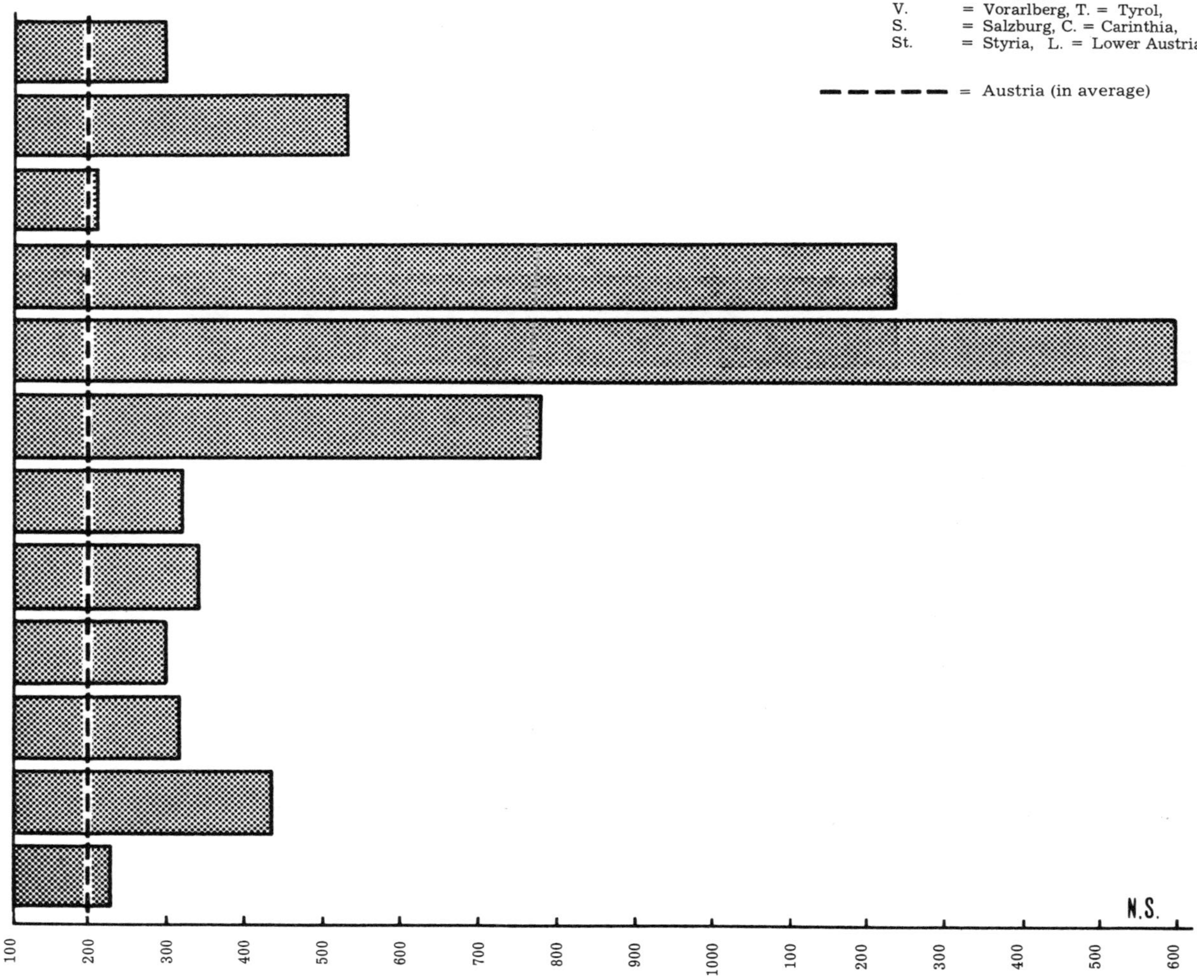

Index: 1964/65 = 100

P. = Province:
V. = Vorarlberg, T. = Tyrol,
S. = Salzburg, C. = Carinthia,
St. = Styria, L. = Lower Austria

– – – – = Austria (in average)

The impact of cableways was greater in those communities, which already had considerable summer tourism. There, much of the necessary equipment was already existent and only had to be adapted for winter use.

By contrast, cableways had very little effect on the summer season. This is true also of those cableways which have valuable summer recreational functions (e. g. to reach look-outs). In summer a cableway is considered an additional attraction, but not a necessary condition for spending a vacation in a resort.

However, there is one important exception i. e. cableways opening up glacier areas for summer skiing. Here the course of tourism throughout the year is changed. This does not mean that there is much tourist growth in the peak summer season, that is in July and August. But in the other months of the summer period when skiing is possible on the glaciers (before and after July and August), there is considerable growth. This is precisely the time, which previously was a quiet season, for example, late spring or autumn.[3]

The *economic multiplier effect* of tourism has often been treated in the literature.[4] In the Austrian skiing resorts too, there are considerable economic benefits for winter tourism, brought about by cableways. This can be shown by a number of criteria. I have selected three, and have used them in my example of 15 typical Austrian skiing resorts. These are:

1. The development of population
2. The development of number of houses
3. The per-capita-tax-yield

Changes in these criteria become apparent only after a time-lag of several years after the development of winter tourism. Therefore it is possible that a skiing resort already has passed the optimum point of its development (i. e. that the growth in number of overnights is below the average or that there even is a decrease of visitors), while the three criteria mentioned still show a tremendous growth.

Growth of population in all fifteen communities was above the average between 1961 und 1971 (graph 2). The year 1961 is used as base. Since development of population varies greatly throughout the Austrian provinces, not only the federal average but also the respective provincial average is indicated.

It is remarkable that population is growing in regions which only a few decades ago were threatened by out-migration.

Building activities in skiing resorts are particularly notable. Mountain villages which had almost the same number of buildings for hundreds of years, are suddenly "exploding". From the selected resorts, 13 are over the national average (graph 3), according to building activity.

Most new buildings are directly or indirectly connected with tourism. The housing standards and housing demands of the local population are increasing. In the village of Lech, for instance, farmers rent their old farmhouses to youth

---

[3] See for example:

BARNICK, H.: *Sommerschigebiete in den Alpen und ihre Einzugsbereiche.* Berichte zur Raumforschung und Raumplanung, Wien 1970, 3, pp. 30–42

BARNICK, H.: Sommerschigebiete in Österreich – Erfahrungen und Ausblicke. *Berichte zur Raumforschung und Raumplanung,* Wien 1974, 3, pp. 25–36

HAIMAYER, P.: Zur Frage der Ganzjahresschigebiete: Das Beispiel Hochstubai/Tirol. *Berichte zur Raumforschung und Raumplanung,* Wien 1977, 1, pp. 5–13

[4] See for example:

JÜLG, F.: *Die Bedeutung der Bergbahnen für den Fremdenverkehr in Österreich* (hier dargestellt an Hand des Beispieles Westendorf, Tirol). Diss. Hochschule für Welthandel, Wien 1964

MAIER, J.: Die Leistungskraft einer Fremdenverkehrsgemeinde. Modellanalyse des Marktes Hindelang/Allgäu. „*W.G.I.*" – *Berichte zur Regionalforschung,* 3, München 1969

KRÖNER, A.: Grindelwald. Die Entwicklung eines Bergbauerndorfes zu einem internationalen Touristenzentrum. *Stuttgarter Geographische Studien,* Bd. 74, Stuttgart 1968

Graph 2: Population in selected resorts 1971

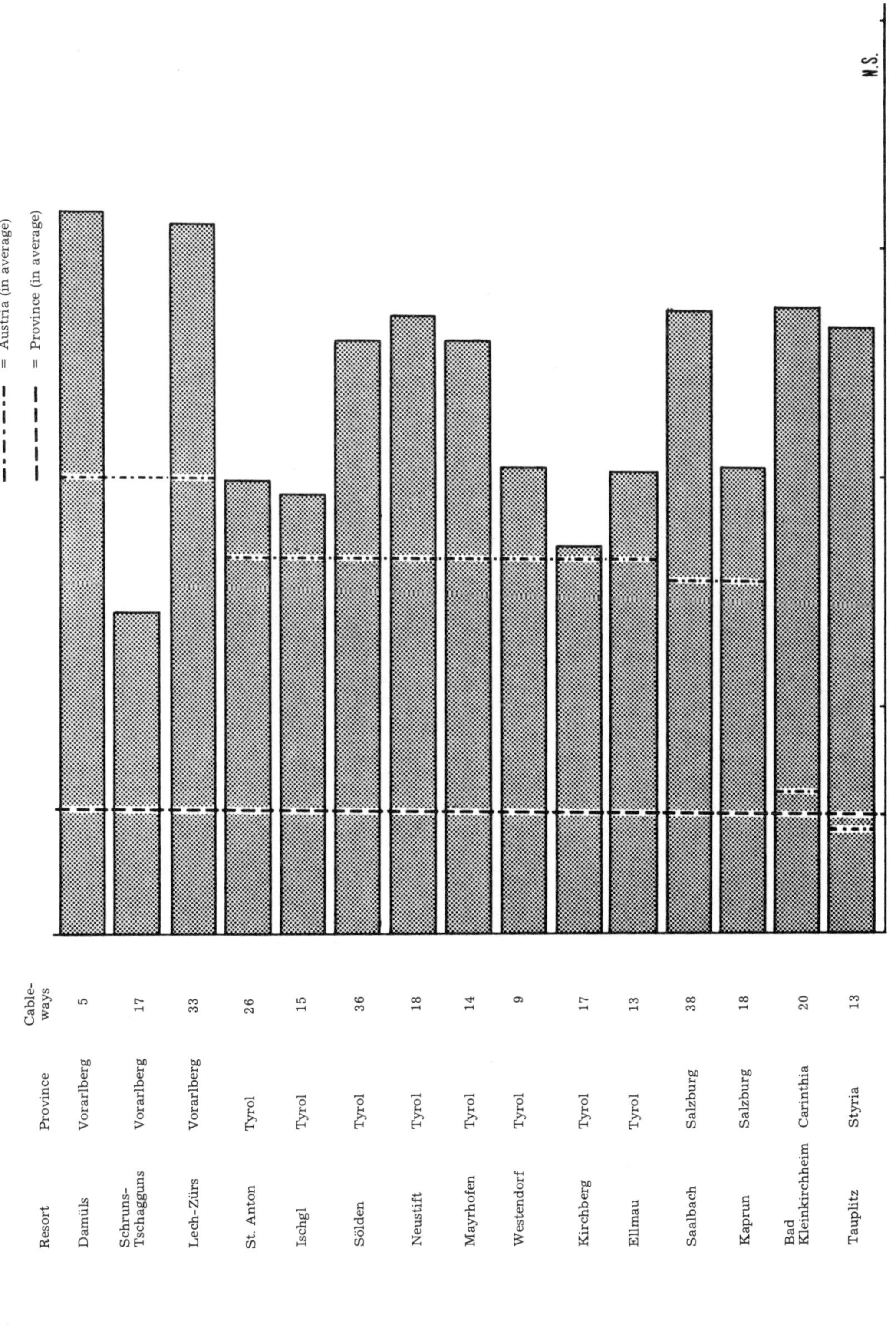

Graph 3: Number of houses in selected resorts

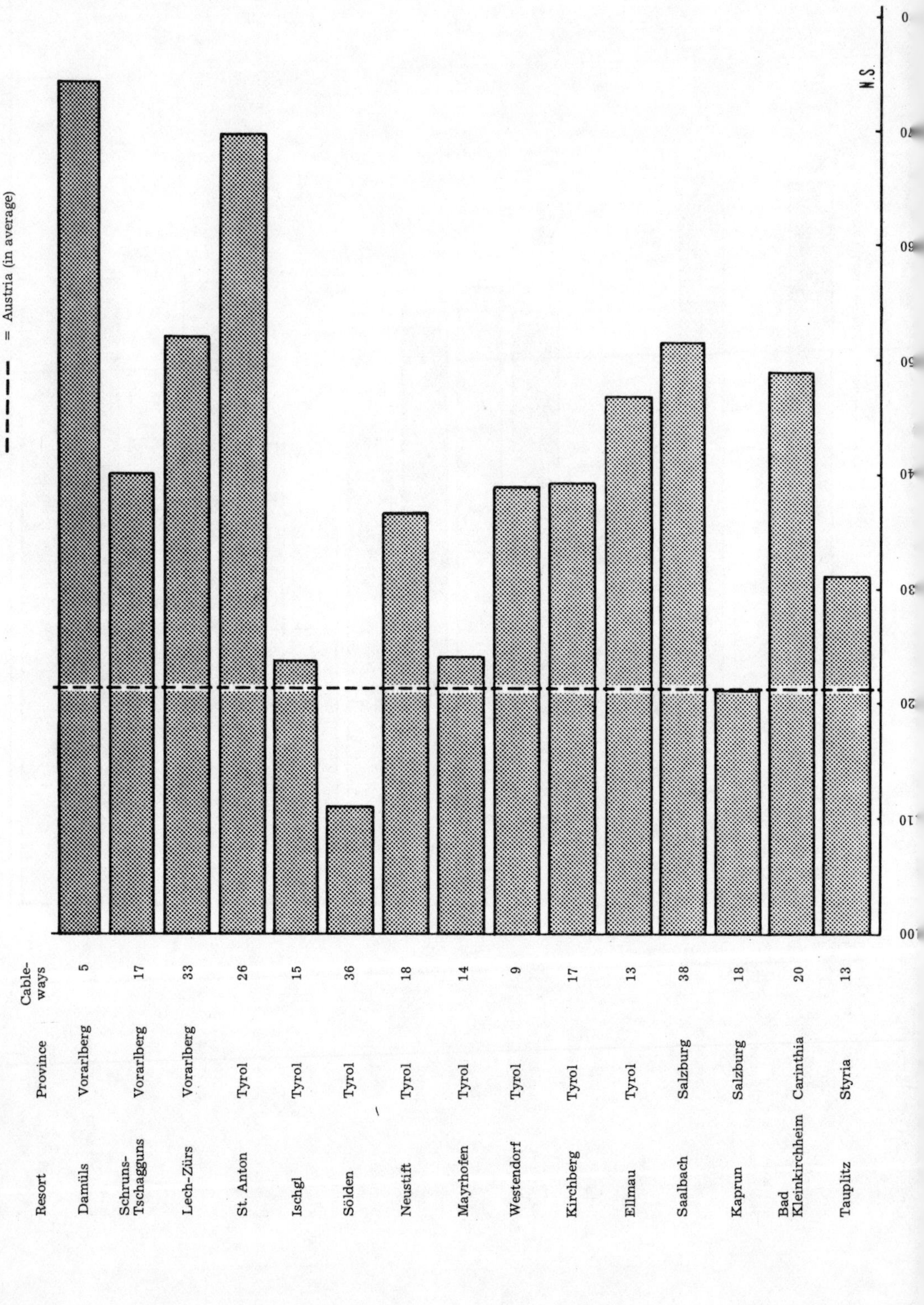
Index: 1961 = 100
= Austria (in average)
Resort
Province
Cable-ways
Damüls
Vorarlberg
5
Schruns-Tschagguns
Vorarlberg
17
Lech-Zürs
Vorarlberg
33
St. Anton
Tyrol
26
Ischgl
Tyrol
15
Sölden
Tyrol
36
Neustift
Tyrol
18
Mayrhofen
Tyrol
14
Westendorf
Tyrol
9
Kirchberg
Tyrol
17
Ellmau
Tyrol
13
Saalbach
Salzburg
38
Kaprun
Salzburg
18
Bad Kleinkirchheim
Carinthia
20
Tauplitz
Styria
13
100
110
120
130
140
150
160
170
N.S.

groups, whereas they themselves live in new boarding houses and from there carry out their farming activities. These activities themselves have been modernised and rationalised.

Building activities affected by cableways are limited to areas near the centre of the village and the cableway. More distant parts of the community often do not participate in these activities. In the centre, however, places and streets are beginning to resemble those of towns. The traditional architectural style prescribed by the regional authorities is copied by tourist buildings in dimensions which destroy the traditional village scene, which comprises such an important part of the tourist landscape. Near the run of cableways the arrangement of buildings is such that much space is wasted. The near-by skiing slopes before the village edge are being divided into plots. Even the run to the cableway station is in danger of being obstructed.

Tax laws in Austria are such that *per-capita-yield of local taxes* is an important criterion of local economic development. Among the taxes, whose income is ascribed directly to the communities, are the trade tax, the real estate tax, the beverage tax, the taxes for entertainments and others. The income from the real estate tax, for example, shows the increase on properties in areas where cableways are operated. In fact, all but two selected communities recorded a per-cap-

Table 6: Per-capita-income from local taxes in 15 selected Austrian winter-resorts 1973

	Per-capita-income from local taxes 1973	Beds per resident	Per cent. of winter overnight-stays of total overnight-stays 1974/75
Damüls	4.226,—	3,1	63,2
Schruns-Tschagguns	2.751,—	1,0	42,7
Lech-Zürs	11.985,—	4,9	82,8
St. Anton a. A.	3.797,—	2,7	70,2
Ischgl	2.170,—	3,0	72,7
Sölden	5.022,—	4,1	63,2
Neustift i. St.	1.188,—	1,5	31,6
Mayrhofen	4.142,—	2,3	31,6
Westendorf	1.330,—	1,2	43,3
Kirchberg, T.	1.926,—	2,0	54,7
Ellmau	2.278,—	2,4	35,9
Saalbach	5.350,—	4,6	59,7
Kaprun	6.591,—	1,3	46,1
Bad Kleinkirchheim	5.819,—	2,3	29,3
Tauplitz	1.673,—	1,4	64,9
Average for Austria	1.370,—	0,1	30,4

Source: Verbindungsstelle der Bundesländer beim Amt der N.Ö. Landesregierung: *Das Steueraufkommen der Gemeinden im Jahre 1973,* Wien 1975

Österr. Stat. Zentralamt (ed.): *Der Fremdenverkehr in Österreich 1975,* Wien 1976 ita-income of local taxes above the federal average. Some highly developed resorts, where already a danger of overdevelopment is present, have attained top ranks in the per-capita-income from taxes, often ranking above communities with flourishing manufacturing industries.

However, these communities are not free from debts. In keeping with the development of tourism their responsibilites also have grown. Expensive investments, especially for infra-structure, were necessary to establish installations which often are only used for a few months of the year.

These three criteria were chosen as examples. Limited time does not allow my going into further details on the economic effect of cableways. In fact, almost the whole local economy is influenced, beginning with tourist businesses through trade, local industries and crafts and farming (here including the letting of rooms and the possibility of selling home-made products).

For our purposes, *the key question is why the development of cableway-induced winter tourism is so successful.* This depends on three items:

1. Many tourist enterprises do not reach a satisfactory utilization of capacity, and therefore break-even-point, before a second season, the winter season, is developed. In the light of today's tourist market and cost structure, a one-season-business of high standards hardly covers its costs. *A second season,* however, *brings profits and stimulates investment expenditures.*

2. *The average receipt per tourist and day in winter is considerably higher* than in summer. There are additional expenditures to be met, such as cableways, après-ski activities and also an accomodation, because during wintertime one has to spend more time indoors.

3. In Austria at least, *higher income groups participate in winter sport.* According to their functional classification, cableways which were predominantly or exlusively for winter sport, had the greatest impact. Nearly all cableways opened during the last four years were of this type.

The impact of cableways was greater in resorts where passengers were tourists on an extended vacation. In places where short-time excursionist tourists played a great role, the impact was less.

In the development of cableways there are a *lot of problems;* the most important of them should be briefly pointed out:

1. There is something which could be called an "*armaments race*" in the whole Alpine region. The precious buying power of winter tourists leads to a strong competition between states, regions and resorts. More attractive, diversified and spacious constructions are established, but the economic results are deteriorating. This "armaments race" is promoted by optimistic estimates of growth of winter tourism, based upon a favourable future economic situation which will allow more and more people to take part in winter tourism. The growing market share of other winter destinations, viz. the warm southern coasts for instance, are not being considered to the necessary extent.

2. The *state of euphoria* despite unfavourable economic results has already been pointed out. This state, of course, is partly caused by the "armaments race". On the other hand, a false estimation of the economic situation in the cableway business is responsible for the growth in construction. When constructing new additional cableways, provision for renovation of the existing ones is forgotten. Often bad investments are made, hoping that an additional cableway will bring profitability to the existing ones. In this way, a lot of businesses are founded which may have to be subsidised in the future.

3. The *danger of overdevelopment* has also been pointed out. It is generally

Graph 4: Winter overnight-stays in ,,winter-centres" 1974/75

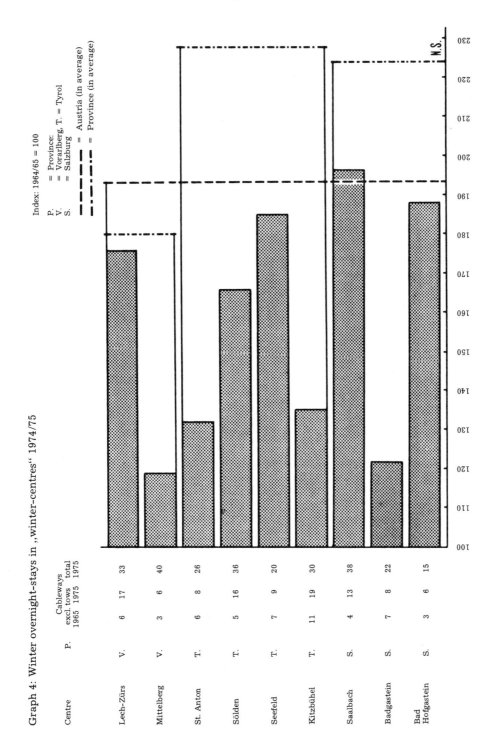

Index: 1964/65 = 100

P. = Province:
V. = Vorarlberg, T. = Tyrol
S. = Salzburg

— — — = Austria (in average)
—·—·— = Province (in average)

Centre	P.	Cableways excl. tows 1965	Cableways excl. tows 1975	Cableways total 1975
Lech-Zürs	V.	6	17	33
Mittelberg	V.	3	6	40
St. Anton	T.	6	8	26
Sölden	T.	5	16	36
Seefeld	T.	7	9	20
Kitzbühel	T.	11	19	30
Saalbach	S.	4	13	38
Badgastein	S.	7	8	22
Bad Hofgastein	S.	3	6	15

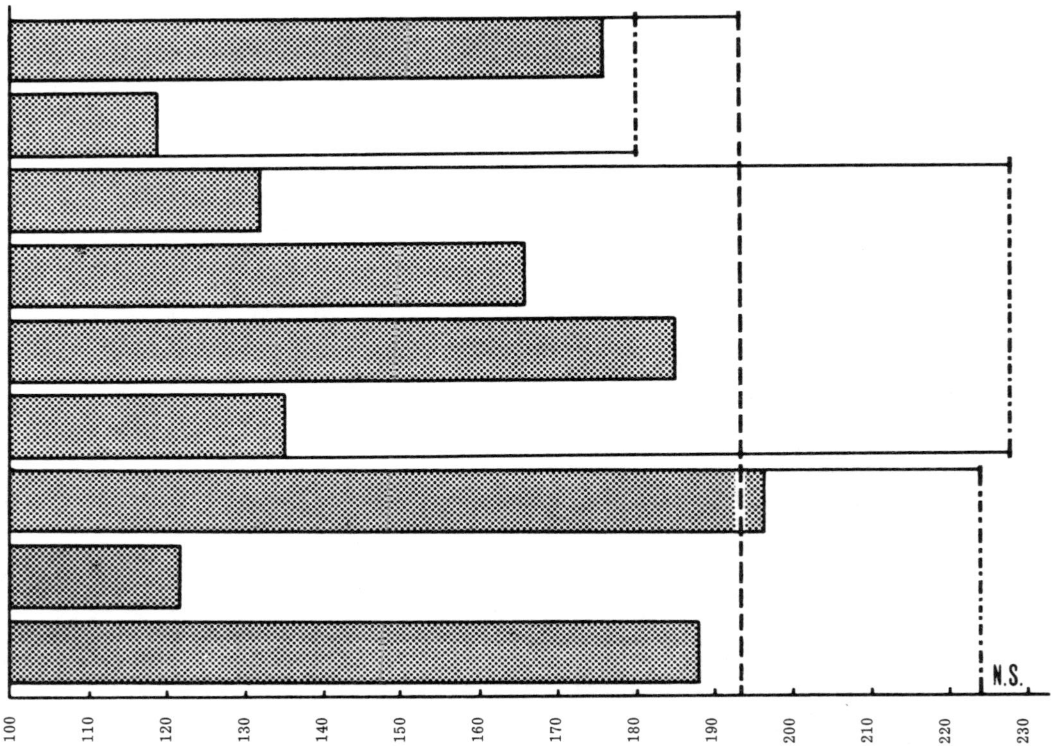

known that tourism, similar to other economic activities, inclines to concentration, although this does not appear to be in keeping with the word recreation. In Austria, for example, there are 2.317 communities, 1.520 of them classified as tourist-communities for statistical use. But 15 per cent. of the tourists nights registered in a year take place in only 11 resorts, 45 per cent. of nights in 89 resorts. This tendency to concentration is more prevalent in winter than in summer, and depends on the necessary facilities for the winter season. An attractive skiing area with many cableways needs large resorts in the valley to utilize its capacity. The dimension of these developments is no longer the best for true recreation in the generally accepted sense.

Investigations conducted for an Austrian Cableway Plan have shown that the growth of overnight stops in centres is below average, but growth in investment in cableways is still continuing unabated. There is now an attempt to connect several smaller resorts with one attractive large skiing area by feeder-cableways.

4. Every cableway development is an *encroachment on the landscape*. For the construction of cableways and the establishing of ski runs earth movement and the uprooting of forests is necessary to an ever-growing extent. Not only is there a detrimental influence on the natural beauty of the landscape, but also an increase in natural hazards, such as avalanches, erosion and so on. The use of slope-grooming-vehicles causes compression of snow. Therefore plants begin to grow later and that means disadvantages for producing cattle. Also the problem

Table 7: Wintertourism in alpine states or regions[1]

State or Region	Year under report	Overnights in millions all-year	Overnights in millions winter half-year	Winter per cent.	Average duration of stay
Austria	74/75	104,6	31,1	29,7	6,1
Bavaria	74/75	64,8	19,0	29,3	4,6
Switzerland	73/74	67,2	27,1[3]	40,3	3,8
Italian Alpine regions[2]	72/73	48,2	11,3	23,3	5,9
Slovenia	74/75	6,4	1,8	27,3	—

[1] Overnight stays recorded at all tourist accomodations.
[2] Including the following provinces: Piemont, Trentino-Southern Tyrol, Valley of Aosta, Friula-Venetia-Julia.
[3] estimated.

Sources: Eidgenössisches Stat. Amt (ed.): *Tourismus in der Schweiz 1974*, Bern 1975

Österr. Stat. Zentralamt (ed.): *Der Fremdenverkehr in Österreich 1975*, Wien 1976

Statistisches Bundesamt Wiesbaden (ed.): *Übernachtungen in Beherbergungsstätten, Mainz 1975 und Winterhalbjahr 1974/75 sowie September 1975 und Sommerhalbjahr 1975*, Stuttgart-Mainz 1975 bzw. 1976

Information provided by the ENIT (Italian national office for Tourism) and the Yugoslavian Tourist advertising office in Vienna of waste in winter sport areas is as yet unsolved. On the Schmiedinger glacier, near Kaprun, contamination of snow, down to a depth of 25 cm was noticed.[5]

In a comparison of winter tourism in Austria with other Alpine states (France excluded because suitable data are lacking), Austria is in a leading position with respect to number of tourist nights. *The share of winter tourism in total tourism increased by 7 per cents. to 30 per cent. since 1961.*68 per cent. of tourist nights registered in Austria during the winter period are spent by foreigners. That means, that a remarkable part of Austria's foreign currency receipts, which are very important for the Austrian balance of payments, stem from winter tourism and thus in the last instance from its cableways.

The economic impact of cableways can hardly be overestimated. It appears to be the most effective factor in the development of the regional economy of mountainous regions suitable for winter sport. However, projectors and constructors of cableways should be more conscious of the possible effects and dangers in the future.

---

[5] MOOR, H.: Der Schisport verursacht Landschaftsschäden. *Neue Zürcher Zeitung*,21./22. 11. 1976. p. 19
TOLLNER, H.: Der Zustand von Gletschern im Großglockner- und Sonnblickgebiet am Ende des Eishaushaltsjahres 1972/73. *70./71. Jahresbericht des Sonnblickvereines für die Jahre 1972/73,* Wien 1974, P. 61

Urbanisation and problems of tourism and recreation in Bulgaria

LJUBOMIR DINEV, Sofia, Bulgaria*

Tourism as a branch of national production begins to form and develop under the conditions of rising capitalism in 19th century. The quick development of industry and transport at that time and connected with them – urbanisation in the economically developed European capitalist countries was a main reason for this. The industrial regions and the big urban centres and agglomerations became the main source of the increasing number of tourists, who are mainly members of the urban bourgeoisie and intelligentsia. The increasing number of tourists and those seeking recreation cause the formation of tourist regions and centres. There the necessary conditions to serve the tourists come into being. All this together with the provision and preparation of further tourist services were factors which little by little turned tourism into tourist industry, an effective economic branch. Its importance quickly increased at the beginning of this century, in the period between the First and Second World Wars and especially after1945. Simultaneously the social spectrum of the tourists contingent was considerably widened.

Bulgaria at that time was an economically backward country as was then the Ottoman Empire. As an independent country Bulgaria arose after 500 years of Ottoman slavery as result of the Russian-Turkish liberation war in 1877–1878 which for Bulgarian was equal to a bourgeois-democratic revolution. Only after that did the young Bulgarian country begin slowly to develop capitalism.

Until World War I the industry and transport in Bulgaria were badly developed. The urbanisation was only at its beginning. Most of the towns were small, mainly agrarian, craft and market centres. At that time without the necessary material basis conditions for the development of tourism in Bulgaria did not yet exist.

Some economic activity began to develop in Bulgaria between World War I and II, but in comparison with some developed European countries Bulgaria at that time lagged behind, with a poorly developed manufacturing industry and transport system.

The socio-economic development of Bulgaria at that period was connected with the establishment of industrial enterprises which were mainly in the towns. The increasing proletarization of the rural population was the reason for migration of people not only from the mountainous unproductive regions towards the plains because of their natural high fertility, but also towards the bigger towns. Urbanisation increased however at a rather slow speed. All this accounts for the peculiarities of the development of tourism in Bulgaria in spite of the presence of the necessary natural and anthropogenous tourist and recreation resources.

The domestic tourism was stimulated, international tourism at that time made its first steps. But the necessary material basis was still absent. Compared with

* Dr.LJUBOMIR DINEV, Professor, Department of Geography, University, Sofia, Bulgaria.

some European countries in which the tourism had already turned into a separate branch of the economy, the national economy in Bulgaria was considerably backward.

The beginning of organized tourism in Bulgaria dates from 1895. After the mass hike organized by the writer Aleko Constantinov to the peak Cherni Vruh (2.290 m) a tourist club was founded in Sofia – the precursor of the Bulgarian Tourist Union (BTU). The members of this club till World War I were mainly part of the intelligentsia of white collar workers in the towns. Between the two World Wars members of the working class began to join. The principal role for the development of the tourism played at that time the Youth Tourist Union (UTU), founded in 1911; its members were pupils. Later the Bulgarian Mountain (later Alpine) Club was founded (1929), the Union for the Protection of Nature (1929), the Bulgarian Ski Union (1931) and others. The Bulgarian Tourist Union helped, as well as the other organisations, in the development mainly for mountain tourism.

After World War I the Bulgarian Tourist Union began to build the first tourist huts in the mountains and the first tourist lodges in well organized tourist centres. It also started the marking of footpaths. This simple material basis played a big role in the development of mountain tourism.

The increased activity of organized tourism and its direction towards the mountains was closely connected with the increasing urbanisation of the country and the aspiration of its citizens to overcome the difficult conditions of life in the towns. For the same reasons the Bulgarian bourgoisie began to build cottages in the mountains, at spas, and at the beaches of the Black Sea. Besides many of the curative baths and springs baths, modern for that time, were built and the villages beside them became well known and much visited resorts. At the Black Sea coast and in the mountains schoolcamps for the pupils from the bigger towns began to be organized.

The beginning of the sea recreative tourism at the Black Sea coast commenced in Varna in the years before the World War I with the opening of the first organized beaches. But its international importance appeared between World War I and II when in 1921 Varna was officially declared a resort. The number of foreign tourists, almost entirely Poles and Czechs, increased in the Black Sea towns of Varna, Bourgas, Nessebar, Sozopol and others, although the material base was rather primitive. In 1928 15.000 foreign tourists were registrated in Varna. Despite of everything pointed out above, domestic and international tourism in Bulgaria were not sufficiently developed before World War II to emerge as a separate branch of the national economy.

The establishment of the socialist conditions for and the socialist way of production after World War II caused radical changes of the socio-economic structure of Bulgaria. The planned economy, socialist industrialization, the co-operative management of the land and the other revolutionary changes brought radical changes of the territorial distribution of the population. The proportion of those employed in agrarian production declined from 82 per cent. of the work force in 1948 to 31 per cent. in 1975, and the ratio between the urban and rural population changed from 24:76 in 1944 to 58:42 in 1975. All these data obviously show the accelerated urbanisation of the country in the years after World War II.

The accelerated urbanization of the country and its socio-economic reorganisation were favourable conditions for development of tourism, due to the politics of its government, Bulgaria, in a short period, became a country of domestic and international tourism. For this purpose the natural and anthropogenous tourist and recreation resources were utilised to the full. For a short period the necessary technical material was built. Tourism changed to be a branch of the national economy.

The international active tourism had become a very big success. While in 1956 Bulgaria had been visited by 8.500 foreign tourists, in 1960 their number had grown to 200.000 and in 1976 they were more than 4 millions. In the international market Bulgaria is a much sought after country. In the field of international tourism the aim is now to develop parallel with the development of the recreative tourism of the seaside, more intensively the mountains, curative, spa, congress and educational tourism, which should help to overcome seasonal tourism and thus use the material bases more extensively. Parallel to building of new modern hotels, the reconstruction and modernisation of the existing material infrastructure is successfully being carried out, service is also being improved. The "passive" tourism is also increasing every year. The number of participants in 1976 was 705.000 persons, in 1960 it had been only 61.000.

Parallel with the development of international tourism after World War II domestic tourism had also a great increase. Special merit for this must go to the Bulgarian Tourist Union (BTU). In comparison with the pre-war period it was popularized and in 1977 counted already 1.650.000 organized members, which represents 35 per cent. of the population able to participate in tourist activities. For the whole period 1972–1977 the Bulgarian Tourist Union and its branches carried out 315 thousand activites with 28.5 million participants but in 1976 alone there were about 30 thousand tourist manifestations with 6.3 millions of participants. Increased to a great extent has the excursion holiday which is taken in mountainous regions along fixed routes. The Bulgarian Tourist Union contributes to the development not only of tourism on foot, but also to the ski-tourism, mountaineering and caving. The influence of the Bulgarian Tourist Union has increased among the various strata of society-factory and agricultural workers, employees, pupils and students. The Bulgarian Tourist Union works at making tourism more a mass movement, for its adoption as the way of life under the slogans "Tourism, the holiday among nature", "Familiarize yourself with your native land in order to love it". The movement for visiting the "100 national tourist places" is of great importance for stimulating tourism. For its spread among the people an important role is played by the combined efforts of the Bulgarian Trade Union and Dimitrov's Communist Youth Union together with the Bulgarian Touring Club and the Ministry of Education. An important role for the development of the holiday business (social tourism) is played by the Bulgarian Trade Union, with its numerous rest houses at the sea side, in mountain resorts and by health resorts of curative waters.

The development of the domestic tourism is facilitated not only by the well developed railway, motorcar, water and air transport, but also due to ample availability of accomodation. The hotels of the State Committee of Tourism are used not only for the needs of international but also for domestic tourism. This Committee in 1976 had 555 well equipped hotels with 91.550 beds at its disposal. For the needs of domestic and international tourism in 1976, mainly in the mountainous regions, 343 tourist huts (in 1944 there had been only 70) with 20 thousand beds were available. 290 of them are run by the Bulgarian Tourist Union. In the tourist huts in 1976 1.335.000 persons had stayed overnight. In the same year social tourism had the use of 1.392 rest houses with 90.700 beds where 841.000 persons stayed as well as a 329.000 pupils in 924 pupil camps.

The emerging mass tourism of the domestic tourism is due to the accelerated urbanisation in Bulgaria. It is characterized not only by the increase in the number of towns and town dwellers, but also by the inculcation of an urban way of life everywhere. Its characteristics make the urban population seek new and different ways of rest and tourism. The short rest has increased very rapidly (week-end rest). For a part of the urban population it is realized in cottage zones near the towns. Another part participates in tourist activities which is realized by both organized and indivudual tourism. During the last years auto tourism has increased considerably.

The different forms of tourism become more and more an integral part of the way of life of the population. For the needs of mass tourism it is necessary to build a good material infrastructure. Hotels, tourist huts, rest houses and cottage zones are insufficient. One way to solve this problem is to build suburban zones for short rests; in those most of the beautiful places of our country should be included. An important role in this direction should be the setting up of campsites in the mountains for use during summer and the building of tourist huts not only in places suitable for the purpose, but also in places connected with important historical events. This building should be linked with tree-planting and improvement works.

The accepted principal directives for further development and improvement of territorial and settlement arrangement of Bulgaria will have a great bearing on the development of tourism and short rest. According these directives the further development of settlements is to be realized not individually but settlement system. The last represents a connection of settlements to each other and inter-creation of territories in which the problems of economic and social condition, social service, rest and technical infrastructure will be solved combined. Settlement systems will offer favourable conditions for improving the quality of life in villages and towns. As a result of this not only the problems of migration and urbanisation but also those of tourism and recreation and environment will be solved far better.

References

DINEV, L. et al.: *Geographia na tourisma.* Sofia 1973 (in Bulgarian)

DINEV, L., MISHEV, K.: *Bulgaria.* Moskva 1973

DINEV, L., MISHEV, K.: *Bulgaria, short geography.* 2nd ed., Sofia 1975 (in Bulgarian)

DINEV, L.: Development and estimation of the migrational processes in Bulgaria. *Geographia Polonica,* 36, Warszawa 1977

Otčet na Centralnija savet na Bulgarskija turističeski sajuz. Sofia 1977 (in Bulgarian)

Osnovni nasoki za po-natatashnoto razvitije i usavarshenstvovane na teritorialnoto i selishnoto ustrojstvo na N. R. Bularia. Sofia 1977, (in Bulgarian)

STEFANOV, I., DINEV, L. KOEV, Z.: *Bulgarien, Land, Volk, Wirtschaft in Stichworten.* Ferdinand Hirt, Wien 1977.

Tourism, Statistics of tourism. Sofia 1977

Les étapes de l'occupation touristique des montagnes moyennes par les sociétés industrielles

L'exemple rhénan

GABRIEL WACKERMANN, Strasbourg, France*

Le processus d'industrialisation modifie fondamentalement les relations entre les principaux centres d'activité et les montagnes qui les entourent. L'urbanisation croissante des plaines étend ses ramifications jusque dans les vallées des massifs tout proches, déclenche en milieu montagnard un mouvement d'exode vers la ville, entraîne l'instauration de réseaux de migrations alternantes de travail et, sous la pression du nombre de citadins, de l'importance des foyers de production et des capitaux à la recherche d'un placement, fait que l'on tend à considérer de plus en plus la montagne comme une annexe territoriale, prête à subir de multiples formes de colonisation en échange d'une assistance économique susceptible de réduire son déclin. L'entassement urbain et la dégradation des conditions atmosphériques par la pollution renforcent progressivement l'attrait des massifs forestiers jusqu'à provoquer en certains endroits une saturation matérielle et morale telle que surgit une nouvelle dialectique entre l'espace vécu par les citadins et l'espace ressenti par ruraux et montagnards.

Le modèle que nous nous proposons de présenter ici, – celui des pays rhénans – se caractérise par une quasi-exclusivité de montagnes moyennes hercyniennes, écrin vert bordant la plaine du Rhin, et n'atteignant en général que des altitudes dépassant rarement 1000 mètres, même au Sud où les crêtes sont généralement plus élevées qu'au Nord. Seul dans la partie méridionale apparaît un relief alpin dont les abords immédiats n'atteignent guère plus de 1800 mètres. Ce cadre montagneux délimite un bassin riche en hommes et en production, sous-tendu par une puissante armature urbaine et des niveaux de vie parmi les plus élevés d'Europe. L'unité physique est cependant compartimentée par de nombreux tracés frontaliers qui attisent la compétition économique et accentuent les contrastes. La récente renonciation à la politique des glacis et la mobilité des personnes due à l'essor de l'après-guerre suscitent depuis quelques années à peine, et de façon limitée, une attractivité rivale de la part des hautes montagnes que complète, plus au sud, le littoral méditerranéen. Mais les liens avec les massifs hercyniens demeurent noués par la plaine industrieuse, tant en ce qui concerne le tourisme de fin de semaine que pour ce qui est des périodes de congés ou de vacances.

1. Les modes bourgeoises

Lorsqu'au XIXe siècle l'industrialisation progresse dans l'espace rhénan, grâce à la découverte de matières premières que recèle son sous-sol et à l'aménagement de grands axes de circulation, la vie urbaine se place sous une dépen-

*Dr. GABRIEL WACKERMANN, Professeur, Institut de Géographie, Université Louis Pasteur, Strasbourg, France dance accrue de la bourgeoisie des affaires qui tend à imprimer à la vie quotidienne une hiérarchie de valeurs fondée sur la réussite sociale. L'image de l'homme „arrivé", de la famille apparemment comblée, se présente petit à petit sous le signe d'une façon de vivre récréative. L'expression de la puissance, la manifestation de la dominance, le culte du prestige, impliquent des attitudes touristiques que facilitent les massifs tout proches nourrissant difficilement des populations très denses, prêtes à monnayer, à faible prix, des sites convoités soit pour des résidences secondaires, soit pour des équipements collectifs de loisirs ou de cure. Le conditionnement mental des couches sociales modestes ou humbles, destiné à faire accepter les stratifications souhaitées apparaît d'autant plus facile que le monde du travail est tributaire des structures industrielles mises en place par les dynasties bourgeoises.

1.1. L'attrait de la double résidence

Conscient d'une supériorité due au succès de ses entreprises, désireux d'émerger de la masse citadine et anonyme par un style d'habitation très personnalisé et recherché, l'industriel, le banquier, le commerçant ou l'un des ses enfants entré dans une carrière libérale ou dans l'enseignement, tend à établir sa résidence secondaire à l'extérieur des agglomérations, *de préférence sur les coteaux le long de la grande faille rhénane ou dans les vallées des monagnes voisines.* Il réalise en cela un vieux rêve, celui d'égaler la noblesse de sang qui, en d'autres temps, s'est volontiers complue dans une mobilité résidentielle oisive. Cette consécration lui confère le surcroît de brillance souhaité et lui permet d'envisager l'organisation de réceptions mondaines qui élargissent, par leur retentissement, sa notoriété régionale.

Ainsi les montagnes moyennes commencent à s'ouvrir lentement et très ponctuellement aux déplacements récréatifs, limités, il est vrai, aux initiatives des catégories les plus favorisées de la population, c'est-à-dire à un taux minimal de personnes: 1% à peine de l'ensemble des habitants dans les secteurs les plus industrialisés: Rhénanie-Westphalie, triangle Francfort-Wiesbaden-Mayence, Sarre. Les »Gutsbesitzer« (propriétaires immobiliers) aménagent fréquemment leur »Résidence« en pavillon de chasse, se rapprochant ainsi davantage encore du modèle nobiliaire qu'ils souhaitent reproduire en nouveaux aristocrates. Les décideurs industriels se constituent des domaines forestiers importants et étendent leur influence à la montagne, posant par là-même les jalons d'une mise en tutelle du territoire. Bénéficiaires de l'ère industrielle, bourgeois des villes et bourgeois des campagnes conjuguent leurs efforts ou rivalisent d'adresse pour acquérir des domaines en moyenne montagne, reflets de leur importance socio-économique. *Le nombre comme la superficie de ces biens est directement proportionnel à celui des grands patrons de la région:* c'est ainsi que le nord et le sud du massif schisteux rhénan se situent en tête du classement, le premier par suite de l'expansion des activités de la Ruhr et des réseaux, urbains animés par Dusseldorf ou Cologne, le second en raison de l'influence des centres liés, à l'est au triangle Francfort-Wiesbaden-Offenbach, à l'ouest à la Sarre et au Luxembourg. Suivent en seconde position l'Odenwald, zone de fixation de Darmstadt au nord, de Mannheim-Ludwigshafen-Heidelberg au sud, ainsi que les massifs proches de Zurich-Saint-Gall. Les autres montagnes sont encore trop éloignées des grands foyers industriels et urbains pour être atteintes par le phénomène ou séparées d'eux par la frontière; c'est le cas de Vosges, de la Forêt Noire du Palatinat

Méridional et de la Forêt Noire qui jouxtent des plaines et des plateaux moins industrialisés, sectionnés en outre par des limites internationales.[1]

L'engouement pour la double résidence se propage souvent, par relais interposés, *dans les stations de cure climatique* (»Luftkurort«) *et thermale* (»Heilbad«) *particulièrement nombreuses dans cet espace.* Celles-ci connaissent un développement rapide lié, bien entendu, à la réputation internationale de certaines d'entre elles (Bad-Godesberg, Bad Ems, Baden-Baden, Vittel, Plombières...), mais surtout à l'environnement industriel et urbain, les brasseurs d'affaires venant solliciter périodiquement le calme et les eaux de ces havres de repos, mais aussi, pendant la bonne saison, de loisir et de vie mondaine. L'habitude se répand dans certains milieux de la haute bourgeoisie de suivre là aussi les traces de l'aristocratie princière et de séjourner quelques semaines par an en station de cure, pas forcément, cette fois-ci, dans la plus proche, mais – »noblesse« oblige, – dans la plus renommée d'entre les moins éloignées. Il est vrai que la hiérarchie bourgeoise classe les stations selon les niveaux de fréquentation: les familles les moins influentes doivent se contenter généralement des lieux les moins recherchés, ce qui les incite couramment à se rendre plus nombreuses dans le voisinage.

La montée rapide des stations balnéaires correspond grosso modo à la consolidation et la prospérite de la société industrielle durant la seconde moitié du XIXe siècle. C'est l'époque où les capitaux investis dans des établissements de cure, les hôtels et autres équipements d'accueil – récréatifs surtout – se retrouvent multipliés par vingt. Les communes transformées et parfois les villages limitrophes fournissent une main d'oeuvre saisonnière touristique importante aux stations, ce bouleversement des habitudes induisant également des activités liées au tourisme: artisanat du bâtiment, production agricole variée. Le pourcentage d'autochtones ainsi concernés, directement ou indirectement, par l'aménagement de stations est relativement supérieur à celui de nos jours, car le recrutement du personnel nécessaire n'exige pas le recours à une qualification professionnelle importante. Bien au contraire, les effectifs sont bon marché et leur genre de vie mixte mi-agricole mi-thermalo-touristique ainsi que la faiblesse des exigences favorisent le travail à mi-temps et l'activité saisonnière. Cette situation explique la raison pour laquelle la plupart des stations engagent alors dix à quinze fois plus d'ouvriers ou d'employés locaux qu'actuellement.[2]

1.2. Les privilégiés des nouveaux moyens de transport

Dès la fin du XIXe siècle et surtout à partir du début du XXe siècle, la pénétration rapide des nouveaux moyens de transport inventés peu de temps auparavant commence à bouleverser les relations entre la société industrielle et la montagne. Le chemin de fer, puis le tramway, l'automobile plus tard, incitent les cadres supérieurs des entreprises privées, des administrations publiques, ensuite certains cadres moyens parmi les plus favorisés, mais surtout les professions libérales et les professeurs bien nantis à suivre l'exemple de la haute société bourgeoise. *Chemin de fer et tramway suburbain relient de plus en plus la plaine urbanisée aux massifs forestiers pour des raisons essentiellement* économiques. Le tou-

---

[1] L'étude cadastrale fait ressortir une occupation moyenne (résidences secondaires et domaines fonciers attenants) de 0,07 à 0,09 hectare de coteau ou de vallée dans la première catégorie, de 0,04 à 0,05 ha dans la seconde et de moins de 0,02 ha dans la dernière catégorie.

[2] Evaluation faite à partir des archives locales ou régionales et les indications fournies par les historiens régionaux spécialisés dans le thermalisme, entre 1958 et 1965, au moment où nous avons commencé à réunir la documentation destinée à notre thèse de doctorat d'Etat intitulée *»Les loisirs dans l'espace rhénan, de la région zurichoise à la frontière germano-néerlandaise – Une analyse géographique dans un espace multinational«*, Service de Publication des Thèses, Université de Lille, 1973

risme bénéficie de cette innovation, surtout les dimanches d'été, au moment où de nombreuses initiatives, inspirées du romantisme et d'une nostalgie de la nature que les concentrations industrielles sont en train de dégrader, aboutissent à la création de clubs de promenades pédestres (»Wandervereine«) qui créent et flèchent des sentiers, installent des bancs de repos, remettent en état les vieilles ruines, les sites historiques et aménagent les panoramas pittoresques. La fraîcheur forestière et plus particulièrement celle de la montagne sont appréciées durant la bonne saison, non seulement pour leur valeur intrinsèque mais aussi à cause de la *donsidération sociale* qui est liée à la »sortie«: on sait être oisif, on doit donc disposer des moyens de l'être; si l'on se promène, on se trouve dans une situation aisée et l'on accomplit un travail hebdomadaire pas trop fatigant; la »Sommerfrische« (la fraîcheur estivale) et le »Sommerfrischler« (celui qui recherche la fraîcheur estivale, l'estivant en somme) sont indissociables de la promotion sociale des nouvelles classes bourgeoises; enviées, jalousées ou haïes, celles-ci font naître en maint endroit un sentiment de xénophobie dans les milieux agricoles, sauf dans les stations touristiques où les retombées financières facilitent l'intégration des autochtones au système mis en place par la société industrielle.

Si la hiérarchie des zones de montagne concernées par le tourisme durant la période précédente demeure pratiquement la même pendant la seconde étape, de nombreuses modifications interviennent toutefois dans la configuration interne de chacune d'entre elles. L'étoffement de la bourgeoisie à la faveur de l'intensification des activités industrielles, la densification urbaine et l'engouement pour un genre de vedettariat dans une civilisation de plus en plus dépersonnalisée, resserrent les liens entre villes et montagne: les résidences secondaires se multiplient; la superficie consacrée aux domaines privés de chasse augmente: elle triple presque dans le nord du massif schisteux rhénan jusque vers les années 1930, double dans le Taunus, le Hunsrück, l'Odenwald et les massifs proches de Zurich-Saint-Gall. Les investissements dans les stations de cure quintuplent en moyenne, le nombre de clients logés à l'hôtel décuple presque. Les particuliers commencent à acquérir des propriétés dans ces stations. Les crises économiques semblent accélérer et raffermir le marché foncier de la montagne[3], surtout dans les vallées pittoresques et sur les coteaux ensoleillés où l'on ne se contente plus de construire des résidences secondaires, mais où l'on installe sa résidence principale lorsque l'entreprise que l'on dirige n'est pas trop éloignée. Le renforcement de la spéculation foncière en période d'instabilité ressemble quelque peu à la roulette où le nombre de joueurs a tendance à augmenter lorsque le monde des affaires se porte mal. Les multiples crises de l'Allemagne weimarienne conduisent ainsi à une surenchère immobilière de la montagne plus ample que dans les autres Etats rhénans.

Malgré l'amélioration des axes de circulation et la multiplication des moyens de transport, dont la bicyclette, il est très rare que l'occupation des massifs forestiers soit prononcée au-delà de 30 à 40 kilomètres de rayon des principales agglomérations urbaines. La montagne »profonde«, peu sollicitée par le tourisme et par l'économie en général, reste inviolée dans les régions francophones plus encore que dans les régions germanophones, davantage portées, de par leur culture, vers le plein air et le culte de la nature; l'exemple vosgien est typique à cet égard: du côté alsacien, l'occupation touristique du massif apparaît dès le départ plus

---

[3] cf. les archives notariales, ainsi que les services cadastraux, après avoir relevé les principales séquences de crise économique ou monétaire.

intense et moins marginale que du côté lorrain. En dépit de ces différentiations, une vaste pression sociale va, à partir des années trente, modifier sensiblement la dialectique entre la société industrielle et la moyenne montagne.

2. Les tentatives de popularisation de la montagne et leurs contradictions

2.1. Les exigences d'une société de masse

Durant l'entre-deux-guerres, les déséquilibres inhérents à l'industrialisation sont d'autant plus inquiétants que leurs conséquences sociales pèsent lourdement sur le climat politique aux prises avec des tensions préjudiciables à l'ordre public. La concentration urbaine demeure l'élément perturbateur majeur:

„La ville n'est plus l'image d'une société inscrite sur le sol exprimant des rapports sociaux, des symboles, un imaginaire. Elle n'est plus un espace vivant, mais une accumulation de moyens techniques, de machines à habiter pour préserver la force de travail, de voies rapides permettant d'accélérer les mouvements d'échange. La ville n'est plus faite pour les hommes, mais les hommes pour la ville. L'espace urbain devient l'expression du non-sens ...

... Même le temps dit libre, le temps des loisirs, est un temps de récupération, et un temps de »consommation culturelle«, source de profit et objet de manipulation.[4]

... Si nous parlons du milieu urbain en général, nous pouvons ... distinguer ... pour faciliter les observations, un environnement urbain marqué surtout par la concentration de l'habitat, des entreprises et du commerce, et un milieu social urbain se rapportant aux relations, aux modes de communication et aux idéologies".[5]

La société industrielle habituellement considérée comme l'expression d'un nouveau progrès social, entraîne dans son sillage des servitudes que la législation essaie de pallier. Les avantages légaux accordés aux hommes sont donc plus des correctifs sociaux et des stimulants économiques intégrés au système de production que des moyens d'émancipation réelle.

Dans l'espace rhénan où l'urbanisation atteint des proportions peu communes avec d'autres espaces européens, -en secteur allemand le plus vaste parmi les secteurs nationaux, les grandes liaisons intercités concernent actuellement 17 villes contre seulement 14 pour le reste de la R.F.A., – les mesures prises depuis les années trente et surtout depuis 1945, favorisent un véritable assaut de la montagne, au moment où de nouveaux moyens de transport individuels viennent compléter les transports publics: deux-roues à moteur d'abord, automobile ensuite. *L'indice d'attractivité récréative le plus élevé des populations urbaines est généralement atteint par les massifs forestiers.*[6]

De nombreux mouvements et institutions contribuent à développer la mobilité, qu'ils soient démocratiques ou autoritaires. Les sociétés philanthropiques associées à celles des amis de la nature, les cercles confessionnels ou laïcs, renforcés à partir des années vingt par les organisations syndicales, sont canalisés par de puissants courants idéologiques qui marquent l'opinion pour que, à travers la détente dominicale, soient atténuées les rigueurs imposées au rythme de travail quotidien. C'est ainsi qu'en Allemagne les dirigeants nazis dès 1933 sub-

---

[4] CHOMBART DE LAUWE,: *La culture et le pouvoir.* Paris 1975, p. 27

[5] cf. CHOMBART DE LAUWE, P.-H.: *La culture et le pouvoir.* Paris 1975, p. 105

[6] cf. e. a. KEMPER, F.-J.: *Inner- und außerstädtische Naherholung am Beispiel der Bonner Bevölkerung – Ein Beitrag zur Geographie der Freizeit.* Bonn 1977, p. 137

stituent au courant très républicain du »Wandervogel« des groupements de tout genre, depuis les jeunesses hitlériennes jusqu'à »Kraft durch Freude« (»la force par la joie«), conscients d'atténuer les effets de la dictature par la systématisation des congés payés et la mise en chantier d'équipements d'accueil récréatifs sociaux. Dans les autres pays du Rhin, les progrès de la législation, – en France notamment celle introduite par le Front Populaire en 1936, – stimulent la mobilité populaire et encouragent l'édification de maisons de week-end et de vacances pour les travailleurs en même temps que celle de colonies de vacances. Après 1945, la généralisation progressive des congés et leur allongement à 3 puis à 4 semaines, l'augmentation des niveaux de vie, la création des routes et les facilités accordées par les transports en commun et l'abaissement relatif du coût des moyens de locomotion individuelle, rendent la montagne de plus en plus accessible aux populations urbaines. Depuis une dizaine d'années environ, l'insertion du troisième âge dans les migrations touristiques augmente encore la clientèle: le prolongement de l'espérance de vie et l'amélioration des budgets des retraités, mais surtout les méthodes de sollicitation psychologique et commerciale élaborées tant par les milieux d'affaires que par les milieux politiques, insèrent dans le circuit récréatif quotidien, notamment en période creuse, des centaines de milliers de personnes. L'apport du tourisme de passage et de séjour qui prend une allure internationale depuis les années 1960, représente actuellement 40% environ de l'ensemble des flux récréatifs de la bonne saison et un cinquième des flux annuels.

Un examen attentif de la situation révèle toutefois que la montagne n'est pas aussi saturée qu'on ne le prétend parfois, ni aussi ouverte aux couches populaires. Elle traduit en effet davantage les contradictions et les antagonismes suscités par la société industrielle qu'une véritable démocratisation de l'occupation ou de l'usage du sol.

2.2. *Le loisir en montagne, reflet des stratifications sociales*

L'observation fine des diverses migrations récréatives montre que les *catégories sociales modestes ou humbles des villes* et même les *couches moyennes de la population ne sont pas les bénéficiaires essentiels du tourisme en montagne.* L'indice de concentration des promeneurs dominicaux est dans l'ensemble plus élevé dans les espaces verts urbains et périurbains qu'en montagne[7]: depuis les années soixante-dix il dépasse couramment 50% dans les premiers pour tomber à moins de 40% en massif forestier, voire 25 à 35% à partir de 600 mètres d'altitude, alors que de 1960 à 1970 il atteint jusqu'à 60 à 65% en plaine contre 15 à 20% en altitude de plus de 600 mètres. Le gros des taux de plaine est alimenté par les catégories socio-professionnelles modestes, alors que plus des deux tiers des taux de montagne se rapportent aux couches aisées de la population. Le fait est particulièrement net dans les lieux touristiques de montagne non desservis par le chemin de fer ou un quelconque transport en commun suburbain: les touristes aisés y atteignent jusqu'à 75 à 85%, notamment depuis la crise du pétrole.[8]

Les zones les plus saturées en touristes résidants ou itinérants demeurent celles situées dans un rayon ne dépassant pas 50 ou 60 kilomètres autour des grandes agglomérations. Le temps de déplacement s'avère coûteux; de nombreux amateurs de loisirs préfèrent alors rester à proximité du domicile où la densité et la variété

[7] cf. KEMPER, F.-J.: *Inner- und außerstädtische Naherholung am Beispiel der Bonner Bevölkerung – Ein Beitrag zur Geographie der Freizeit.* Bonn 1977, pp. 137–138

[8] sondages effectués par l'auteur depuis 1960.

de distractions offertes sont plus conséquentes. Par le fait de cette concentration excessive du tourisme à la périphérie des montagnes moyennes et dans les portions de vallées les plus rapidement accessibles, la pression des prix et la spéculation immobilière sont parfois aussi élevées sinon plus qu'en ville. On a certes souhaité préserver, en territoire allemand surtout, de vastes surfaces de massifs forestiers par la création de parcs naturels; il n'a pas été possible d'empêcher une certaine sursollicitation en équipements touristiques à la périphérie de ces parcs.

Ce déplacement de la demande sociale urbaine vers les marges des montagnes essentiellement réservées, il y a encore quelques décennies, à la bourgeoisie, entraîne donc l'apparition de situations antisociales: renchérissement du foncier et sélectivité des installations touristiques provoquant la disparition progressive des points d'accueil populaires bon marché et bon vivant. Il amorce aussi le processus d'exploration de la montagne »profonde« par les citadins aisés en vue de l'acquisition de terrains ou de fermes, au moment même où le marché est peu tendu et avant la pénétration éventuelle des citadins modestes, comportement qui permet de se procurer des superficies plus vastes que dans l'avant-pays et d'hypothéquer le sol par la spéculation.

C'est déjà le cas des stations de sports d'hiver qui accueillent essentiellement des citadins aisés ou riches et aux alentours desquelles se fixent des résidences qui éliminent agriculture et autochtones. L'été dans ces stations est également réservé en grande partie aux mêmes types socio-professionnels ainsi qu'aux touristes originaires d'autres régions ou d'autres Etats.

Le phénomène de ségrégation et de spéculation est amplifié dans les massifs situés à proximité des grosses agglomérations, dans lesquelles le taux d'activité s'accroît plus qu'ailleurs à la faveur de la diversification des emplois, de leur tertiairisation et du taux croissant de femmes au travail:

». . . dans les villes d'un million d'habitants, le taux d'activité de la population dépasse de quelque 12,5% celui des villes de 100.000 à 200.000 habitants. Pourquoi?

Tout d'abord, parce que la population active croît avec la taille des villes en raison de la conjonction de deux phénomènes, l'immigration de jeunes et l'émigration de personnes âgées. Ensuite, parce que le mode de vie urbain est en lui-même créateur d'emplois. Il entraîne . . . la création de 16% des postes de travail supplémentaires en particulier dans les transports, l'administration et les loisirs.

Plus la ville est importante, plus les activités y sont diversifiées et plus leur nature exige une forte main d'oeuvre. Le secteur tertiaire traditionnellement à forte intensité de main-d'oeuvre représente ainsi 63% des activités urbaines dans les pays développés. C'est d'ailleurs dans les capitales (où le tertiaire occupe la place la plus grande) que le chômage est le moins fort en raison de la concentration de services gouvernementaux qui assurent généralement la sécurité de l'emploi.

Dans les grandes villes, surtout, les femmes sont plus nombreuses à travailler. Entre les villes de 100.000 à 200.000 habitants et celles de plus de 500.000 habitants, le taux d'activité des femmes progresse de 15 à 20%. Cette participation plus forte des femmes à la vie active découle des possibilités d'emploi, notamment dans le tertiaire. Mais il existe également des facteurs sociaux et économiques qui entraînent un désir ou un besoin d'activité plus impérieux dans les grandes villes: l'isolement, le coût de la vie plus élevé (en particulier celui des loyers), l'émancipation sociale, l'indépendance financière.«[9]

[9] BAIROCH, P.: *Emploi et taille des villes.* Bureau international du Travail, Genève, 1977; le passage cité est extrait du résumé de cet ouvrage, paru dans Informations O. I. T., Genève 1977

Cette analyse correspond en moyenne à l'évolution de l'espace rhénan. C'est dans les massifs forestiers proches des grandes métropoles de Francfort et de Zurich d'abord, puis de la région urbaine de la Ruhr à laquelle on peut associer Dusseldorf et même Cologne, que les contradictions sociales évoquées ci-dessus s'expriment avec le plus d'acuité. Viennent en troisième lieu les massifs situés près de Mannheim-Ludwigshafen-Heidelberg, Sarrebruck-Luxembourg, Karlsruhe-Stuttgart. Ailleurs les tendances se précisent et des voix s'élèvent pour éviter que ne se reproduisent un peu partout les mêmes événements. Mais en raison d'une information plus complète sur les problèmes de l'environnement et face aux multiples nuisances observées, une nouvelle étape se dessine dans l'évolution touristique de la montagne moyenne.

3. Les tentatives de rééquilibrage en montagne moyenne

3.1. La contestation du processus d'occupation touristique

Après plusieurs phases d'expansion, le système d'occupation touristique de la montagne est contesté au moment même où la société industrielle, en pleine crise, fournit des arguments déterminants à l'opinion publique.

Quoique les montagnards soient très divisés à propos des attitudes à adopter vis-à-vis de la colonisation touristique – les uns préférant s'installer dans l'atmosphère de spéculation générale, les autres essayant de conserver une certaine identité socio-culturelle – des minorités agissantes, appuyées par des mouvements écologiques régionaux, voire nationaux, s'inspirent de la discussion globale qui s'est instaurée aux niveaux les plus élevés. L'exemple des massifs forestiers moins hypothéqués par le tourisme, notamment dans les Vosges et les Ardennes, soumis à une pression »sauvage«, donne à réfléchir là aussi compte tenu de l'expérience faite ailleurs.

Le recul de la natalité dans l'ensemble des régions rhénanes, la surindustrialisation de la zone allemande et les surcapacités qui en résultent, l'importance croissante des moyennes entreprises, réduisent le rôle joué par les grandes villes dans l'organisation du territoire et rendent sujette à caution leur revendication d'un surcroît d'espace. Dans ces pôles urbains se développent également des associations écologiques qui se concertent avec les ruraux et les montagnards pour créer un front commun d'action sociale. Des contradictions subsistent cependant, une part importante des adhérents de ces mouvements étant des intellectuels qui, à l'occasion, n'hésitent pas à acquérir un terrain ou une ferme dans l'un des massifs contestés, pour placer leur argent, contribuer au démantèlement des vieilles structures locales, participer au maintien plus ou moins factice du folklore ou pour s'y implanter politiquement.

En R.F.A. par exemple se développent vers 1970 des comités de citoyens („Bürgerinitiativen"). D'après une enquête effectuée en 1976, par l'Institut allemand d' urbanistique, 16,9% d'entre eux s'intéressent à l'environnement, 15,8% aux jardins d'enfants, 11,8% aux problèmes de transport, 8,1% aux écoles, 8% au développement urbain, 7,1% aux groupes marginaux de la population, 5,7% aux problèmes culturels et à la défense du patrimoine artistique, 4,9% aux jeunes et aux problèmes de loisirs, 3,9% aux institutions communales, 3,6% à la rénovation urbaine. »Leur caractère informel défie la statistique et l'on doit s'en remettre à des enquêtes partielles pour approcher leur composition sociologique ... Il est admis ... que les „Bürgerinitiativen" attirent surtout les jeunes appartenant aux couches intellectuelles ou aux classes moyennes et ayant un niveau d'éducation moyen ou supérieur«.[10]

Les préoccupations relatives à l'environnement et au changement social apparaissent nettement dans cette enquête. L'époque semble révolue où la population admet docilement les contraintes spatiales imposées par l'économie.

3.2. Perspectives de solutions

»Dans les zones de montagne ... ce sont des réflexions globales, pouvant aller jusqu'à la proposition de ›systèmes de vie‹, d'équilibre d'activités ... (pluriactivité, services polyvalents ...) qui sont à approfondir. Il faudra même probablement remettre complètement en cause le principe libéral de l'initiative privée en matière économique, l'Etat (à tous niveaux: nation, département, commune) prenant à sa charge le maintien de l'activité industrielle ou autre«.[11]

Ce passage résume à la fois les tendances actuelles des montagnards et celles des services d'aménagement conscients des erreurs passées et des conséquences d'une société industrielle livrée à elle-même. Le désordre dû à la spéculation et à une consommation intempestive de l'espace n'est pas propre aux pays rhénans, mais il y trouve une terre d'élection à cause de son haut niveau industriel. Le problème de la friche illustre aussi cette situation. Les propos du ministre français de l'agriculture s'appliquent facilement à ce territoire:

»Dans ce climat de concurrence, ou plutôt de complémentarité entre la forêt, la culture et le pâturage, la friche ne doit pas avoir de place. Rares sont en effet les parcelles qui ne sont pas entretenues uniquement faute d'exploitant décidé à les mettre en valeur, en raison de leur localisation ou par suite de la pauvreté des sols. Beaucoup au contraire sont laissées incultes de par la volonté expresse des propriétaires qui y voient un moyen de conserver un capital foncier susceptible de plus-value«.[12]

La société industrielle urbaine a donc marqué profondément la population montagnarde en l'intégrant à son système de profit. La réarticulation entre le territoire urbain et les massifs forestiers voisins suppose comme préalable un changement des structures mentales fondé sur une rénovation culturelle, c'est-à-dire une politique de respect de la spécificité de chaque espace et de ses composants. Mais, selon MICHEL FOUCAULT[13], »Le problème n'est pas tellement de définir une ›position‹ politique (ce qui nous ramène à un choix sur un échiquier déjà constitué) mais d'imaginer et de faire exister de nouveaux schémas de politisation. Si ›politiser‹ c'est ramener à des choix, à des organisations toutes faites, tous ces rapports de force et ces mécanismes de pouvoir que l'analyse dégage, alors ce n'est pas la peine. Aux grandes techniques nouvelles de pouvoir (qui correspondent aux économies multinationales ou aux Etats bureaucratiques) doit s'opposer une politisation qui aura des formes nouvelles«.

Le monde rhénan exige une pareille remise en cause de la société industrielle. L'essence même du loisir et de ses diverses échelles, dont le tourisme tout particulièrement, implique une prise en considération plus prononcée des impératifs humains et spatiaux. Dans un périmètre aux nombreuses frontières, des expériences originales mériteraient d'être tentées si l'idée d'une meilleure cohésion européenne doit se concrétiser réellement.

---

[10] VERNET, D.: *Les comités des citoyens et la désobéissance civique*, dans: Documents – Revue des Questions Allemandes, 4, Paris 1977, 2, pp. 29–30

[11] Bulletin d'Information de l' ACEAR (Atelier Central d'Etude d'Aménagement Rural), fasc. 13104, juillet, Paris 1976

[12] Congrès de la Fédération Française d'Economie Montagnarde, Colmar, 2–5 juin 1977.

[13] La Quinzaine Littéraire, nr 247, Paris 1977, p. 6

Ranges and catchment areas of selected recreation facilities in Bavaria

GÜNTER HEINRITZ, Munich, Federal Republic of Germany*

1. *Introduction*

To apply the concept and questions of central place research to facilities for recreation, i. e. to objects that are usually studied within a geography of recreation behaviour, may seem inappropriate, even paradoxical at first sight. "Central places" and recreation areas were all too often thought of as antipoles; central place amenities on the one hand and recreation facilities on the other hand seemed to be essentially different. This rather intuitive approach, however, should not make us forget that it is essentially the same problem that geography has to study when dealing with central places as well as recreation areas. New terms like holiday centre, recreation centre, youth or sports centre, indicate that the functional locations of recreation facilities can be considered as "central facilities". And in fact, they satisfy all the criteria found in K. GUSTAFSSON's[1] definition of the term "centrality": "A place is central, if at least one of the spatial interactions observed within a well defined region is directed towards this place." If "place" in this definition is substituted by "facility", indoor swimming pools as well as deer parks, pony tracking areas, keep-fit paths or minigolf courses prove to be central amenities just as much as a department store or a bank. In practical work, for example in the field of locational planning, issues and methods of central place research have therefore been applied to recreation facilities for a long time. Whether the minimum turnover can be reached, or exceeded, i. e. whether a sufficiently large catchment area can develop essentially depends on the location of the respective facility. Indeed the factors determining the formation of catchment areas have received more and more attention in private enterprises or locational planning teams. Even for non-profit making public facilities planners must prove a certain minimum effective use of the recreation facilities they have demanded, of implemented, often for prestige reasons. Needs and accessibility are often determined normatively, and such norms are then applied as standard values or estimates. It has to be asked, however, how useful such estimates are. What does it mean, for example, when the catchment area of an indoor swimming pool is claimed to extend over an area with a radius of 5–10 km [2] or when the radius of a catchment area of a teaching pool is set at 3 km.[3] The search for such data implicitly assumes that such values specific to facilities do exist in reality.

---

* Dr. GÜNTER HEINRITZ, Professor, Institute of Geography, University of Technology of Munich, Federal Republic of Germany

[1] GUSTAFSSON, K.: Grundlagen der Zentralitätsbestimmung, dargestellt am Beispiel der Region „Westküste Schleswig-Holstein". *Veröffentlichungen der Akademie für Raumforschung und Landesplanung.* Abhandlungen 66, Hannover 1973, p. 19

[2] SCHAEFLER, H. O.: Gedanken zur Planung von Hallenbädern. *Deutsche Bauzeitschrift,* Gütersloh 1964, pp. 1193–1198

[3] CASPAR, H.: Bäderbau, Bäderplanung, Planungsrichtzahlen für Normal-, Kleinschwimmhallen und Lehrschwimmbäder sowie medizinische Bäder. *Archiv des Badewesens. Zeitschrift für Praxis, Technik und Wissenschaft des Badewesens,* Essen, 18. 8. 1965, pp. 211–212

To test that assumption by empirical means would be of considerable use for planning.

The studies that are reported below started with this question. By means of inquiries at several locations of recreation facilities of the same type, their ranges or catchment areas were investigated with the aim of obtaining specific ranges for each of these facilities. This demands, first of all, a clear definition of the terms range and catchment area. According to CHRISTALLER's definition, the range is the maximum point in a time-cost-effort-scale which a consumer is prepared to tolerate when travelling to a certain facility. In order to prevent extreme findings (for whose occurrence we cannot assume regularity) from distorting the empirical calculation of this critical value, it is advisable to take a large number of observations as a basis and to calculate a suitable figure.[4]

Thus, the decisions of the research worker, concerning data gathering and computing will exert considerable influence on the calculation of the ranges of the facilities under study; for this reason they have to be explicitly stated.[5]

The catchment area is that area in which the homes of the visitors to a facility are situated. Assuming a homogeneous surface (e. g. equal distribution of population and functional locations), it forms a circle the radius of which equals the range. In reality, of course, a homogeneous surface does not exist. Because of differential conditions as to population density, transport facilities and their accessibility, or relative location to competing facilities, differences between the ranges of recreation facilities of the same type are to be expected as well as irregular and asymmetrical shapes of catchment areas.

2. *The obtaining of the ranges*

The initial assumption of our empirical studies was that influences caused by the geographical position of a recreation facility are rather small, that differences between ranges remain within such narrow limits that the arithmetic mean can well be interpreted as the "average range". For testing this hypothesis all the other factors which by themselves might affect the ranges of facilities of the same type had to be excluded. This applies particularly to factors which influence the ranges because of different standards of equipment and attractiveness of the facilities; this can be achieved by holding the variable "attractiveness" as constant as possible. For different recreation facilities this poses difficulties of varying degree. It is nearly impossible in the case of facilities such as excursion cafés or dancing-halls, i. e. facilities that derive their attractiveness not only from their material furnishing, but also from aesthetic qualities and the quality of the services they offer. On the other hand problems are less serious in the case of monofunctional recreation facilities, which present standard offers, i. e. have more or less equal fixtures and offer little service. This holds good – with certain qualifications – for example for recently built public indoor swimming pools, with "normal" equipment and, with even higher probability, for keep-fit paths and minigolf courses. Therefore, these three types of facilities were chosen for the empirical investigations. In many contributions to the geography of recreation behaviour it has been justly pointed out that – compared to other fields of

[4] It could, for example, be the first number of the 6th sextile. Since in this paper the original data were aggregated, the mean of all distances covered by all the respondents had to be used to define the range of the leisure time facilities. The author is fully aware of the fact that it has only limited value as the above mentioned critical figure.

[5] HEINRITZ, G.: Einzugsgebiete und zentralörtliche Bereiche. Methodische Probleme der empirischen Zentralitätsforschung. *Münchner Geographische Hefte 39,* München 1977.

human activities – travelling for holiday or local recreational purposes, is evaluated in a completely different way. In a way the covering of even long distances will be given a certain value of its own. The time-cost-effort-relation is not exclusively evaluated in economic terms; what is more, time considerations are less important than in other activities.

With the assumption of the consumers economic and rational behaviour being dismissed to a degree, they can obviously not be expected to visit the nearest location only – as was originally assumed in central place research. But how do they behave in the case of the facilities chosen for our study? Swimming pools, keep-fit paths and minigolf courses are, after all, often visited within the limited spare time of a working day, so that the small time budget available could well be a factor influencing the choice of the location to be visited.

As map 1 shows, these present a pattern far from uniform. Catchment areas of the facilities often overlap and the ranges of the keep-fit paths under study show considerable differences. A uniform range specific to this type of facility, as assumed in our working hypothesis, does not exist. Of course, the arithmetic mean of the ranges can be calculated for all the keep-fit paths; but the variance

Fig. 1: Average travel distance of visitors to the indoor swimming pool at Helmbrechts during normal hours and hours with wave service

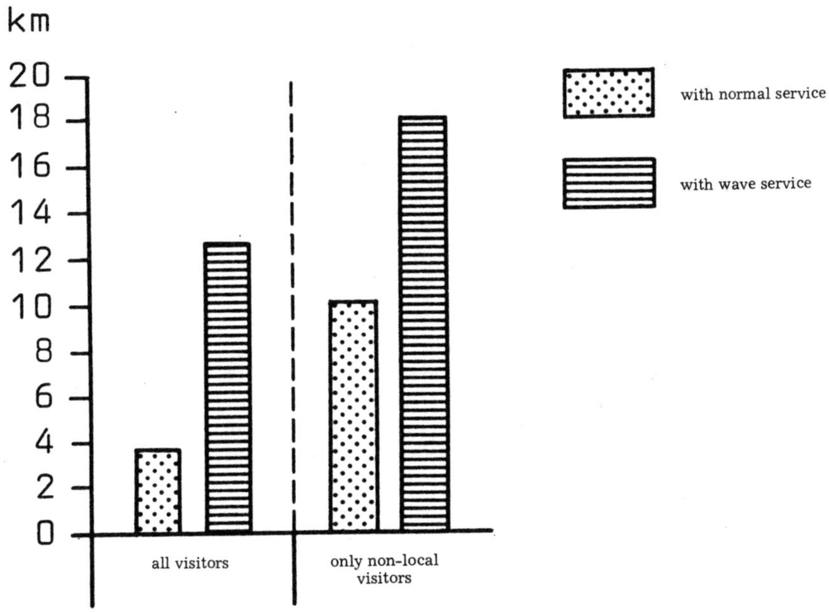

Source: GÜNKEL, R.: *Waldsportanlagen im Raum Nürnberg-Erlangen-Forchheim.* Staatsexamenarbeit, Erlangen 1976

Table 1: Occupational groups and average travel distance of visitors to indoor swimming pools

Usable questionnaires of 1014 persons questioned in the swimming pools of Bad Berneck, Steinwiesen, Marktredwitz, Rehau, Selb, Schwarzenbach/Saale, Hof/Saale, Gefrees, Münchberg and Kronach

Occupational groups	all visitors			non-local visitors only	
	number (abs.)	in per cent.	av. km per person	in per cent. of all visitors	av. km per person
school children/apprentices	268	27,1	3,332	32,8	8,102
housewives	128	13,0	3,480	25,0	10,922
1) lower occupation gr.	158	16,0	4,050	31,6	10,640
2) medium occupation gr.	303	30,7	4,580	41,9	9,543
3) higher occupation gr.	95	9,6	3,679	30,5	9,775
pensioners	36	3,6	3,722	33,3	9,166
altogether	988	100,0	3,897	34,2	9,467

1) = semiskilled workers, lower white collar workers and clerks
2) = skilled workers, medium grade employees, self-employed persons
3) = higher grade employees, professional people

Source: HAHN, H(olger): *Die öffentlichen Hallenschwimmbäder im Fichtelgebirge und in Frankenwald.* Staatsexamenarbeit, Erlangen 1976

(of the data represented by the mean) would be so large that the mean could not possibly serve as a criterion for planning purposes.

A closer look at the map shows that residential areas in close vicinity to a keep-fit path account for a rather high percentage of visitors to this keep-fit path. The larger the distance between a residential area and a keep-fit path, the less distinct is the orientation to the nearest facility. The advantage of a short distance apparently works only within narrow limits and becomes ineffective beyond these limits.

Similar results were obtained in the studies of minigolf courses in the Munich and Nuremberg-Erlangen area. The values of the ranges of about 40 facilities chosen have such a large variance that their arithmetic mean cannot be interpreted as a value "specific to a facility". However, if the facilities are grouped according to their locations, the variance of the ranges within these groups are only small. In this case, the mean of the ranges represents a value meaningful and useful for planning. If, for example, locations in larger or smaller conurbations are separated (Munich and Nuremberg-Erlangen respectively) the variance of the respective range values is considerably reduced. This is even more the case by separating locations within from those outside a conurbation area. If the two grouping criteria are combined and if those minigolf courses that are situated outside the conurbation area and inside small towns are excluded, this produces means which represent a high percentage of the respective cases and, at the same time, differ from each other distinctly. In this context it is noteworthy that the relation between the ranges of facilities inside the conurbation area and of those outside is the same for the Nuremberg and the Munich areas, although the absolute values for the Munich area are much higher.

If we summarize the results so far, we have to state that even in the case of recreation facilities with only small differences in attraction, the identification of a range specific to that facility is not meaningful; such a value is only meaningful if calculated for facilities of exactly the same type and in similar locations. A possible explanation for such locational differences can be found in the observation that only small proportions (20 per cent. of the 1.360 cases observed) of the visitors come directly from their homes to the minigolf course or go home directly after the game. The rest combined minigolfing with other activities, performed partly before and partly afterwards. In these cases, the distances between locations visited immediately before or after the game of minigolf and the minigolf courses are much smaller than those between home and minigolf course. It is an interesting fact that for the "home-minigolf" distances the ratio between courses inside the conurbation *vs.* those outside is 1:3.3, whereas the same ratio for "last activity-minigolf" distances is only 1:1.8. If we assume that the attraction of a minigolf course has, after all, reached only the location of the "pre minigolf-activity", the wider range of the minifolg courses outside the conurbation is reduced considerably. Moreover, the number of visitors who leave their homes to play minigolf only and return immediately afterwards, is much smaller in the case of the courses outside the conurbation than of those inside. On the other hand, the number of visitors to minigolf courses who did not come intentionally, but by chance, is much higher outside the conurbation. When asked "Did you intend to play minigolf here, when you left home, or did it occur to you by chance?", 68 per cent. of the visitors to minigolf courses inside the conurbation answered "intended", as compared to 52 per cent. of the visitors to courses outside the conurbation. This implies that for people, who passed by chance, the minigolf course did not play a part in the decisions as to their spatial behaviour. This again leads to the conclusion that it is rather doubtful whether the calculation of the ranges of such facilities ought to be based on the distance home – functional location. The attraction of the minigolf course itself was obviously not sufficient to attract the visitors. This was rather achieved by the minigolf course, if at all, in combination with other facilities, if not other facilities alone determined the willingness to cover a certain distance. Here we encounter a phenomenon that has been known for a long time in central place research as "coupling", and which, without doubt, has an important part in the field of recreation facilities, too.

3. *The patterns of the catchment areas*

As we turn to the catchment areas of the facilities, we have to remember that the ranges of the respective facilities are calculated as means, so that a certain amount of doubt seems justified as to whether they are suitable to represent reality. If we test this for some facilities in equal locations and with similar ranges, we find that the distances between home and functional location have a large variance. If the respective answers are mapped, the range of the functional location will often extend into one or two directions much farther than into all the others.

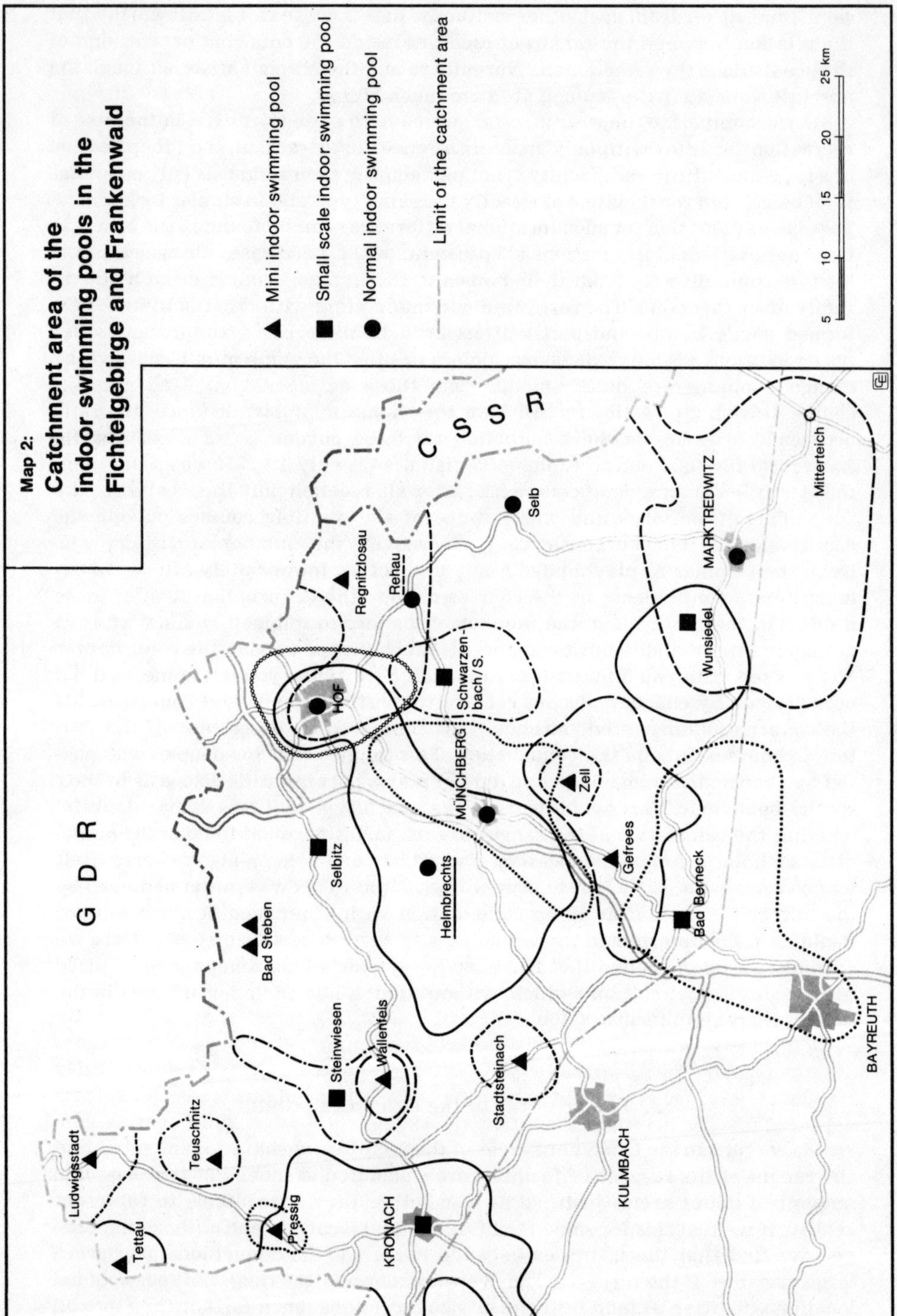

Map 2:
Catchment area of the indoor swimming pools in the Fichtelgebirge and Frankenwald

The mean of all the distances can therefore not be used as the radius for delimiting the catchment areas. The observed catchment areas are practically never, and not even roughly, circular, but show distinct asymmetrical shapes, that primarily reflect different population densities, conditions of accessibility and spatial relations to competing locations. The effect of competing locations on the pattern of the areas of influence can be very well demonstrated by the example of the indoor swimming pools in north-eastern Upper Franconia. The swimming pool in Kronach, for example, does not have many competing facilities in its vicinity – as opposed to that of Münchberg, which faces an equivalent one in Helmbrechts at a distance of only 8 km in the northwest and three other such swimming pools in Gefrees, Zell and Schwarzenbach/Saale in a south-westerly direction. In contrast to the Kronach pool, which has an influx of visitors from all directions, the density of swimming pools in the Münchberg area is already such that for the one at Münchberg no circular catchment area "is left", but one with a marked lenghthening from northeast to southwest.

A similar asymmetry, caused by the competing location in Gefrees, can be observed in the cases of the swimming-pool in Bad Berneck and that of the small school swimming pool in Wunsiedel, for which the bath in Marktredwitz, with better facilities, causes an asymmetrical shape of catchment area. The comparison between the pools of Marktredwitz and Münchberg, which are equivalent as to standards, strongly exemplifies the effects of competing equipment in the vicinity, as the Marktredwitz catchment area is twice as large as that of Münchberg.

The map also shows that the Marktredwitz catchment area is only slightly affected by the existence of the nearby pool in Wunsiedel. Apparently the Wunsiedel school swimming pool with much simpler facilities, does not represent any effective competition for the bigger, and more attractive pool in Marktredwitz. The close proximity of two swimming pools affects the shape of the catchment areas only if they are equivalent or equally attractive. In such cases the visitors tend to visit the nearest bath – except for a small overlapping area. If, however, swimming pools of unequal attractiveness are situated close to each other, the rule of orientation to the nearest swimming pool holds good for that proportion of visitors only, who do not have a car at their disposal, i. e., generally speaking, for children and adolescents, who will visit the swimming pools of their own communities, whilst the visitors with cars at their disposal will prefer the pool with the higher standard of facilities.

Such group-specific differences have been known for a long time in social geography; in fact the example of recreation facilities can particularly well demonstrate, that their significance to different social groups varies. As to their social structural characteristics, the visitors to a swimming pool will deviate from the total population just as much as the visitors to keep-fit paths, excursion cafés, minigolf courses or recreation parks. More often than not this is an effect of preferences specific to groups, classified, for example, by age, sex, occupation, education, or income.

For the recreation facilities under study we can also show that certain groups of the population are overrepresented at the respective facilities; that they obviously give a higher priority to the visit of this particular facility than do other groups. Obviously these groups are prepared to tolerate longer distances, when visiting the same facility than other groups. If this holds true the ranges of the facilities studied would not only have to be differentiated according to direction, but also according to social groups.

Table 2: Occupational groups by distance categories of the visitors to 17 keep-fit paths

Occupational groups	0,1–2,5 kms		2,5–5 kms		5–10 kms		10–20 kms		>20 kms		altogether	
	absolut	in per cent.	absolut	in per cent.	absolut	in per cent.	absolut	in per cent.	absolut	in per cent.	absolut	in per cent.
school children/ apprentices/students	55	12,7	31	10,9	44	8,5	7	6,9	6	13,0	143	10,3
housewives	29	6,7	21	7,4	30	5,8	4	4,0	4	8,7	88	6,4
1) lower occup. gr.	132	30,4	82	28,9	191	36,9	42	41,6	10	21,8	457	33,0
2) medium occup. gr.	119	27,4	98	34,5	162	31,3	30	29,7	14	30,4	423	30,6
3) higher occup. gr.	58	13,4	37	13,0	66	12,7	13	12,9	10	21,8	184	13,3
pensioners	41	9,4	15	5,3	25	4,8	5	4,9	2	4,3	88	6,4
altogether	434	100,0	284	100,0	518	100,0	101	100,0	46	100,0	1383	100,0

1) = semiskilled workers, lower white collar workers and clerks
2) = skilled workers, medium grade employees, self-employed persons
3) = higher grade employees, professional people

Source: GÜNKEL, R.: *Waldsportanlagen im Raum Nürnberg–Erlangen–Forchheim.* Staatsexamenarbeit, Erlangen 1976

Table 3: Age groups and average travel distance of visitors to indoor swimmingpools

Total: 1927 persons questioned in the pools of Augsburg-Stadtbad, Augsburg-Spickelbach, Augsburg-Haunstetten, Füssen, Pfronten and Oberstdorf

Age group	per cent.	av. kms per person	av. kms per local resident	av. kms per holiday maker
up to 16 years	10,9	5,017	4,110	6,768
17–25 years	25,9	7,202	6,648	8,842
26–45 years	39,3	6,390	5,697	7,640
46–65 years	18,4	4,773	4,798	4,724
66 years and older	5,5	2,863	2,846	2,942

Source: JAROSLAWSKY, M.: *Hallenbäder im Schwäbisch-Allgäuerischen Raum und ihr Einzugsgebiet.* Magisterarbeit, Erlangen 1976

However, if the average travelling distance is studied for particular groups of visitors, the differences are not at all impressive. Whereas they are most obvious for age groups, such differences are scarcely to be found, when variables such as sex, occupation, income or education are applied. In other words: if people visit a swimming pool, use a keep-fit path or a minigolf course at all, they are willing to cover equal distances – by and large independently of their sex, education and occupation. On the other hand, group-specific differences can be proved, to exist as mentioned above, for the spatial behaviour of age groups and the groups "local residents" as against "holiday makers". Thus, for example the local population visiting swimming pools in the Allgäu or in Augsburg, are, according to M. JAROSLAWSKY's studies,[6] by and large slightly more sensitive to distance than holiday makers. As for the age groups, differences exist between the children and adolescents, on the one hand, and old people (over 65 years old) on the other hand, whereas the average travelling distance is more or less the same for all age groups between 20 and 65 years. The same is true of the behaviour of visitors to keep-fit paths and minigolf courses. In other words: it is impossible to identify in a catchment area of a facility more or less concentric or parallel belts corresponding to a specific group of the population.

Findings on distance sensitivity are, however, completely different, if we include the dimension of time, i. e. if we consider the frequency of the visits. Here it can be clearly seen that the frequency of visits decreases with increasing distance. But here again considerable differences between social groups (cf. table) can be detected. The different constraints of the social groups as to means, i. e. the different amount of time or money or means of transport etc. at their disposal, have a notably differentiating effect on the frequency of visits. The data available are not sufficient to analyse the "constraints" affecting each of the social groups. A more detailed study of the variables that produce the differences of frequencies has to be left to future work.

[6] JAROSLAWSKY, M.: *Hallenbäder im Schwäbisch-Allgäuerischen Raum und ihr Einzugsgebiet.* Magisterarbeit, Erlangen 1976.

Fig 2: Frequency of visits and average travel distance of visitors to 17 keep-fit paths in the area of Nuremberg-Erlangen

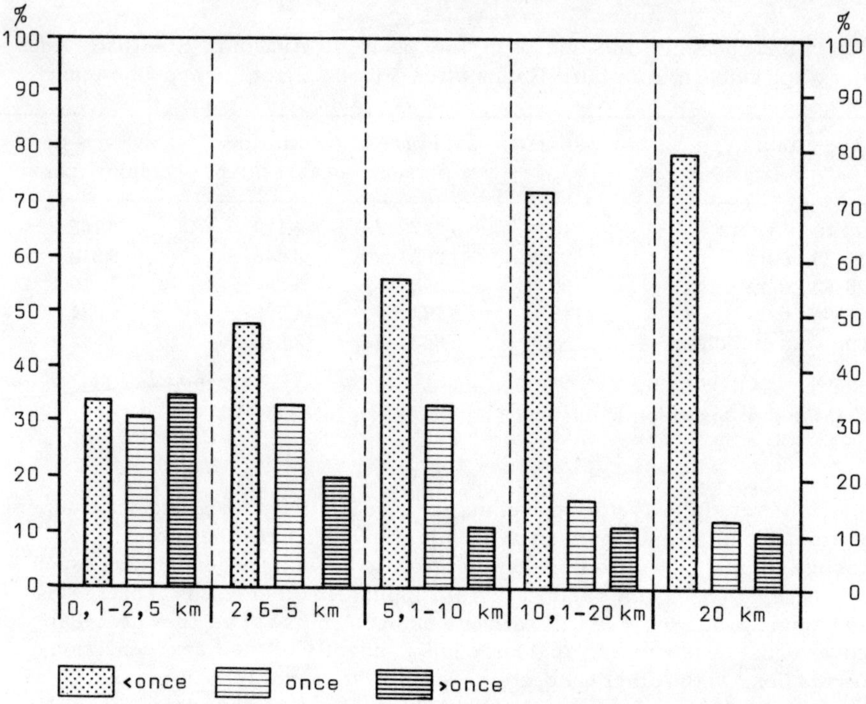

Table 4: Frequency of visits and average travel distance of visitors to indoor-swimming pools in northeast Upper Franconia and Swabia

Frequency (per week)	Northeast Upper Franconia[1]			Swabia[2]		
	in per cent.	av. kms per person	proportion of males	in per cent.	av. kms per person	proportion of males
<once	24	8,949	56 out of 100	34	8,193	58 out of 100
once	47	6,303	52	38	5,150	59
>once	29	3,021	64	28	3,633	66
	100	5,978	58	100	5,762	61

Source:

[1] HAHN, H(olger): *Die öffentlichen Hallenschwimmbäder im Fichtelgebirge und im Frankenwald.* Staatsexamenarbeit, Erlangen 1976

[2] JAROSLAWSKY, M.: *Hallenbäder im Schwäbisch-Allgäuerischen Raum und ihr Einzugsgebiet.* Magisterarbeit, Erlangen 1976

Map 1 of this paper is in pocket in the inside back over.

Veuillez trouver la carte 1 (carte pliante) dans la couverture en fin du volume.

Karte 1 dieses Beitrages befindet sich in einer Tasche im hinteren Umschlagdekkel.

The impact of recreation on life styles of rural communities

A case study of Sleat, Isle of Skye

RICHARD W. BUTLER, London, Ontario, Canada*

1. Introduction

Increasing attention has been paid by researchers in recent years to the impacts of recreation and tourism upon destination areas. The emphasis in research has been shifting noticeably from an almost total economic orientation found in those studies conducted in the 1960s and earlier,[1] to a more critical examination of the costs or negative effects of recreation and tourism, particularly from environmental, social and cultural standpoints. Studies such as those conducted by the I.U.C.N and NELSON[2] represent some of the earliest acknowledgements of the environmental impacts of recreation, land management agencies in many countries are now examining with increasing concern the need for environmental planning and control of natural and scenic areas which are often those areas most exposed to tourist pressure.

Studies identifying the social and cultural impacts of recreation, i.e. the effects of recreation upon the permanent residents of destination areas are, in the majority of cases, much more recent. Such studies have been conducted by researchers in several fields including anthropology, sociology and geography, and perhaps as a result, no generally agreed upon procedures have been forthcoming and there has been considerable variation in scale, approach and aspects of problems examined. Recent reviews of the literature,[3] have demonstrated the breadth of problems examined and the seriousness of the problems encountered. Despite the wide acknowledgement of problems resulting from the development and growth of tourism, as YOUNG[4] has vividly illustrated, government policy is generally in favour of the development of tourism, and in some cases, apparently blind to its non-economic, or even some of its economic costs. Considerable attention[5] has been focused on the social, cultural and political impacts of tourism and recreation development in the developing world, where

---

* Dr. RICHARD W. BUTLER, Associate Professor, University of Western Ontario, London, Ontario, Canada.
The author wishes to acknowledge the financial support of the *Scottish Tourist Board* and the *Canada Council* in the preparation of this study. Mr. J. E. BROUGHAM conducted the field interviews and was a joint author of the complete report.

[1] RATHMELL, J. M.: *The economic impact of recreational travel on a local community.* New York, 1956
CLAWSON M. and KNETSCH J.: *Economics of outdoor recreation.* Baltimore 1966

[2] International Union for the Conservation of Nature (I.U.C.N.): *The ecological impact of tourism and recreation in temperate lands.* No. 7, Morges 1967
NELSON J. G. (ed.): *Canadian parks in perspective.* Montreal, 1973

[3] NORONHA, R.: *A review of the sociological literature on tourism.* International bank for development and reconstruction, Washington, D.C., 1975
THUROT, J. M.: *Impact of tourism on sociocultural values.* Centre d'etudes du tourisme, Aix-en-Provence 1975

[4] YOUNG, C.: *Tourism. Blessing or blight?* Harmondsworth, Middlesex 1973

[5] BRYDEN, J. M.: *Tourism and development,* London 1973
JAFARI, J.: The socio-economic costs of tourism to developing countries. *Annals of Tourism Research,* Menomonie, Wisc., 1974, pp. 227–262
OUMA, P.: *The evaluation of tourism in East Africa.* Nairobi 1970

the differences between the visitors and the visited is most marked. In many cases however, the social, cultural, and sometimes political impacts of recreation can be seen closer to home. GREENWOOD[6], noted the effect of tourism as an agent of social change among the Basques, and it would be unreasonable to expect that the thousands of recreationists who visit rural Britain both on weekends and during the summer holiday periods do not have some effect at least upon the social and cultural patterns of rural residents. The differences may be greater between white Americans earning $ 50.000 a year and a black Jamaican cropper earning $ 500 a year, than say, between a Coventry car worker earning £ 5.000 and a Gaelic speaking crofter in western Scotland earning £ 1.000, but they may be great enough in the latter case to cause some potential conflicts. Cultural, linguistic and residential differences apart, the fact that one individual is on holiday and views his recreation area in one way, with a specific set of desires and expectations, and the fact that the other individual is living permanently in the destination area, making a living from the environment, with a different set of expectations and desires from that area means that their reactions and requirements are likely to be different. The requirements of the visitor, often resulting in the development or improvement of facilities (e.g. transport and accommodation) may not be sympathetically viewed by the permanent resident, or may even be actively opposed. At the very least one might expect local residents to have some opinions with respect to maximum numbers of tourists and facilities they find acceptable in their area. As BROWNRIGG and GREIG have written in the context of Western Scotland:

> "when tourist numbers are relatively small, there is a guest/host type of relationship, a genuine welcome, hospitality and warmth. However, as numbers rise, it becomes physically important to maintain this relationship. Then, as locals become more commercial, tourists feel cheated by the absence of the promised welcome and their disappointment can easily develop into resentment, which can often become mutual."[7]

In the majority of cases of tourist development, however, little or no effort has been made to forecast or examine from a hindsight position any social and cultural impacts which may occur. The study discussed in this paper falls into the category of hindsight study, as tourists have been visiting the Isle of Skye for some two hundred years, albeit in large numbers only over the last half century. No single major tourist development has taken place in the area studied, but major improvements in transportation and a rapid growth of tourism in the western highlands of Scotland generally[8], have occurred along with extensive development of second homes or cottages.

2. *The case study*

The study discussed in this paper was an attempt to identify the social, cultural and linguistic impacts of recreation in a rural insular crofting[9] parish in Scotland. The parish of Sleat covers the southwestern peninsula of the Isle of Skye,

---

[6] GREENWOOD, D.: Tourism as an agent of change. *Annals of Tourism Research,* Menomonie, Wisc., 1976, pp. 128–142

[7] BROWNRIGG, M. and GREIG, M. A.: *Tourism and regional development.* Glasgow 1976, p. 12

[8] BUTLER, R. W.: *The tourist industry of the highlands and islands.* Ph. D. thesis, University of Glasgow 1973

[9] Crofting is a unique form of tenant agriculture, limited legally to seven countries of Highland Scotland, usually practised part time. A croft is less than 50 acres in size and has hereditary tenure

an island noted for its romantic historical image, and much frequented by tourists. The peninsula is some 15 kilometres from south-west to north-east, and 8 kilometres at its widest. It is accessible by roll-on-roll-off car ferry from the nearest railhead, Mallaig, and by road to the rest of Skye. The population, which has declined from a peak of 2531 in 1891 to a little over 400 today, is predominately Gaelic speaking, and shows the typical west highland patterns of large proportion of elderly residents, with women outnumbering men. Until very recently the parish has seen continuous outmigration, particularly of young people in search of employment. In the last few years this trend has been reversed, and other people have come to settle in Sleat, finding it a pleasant alternative to urban areas to retire in, or to live "away from it all". Much of the present social pattern is of the traditional Gaelic type with house gatherings and ceilidhs (Gaelic evenings of musical entertainment) being of great significance, particularly in the more isolated communities, and less so in the case of larger communities such as Ardvasar, reflecting a higher proportion of newcomers and the presence of facilities such as hotels in these latter centres.

An in-depth survey was made of over 75 per cent. of the households in Sleat, using a bilingual (Gaelic, English) questionnaire, to determine the attitudes of the residents towards tourism and their perceptions of impacts and changes caused by the industry. (For copies of the questionnaire and a complete tabulation and discussion of results the reader is referred to the full report of the study).[10]. Sleat was chosen for several reasons, the major ones being the establishment of a Gaelic College in 1974 to further the Gaelic language and culture, and the completion of a survey of the economic impact of tourism on Skye in 1974[11]. It was expected that awareness of and attitudes towards tourism would vary between residents depending upon a number of variables such as their involvement and contact with tourists, their location, and whether they were Gaelic speaking or not and these initial hypotheses were substantiated, in general terms. It is necessary first to summarize the overall reactions of the residents towards tourism before discussing the impacts resulting from increasing numbers of tourists.

2.1. *Residents' attitudes and perceptions*

While general awareness of increases in numbers of visitors to Sleat was high, perception of any changes brought about by tourism was noticeably lower, with a quarter of the population not aware of any changes. Some changes were perceived as being for the better by some individuals and in a negative light by others, while in general almost two thirds of the responses felt changes noted were positive, citing increased revenue as by far the most important.

Perception of contact with tourists varied very widely, with a quarter of the respondents claiming only visual contact with tourists, while those actively involved in the tourist industry, such as offering accommodation had much higher levels of contact (20 per cent.). Not surprisingly, however, only 40 per cent. of respondents felt they experienced disbenefits. Major benefits perceived were increased revenue, seeing new faces and employment (see table 1), while major disbenefits were associated with traffic, invasions of privacy and changes in be-

---

[10] BROUGHAM, J. E. and BUTLER, R. W.: *The social and cultural impact of tourism: A case study of Sleat, Isle of Skye.* Edinburgh 1977

[11] BROWNRIGG, M. and GREIG, M. A.: The economic impact of tourism spending in Skye. *Highlands and Islands Development Board Special Publication.* No. 13, Inverness 1974

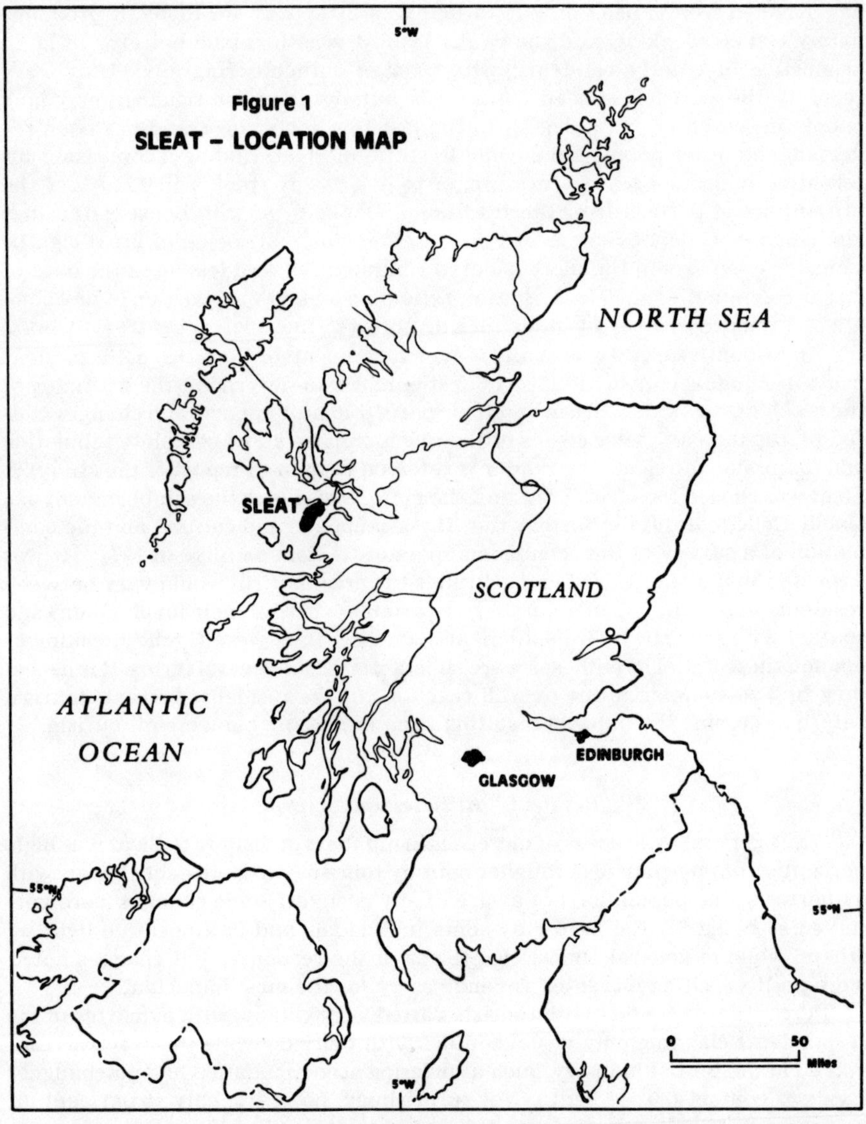
5°W
Figure 1
SLEAT – LOCATION MAP
NORTH SEA
SLEAT
SCOTLAND
ATLANTIC
OCEAN
EDINBURGH
GLASGOW
55°N
55°N
0
50
Miles
5°W

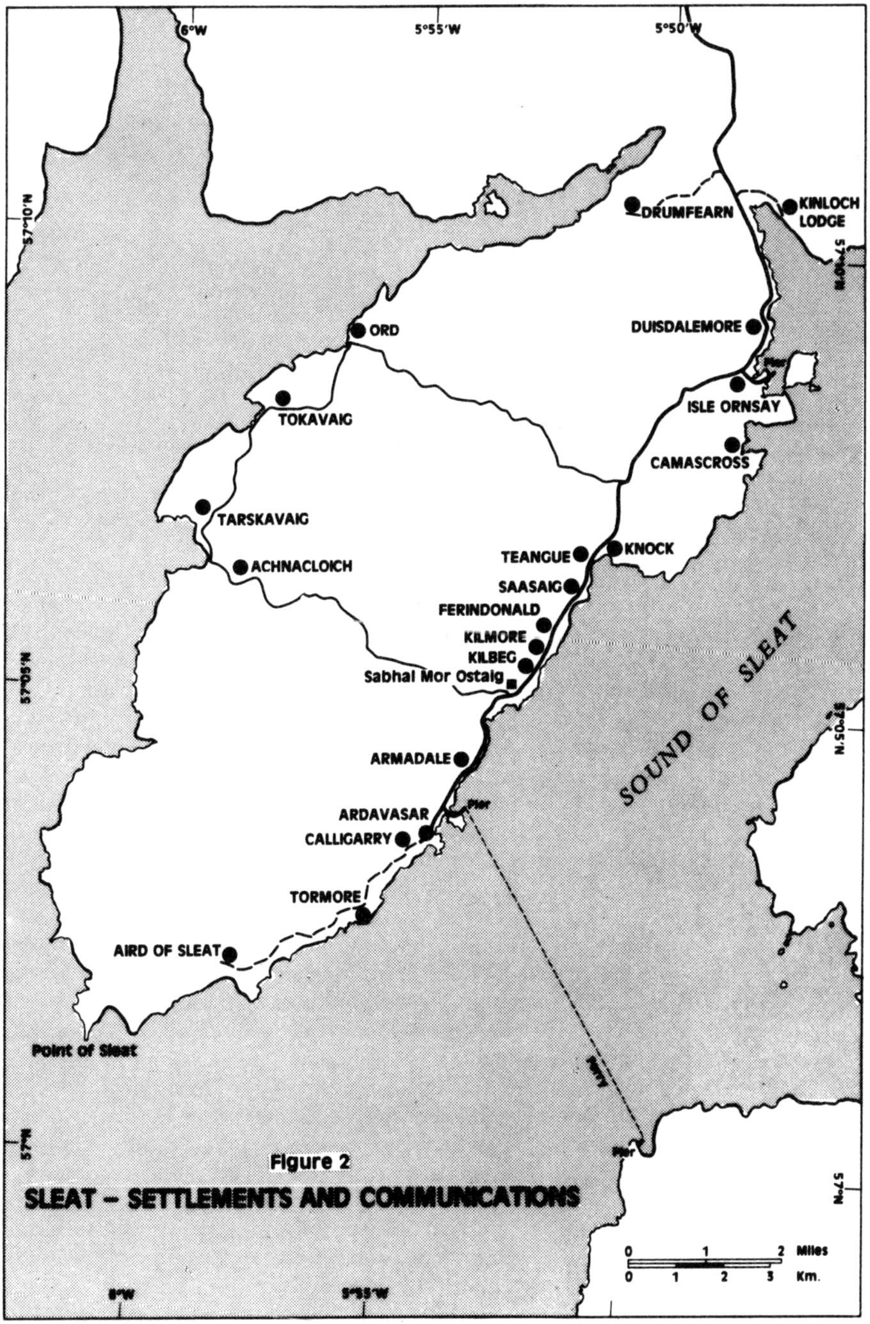

Figure 2
SLEAT – SETTLEMENTS AND COMMUNICATIONS

haviour patterns. A consistent finding applicable to all subgroupings as well as the total set, was the fact that respondents were prone to attribute benefits far more readily (78 per cent.) to other people than to themselves, perhaps indicating an optimistic view of tourism in the area.

Table 1: Benefits and disbenefits resulting from tourism in per cent.

Benefit	41.7	Neither	34.8	Disbenefit	23.5
increased revenue	38.5			traffic roads	49.1
employment	25.6			disturbance	21.8
company	28.2			litter	10.9
other	7.7			damage	7.2
				crowding	5.5
	100			other	5.5
					100

7.3 per cent. of respondents reported experiencing both benefits and disbenefits.
Source: Data collected by the author

Attitudes towards second homes produced perhaps the strongest responses, with only a quarter of respondents in favour of such development. Sleat has a greater proportion (20 per cent.) of residences used as second homes than any other parish in Scotland[12] and competition for houses is high, with local people being unable to afford the considerable prices properties are sold for, a factor which it is felt locally has contributed to a declining population. Contact with second home users was in general extremely low.

Rather suprisingly a slight majority of respondents felt that tourism had no impact upon the Gaelic language and culture, or upon other activities, e.g. agriculture in the area. Of those who did feel there was an impact, however, the majority felt this to be negative towards Gaelic, primarily because it was felt the presence of tourists inhibited the use of Gaelic. Those who felt the impact to be positive most frequently quoted the example of students attending the Gaelic College in Sleat, who are learning Gaelic and therefore use the language in conversation with locals as much as possible, thus promoting its use.

An overwhelming majority of respondents favoured measures to strengthen the Gaelic language, but a smaller number felt that this would make the area more attractive to tourists. No one felt such a move would reduce attractivity for tourists however. While few respondents indicated they were not looking forward to the arrival of tourists, a much larger proportion stated they would be pleased to see the last of the tourists leave at the end of the summer.

As was indicated earlier, some noticeable differendes in opinions and attitudes emerged when the sample was broken down into specific subsets, and it is only possible to summarize these very briefly here. Respondents less aware of changes in numbers of tourists, normally either recent immigrants or isolated residents had less favourable attitudes towards tourism, experiencing fewer

[12] BROUGHAM, J. E. and BUTLER, R. W.: *The social and cultural impact of tourism: A case study of Sleat, Isle of Skye.* Edinburgh 1977

benefits and more disbenefits. They were more sympathetic towards second homes, however, in part perhaps because some of the immigrants had retired or settled permanently in what used to be their second homes.

Those respondents who took in paying guests, not surprisingly were most positive about tourism, viewing changes as being for the better, and feeling almost unanimously (96 per cent.) that other people in Sleat benefited from tourism also. No one in this group indicated they experienced disbenefits alone, the benefits they derived apparently compensated for any inconvenience. Of interest is the fact that attitudes towards the impact of tourism upon Gaelic were much more strongly held by this group, over half (compared to 35 per cent. of the total) feeling tourism did have an impact and two thirds feeling this to be negative. The fact that this group has the most contact with tourists and in general is the strongest proponent of tourism gives these comments added significance.

The Gaelic speaking respondents were generally older, and more aware of changes brought about by tourism. No one felt tourism had improved the social life in Sleat, with almost a quarter feeling it had caused it to decline, a view exactly reversed by the non-Gaelic speakers. Gaelic speakers were more opposed to second homes, felt tourism had less impact on Gaelic, and were more inclined to view the impact as positive. This is explained by the fact that Gaelic speakers in general have less contact with tourists, can use Gaelic to obtain increased privacy, and have more contact with students from the Gaelic College, and thus converse in Gaelic to some visitors.

The respondents with little contact with tourists felt they benefited little from tourism, as opposed to those with more contact. However, when it came to attributing benefits to others, those with little contact attributed benefits at the highest rate and disbenefits at the lowest. It would appear that those with little or no contact with tourists assume the benefits to other people are close to universal. Those with least contact felt tourism had an influence upon Gaelic in the order of six to one compared to those with frequent contact, and considered the effects to be negative rather than positive in rates of two to one.

Finally variation in responses occurred with respect to location of respondents. Those living in the more remote communities (fig. 2) were less exposed to, and less favourable to tourism. These are the more traditional crofting Gaelic-speaking areas. Other communities, especially Ardvasar, are more aware of and positive towards tourism, reflecting perhaps the greater contact with tourists and greater economic benefits.

More detailed analyses of the data showed that substantial variations in opinion, awareness and attitudes towards tourism do occur, and that these variations are related to a number of factors including personal characteristics, exposure to and reliance on tourism, and location and that these factors in turn are also inter-related. Further analysis is continuing on this part of the data.

2.2. The impacts of recreation in Sleat

As was noted earlier in some instances impacts were perceived as both benefits and disbenefits in different individuals. The most universally acknowledged impact was the economic one, but even here the benefits accrue to a small proportion of the population only. Leakage of money out of the area is relatively high because almost all goods supplied to visitors are imported to Sleat, even such staples as milk, eggs and bread, and the multiplier effect is relatively low.

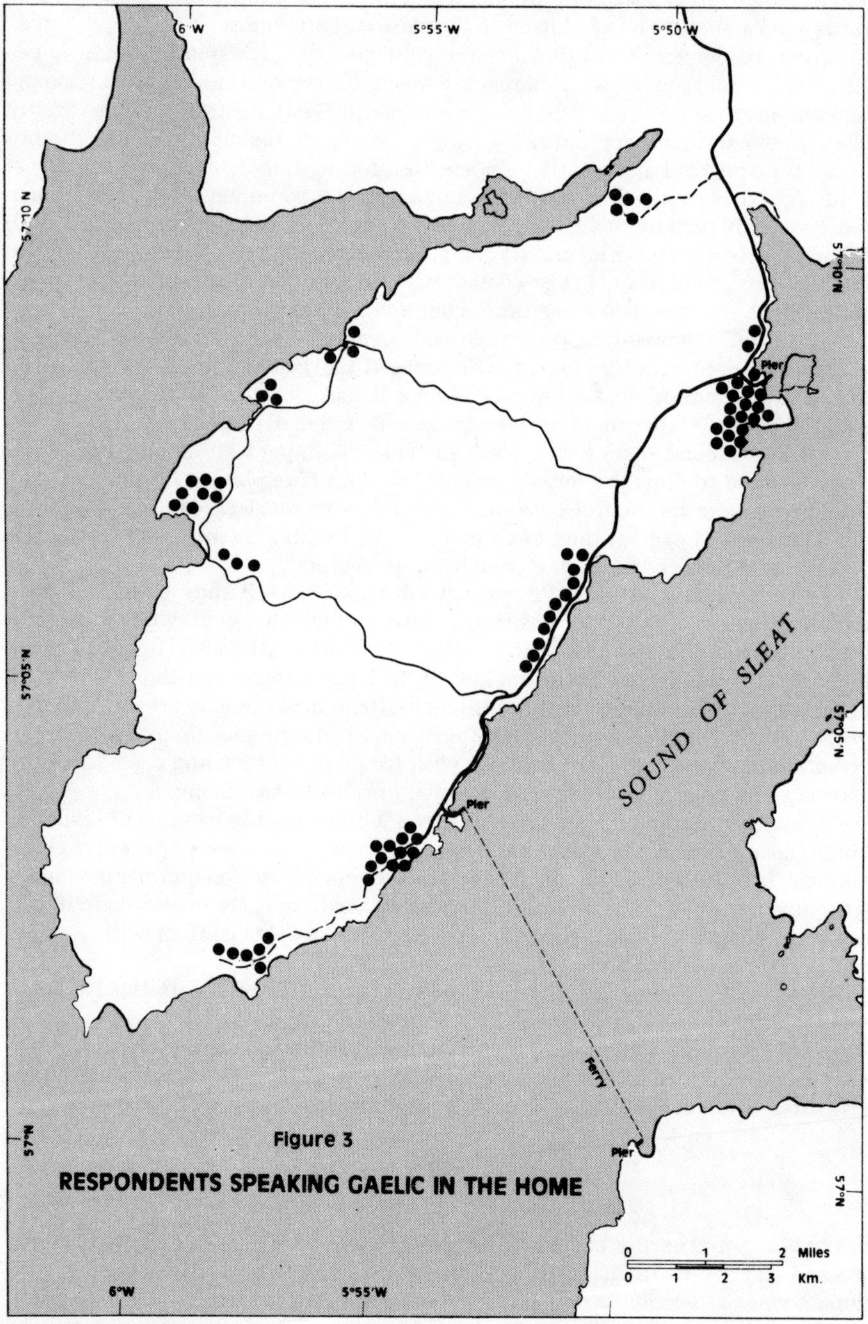

Figure 3

RESPONDENTS SPEAKING GAELIC IN THE HOME

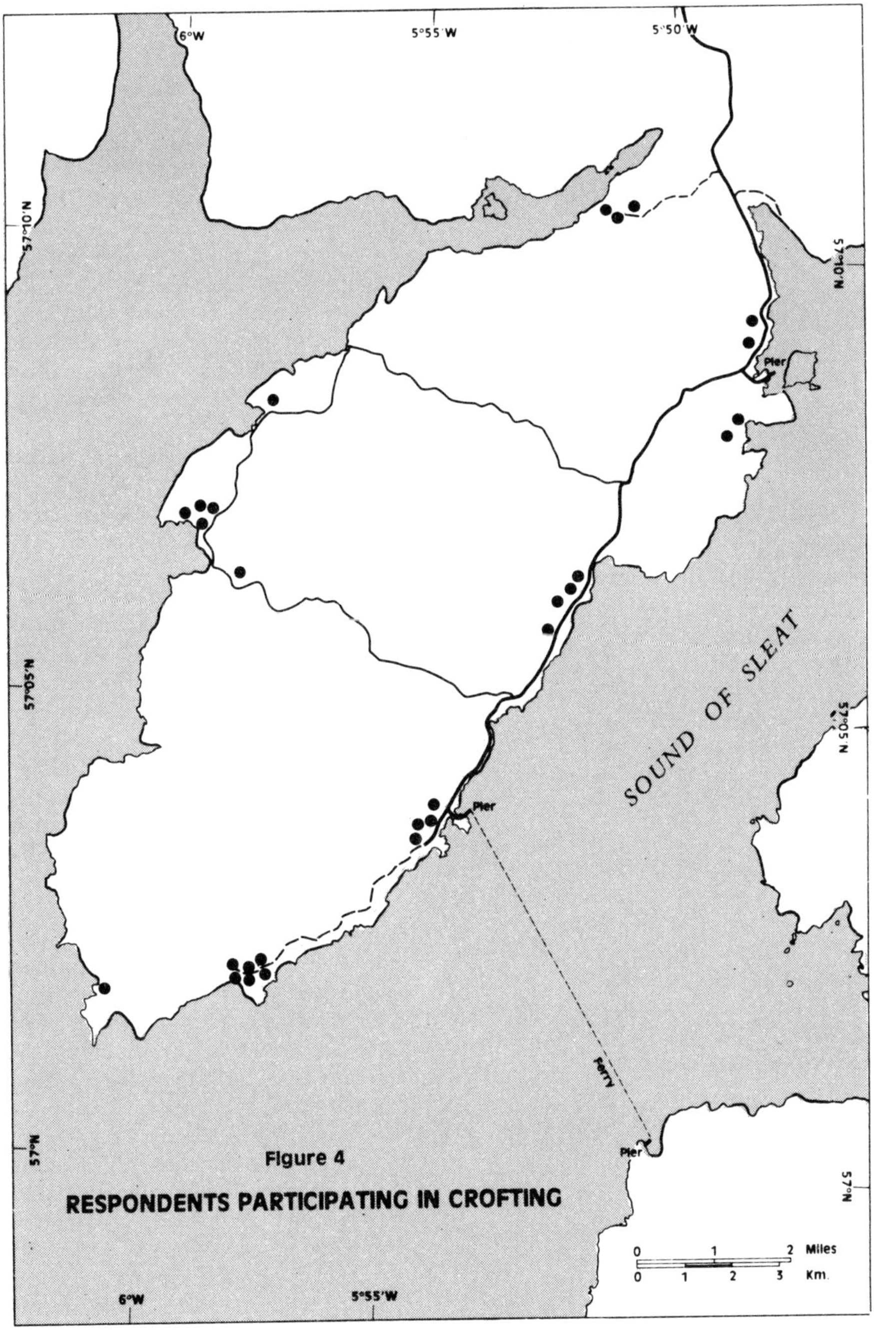

Figure 4

RESPONDENTS PARTICIPATING IN CROFTING

Tourists would appear to attempt to minimize local purchases as much as possible by bringing items with them. Tourism generates approximately 20 jobs, primarily in hotels, but while hotel employment triples in the summer, about half of the temporary positions are filled by people from outside Sleat. Employment is predominately female, as males can find some employment in the summer in agriculture and construction. Some limited additional employment has been provided in the past by renovations to second homes, to hotels, and lately to the Gaelic College and Armadale Castle Visitor Centre.

The social benefits of tourism are quite well appreciated on Sleat, with many residents enjoying the additional company. As most tourists are transient, however, contact between individuals is relatively brief, and in most cases confined to casual meetings in hotels and shops, or when visitors are staying overnight in private homes. More contact is made in the case of a few residents with visitors to Armadale Sailing Club facilities. Major contact occurs between students attending the language courses at the Gaelic College. These courses run over a period of eight weeks, for two or four weeks duration, and students are accommodated with local Gaelic speaking families in order to be able to use their new language skills. Various lectures, concerts and dances at the College are attended by locals as well as students and thus considerable contact occurs. The students represent a reliable source of income to some residents, although in a few cases having people stay for 8 weeks and having to provide accommodation on Sunday are regarded as necessary disbenefits.

Various improvements in transportation have occurred because of the rise in tourist numbers, the most important being the institution of a roll-on-roll-off car ferry on the Mallaig-Armadale run during the summer. Many locals, however, were more indignant that this service was not maintained in the winter than grateful for its presence in the summer. The main road through Sleat has been considerably improved because of the traffic it has received since the ferry service began in 1964, as have other roads on Skye and the main road to Mallaig.

The benefits resulting from tourism therefore are principally economic, (limited to a minority of residents) social, (for the majority of residents, although a disbenefit to some), through improvements in services, particularly transportation and the addition of services, generally tourist related but utilised by some locals, e.g. the Sailing Club Clubhouse.

The disbenefits or negative impacts of tourism are somewhat more nebulous and inevitably in some cases, the results of individual biases and perhaps unreasonable expectations. The development of second homes is undoubtedly a major disbenefit to the area at the present time. When many houses were acquired in the 1960s as a result of the sale of MacDonald estate properties, there was little local interest in the properties. Subsequently, however, with increases in employment opportunities in Sleat, local people or potential residents find it almost impossible to acquire a house, either because none are available, or because when a property is available they cannot compete economically with affluent "outsiders". (This problem is of course not confined to Sleat, but is particularly serious here because over 20 per cent. of the properties are already second homes). The process of people ultimately retiring to their second home, combined with the use of the property by visitors before this occurrence make the second home probably the single most negative aspect of tourism with respect to the Gaelic language. Owners and users of second homes are almost entirely monolingual Anglophones and thus approximately a quarter of the residences can be classified as English speaking directly as a result of tourism. This proportion is likely to rise in the future as the Gaelic population is older and will decline naturally, and at the moment is being replaced by English speaking immigrants in most cases.

A second major disbenefit is related to the sheer numbers of tourists who visit Sleat, and who cause considerable crowding on the narrow roads. This can cause delays in travel, disruption of livestock movement and livestock casualties, frustration and resentment at the additional traffic, and obvious safety problems. To the residents of those settlements lying on the main road, the increase in traffic in the summer (over three times the average winter level), particularly prior to and following the ferry arrival, represents a real reduction in the quality of life.

All respondents engaged full time in agriculture (a small minority admittedly), indicated a strong opposition to tourism because of occurrences of crop damage, stock chasing, fence damage, and litter. Other disbenefits were related to changes in the social patterns and life styles as a result of tourism. The development of second homes was felt to be partly responsible for the reduction in social life, as most second home owners wish to "get away from it all" and in any event could not participate in a Gaelic ceilidh if they wished. Involvement of residents in tourism during the summer has reduced this opportunity to engage in social activities, however, the existence of the College has increased opportunities for some social gatherings.

Opinions varied with respect to the influence of tourism on Sunday observance; while there is general but not spontaneous agreement that Sunday observance has declined, it is difficult to assess the role of tourism in such a trend and in some resident's eyes, this was regarded as a benefit. The offering of some services in English in the summer rather than Gaelic as in the winter is perhaps another minor example of the reduction of Gaelic spoken as a result of tourism.

The impact of tourism on lifestyle is obviously complex, and perhaps, compared to other influences not very great. Most tourists spend little time in the area and individual contact is brief. One has to feel, however, that the impact such as it is, is cumulative. Many residents feel that the tourists respresent the way of the future, and that the visitors' needs and expectations may eventually replace their own. In the case of the Gaelic language this is clearly the case, since to converse with the tourist the resident must use English, and the Gael is traditionally reluctant to use Gaelic in the presence of English speakers. One researcher, however, has noted that of late this trend may be reversed and Gaelic used more because of the privacy it can afford.[13]

It is important to note, however, that even in an area as small as Sleat, there is considerable spatial variation with respect to the impacts of tourism and parts of the peninsula, particularly the extreme south and the west experience very little visitation from tourists. This variation in impact, as discussed earlier, is matched by variations in attitudes and perception of the residents themselves. In any area, the results and changes brought about by the impact of tourism will be dependent upon the capacity of the area to absorb such impacts.

Capacity is a function of a number of variables, ecological capacity, capacity of man-made facilities, tourist perception of crowding and local receptiveness to tourists. At any given point in space and time the number of tourists capable of being absorbed without significant change in the local environment depends on the most limiting of these four factors. If this level or threshold is exceeded, then

[13] WARDROP, K.: *The geography of Gaelic*, B. A. thesis, University of Edinburgh, 1974, p. 78

significant change in the local environment will occur, a new equilibrium may be reached and the situation may remain stable.

Local receptiveness to tourism has rarely been considered by those planning and developing tourism and yet it is of crucial importance to the establishment and continued existence of a successful tourist trade. It must be accepted that individuals will have different levels of receptiveness, and while some local residents may be content to see an unlimited number of tourists, others may object to the presence of even a few visitors. There exists a threshold, however, beyond which a significant proportion of local residents feel there are too many tourists in their community. It is felt that this situation is approaching, or may have been reached in Sleat. Certainly from some individuals, this is the case, as shown by comments made by residents in Point of Sleat, and in the responses of a larger number to the question on their attitudes to the coming of tourists. While the vast majority indicated they were looking forward to the visitors, a sizeable proportion added qualifications to the effect that they would also be glad to see tourists depart at the end of the season or that they felt that capacity had been reached. This was particularly true for those actually involved in tourism. It implies quite clearly that "enough is enough" and that a limitless number of tourists staying in Sleat for a much longer season is not desired.

This receptiveness has nowhere reached the levels of anti-tourist feeling reported as being present in Portree or elsewhere, and is certainly far removed from any real display of hostility as shown in other parts of the world. It is rather at the stage of limiting hospitality and assuming a more urban level of sociability, i.e., acknowledging the presence but not the desirability of the visitors.

As is stated earlier, however, these comments do not apply to all residents, and obviously some further increases in numbers, especially of transient tourists can be tolerated without major change. It should be borne in mind that the physical plant aspect of capacity, e.g. the car ferry, imposes a very real finite limit on numbers of tourists, especially those travelling by car, and this limit has been reached on many days during the peak summer months. Additional services, the introduction of a larger vessel, and Sunday services would increase this figure but are not immediately likely. Any further increase in tourist numbers will probably result from day visits from tourists from elsewhere on Skye, or, and this is unlikely from the survey results, a large increase in overnight accommodation until a new threshold, possibly involving a different variable is reached. The system would presently appear to be in a state of equilibrium, with the limiting factors now consisting both of man-made facilities in the shape of roads, ferry service and accommodation, and of local receptiveness.

3. Conclusions

This study of the population of a small rural area has illustrated the variations in perceptions and attitudes which exist among such a population with respect to tourism. It is clear that people have different ideas about the impacts of tourism and recreation on their local area and their neighbours, and these viewpoints do not always agree with the aims and goals of those in charge of regional development or tourist promotion. If tourism is to be developed to aid local economies and to make certain areas more attractive to the local population as a place to live, then more attention should be paid to the opinions of the local inhabitants, and efforts made to identify aspects of existing ways of life which may be susceptible to change by the development of tourism. The two major aspects of life in Sleat that appear to be most vulnerable to the pressures of tourism are the patterns of normal social intercourse during the summer, and the amount of Gaelic spoken in an area in which its use is already declining.

The pattern of social intercourse is disrupted by people being accommodated in private homes for two reasons. The presence of guests, even paying ones, deters people from leaving their homes to visit others, either in their homes or at public meeting places, e.g., hotels and village halls. Secondly, the presence of visitors may deter hosts from hosting a ceilidh because of the risk of disturbing visitors or possibly of having them wish to participate in otherwise personal intimate groups normally speaking in Gaelic.

Perhaps the most fundamental characteristic of life in Sleat which is vulnerable to tourist pressure is the pace and quality of life itself. Large numbers of people, even transients, in an area over several months of the year, do undoubtedly change the pace of life. As was shown by responses to questionnaires, increased traffic on the roads, increased custom in shops reducing opportunities for casual talk among locals, the meeting of large numbers of strangers, all increase stress levels of the local population. This is reflected in responses in interviews indicating that although most people expressed a desire to see visitors, many also expressed the opinion that they would be glad to see the tourists depart. Many writers and others involved in tourism have indicated the danger of tourists spoiling that which they come to experience, either by destroying the attraction through overuse or sheer weight of number, or by replacing the original attraction with pseudo or non-related substitutes. This threat is certainly realistic in parts of Western Scotland, where people come in part to "get away from it all", and escape from the stress, overcrowding and large numbers of people the experience in their normal working environment.

The crucial question is the ability of the communities in Sleat to withstand the temporary but increasing summer pressures which are put upon them. Because the growth of tourism has been primarily in transient traffic, much of which passes through the area without pausing, the impacts have not been as severe as in other places which are major destinations of tourists and in which tourists stay for considerable periods throughout the year. Sleat is not likely to experience such pressures and from that aspect is perhaps less likely to experience sudden major changes. Over the years, however, certain changes have resulted from the development of tourism and its facilities, the most noticeable being the existence of hotels and associated facilities, which, in winter particularly, become social centres for local communities.

The traditional forms of activity in Sleat, agriculture and to a lesser extent fishing and home craft industries, are unlikely to be threatened by tourism in the foreseeable future. There is no doubt that tourists can be annoying and disturbing to those engaged in agriculture, as discussed earlier. However, there is little direct competition between these two activities for labour, land or other facilities. The growth of summer homes at the expense of permanent settlement, through the changeover in existing houses, is a matter already dealt with and is causing more concern.

The possibility of competion for labour between tourism and other activities is often raised in rural, thinly populated areas. This is not viewed as a major problem in Sleat, or other areas in Western Scotland for a number of reasons. Employment in tourism is highly seasonal, not well paid compared to other occupations, and is predominantly female oriented. It is therefore unlikely to attract many males away from other, more regular employment, even if vacancies existed. It is possible that tourism allows additional part time employment for a limited number of men by way of boat-hiring for fishing and sightseeing trips, and in other areas as ghillies (assistants of fishermen and shooters) and stalkers, but in Sleat this is extremely rare.

In the area of female employment there is the possibility of some competition for labour by tourist establishments, which in Sleat are almost entirely hotels, but other opportunities for employment are few. The majority of shops are family owned and operated, and the woollen mill, the only other major source of female employment, has not faced any problems because of competition of labour. The involvement in the bed and breakfast trade may have some effect on crofting, in that women may not be able to help on crofts when busy catering for tourists, but when such a situation is critical, the decision is invariably made not to take in visitors.

While the future of Sleat and other parts of the Western Isles cannot be said to be secure in the long term, this situation is not the result of the development of tourism, and is not being made appreciably worse by the presence of a growing trade in tourism. As was indicated earlier it is in the area of social patterns and pace of life that tourism makes a noticeable impact, and even in this respect opinions are divided among local residents.

The impact of tourism on the Gaelic language itself is difficult to assess from one point in time, particularly when tourists are not present. It has been suggested[14] that tourism can be a strong influence in the process of Anglicisation of Sleat, by turning primarily Gaelic speaking communities into predominantly English speaking ones for several months each year citing the natural reluctance of the Gael to speak Gaelic when in the presence of non-Gaelic speakers as a major factor in this process. There is some doubt whether this point is as valid in private houses as in public situations, and people may well use Gaelic in their own homes to secure some degree of privacy.

WARDROP suggests that summer homes are particularly effective in the displacement of Gaelic by English where such residences become retirement homes, thus increasing the proportion of permanent English speakers in this community. In larger communities a sizeable influx of non-Gaelic speaking temporary workers in the hotel and catering trade would also be a factor in the decline in use of Gaelic, by requiring otherwise Gaelic speaking staff to use English. This is a present but minor problem in Sleat because of numbers involved and because not all of the permanent hotel staff are Gaelic speaking.

In general therefore the direct impact of tourism on Gaelic, particularly in the home, where it is spoken most, is probably low especially when compared to the influences of the mass media, the education system, and mixed language marriages. The exception to the above being the conversion of second homes into primary retirement residences.

There are clearly divergent views held by the Sleat residents about the tourist industry. A minority feel its most positive social and cultural contribution would be for it to disappear. Such a situation ist neither practical nor desirable given the proportion of the population who do derive economic benefits from the industry. On the other hand, there is little justification on social, cultural or economic grounds for increasing the dimensions of the tourist industry, particularly the summer cottage element, from the point of view of the indigenous popula-

[14] WARDROP, K.: *The geography of Gaelic,* B. A. thesis, University of Edinburgh, 1974

tion. Given the age of many of the long time residents, and the present level of involvement, any further significant involvement in tourism by this population is unlikely to be practical. Most, if not all benefits from further developments would therefore accrue to incomers, and in fact, as has been the case provide the stimulus for immigration by non-Gaelic incomers. Such a situation is not necessarily wrong or an unwise use of resources, but one can make a strong case that regional and particularly local development should be primarily for the benefit of existing residents, to improve their economic and social well-being. It is highly unlikely that further development of tourism in Sleat will have that effect, and more likely that it will reduce the quality of life from a social and cultural viewpoint.

Attempts to limit the growth of tourism in Sleat would be difficult to impose, unless efforts were made to limit numbers of tourists to the whole of the Scottish Highlands, a move which is unlikely, to say the least, given the development policies of many bodies involved in this area.

Indications are that tourist numbers will continue to increase, although at a slower rate than in the previous decade. Ferry and accommodation capacities are limited, and no new major developments are likely in the area to change these factors, and growth in numbers of second homes has slowed noticeably. Increased publicity for the Gaelic College, the Clan Donald Centre and the woollen mill, however, will add to the attraction of Sleat for tourists. The relative isolation of Sleat compared to more accessible and crowded parts of the Scottish Highlands will also make it more attractive in the future.

The pressures upon Sleat, and upon the Gaelic culture are therefore likely to be at increased levels in the foreseeable future, unless the level or type of tourism can be changed. As it is unlikely, for the reasons noted above, and others (e.g., worsening devaluation of sterling encouraging British people to holiday in Britain, and making Britain excellent value to foreign visitors), that the level of tourism will decline, it becomes much more important to consider ways of making tourism and tourists more culturally sympathetic with the local language and life style. To fail to so invites either eventual cultural extinction by assimilation or enforced changes, as has happened in other parts of Scotland, or antagonism towards tourists resulting in a diminishing tourist industry and inevitable financial hardship for some elements of the community, as seen in other parts of the world. This latter situation would symbolise the final disappearance of the Gaelic way of life, for hospitality towards visitors has always been one of its most attractive and consistent elements.

Planning for outdoor recreation at the local government level in Sweden

Some thoughts on the institutional framework of communal involvement

HANS ALDSKOGIUS, Uppsala, Sweden*

1. Introduction

In this paper I wish to consider some of the problems which relate to the role that planning for outdoor recreation plays at the local government level. The discussion refers specifically to the situation in Sweden. Obviously, a number of geographic and institutional factors which are characteristic of this regional setting may reduce the degree of general applicability of such a discussion of outdoor recreation in the context of local planning. Nevertheless, one purpose of the paper is to present an argument of more general nature, and, in particular, to draw attention to the importance of considering the institutional structure within which the recreational landscape and people's recreational behaviour is shaped, and to suggest a possible framework for studies of local situations.

For the purposes of this discussion I define *outdoor recreation* so as to include primarily those activities which take place outdoors and beyond the confines of the home, which involve at least a moderate degree of active participation, which are informal in the sense that they typically require little organization beyond the level of the individual or household, and which are oriented towards land and water resources for informal recreation in the countryside around built up urban areas – natural resources, as it were, rather than specialized, created facilities. This broad definition of outdoor recreation includes, in the context of the Swedish recreational life style, such activities as outdoor swimming, hiking and rambling for general recreational purposes, or in connection with berry- and mushroom-picking, cycling for pleasure, fishing, cross-country skiing, lake skating, boating, canoeing, and so forth.

The local government level in Sweden is represented by the commune. There are now 277 communes in the country. They range in size according to population from 4.000 to close to 700.000 inhabitants, and in area from about 10 to 19.000 square kilometres. Generally speaking, population densities are low – about 19 inhabitants per square kilometre for the whole country, and ranging from less than 1 to about 3.600 persons per square kilometre in the individual communes. There is thus a considerable variation between communes in terms of their size as political and economic organizations as well as with respect to the relationship between population and environmental resources. The communes have rather extensive decision-making powers e.g. in land use planning. They raise taxes – roughly 30 per cent. of the direct taxes on personal income – and in principle, and also in practice, must be considered quite powerful political units, which can plan and act quite independently in many areas of social, economic and physical planning. This is definitely the case as far as what we might loosely call the "leisure

*Dr. HANS ALDSKOGIUS, Docent, Department of Human Geography, University of Uppsala, Sweden

sector" is concerned. Each commune decides upon the extent of the communal involvement in the provision of facilities and the organization of activities. Variations in these respects between communes therefore reflect not only differences in local conditions with respect to environmental resources, size and spatial distribution of the population, and financial resources, but also the degree to which an active commune policy for the leisure sector has been formulated and carried out.

With respect to outdoor recreation, local government authorities might become involved in the following ways:

1. by following the development of leisure activities on the local scene and analysing the need for political action in order to improve the opportunities for recreational activities;

2. by planning for the creation, location and management of facilities such as swimming pools, bathing beaches, trails for hiking and skiing, cycle paths, ski lifts, open-air sports centres, marinas for small craft, roadside parking areas, and so forth;

3. by land use zoning (and acquisition of land) for the purpose of preserving areas of particular value for outdoor recreation;

4. by servicing and giving financial support to local organizations which are active in the field of outdoor recreation;

5. by organizing outdoor recreation activities, e.g. for specific age groups;

6. by putting together and distributing information about opportunities for outdoor recreation in their area.

2. An overview of communal involvement in outdoor recreation infrastructure

Unfortunately, there is a noticeable lack of statistical informtion about variations within the universe of Swedish communes with respect to different forms of communal involvement in outdoor recreation, and what does exist on a nation-wide basis is in some ways of dubious accuracy. For the purposes of an explorative analysis I have used data from a survey of communal installations in 1975.

I have selected four types of installations or facilities for analysis: *bathing beaches,* which have been improved in some way, e. g. by clearing of vegetation, installation of jetties, diving-boards, toilets etc., *illuminated hiking and/or skiing trails, ski lifts* and *open-air sports centres.* The survey only reports the number of such installations; there is no information on say size or quality of the installations, or length of trails and capacity of lifts. These four indicators of public investment in outdoor recreation infrastructure have been crosstabulated with three variables for which Census data on each commune are easily available – *"urbanity"* (proportion of population living in densely built-up localities with more than 200 inhabitants), *total population,* and *population density,* and one variable, reported on in the survey, which like total population serves as a commune size index, namely *leisure sector budget* (total budgeted expenditure for the leisure sector, a measure that includes a great deal more than expenditures for outdoor recreation purposes). – Neither the four selected facilities, nor the four background variables are ideally suited to the purposes of this study. Perhaps the major weakness in the survey data is that only installations and facilities which are operated by the communes themselves are included. Facilities which are owned and managed by youth organizations, sports clubs, tourist associations, and so forth, are not included, even though the total public funds allocated to support the operation of such installations may well exceed what a commune budgets for its own installations.

Given the rather unsatisfactory selection of variables and deficiencies in the data, and acknowledging that the outcome of a crosstabulation between indicator and background variables in several instances is predictable, perhaps the most rewarding approach would be to look for deviations from the expected relationships which may suggest additional explanatory factors or questions that would be interesting to pursue further.

In the case of bathing beaches and ski lifts, environmental factors obviously explain a major portion of their regional distribution and relative frequency in different types of communes. The opportunities for outdoor swimming are adequate in most parts of Sweden, a country which is rich in lakes and has a long coastline. There are, of course, spatial variations in environmental resources and these are reflected in the regional distribution of bathing beaches, but there is also a positive relationship between population size and number of such beaches. In the case of ski lifts, the environmental factor is much more dominant. In just over 50 per cent. of the communes there is no ski lift at all, and it is only in the northern parts of the country, and in a few large communes in central Sweden, that the number of lifts exceeds five. It is obvious that in the north communal investments in ski lifts are related to the demands of the tourist industry. The degree to which communal investment in outdoor recreation infrastructure reflects the needs of the local population and the interests of other users, respectively, and the possible conflicts that might arise in tourist regions because of this, is an interesting question which merits further consideration.

The relationship between the number of illuminated hiking and/or skiing trails and population is not as strongly positive as one might perhaps expect. Rather it seems as if this type of facility, relatively speaking, is most frequent in communes with fairly small populations, an only moderately high degree of urbanity, large areas and thus low population densities. Communes in the north generally rank quite high on this variable, which indicates that many of the trails are laid out primarily for skiing. Twenty per cent. of all communes have no commune-operated trails at all, the median value is 2.3 and the maximum number of trails in a commune is 20. Illuminated trails are generally rather short and tend to be heavily used for high-tempo exercise. It would have been interesting also to be able to analyse data on the existence and length of marked trails which are primarily intended to provide opportunities for hiking and skiing excursions and to connect residential areas with excursion areas and outdoor recreation centres, but the survey did not include such information.

Open-air sports centres are non-existent in as many as 62 per cent. of all communes and this facility is therefore not a very useful indicator of differences between communes. Where they exist, the relationship between number of centres and size of commune population is quite clear and positive. Only about 10 per cent. of all communes have more than two such centres.

The observations made in the preceding paragraphs on the basis of available, but rather unsatisfactory survey data at least indicate that there is considerable variation in the extent to which communes have involved themselves directly in provision of outdoor recreation facilities and activities. Variations in this respect are greater than variations in communal per capita expenditure for the total leisure sector, although this also differs considerably, with high values occurring in communes with large urban populations and in communes in tourist regions, and low values in rural, low-density communes. I have already indicated that these variations reflect basic differences in population size, economic resources, environmental characteristics, and the extent to which non-public organizations are active in the leisure sector. What, then, is the role that local government policy plays in the development of the leisure sector, and particularly with regard to outdoor recreation?

3. Towards a format for studies of communal involvement in the outdoor recreation sector

Traditionally, the leisure sector was often regarded as a "non-partisan" area in local politics, where problems could be solved harmoniously across party lines. In retrospect, leisure planning in Sweden up into the 1960s has been characterized as *ad hoc* and crisis-solving rather than anticipatory, and as too responsive to the demands of active but small and specialized pressure groups. This situation is changing, however, and for several reasons. Communal expenditure in the leisure sector increased tenfold between 1960 and 1970, the growing importance of leisure activities have made such matters politically more substantial and "rewarding", while the combination of new demands for communal involvement in planning for recreation and, at the same time, a tight economic situation brings forth more sharply questions of priorities which have to be resolved in the political process. In an attempt to come to grips more efficiently with problems in the leisure sector, many communes have reorganized the political and administrative machinery, replacing several more specialized boards and committees by a "leisure committee" which is responsible for the whole leisure sector and carries more political weight.

We can assume that communal policy will reflect positions taken with respect to:

1. the needs of the outdoor recreation sector in relation to other recreational activities,
2. the relative importance of different types of outdoor recreation activities,
3. the needs of specific groups of individuals (e.g. age groups),
4. the balance between direct and indirect public involvement in the provision of facilities and organization of activities in the outdoor recreation sector.

In figure 1 I have made an attempt to sketch, in a highly condensed form, a local system of institutions within which communal outdoor recreation policy is formulated and implemented. The diagram includes a set of "actors", some of the types of activities in which they may become involved, and an indication of how these activities affect some of the elements which determine the opportunities for outdoor recreation, as perceived by recreationists. I want to make only two points in reference to this diagram. The first point is that as a rule several different institutions will be involved in decision making with respect to each type of activity. The second point, which follows logically from the first, is that, whenever two or more arrows meet at one of the "activities" boxes (e. g. "establishment of facilities"), there is an opportunity for cooperation between decision-making units, or, alternatively, a potential conflict situation. Real-world local systems are of course infinitely more complex; if, e.g., the "black box" labelled "commune" were opened up, we would find a hierarchy of political and administrative institutions which cooperate and compete with each other. The outdoor recreation sector is thus a subsystem within the leisure sector, itself a subsystem within the commune system, which in turn operates subject to developments in larger regional and sectoral systems at the provincial and national level.

Figure 1: A diagrammatic sketch of the framework within which communal involvement in outdoor recreation planning develops

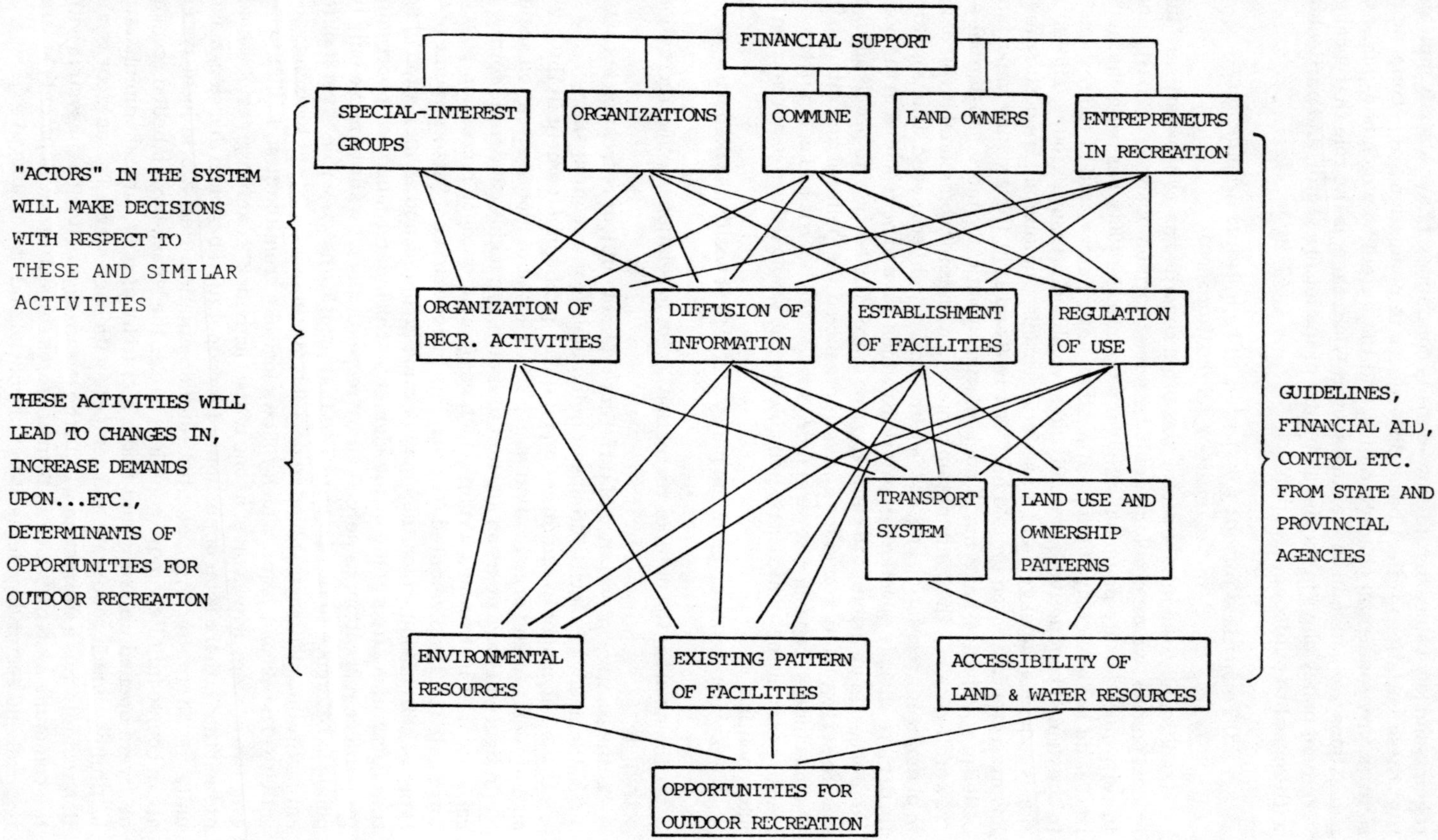

The diagrammatic sketch in figure 1, although trivial in itself, raises questions about how the supply side in the outdoor recreation equation develops. The machinery of local government occupies a central position in the system. This is the case even where direct communal involvement in the provision of facilities and activities is modest, not least because of communal control of land use planning. Where communal investment in outdoor recreation infrastructure becomes more extensive and takes such forms as the development of open-air sports centres with catering facilities, prepared trails, bathing beaches, picnic places and so forth, it is clear that they have considerable impact upon the pattern of recreational day trips. In comparison with the situation in more densely populated countries, urban populations in Sweden are priviledged from the point of view of access to areas for outdoor recreation, both in terms of sheer space and because Swedish common law implies an exceptionally liberal attitude with respect to the general public's right of access to land and water. One would assume that public policy plays an even greater strategic role in shaping patterns of recreational use of day trip areas in countries less generously endowned with space for recreation, and with greater pressure on environmental resources.

Against the background of this brief discussion I would like to offer the following suggestions.

1. Spatial patterns of facilities for outdoor recreation can be expected to be the product not only of rational judgments about "best" or satisfactory locations, but also of land use competition and policy compromise. Institutional factors in all probability will play a significant role in the emergence of such patterns of recreational infrastructure and therefore must be considered in studies of the development of recreational landscapes.

2. There is a case to be made for studies of these problems at the local government level, since it is at this level where most decisions which regulate and coordinate land use are made. It is also in the local situation that the complexities of the institutional structure become most obvious, because the full range from informal *ad hoc* special-interest groups to central government agencies might become involved in the process.

3. The rationale for considering the role of institutional factors is not only that it may lead to deeper insights into the development of the recreational landscape, but also that comparative studies of different areas might provide object lessons for other areas and future situations.

4. A closer look at the structure and workings of institutional systems will provide opportunities for cooperation with researchers in other fields, such as political science and public administration. Such cooperation should be welcomed and undoubtedly will provide stimulating impulses for studies in the geography of outdoor recreation.

References

Fritidsverksamhet för barn och ungdom den 1 april 1975. *Statistika meddelanden*, Sveriges officiella statistik, Statistiska C'entralbyran Stockholz 1976, 10

PALMER, J. and BRADLEY, J.: Planning for outdoor recreation. *Recreational geography*. Newton Abbot 1975

Planering för friluftsliv. *Statens naturvårdsverk publikationer*. Stockholm 1971, 7

Turism och rekreation i Sverige. *Statens offentliga utredningar*. Stockholm 1973, 52

Tourists and recreation facilities in the Western United States – use and misuse

BURKHARD HOFMEISTER, Berlin (West)*

1. Introduction

In the era of mass tourism more leisure time and higher mobility made the annual numbers of visitors to some of the popular tourist attractions in the Western United States rise tenfold during the post-war period. During the 1960s the authorities in charge were still more or less inclined to let such development have free play. Around 1970, however, problems had grown to the extent that serious consideration had to be given to them and measures were taken to cope with at least some of them. Such measures had, of course, an impact on the land use of the areas in question, and the present report focuses upon the most conspicuous results with regard to spatial changes within such tourist and recreation areas.

A sample study carried out in the Western United States from mid-June till mid-August, 1977 included a limited number of tourist and recreation areas in the states of California, Nevada, Arizona, Utah, Wyoming and Oregon falling under four categories (fig. 1):

Fig. 1 Location of Sample Areas

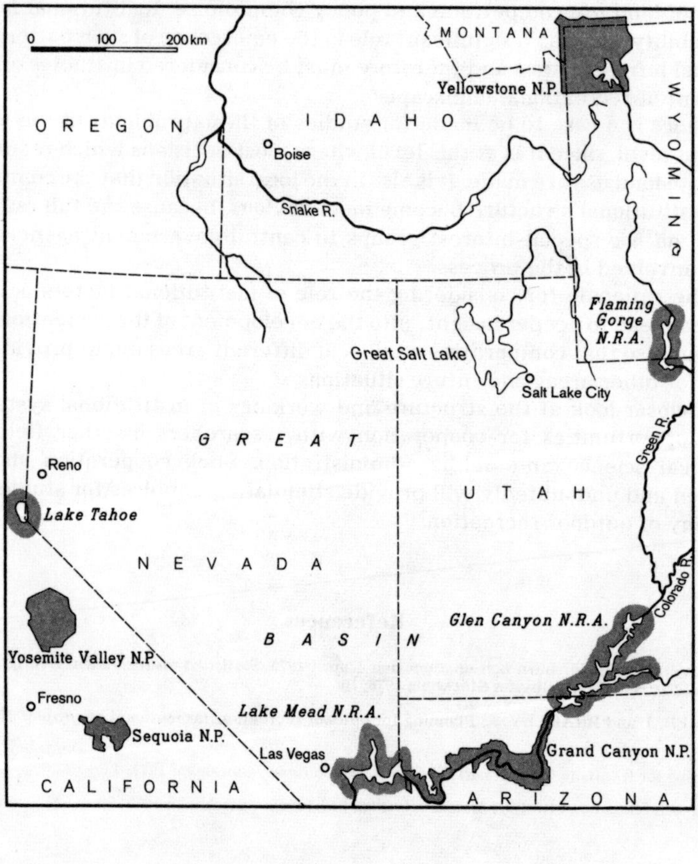

First, *National Parks* (N. P.) under the jurisdiction of the National Park Service (N. P. S.). They are, generally speaking, major tourist attractions for brief visits by a large number of people stopping by during a longer vacation trip because of their outstanding natural features. Included were Yosemite Valley and Sequoia N. P.s in California, Grand Canyon N. P. in Arizona, and Yellowstone N. P. in Wyoming.

Second, *National Recreation Areas* (N. R. A.), which are, with few exceptions, also administered by the N. P. S. They serve, however, quite a different purpose as compared with the National Parks. Usually located along river banks or lake shores, mainly artificial lakes or reservoirs behind some dam, they are visited by people over the weekend or by vacationists staying for a longer period for boating, fishing, swimming, and also hiking. Included were the Lake Mead N. R. A., the Glen Canyon N. R. A. and the Flaming Gorge N. R. A. on the Colorado and Green River respectively.

Third, *National Forests* (N. F.) under the jurisdiction of the United States Forest Service (U. S. F. S.) that has, in certain favourable locations, established picnic areas for day use and camp-sites for overnight stays. The areas devoted to such recreational uses are comparatively small portions of the total forest lands organized as National Forests. Included were Ashley N. F. adjacent to the Flaming Gorge N. R. A. in northern Utah and Winema N. F. in southern Oregon.

Fourth, *State Parks* (S. P.) which are administered by the Department or Division of Parks and Recreation of one of the several states and which serve various purposes within the respective State Park system. Some are, like the N. R. A. s, located along lake shores offering picnic areas or camp-sites or both to the vacationist. Some are natural attractions like most of the National Parks; some are ghost towns which are preserved from further decay through the effort of the respective state agency. Included were the State Parks of California and Nevada along the shores of Lake Tahoe in the Sierra Nevada and the ghost town of Bodie reached by a gravel road of 13 miles branching off California highway 395, near the Nevada boundary.

This being a preliminary report on some general findings, I shall restrict myself to the above mentioned types of tourist and recreation areas and not touch upon other types of facilities like privately developed camp-grounds along natural or artificial water bodies, privately developed ski resorts like Snowbird in Little Cottonwood Canyon in the Wasatch Mountains near Salt Lake City, Utah, or the ski resort of Squaw Valley near Lake Tahoe which, after having served as the place for the Olympic Winter Games, is now operated by the U.S. Olympic Training Center and whose architectural facilities are used for congresses related to the topics of sport and health.

2. *Visiting trends*

The growing demand for recreational facilities and the increasing pressure on the existing tourist and recreation areas is best appreciated against the background of visitor statistics. These are, however, extremely deficient so that all figures compiled in the following tables are not more than very coarse approximations. Why should this be so?

There are, till the present day, hardly any exact counts of persons entering the various units of the Parks, Forest, and Recreation Area systems. Of course, people staying overnight on camp-grounds are registered. In most cases prospective campers will even register well in advance. They are for instance urged by the State of California Department of Parks and Recreation to do so 90 days ahead of time in order to secure a camp-site for the exact date wanted, and they are then assigned to a specific camp-site according to the particular circumstances such as type and size of their camper or caravan by a computercontrolled registration system called *Ticketron.*

Except for such figures on overnight stays on individual camp-sites there are *hardly any reliable data* available, and there are lots of sources for errors of enumeration. To mention just a few:

1. The National Recreation Areas as well as many State Parks have a considerable number of entrance roads only few of which are observed as to the number of cars driving in either direction. So, to begin with, the enumeration system is *incomplete,* and for some entrance roads there are but rough guesses.

2. The other entrance roads are equipped with devices counting the axles of cars. The administrations use a certain ratio which usually is 3.5 persons per car. This is certainly a rather coarse method. The haedquarters of Yosemite Valley National Park initiated, after certain doubts, a survey that was to find out whether this ratio was realistic and thus justified or not. Having used the factor of 3.5 till 1976 they started, in 1977, to use the lower factor of 2.8 persons per car. As a result, figures of former years are not comparable and, before all, are very likely not to come close to reality.

Table 1 shows the visits to Yosemite Valley National Park during the month of May for the years 1970–1977.

Table 1: Visits to Yosemite Valley National Park in May

1970	1971	1972	1973	1974	1975	1976	1977
299.337	289.783	283.633	223.118	237.029	259.537	321.818	239.462

The remarkable downward trend in 1973 was, of course, due to the energy crisis and the sudden change in behaviour of many Americans as to the way they would spend their vacations in that year. While there has again been a strong upward trend till 1976 the low figure for 1977 is mainly due to the new ratio applied for the first time in that year; the adjusted figure would read 299.327.

3. The chances are high that cars or people are counted more than once or not at all without these errors being corrected. Because of a shortage of accommodation within the park people will stay overnight outside, as they do for instance in the case of Yellowstone National Park where many people spend a couple of nights in the village of West Yellowstone just outside the park boundary and then enter the park on several consecutive days: they are counted each time at the gate thus making for a much *higher visitor's figure* as compared with reality. On the other hand there are, for the same reason, illegal overnight stays in the park by people parking their campers on parking lots not designated for overnight camping or staying on camp-grounds without having received a wilderness permit thus making for a *lower figure of overnight stays* as compared with reality.

This is why I shall just give rounded up figures for the visitors to selected National Parks and National Recreation Areas (table 2).

Table 2: Number of visitors to selected recreation areas in the Western United States of America

Unit	Visitors in 1.000.000			1976	
	1960	1970	1976	1960 = 100	1970 = 100
National Parks					
Yellowstone	1.4	2.3	2.5	180	109
Grand Canyon	1.2	2.3	3.0	250	130
Yosemite Valley	1.2	2.3	2.8	233	122
Sequoia	0.6	0.9	1.0	167	111
National Recreation Areas					
Lake Mead	2.3	.	6.9	300	.
Glen Canyon	0.7	0.8	1.1	157	138
Flaming Gorge (1965)	0.8	2.0	2.5	313	125

According to table 2 four of the seven areas experienced an increase in visitors since 1960 of 100 per cent. or more. However, visitation curves have levelled off since 1970. During the 1970s numbers of visitors have increased at a lower rate or have even temporarily decreased due to the petrol shortage of 1973 and the high petrol prices in recent years.

National Recreation Areas have experienced a more rapid increase of visitors than have the National Parks, above all the Lake Mead National Recreation Area which is closest to the huge population cluster of the California metropolitan areas.

This brings us to the next aspect: regional variations in terms of varying degrees of *attractiveness* and of *accessibility* which, in turn, is highly dependent upon the distance to major population concentrations. Thus, Grand Canyon National Park, Yellowstone National Park, and Yosemite Valley National Park with their world-famous features draw much larger numbers of visitors than the less known Sequoia National Park, not to mention the fact that giant redwood trees can be observed at quite a few locations outside the Sequoia National Park area. The first two parks drew visitors from places farther away and even from overseas while the vast majority of visitors to Yosemite National Park and to Sequoia National Park and also to the Lake Mead National Recreation Area originate in the State of California. Around 80 per cent. of the visitors to Yosemite Valley come from places in California, while only 21 per cent. of the visitors to Grand Canyon National Park are Californians!

A survey carried out during three days in July 1970 in Yellowstone National Park showed that 9 states of the United States and Canada ranking 10th accounted for 53.3 per cent. of all private (non-commercial) vehicles entering the park (table 3). The next ten states were Washington, Wisconsin, Idaho, New York, Iowa, Missouri, Pennsylvania, Indiana, Wyoming, and Oregon, accounting for another 27 per cent., while all the other several states of the United States and all other foreign countries just accounted for 19.7 per cent. Of the states sharing the park area, Montana ranks 4th, while Idaho ranks 13th and Wyoming only 19th. If these figures are, however, weighted according to the total numbers of private cars registered in each respective state (ratio per 10.000 registered cars) one realizes that the nearby states rank highest.

Table 3: Number of cars entering Yellowstone National Park on July 22nd, 24th and 27th 1970

State	No. of cars	per cent.	Cars/10.000 registered cars in State	
			Index	Rank
1. California	2.790	13.19	2.5	11
2. Utah	1.277	6.04	22.8	3
3. Illinois	1.242	5.87	2.3	12
4. Montana	927	4.38	25.0	1
5. Ohio	924	4.37	1.5	16
6. Michigan	911	4.31	2.0	14
7. Texas	885	4.18	1.4	17
8. Colorado	799	3.78	5.6	5
9. Minnesota	779	3.68	4.0	7
10. Canada	747	3.53	0.9	19
11. Washington	719	3.40	3.9	8
12. Wisconsin	712	3.37	3.4	9
13. Idaho	704	3.33	16.8	4
14. New York	654	3.09	1.0	18
15. Iowa	626	2.96	4.0	6
16. Missouri	485	2.29	2.3	13
17. Pennsylvania	472	2.23	0.8	20
18. Indiana	468	2.21	1.8	15
19. Wyoming	452	2.14	23.7	2
20. Oregon	417	1.97	3.0	10
Total	16.990	80.32		

Sources: for the US States: US Bureau of the Census: *Statistical Abstract of the United States 1975*, Washington D.C. 1975, p. 573;

for Canada: United Nations: *Statistical Yearbook Annuaire Statistique 1975*, New York 1976, p. 492

Assuming that the greater number of comparatively small and widely scattered State Parks serve to a much higher degree the *local population*, i. e. the population of the respective state, this will especially hold true for a densely populated state like California. Table 4 shows the results of a survey carried out in the summer of 1970. Data are given for D. L. Bliss and Emerald Bay State Parks on the south west shore of Lake Tahoe and for the ghost town of Bodie (Bodie S. H. P.).

Table 4: Origin of visitors to three California State Parks in the summer of 1970 in per cent.

Area of origin	D. L. Bliss S. P.		Emerald Bay S. P.		Bodie S.H.P.
	day use	overnight	day use	overnight	day use
San Francisco Bay Metropolitan Areas	51	43	40	26	22
South Metropolitan Areas	9	20	9	36	48
Central Valley Metropolitan Areas	19	22	17	8	14
North Non-Metros	–	–	–	3	–
South Non-Metros	–	–	1	–	5
Central Valley Non-Metros	7	2	9	7	3
Out of State	14	13	24	20	8

Between 66 per cent. and 85 per cent. originated in California's metropolitan areas with the San Francisco Bay area leading in the case of Lake Tahoe and the Los Angeles metropolitan area leading in the case of Bodie. Only between 8 per cent. and 24 per cent. came from out of state. On the Nevada side of Lake Tahoe there are, within the Nevada State Park system, two State Parks which accounted for approx. 800.000 out of a total of 1.4 million visitors in 1976. They are for day use only and are to a high degree used by the California population. While in the rest of Nevada's State Park visitors from nearby places (Nevada population) is approx. 85 per cent. it is down to 55 per cent. in the two parks at Lake Tahoe due to the high influx of Californians making use of the beaches on the Nevada side as well as of the nearby casinos.

A last aspect is the *seasonality of visits.* While cross-country skiing and snowmobiling have become very popular in recent years and have made for rising numbers of visitors to the National Parks and National Forests in the winter season there is still a marked difference between places farther north and those farther south. This is demonstrated by a comparison of Yellowstone and Yosemite Valley National Parks (table 5).

In contrast to Yosemite Valley with its somewhat more balanced number of visitors throughout the year Yellowstone National Park is characterized by a rather pronounced seasonality. The months of July and August account for over 50 per cent. of the total visits (1.469 million out of a total of 2.525 million), the four months from May to August account for four fifths (2.023 mill. out of 2.525 mill.) while during the six months from November to April slightly more than 100.000 visitors were registered. This means, of course, that the *problem of overcrowding is much more severe in Yellowstone National Park* than in those other parks with more balanced visitation figures.

It has become obvious from the above data that

1. there has been a tremendous increase in the numbers of visitors to many National Parks and National Recreation Areas during the 1950s and 1960s;

Table 5: Number of visitors to Yellowstone and Yosemite Valley National Parks in 1976

Month	Yellowstone N. P.	Yosemite Valley N. P.
January	17.088	68.771
February	23.268	95.957
March	13.372	70.170
April	12.357	166.652
May	155.222	321.818
June	418.403	391.012
July	764.486	434.273
August	704.871	463.319
September	310.893	292.518
October	87.263	186.394
November	28.835	125.644
December	9.086	100.889
Total	2,525.144	2,717.417

2. the further increase during the 1970s has not much aggravated the problem any more;

3. the various tourist and recreation areas included in the sample show rather different rates of increase, so that some of them face the problem of overcrowding while others do not;

4. the problem of overcrowding is especially severe in those areas (a) with outstanding natural features that make for a very high attractiveness like the Grand Canyon, (b) with high accessibility from nearby metropolitan areas like the Lake Mead National Recreation Area, (c) with a strong seasonality in the number of visits like Yellowstone National Park.

3. *Adjustments to crowding conditions*

What adjustments have been made so far and what others have been considered for the future management of the various tourist and recreation areas? This question will be discussed under four aspects.

3.1. Areas with recreation being the predominant but not the only use

Not all the areas included in the sample are recreational areas in the sense that they have exclusively been set aside for recreational purposes. Especially as far as the National Forests are concerned Public Law 86-517 was enacted in 1960 "to authorize and direct that the National Forests be managed under principles of multiple use and to produce a sustained yield of products and services, and for other purposes". The catchword "Land of many uses" is found on all signs announcing the entrance to a National Forest.

This *multiple use concept* is, apart from the N.F.s themselves, also applied to the Flaming Gorge National Recreation Area at the Utah-Wyoming boundary which is not, as are other National Recreation Areas, under the jurisdiction of the National Park Service, but rather under that of the U.S. Forest Service for the supposed reason that until 1971 the Flaming Gorge Area used to be part of the adjacent Ashley National Forest.

To be sure, recreation is given priority over other uses in the Flaming Gorge National Recreation Area by means of the so-called "Environmental Statement and Management Plan of Flaming Gorge". Other uses are, however, not excluded, especially in the less frequented portions of the area. Strip mining is absolutely prohibited, while other kinds of *mineral exploitation* are permitted as far as they are compatible with the recreational function of the area. Transhumance of sheep and cattle is very much restricted, in 1975 nine ranchers were given *grazing permits* for a total of 566 Animal Unit Months (AUM) for sheep and 363 AUM for cattle within the area. As to *forest economy* lumbering is not a major issue within the recreation area, but is permitted to the extent that sick trees are cut especially if they become a hazard for the visitors, that an aesthetic landscape and a favourable mixture of age classes of trees are maintained.

As far as any further expansion of recreational areas is concerned the National Forests have probably got the *highest future potential* which, of course, could only be developed at the expense of other uses such as lumbering, drainage functions, wildlife refuges. Whether this is desirable or not and whether the nation can afford to devote a still greater portion of the land surface within the national boundaries to recreation and tourism is, in the long run, a political decision.

We shall see what other chances there are to cope with the growing demand for recreational facilities.

3.2. Areas with varying intensities of recreational use

According to the management plans of the various National Parks the *further development of certain heavy-use areas* is promoted in favour of the much larger low-use areas of the so-called backcountry. The latter may only be used for extensive hiking or excursions on horseback including overnight camping with special *wilderness permits* of the Park Service or the Forest Service. The restrictive measures that have been applied at least during the high season from mid-June through mid-September are, however, not based on any sound scientific investigations; rather has the backcountry policy so far been in an experimental stage.

Three systems of backcountry mangement have been tried out more or less successfully in various parks at various times: first, *trail head quotas* which allow, during a certain period of time, a limited number of people to enter a certain area on marked trails; second, the *zone system* assigns a maximum number of visitors to a specific area or zone within which there is freedom of movement; third, the *camp-site system* which is highly restrictive inasmuch as it assigns visitors to specific camp-sites within the area.

The areas or zones for each of the three systems have been delimited either on the basis of *vegetation zones or of watersheds*. This device is very pragmatic rather than sophisticated. The Flaming Gorge National Recreation Area for instance, has been broken down into three management areas: The Northern Desert Management Area characterized by stands of pinyon-juniper, the Conifer Forest-Canyon Management Area with prevailing stands of lodgepole and yellow pines and Douglas fir, and the Green River Management Area. For practical purposes there is a further breakdown into subareas. The quotas for each zone or trail head respectively have been derived from three factors at least two of which are easily quantified: the size of the area, the trail length within the area, and the durability of the vegetation cover.

Since, in recent years, the numbers of recreation vehicles have very rapidly increased, outlying camp-grounds at the margin of the heavy-use areas and at the beginning of the backcounty have been more frequently used.

Despite the lack of scientific investigations on the *carrying capacity* of the various portions of the National Forests and other recreational areas a number of measures have been undertaken, the most important of which will be mentioned in the following paragraphs.

3.3. Measures undertaken in heavy-use areas

3.3.1 Restrictions regarding parking space and overnight accommodation

In the many units of the National Park Service, the U.S. Forest Service and the State Park systems *no further development of commercial accommodation and camp-sites* will occur. Camping is usually limited to two weeks during the high season. The numbers of beds in lodges and cottages are frozen or even slightly reduced like in Yellowstone National Park by closing down the facilities at Fishing Bridge and other places thus making for a future concentration of overnight facilities at two points within the park area only. Increasing numbers of visitors will have to find overnight accommodation elsewhere. The data at my disposal are, unfortunately, not sufficient to prove the assumption of an increasing gap between the numbers of visitors and those who can be accommodated within the boundaries of the recreation areas. There was no evidence of the areas outside the National Park boundaries having experienced a recent motel boom. In the high season, however, all the motels within a radius 60 miles outside the park boundaries of Yellowstone National Park have a full house. And there will certainly be some more *motel construction* in the future in response to the restrictive policy regarding overnight accommodation mentioned above.

Overcrowding has, to a greater extent, only occurred on the three *critical weekends* of Memorial Day (at the end of May), Independence Day (July 4th), and Labor Day (first Monday in September). This is when many day use areas temporarily closed their gates to accept visitors simply on the basis of the number of parking lots available. The statements made for backcountry use in chapter 3.2. also hold true for the day use areas inasmuch as there is up-to-date no sophisticated system to assess their carrying capacity. Nobody can really tell whether there could be more parking lots and, consequently, more visitors at any one time without doing harm or still more harm than has already been done to the landscape. In the Flaming Gorge National Recreation Area, however, the U.S.F.S. operates a so-called *overflow camp-ground* which is usually closed from Monday till Friday noon but opens on Friday afternoon to cope with the higher demand for camp-sites over the weekend.

3.3.2. Restrictions regarding vehicular traffic

Certain portions of the heavy-use areas have been reserved for cycling and riding on horseback whereas *vehicular traffic has been prohibited* except for emergency and maintenance vehicles and special *shuttle buses* that are usually operated by the concessioners for transporting visitors to various points of interest (fig. 2). In addition some highways or portions of loop roads have been converted to one-way traffic. An extension of restricted and one-way zones is under discussion.

Fig. 2 Shuttle Bus System in the Grand Canyon National Park

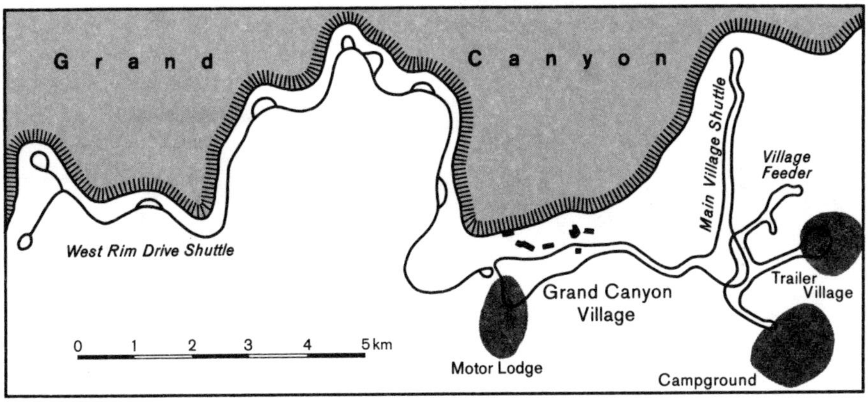

Traffic conditions are, however, different in the various recreation areas and do not always lend themselves easily to such measures. While the south and east entrance roads to South Rim Grand Canyon are dead-end roads and restrictions could be introduced rather easily the entrance roads and loop roads in Yellowstone National Park serve at the same time as highways for through-traffic and are thus important links within the inter-regional highway system of the United States' Northwest (fig. 3a and 3b).

In some locations bypass routes have been constructed at neuralgic points to make vehicular traffic somewhat more fluid. According to the park policy of Yellowstone N.P. this is the only measure of highway construction which is being undertaken at the present time.

Fig. 3a u. b Road System in the Yellowstone Park Region and the Grand Canyon Park Region

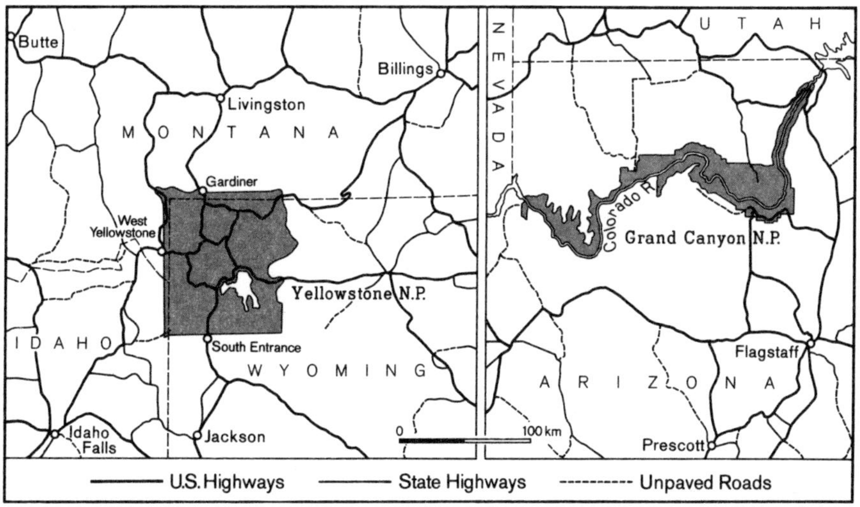

Fig. 4 Lake Tahoe Shoreline-Properties

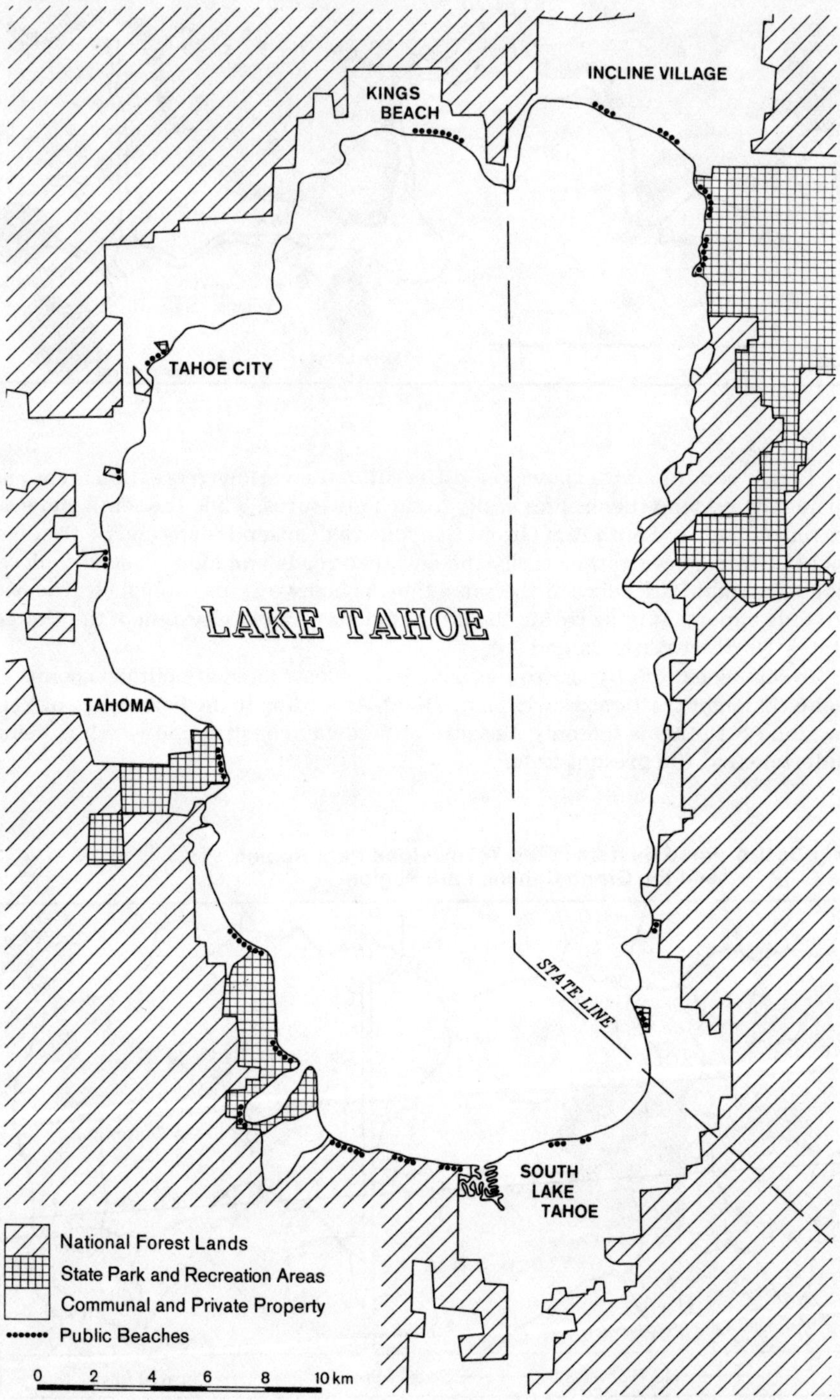

3.4. Measures of a general scope
3.4.1. New recreation areas

The acquisition of new recreation areas has increased the opportunities for the prospective tourist to find places where to go and where to find overnight accommodation. A good example are the once privately owned estates on the southwest shore of Lake Tahoe in the Sierra Nevada which were bought by the State of California in the 1950s and added to the California State Park System thus making a greater portion of the lake shore accessible to the public (fig. 4). Many Americans had, prior to the acquisition, complained of too much of the shore line being in private ownership and thus unaccessible. Today a considerable portion is in public ownership while much of the east shore (on the Nevada side) is relatively unaccessible because of the rough terrain and steep slopes.

3.4.2. Carrying capacity studies

Carrying capacity studies have recently been initiated, among others a study for South Rim Grand Canyon by a special research team affiliated with the Denver Service Center of the National Park Service. Such studies are supposed to offer a sounder basis for all decisions to be made with regard to numbers of visitors that may be admitted and to the kinds of uses that may be permitted in any particular portion of the respective recreation and tourist areas.

At the beginning of the next decade the conclusions drawn from those studies may very well initiate a somewhat modified policy for the vacation lands of the American West.

Acknowledgements:

Thanks to a travel grant of the *Deutsche Forschungsgemeinschaft* (German Research Society) I was able to carry out field work in the United States during the summer months of 1977 and to gather the data and facts on which this paper is based. I am grateful to the *Chief Rangers* and *Resource Management Specialists* of various National Parks, the *Rangers* of several National Forests and State Parks who by permitting interviews and generously supplying statistical and other material made this research report possible.

Recreation in the self-managing socialist society

Contemporary theory and practice in the Socialist Federal Republic of Yugoslavia

MOMČILO VUKIĆEVIĆ, Novi Sad, Yugoslavia*

1. The setting of the problem[1]

Under socialism conditions are being created in which the various needs of working people are gradually developed and covered, both quantitatively and qualitatively. Although this process does not move quite straight in all stages of the building of socialism i. e. in all socialist countries, in the long run its trend is positive and it is connected directly with the building of the socialist community. Similar to other socialist countries, in Yugoslavia too the "trade-union" tourism has been developed. As a form of democratization of tourism it has been accorded special attention for a long time and has been classified as one of the factors which influence advantageously the living standard of the working people. Yet, the "trade-union" tourism in our country has been different from other national models. That difference has been increasing gradually and in the present stage of development these quantitative changes have resulted in a new quality: out of "trade-union" tourism "worker" tourism has emerged, as a particular form in the current process of the democratization of tourism in the world.

2. The working people and tourism

2.0. The economic determinants of the development of "trade-union" tourism

Up to the last decade of our development tourism has been lagging quantitatively behind the other branches of the national economy, especially those whose building up was one of the primary aims of our post-war economic policy. Only at the present stage of our development is the structure and other qualitative elements of tourism undergoing positive changes. But there is a marked discrepancy in the dynamics of development and changes. This discrepancy was not always of the same intensity and at different stages it had different forms.

2.1. The socio-political determinants of the "trade-union" tourism

The basis i. e. the starting point of the development of Yugoslav tourism has undergone considerable quantitative and qualitative changes in the post-war years. Since the beginning of its socialist development the needs for tourist-recreational activities have been, in principle, considered one of the components of the people's living standard. The fact that the tourist-recreational activity of the

---

* Dr. MOMČILO VUKIĆEVIĆ, Assistant Professor, Institute of Economics and Jurisprudence, Law School of the University of Novi Sad, SFR Yugoslavia

[1] The analysis in this paper is directly connected with the author's article "Demokratizacija turizma (Prilog obradi savremenih oblika demokratizacije u socijalizmu i kapitalizmu)", in *Zbornik radova Pravnog fakulteta u Novom Sadu,* Novi Sad 1974, pp. 421–441

resident population in general was accorded this place and importance brought about as a result its special treatment. These needs, however, as needs in general, were covered then and to such an extent, when and to which extent the level of economic development achieved permitted. Later on these activities were classified as secondary needs and thus did not receive special treatment any more; to what extent they were covered was determined by economic factors alone. This conception and treatment of the needs for tourist and recreative activity has directly affected the basis i. e. the starting point of the development of tourism. In other words this may be defined as an effort to make tourism one of the branches of national economy.

During the last ten years or so tourism has been treated and developed as a function of priority branches but now it is considered a propulsive branch of our economy and is included in the basic trends of its development.

In the programme of tourist development there are depending on the stage in question, two theoretically possible variants of the correlation of domestic and international tourism. For some time these two variants were relatively closely coordinated but in general foreign tourism has always been favoured in the Yugoslav development conception. The same tendency is reflected by the proposal for the basis of the long-range development of Yugoslav tourism up to 1985, but that proposal is at the moment being critically analyzed.[2]

For a long time the essential meaning and contents of the tourist policy has been to support, regulate, control, develop and promote tourism with the intention of creating conditions for the optimum manifestation of its functions connected with health and recreation, cultural education and politics. It was a specific policy of the organization of tourism, or to be more exact, qualitative structural measures taken by the government departmens. In this way the social and commercial tourism policy was subordinated to the official policy. The basic scope of action of official policy has been the building up of the financial basis of tourism, the tourist propaganda and the actual tourist economy, and partly the training of skilled personnel for tourism, to watch, to record and to evaluate the results of tourist traffic and to plan the development of tourism. Practically a complete tourist cycle exists, but the range and effects of state intervention are different in some of its sections. It was just the official tourist policy that represented one of the major factors in the development of tourism under the conditions of formerly existing starting points and general programmes of tourist development. It was in fact a complex, coordinated and efficient system of measures with its economic-financial measures being the most important. The latter are to a certain extent accompanied by the most urgent legal and administrative measures concerning tourism. The socio-political management of tourism is still at its beginning. Tourism classified as belonging to the group of tertiary activity, had its development determined indirectly by the plans for the entire field of service industries. In a later stage tourism acquired the qualities of tourism policy, a process aiming at bringing about quantitative changes in the tourism of our country. Its corollary, the formerly mentioned modified basis and the qualitatively new development programme have an influence on the change of all elements of tourist policy: the relation of the three major factors of tourism – the subjects of the tourism policy are relatively brought into a harmony (i. e. the majority of the various government bodies concerned has been abolished); the tour-

---

[2] The Federal Executive Council, *Basis of the policy of long-ranged development of the SFR of Yugoslavia up to 1985.* A proposal for discussion, Belgrade 1974, section about tourism, pp. 51–53

ism cycle, the object of the activity of tourism policy is being completed (in the sense of levelling the development stages of its parts); and there is a better balance in the structure of the means of tourism policy i. e. the basic (legal, economic and financial) and the supplementary (administrative and socio-political) measures.

2.2. Other rational factors determining the development of "trade-union" tourism

Yugoslav tourism, situated in the formerly economic and socio-political framework outlined above, has been influenced by a wide range of rational and irrational factors. On the one hand the character of their influence has been different, depending on the development stage of tourism. On the other hand, the principles of social welfare policy being included in the basis of "trade-union" tourism, the role and significance of certain rationally determining factors have been very different and their influence relatively small. That is the reason why this paper gives a theoretical explanation of the influence of only some of them – of the standard of living and the available amount of leisure time.

Living standard

Living standard is one of the major determining factors both of initiative and of receptive tourist activity in general. If we limit the object of this analysis to our country, we shall see that in the post war period the effect of most of the components of living standards of the resident population on the development of "trade-union" tourism is noticeable:

1. the national tourist potential consisting of natural resources, significant both qualitatively and quantitatively; they were the naturally attractive factors of our country with a great general tourist value and significance.

2. the continous improvement of working conditions leading to results affecting the development of "trade-union" tourism in two ways: (1) the working hours becoming shorter, the amount of leisure time increasing and the latter being most conveniently spent in tourist and recreational activities; (2) the permanent improvement of the hygienic and technical conditions of labour and human labour being increasingly replaced by machines thus becoming the "driving power" of the process in which the structure of spending of leisure time was changed by the tourist – recreational activity: instead of being spent in different kinds of rest its structure has gradually come to consist of recreation, entertainment and many sided developments of the personality.

3. the continous rise of individual standards as the component of the domestic population's living standard which affected decisively its tourist-recreational activity; the earnings of the workers which determine the volume and kind of their personal consumption having grown so much that at definite stage their personal consumption gradually included not only the needs of the first grade (the so-called bare necessities), but also the needs of second grade (the so-called indispensable needs: cultural-, sport- and tourist recreation) and finally the third grade needs (the so-called luxury needs – the durable consumer goods); the nominal and real earnings of the workers in our country rose at such a rate that this had a favourable effect on the participation of all categories of the population in the tourist industry (to a greater extent in domestic and to a lesser extent in international tourism); so in 1973 there were about 32 million registered tourist-days spent in domestic tourist facilities; if we add to this a further

86 million tourist-days unregistered, but established by means of sample surveys, we obtain the impressive figure of 118,1 million tourist-days; that means an average of 6 tourist-days per capita;[3] still more impressive are the data about their estimated tourist expenditure.[4]

Table 1: Expenses of Yugoslavian tourists in Yugoslavia (1973)

Indicators	average daily consumption		expenses of whole stay	total expenses	
	dinars	per cent.	dinars	thousand dinars	thousand US Dollars
"great" tourism					
a) in place of residence	12,30	16,30	167,40	1.236.400,00	73.000
b) during travel	8,90	11,80	121,70	894.600,00	53.000
c) in place of temporary residence	54,10	71,90	738,30	5.439.000,00	320.000
d) total	75,30	100,00	1.027,40	7.570.000,00	446.000
"small" tourism	60,00	100,00	—	4.620.000,00	272.000
total	—	—	—	12.190.000,00	718.000

1 US Dollar = 17,00 dinars

In spite of the daily expenditure being small both absolutely and relatively, the volume of tourist spending of the domestic population in the country was 4 per cent. of the national income of Yugoslavia.

At the end of this analysis it should be mentioned that the other components of living standard had also an effect on the development of "trade-union" tourism: firstly, the twofold significance and effect of the social standard on the initiative tourism activities has been put into practice – i. e. the increasing level of material wealth influenced the continous growth of the expenditure of the Yugoslavs and an increasing amount of this expenditure is connected with cultural-, sport- and tourist recreation; secondly the development of the communal and food-supplying services (the function of which is to cover the various needs of tourists) is at the same time the development of a very important part of tourist supply – the tourist infrastructure; thirdly the situation of the people in Yugoslavia has an indirect but positive influence on their participation in tourism.

Leisure time

The reduction of the working hours and the lengthening of leisure time are some of the results of the technological progress of mankind. Now we have the so-called classical structure of the spending of a day: eight hours work, eight

[3] These data do not include the 8,6 million days spent abroad by citicens of Yugoslavia

[4] FRANJEVIĆ, L., TKALAC, D.: *Karakteristike stanovništva u turizmu,* Zagreb 1974, p. XI–XII/6–8, tab. 2, 3, 4

hours free time, eight hours sleep. The weekly amount of leisure time has also shown an increasing tendency:[5]

Similarly positive are the tendencies which determine the amount of leisure time in the course of the year. Apart from the two processes already mentioned, the increasing amount of leisure time during the week and the year, this tendency has been affected by the process of increase of the number of other days on which one does not work (various national, religious and other holidays) and of annual holidays. In this way free time has in the last decades obtained the qualities and the value of an autonomous factor i e. of a special force of modern society which begins to influence the change of human habits and needs. From the theoretical point of view tourism is one of the most successful and to modern man most acceptable ways of fulfilling the three functions of such an ample amount of leisure time.

Table 2: Reduction of working hours and lengthening of leisure time since 1840

Indicators	Year				
	up to 1840	1840	1890	1962	1968
	in hours per week				
leisure time	0	12	24	36	42
working hours	84	72	60	48	42
sleep	84	84	84	84	84

Leisure time is one of the fundamental constitutional rights of the citizens of our country. The legal formulations unambiguously state the place, role and significance attributed to it.[6] (1) "The worker has a right to limited working hours . . ." which "cannot be longer than 42 hours a week" except in the case determined by the Constitution (article 162/1 and 2 of the Constitution of SFRY); "The conditions for reduction of working hours may be fixed by law" – article 162/3 of the Constitution of SFRY; (2) "The worker has a right to daily and weekly free time as well as to annual holidays of at least 18 working days (article 162/4 of the Constitution of SFRY). During the post-war development of our country the degree and way of using the amount of free time guaranteed by the Constitution depended directly and continually on a number of objective and subjective factors. These can be divided into two basic groups – the group of social, political and cultural and educational factors (way of life, the awareness of the need of using the leisure time, the development of tourist traditions and culture, etc.) and the group of financial-material factors (the achieved level of living standard, the development and number of institutions for sports and initiative tourist-recreational activity). Having in mind that the mentioned factors, of their groups i. e. their configuration are different in the republics and provinces, it has been established by analysis that both the degree of use of leisure time and how this constitutional right is used are very different in different parts of the country.

[5] MIHOVILOVIĆ, A. M.: *Slobodno vrijeme odraslih stanovnika gradova Jugoslavije.* Izd. Institut za društvena istraživanja Zagrebačkog sveučilišta. Zagreb 1972, p. 138

[6] *Ustav SFRJ,* Izd. Komunist 1974

On an national level (a kind of Yugoslav average) the activity displayed by the Yugoslavs in their daily, weekly and annual leisure time shows the following quantitative and qualitative characteristis:

Daily leisure time

The share of recreational activities in the structure of the activities which make up the contents of daily leisure time is relative and very small.

Recreation as a function of the daily leisure time is more directly found with the older groups of the population.

Weekly leisure time

The various tourist-recreational activities have, in general, a larger part and are of greater significance in the structure of the basic ways of using the weekly free time than was the case with the daily leisure time.

This conclusion may be drawn from the statistical data as regards age groups of the population; thus, all categories of the population of work age, without exception, consider tourism as a convenient means for the fulfilling of the basic functions of leisure time and they make use of it accordingly.

Table 3: Way of spending the weekly leisure by age groups

age group of population	way of spending the weekly leisure time		
	one-day excursions	half-day walks	shooting and fishing
up to 20 years	35,0	22,6	—
21–30 years	29,4	34,9	3,2
31–40 years	29,7	22,4	4,9
41–50 years	22,3	19,5	4,6
51–60 years	11,0	12,8	2,7
over 60 years	3,1	5,0	2,3

The situation is similar from the point of view of other, selected qualities of population, their social origin and average monthly income.

Annual leisure time[7]

The relationship between the annual holidays and the tourist-recreational activity (as one way of its use) is not satisfactory; although in the post war period tourism had for a long time been considered to be identical with annual holidays, the share of so-called great-tourism in the structure of using leisure time, which some time ago had reached a maximum of 33 per cent. has not yet been exeeded; this quantitative indicator shows fullly the real situation, namely that $^{2}/_{3}$ of the Yugoslavs use their annual holidays with other activities:

[7] "Annual leisure time" = that part of the leisure time of the population which we obtain when we deduct from the whole amount of its leisure time the daily leisure time, the weekly leisure time (in average 52 saturdays + 52 sundays) and the days on which one does not work because they are holidays; that is in fact the annual holiday being determined by the Constitution of at least 18 work days.

Table 4: Use of annual holidays for tourism in per cent.

completely used annual holiday	partly used annual holiday	not used annual holiday
67,0 per cent.	19,0 per cent.	14,0 per cent.

This, for tourism very unfavourable situation gets still worse when another factor is included in this analysis – the high rate of unused annual holidays (which was 18–29, i. e. in average 24,5 days).

It must be pointed out that this tendency is present in spite of the fact that the framework for the development of tourism in the function of the annual holidays is very favourable (in 1973 71 per cent. of the workers received a holiday pay the average of which was 696,40 dinars); the beneficial effect of it being seriously reduced by the behaviour of the receivers of this sum, since namely a mere 33 per cent. of it was used for tourist purposes.

Finally, one of the major obstacles in the way of wider and more direct introduction of tourism into the structure of "spending" the annual leisure time has been the regional heterogenity of our country in respect of the selected data (table 5).

Such are the quantitative-qualitative characteristics of the connection and correlation between tourism and the basic categories of leisure time; behind it lies with a rather negative effect the group of rational and irrational factors, such as the achieved level of urbanization, the level of tourist culture, the development of tourist traditions etc.

3. *"Worker"-tourism*

3.0. The contents and characteristics of "worker"-tourism as a form of tourist-recreational activity

By "worker"-tourism is meant, somewhat over-simplified, the complex of the tourist-recreational activity of the workers in the place of their residence, and also the phenomena and relations resulting from their travel away from their place of residence.

The basic characteristics in which "worker"-tourism differs from the other forms of people's tourist-recreational activity, and which were the basis of the process of its becoming independent in the framework of the contemporary forms of tourism are the following:

1. A typical un-balanced relation of economic and non-economic functions (with the "worker"-tourism the point lies in its effect in the non-economic fields).

2. The special structure of this tourist-consumer with pronouncedly individualized socio-economic characteristics.

3. An over-simplified set of motives which induce the workers to join tourist-recreational activities.

4. The "legal" linking of the subjects of "worker"-tourism to certain forms of tourist-recreational activities already proved effective in practice.

5. The over-simplified structure of the tourist economy in the function of "worker"-tourism.

6. Finally, the quantitatively and qualitatively transformed tourist cycle connected with "worker"-tourism.

3.1. The functions of "worker"-tourism

"Worker"–tourism has a limited effect in the material basis of the society, where a good deal of the various positive results of the tourist activity can be found. The exceptions are the inductive and partly, the multiplicative effects. On the one hand the demand in "worker"-tourism has little significance for the process of moving the human factor and its entering the economy of non-productive goods and activity. On the other hand this quantitatively and qualitatively specific supply has also only a slight effect on the initiation of investment activity and does not contribute significantly to either the regional or national economy (to the development of underdeveloped areas, the building up of tertiary economy, the increase of the development-rate of tourist generating areas, the coordination of the commodity-money relationship and the market, the formation and territorial re-distribution of the national income, etc.). The same is true of the relationship of the "worker"-tourism and the international-economic relationships of a country, i. e. her foreign trade and balance of payment.

This and such underdevelopment of the economic functions of "worker"-tourism is a relatively constant quality which results from its very nature and other characteristics (owing to which it became independent in the system of tourist-recreational activities). Today in our country "worker"-tourism is near the limit which marks the almost total absence of economic functions. The future development of "worker"-tourism, which should be based on a special programme and regulated by a new, active tourism policy, will contribute to the enlargement of the sphere of influence of "worker"-tourism in the economic field. However, this influence of "worker"-tourism will in the future also remain primarily indirect, quantitatively and qualitatively smaller than the economic effects of the other forms of tourism and it will be subordinated to the effects of social, cultural and political fields.

The non-economic functions of the "worker"-tourism are very outstanding. To a greater or lesser extent this imbues almost all parts of the social superstructure:

Function in the field of health and recreation

Preventive and curative protection of the psycho-physical abilities of the individual workers, that is of the health and working capacity of the population.

Cultural and educational function

A contribution to the many-sided development of the worker, a function which is complementarily linked to the basic educational process.

Political function

The best school of patriotism in time of peace.

Social function

Suitable means in the process of balancing the social position of producers i. e. their relationship with the other parts of the population in a socialist community.

Entertainment function

A successful way of dispelling the boredom of workers in the time when they are not in the production process – a function that is directly connected with the cultural, recreational as well as sport-recreational activities of workers.

Considered as a whole, the informatively presented complex of non-economic functions gives the "worker"-tourism that quality which makes it, as well as tourism in general, a part of the group of the most suitable and to modern man most acceptable ways of spending his leisure time, i. e. fulfilling its basic functions in the society.

3.2. The motives of workers in entering tourism

One of the characteristics of the development of "worker"-tourism up to now has been the fact that in the background of tourist activities which make up its contents there is such a set of motives of the workers for entering tourism which is similar with the level of the initial stage of tourist development in general. The workers join the tourist-recreational activities either to meet their needs for health purposes i. e. curative, or by reason of the so-called psycho-physical recreation. There may be some other motives, such as entertainment, return to nature, learning, becoming acquainted with one's cultural and historical heritage, but they are present merely now and then and only individually.

3.3. The basic forms of the "workers" tourist recreational activities

The workers enter mainly domestic tourism, the reason for that being their socio-economic characteristics and the effect of a number of objective factors. Only recently have they participated to a greater extent in the international tourist traffic. The worker as the subject of domestic tourism is a permanent phenomenon with a tendency to qualitative and quantitative improvement, which is not the case with transit-tourism. But the structure of their tourist-recreational activities differs from the structure of general tourist-recreational activities. While the latter consists of a balanced proportion of half-day and weekly tourism as well as the tourism of annual holidays, "worker"-tourism may be said to be identical with the last only.

Tourism connected with shooting and fishing, sailing, motoring, business and cultural manifestations are tourist forms only slightly represented in "worker"-tourism. Finally, speaking about its qualitative characteristics it must be pointed out that in the structure of "worker"-tourism there is no balance between the initiative and the receptive tourist-recreational activities. The former, although only slightly developed, are superior to the latter, which come at the very beginning of tourist development.

As regards expansion in space, "worker"-tourism is, contrary to the current expansion of tourism in general, limited. Workers generally go in for those forms of tourism which are present in their place of residence or in its neighbourhood. The same is true for the time-aspect of "worker"-tourism. The tourist-recreational activities which make up its contents are as a rule long-range, they are reduced to longer stay, i. e. to the annual-holiday tourism. Finally, there is an almost "regular" tendency of the workers participating primarily in those forms of tourism in which the daily expenses, the board and lodging, are less than the average in the domestic tourist economy, and in which there are almost no other expenses.

3.4. Supply in the function of "worker"-tourism

The observed qualitative and quantitative differences between tourist demand in the "worker"-tourism and tourist demand in general had corresponding consequences on the other side of the tourist market – in tourist demand.

From the very diverse and numerous group of factors of attraction which might be the ultimate aim of the worker's tourist travel, up to now the natural beauty spots had a much more pronounced significance than the social ones. The climate and hydrography, the flora and fauna and the natural beauties of an area belong to the group of factors that determine the various forms of initiative tourist-recreational activities of workers i. e. their excursion- and holiday-tourism. The space and time limit of "worker"-tourism as well as the specific quality of workers as tourist consumers have also contributed to the significance of natural factors. Contrary to this the effect of social attractive factors are insignificant, almost negligible. But very soon this situation which displays a limiting effect on the further development of "worker"-tourism and tourism in general will change. The current process of turning the simple set of motives of the workers' entering the tourism into a complex one will naturally bring along corresponding changes in their tourist-recreational activities. The predominance of this tendency will mean the gradual and equal introduction of the social attractive factors into the primary supply in the "worker"-tourism.

As to communications, only some influence the tourist-recreational activities of the workers. Only recently they have began to use air-traffic and the private motor car.

Up to now in the development of "worker"-tourism its subjects, the workers, have satisfied their needs by using the services provided only by some definite tourist receptive objects:

1. tourist suprastructure

receptive services (supplementary objects for lodging-hotels, rest-houses, camps, restaurants, inns and other permanent and provisional accomodation) catering services (restaurants which provide simple services – inns, snack bars etc.)

2. tourist infrastructure (in a narrow sense)

partly with the exception of the network of roads and the objects connected with it, the services of the other elements of tourist infrastructure in the narrow sense – water-supply, sewerage, supply of electricity are equally used in "worker"-tourism as in other forms of tourism

3. tourist infrastructure (in a wider sense)

the degree and character of the connection between workers' tourist-recreational activities and some parts of the tourist infrastructure in a wider sense are different. This relation is direct (the workers use parks, beauty-spots, places for excursions, sports-objects and public cultural establishments) or indirect (congress halls, the services and partly the airport).

This kind of use of the tourist receptive objects in "worker"-tourism is falling increasingly behind current practice. In the current process of democratization the doors of all the objects of tourist infra- and suprastructure are open to the workers as tourists.

3.5. Tourist economy in the function of "worker"-tourism

"Worker"-tourism uses only certain parts of tourist economy. Hence its specific structure which fulfils the function of the tourist-recreational activities of the workers: 1. the economic activity is mainly complete; 2. the share of social activity is absolutely and relatively smaller compared with the structure of tourist economy in the function of other forms of tourism; finally, the share of non-economic activity and the value of its participation in covering the needs of "worker"-tourists is quite negligible.

3.6. Tourist-cycle connected with "worker"-tourism

There is a considerable difference between the tourist cycle in the part of tourist economy the function of which is "worker"- tourism and its general model. In the part of tourist economy which has the function of "worker"-tourism during its development up to now some stages of the tourist cycle have been

Table 5: Regional heterogenity of selected tourism data in Yugoslavia (1973)

indicators	area	SR Bosnia and Herczegovina	SR Crna Gora	SR Croatia	SAP Kosovo	SR Macedonia	SR Slovenia	SR Serbia (without provinces)	SAP Vojvodina	SFR Jugoslavia (∅)
		republics i. e. provinces								
1. use of the ann. holidays (in per cent.)	wholly	67,0	69,0	66,0	86,0	72,0	52,0	71,0	72,0	67,0
	partly	14,0	14,0	22,0	7,0	11,0	36,0	17,0	13,0	19,0
	unused	19,0	17,0	12,0	7,0	17,0	12,0	12,0	15,0	14,0
2. way of use of ann. holidays (in per cent.)	for tourism	38,0	34,0	31,0	30,0	26,0	43,0	34,0	20,0	33,0
	for other purposes	62,0	66,0	69,0	70,0	74,0	57,0	66,0	80,0	67,0
3. right to annual holidays (number of days per worker)		25,0	25,4	24,5	24,9	24,4	24,3	24,5	24,1	24,5
4. holiday pay										
4.0. grants of holiday pay (in per cent.)										
got holiday pay		60,0	60,0	75,0	68,0	71,0				
got no holiday pay		40,0	40,0	25,0	32,0	29,0				
4.1. the sum of holiday pay (∅ in dinars)		709,4	549,2	810,0	586,2	658,1	671,6	685,8	708,1	696,4
4.2. the way the holiday pay was used (in per cent.)										
for tourism		38,0	34,0	31,0	30,0	30,0	43,0	34,0	20,0	33,0
for non-tourism		62,0	66,0	69,0	70,0	70,0	57,0	66,0	80,0	67,0

completely missing (the systematic monitoring, recording and evaluating of the traffic connected with the tourist-recreational activities of workers and the promotion of "worker"-tourism). On the other hand the other stages are now being worked out. As a consequence of these natural facts even now there is no circular motion of the part of tourist economy in the function of "worker"-tourism. Practically this means that there is no object of the regulatory and directing effect of the three main factors of tourism. Up to the most recent days of our tourism there have been neither special programmes nor active (official, social and business) policy in the field of "worker"-tourism. Lacking the positive effect of the economic and socio-political determinants of the development of tourism in general, "worker"-tourism as one of its contemporary forms, has naturally been lagging behind in its development.

Adresses of the authors
Adresses des auteurs
Adressen der Autoren

Prof. HANS ALDSKOGIUS, Department of Human Geography, Uppsala Universitet, Box 544, S-75122 Uppsala, Sweden

Prof. BERNARD BARBIER, Institut de Géographie, Université d'Aix-Marseilles, 29, Av. Robert-Schuman, F-13100 Aix-en-Provence, France

Prof. RICHARD W. BUTLER, Department of Geography, University of Western Ontario, London, Ontario, Canada N6A5C2

Prof. ALICE COLEMAN, King's College London, Strand, London WC2R2LS, Great Britain

Prof. LJUBOMIR DINEV, Institut de Géographie du Tourisme, Université Clément d'Ochrida, 15, Ruski Blvd., BG-1000 Sofia, Bulgarie

Prof. GÜNTER HEINRITZ, Geographisches Institut der Technischen Universität München, Arcisstraße 21, D-8 München 2, BRD

Prof. BURKHARD HOFMEISTER, Institut für Geographie, Technische Universität Berlin, Kurfürstendamm 196, D-1 Berlin 15, BRD

Dr. FELIX JÜLG, Geographisches Institut, Wirtschaftsuniversität Wien, Franz-Klein-Gasse 1, A-1190 Wien, Österreich

Dr. PETER MARIOT, Geografický Ustav Sav, Obrancov Mieru 49, CS-88625 Bratislava, CSSR

Prof. JOSEF MATZNETTER, Seminar für Wirtschaftsgeographie, Johann Wolfgang Goethe-Universität, Bockenheimer Landstraße 140, D-6 Frankfurt am Main, BRD

Prof. ALEXANDER MELAMID, Department of Economics, New York University, New York 10003, USA

Prof. TED MIECZKOWSKI, Department of Geography, The University of Manitoba, Winnipeg, Manitoba, Canada R3T 2N2

Prof. LISLE S. MITCHELL, Department of Geography, University of South Carolina, Columbia, South Carolina 29208, USA

Prof. KARL A. SINNHUBER, Geographisches Institut, Wirtschaftsuniversität Wien, Franz-Klein-Gasse 1, A-1190 Wien, Österreich

Doz. MOMČILO VUKIĆEVIĆ, Institute of Economics and Jurisprudence, University of Novi Sad, Svetozara Markovića ul. br. 6/I, Y-21000 Novi Sad, SFR Yugoslavia

Prof. GABRIEL WACKERMANN, Institut de Géographie, Université Louis Pasteur, 43, rue Goethe, F-67083 Strasbourg-Cedex, France

Prof. ROY WOLFE, Department of Geography, York University, N 417 Ross, 4700 Keele Street, Downsview, Ontario, Canada M3J 1P3

WIENER GEOGRAPHISCHE SCHRIFTEN

GEGRÜNDET VON LEOPOLD G. SCHEIDL

HERAUSGEBER KARL A. SINNHUBER. SCHRIFTLEITER: KARL A. SINNHUBER UND HERWIG LECHLEITNER
KARTOGRAPHISCHE BEARBEITUNG: KARL SCHAPPELWEIN, NORBERT STANEK

IEGENTÜMER: GEOGRAPHISCHES INSTITUT DER WIRTSCHAFTSUNIVERSITÄT WIEN, 1190 WIEN, FRANZ KLEIN-G. 1

ZUSCHRIFTEN BEZÜGLICH DES SCHRIFTENTAUSCHES AN DAS INSTITUT
BESTELLUNGEN AN DEN VERLAG FERDINAND HIRT, 1090 WIEN, WIDERHOFERGASSE 8

1	JOACHIM KULIGOWSKY:	Die Seehäfen des österreichischen Außenhandels. 1957. 54 Seiten, 6 Karten und Pläne.
2	KARL KNOBLEHAR:	Die oberösterreichische Industrie. Standort, Entwicklung und Leistung. 1957. 56 Seiten, 1 Karte.
3	JOSEF MATZNETTER:	Der Seeverkehr der Kanarischen Inseln. 1958. 56 Seiten, 4 Karten und Pläne.
4	JOSEF DORNER:	Wiener Neustadt — Wiederaufbau einer Industriestadt. 1958. 51 Seiten, 5 Kartenskizzen und 1 Plan.
5	HELMUT SCHMID:	Das Autobusnetz Österreichs. 1958. 62 Seiten, 2 Diagramme und 1 Karte.
6	MATTHIAS SAILER:	Der Hafen Wien. 1959. 48 Seiten, 4 Karten und 1 Diagramm.
7	ADOLF TSCHEITSCHONIG:	Die Magnesitwirtschaft Österreichs. 1959. 62 Seiten, 1 Karte, 3 Profile, 2 Diagramme und 4 Bilder.
8	ELFRIEDE KLEE — RUDOLF BÜTTNER:	St. Pölten als Industriestandort. 1959. 67 Seiten, 5 Karten und Pläne.
9	PETER H. BENDA:	Die Industrie- und Gewerbebetriebe in Wien. 1960. 58 Seiten, 1 Kärtchen, 6 Diagramme und 1 Karte.
10	FRANZ LANG:	Der Güterverkehr der österreichischen Eisenbahnen. 1960. 80 Seiten, 4 Kartenskizzen, 2 Diagramme und 1 Karte.
11	FRIEDRICH JAUSZ:	Die Elektrizitätswirtschaft Kärntens. 1961. 64 Seiten, 3 Diagramme, 1 Kartogramm, 1 Karte und 5 Kraftwerksbeschreibungen.
12 13	ERHART WINKLER:	Die Wirtschaft von Zonguldak, Türkei. Eine geographische Untersuchung. 1961. 127 Seiten, 4 Kartenskizzen, 1 Diagramm, 1 Profil, 2 Karten, 1 Plan und 16 Bilder.
14	EUGEN SWOBODA:	Die Standorte der Elektroindustrie Österreichs. 1962. 77 Seiten, 3 Diagramme, 1 Karte und 11 Bilder.
15	ELMAR SCHNEIDER:	Die Wirtschaftsgeographie des Arlbergs. 1962. 63 Seiten, 3 Karten und 12 Bilder.
16	LEOPOLD SCHEIDL:	Die Probleme der Entwicklungsländer in wirtschaftsgeographischer Sicht. 1963. 67 Seiten.
17	KURT SCHÖMIG:	Österreichs Buntmetallwirtschaft. 1963. 77 Seiten, 1 Kartenskizze, 5 Diagramme und 4 Bilder.

18
23 Festschrift — Leopold G. Scheidl zum 60. Geburtstag, I. Teil. 1965. 32 Beiträge, herausgegeben im Auftrag des Vorstandes der Österreichischen Gesellschaft für Wirtschaftsraumforschung von H. BAUMGARTNER, L. BECKEL, H. FISCHER, F. MAYER und F. ZWITTKOVITS. 396 Seiten, 31 Karten und Kartenskizzen, 8 Diagramme und 3 Bilder.

24
29 Festschrift — Leopold G. Scheidl zum 60. Geburtstag, II. Teil. 1967. 27 Beiträge, herausgegeben im Auftrag des Vorstandes der Österreichischen Gesellschaft für Wirtschaftsraumforschung von L. BECKEL und H. LECHLEITNER. Kartographische Bearbeitung: F. MAYER und K. SCHAPPELWEIN. 398 Seiten, 93 Karten und Kartenskizzen. 12 Diagramme und 30 Bilder.

30 Franz Lugmair: Die Landmaschinenerzeugung in Österreich. 1968. 95 Seiten, 1 Karte, 1 Kartenskizze, 4 Diagramme und 23 Bilder.

31
32 Otmar Kleiner: Österreichs Eisen- und Stahlindustrie und ihre Außenhandelsverflechtung. 1969. 184 Seiten, 1 Kartenskizze und 9 Diagramme.

33 Alice Bargiel: Die Standorte der Wirtschaftstreuhänder in Österreich. 1969. 19 Seiten und 1 Karte.

34 Stefan Skowronek: Die Standorte der österreichischen Kreditunternehmungen. 1970. 59 Seiten und 1 Karte.

35 Klaus Nozicka: Die österreichische Ziegelindustrie. 1971. 90 Seiten und 1 Kartenskizze.

36
37 Herwig Lechleitner: Die Rolle des Staates in der wirtschaftlichen und sozialen Entwicklung Libanons. 1972. 171 Seiten und 5 Kartenskizzen.

38
39 Peter Schnitt: Die Regionalstruktur des Außenhandels Belgien—Luxemburgs. 1973. 126 Seiten.

40 — Zehn Jahre Österreichische Gesellschaft für Wirtschaftsraumforschung. 1973. 36 Seiten.

41
42 Leopold Scheidl: Die Wirtschaft der Republik Südafrika. 1976. 173 Seiten, 18 Karten.

43
45 Festschrift — Leopold G. Scheidl zum 70. Geburtstag. Beiträge zur Wirtschaftsgeographie, 1. Teil. Herausgegeben von E. Winkler und H. Lechleitner. 1975. 296 Seiten, 22 Karten, Skizzen und Diagramme.

46
48 Festschrift — Leopold G. Scheidl zum 70. Geburtstag. Beiträge zur Wirtschaftsgeographie, 2. Teil. Herausgegeben von E. Winkler und H. Lechleitner. 1976. 231 Seiten, 31 Karten, Skizzen und Diagramme, 4 Bilder.

49
50 Wolfgang Entmayr: Der Hafen von London. 1977. 128 Seiten, 11 Abbildungen und Karten.

1—3, 8 und 9: vergriffen. 4: S 40,—. 5, 7 und 16: S 52,—. 10, 11, 14, 15 und 17: S 73,—. 12/13: S 145,—. 18/23 und 24/29: broschiert S 300,—, Ganzleinen S 340,—. 30: S 120,—. 31/32: S 190,—. 33: S 80,—. 34: S 180,—. 35: S 120,—. 36/37: S 273,—. 38/39: S 190,—. 40: S 48,—. 41/42: S 272,—. 43/45: S 483,—. 46/48: S 373,—. 49/50: S 298,—.